INTERMEDIATE GRAMMAR

From Form to Meaning and Use

SUSAN KESNER BLAND

Su hao Lee

Oxford University Press

OXFORD
UNIVERSITY PRESS

198 Madison Avenue
New York, NY 10016 USA

Great Clarendon Street
Oxford OX2 6DP England

Oxford New York

Auckland Cape Town Dar es Salaam Hong Kong Karachi
Kuala Lumpur Madrid Melbourne Mexico City Nairobi
New Delhi Shanghai Taipei Toronto

With offices in

Argentina Austria Brazil Chile Czech Republic France Greece
Guatemala Hungary Italy Japan Poland Portugal Singapore
South Korea Switzerland Thailand Turkey Ukraine Vietnam

OXFORD is a trademark of Oxford University Press.

Library of Congress Cataloging-in-Publication Data
Bland, Susan Kesner.
   Intermediate Grammar: from form to meaning and use /
Susan Kesner Bland.
      p. cm.
   Includes index.
   ISBN : 978 0 19 434366 4

   1. English language — Grammar.
   2. English language — Textbooks for foreign speakers. I. Title
PE1112.B57 1996
428.2'4 — dc20   93-44670

Copyright © 1996 Oxford University Press

Editorial Manager: Susan Lanzano
Art Director: Lynn Luchetti
Production Manager: Abram Hall
Project Manager: Jane Sturtevant

Content Editor: Marietta Urban
Production Editor: Janice L. Baillie
Designer: Alan Barnett
Senior Art Buyer: Alexandra F. Rockafellar

Cover design by: John Daly

Illustrations by: Dean Rohrer

Realia by: Todd Cooper, Maj-Britt Hagsted, Claudia Kehrhahn,
Scott MacNeill/MacNeill+Macintosh, VHL International, Inc.

Printing (last digit): 20 19 18 17 16 15 14

Printed in China

This book is printed on paper from certified and well-managed sources

The publisher wishes to thank these people for their help in
developing this book: Mary Billings of the ESL Program,
University of Washington Extension, Seattle; Carol Keiser Bishop
of the English Language Center at Michigan State University,
East Lansing; Debra Denzer of De Kalb College, Clarkston,
Georgia; Pam Fenstra of Manhattanville College, Purchase, New
York; Patricia Freeland of Temple University, Philadelphia;
Vasiliki Karras-Lazaris of California State University, Northridge;
Nyla Marnay of the University of California, Berkeley Extension,
English Language Program in Berkeley; Suzan Ormandy of the
University of California, Berkeley Extension, English Language
Programe in San Francisco; Marnie Ramker of the Tutorium in
Intensive English, University of Illinois at Chicago; the late John
Rittershofer of Hostos Community College of the City University
of New York; Karen Stanley of Central Piedmont Community
College, Charlotte, North Carolina; Cheryl Wecksler of the
American Language and Culture Institute at California State
University, San Marcos

Contents

Acknowledgments viii

To the Student viii

To the Teacher ix

**1. Expressing the Present: The Simple Present,
the Present Continuous, and Stative Verbs** **1**

The Simple Present 2

The Present Continuous 9

Stative Verbs 15

Summary 21

2. Adverbs of Frequency, *There Is* and *There Are*, and Imperatives **25**

Adverbs of Frequency 26

There Is and *There Are* 32

Imperatives 36

Summary 40

**3. Expressing Past Time: The Simple Past,
Used to, and the Past Continuous** **43**

The Simple Past of Regular and Irregular Verbs 44

The Simple Past of *Be* 50

Focus on Vocabulary: Prepositions of Time 60

Used to 62

The Past Continuous 67

Summary 71

**4. Expressing Future Time: *Be Going to, Will*, the Present Continuous,
and the Simple Present; Connecting Sentences** **75**

Be Going to 76

Focus on Vocabulary: Future Time Phrases 78

Will 82

The Present Continuous as a Future Form 94

The Simple Present as a Future Form 95

But 98

And...Too/And...Either 99

And So…/And Neither… 101

But/And 102

Summary 105

5. Complex Sentences: Past Time Clauses, Future Time Clauses, and Real *If* Sentences **109**

Past Time Clauses 110

Future Time Clauses. 118

Real *If* Sentences 122

Summary 129

6. Connecting the Past and the Present: The Present Perfect and the Present Perfect Continuous **133**

The Present Perfect 134

The Present Perfect versus the Simple Past. 147

The Present Perfect Continuous 150

Summary 161

7. Social Modals: Requests, Permission, Suggestions, Advice, Opinions, Obligations, Necessity, Lack of Necessity, and Prohibition **163**

Requests: *Can, Will, Could, Would*. 166

Permission: *Can, Could, May* 171

Suggestions, Advice, Warnings, Instructions: *Could, Might, Should,*
   Ought to, Had Better, Have to, Have Got to, Must. 176

Opinions, Obligations, Necessity, Requirements, Rules, Laws: *Should,*
   Ought to, Have to, Have Got to, Must 184

Lack of Necessity and Prohibition: *Don't Have to, Must Not* 191

Summary 195

8. Modals of Ability and Belief; Past Modals **199**

Present Ability: *Can* 200

Past Ability: *Could*. 201

Present, Past, and Future Ability: *Can, Could, Be Able to* 203

Modals of Belief: *Could, Might, May, Should, Must, Will* 209

Certainty About the Present: *Could, Might, May, Should, Ought to,*
   Have to, Have Got to, Must. 211

Certainty About the Present (Negative): *May Not, Might Not,*
   Must Not, Can't, Couldn't 218

Certainty About the Future: *Could, Might, May, Should, Ought to, Will* 221

Past Modals: *Should Have, Could Have, Might Have, May Have, Must Have* 224

Ability and Belief Modals: *Could Have, Might Have, May Have,*
   Must Have, Have to Have 226

Social Modals: *Should Have, Ought to Have, Could Have, Had to.* 229

Summary. 233

9. Relative Clauses   239

Restrictive Relative Clauses. 240

Subject Relative Pronouns 246

Object Relative Pronouns. 250

Object Relative Pronouns with Prepositions. 254

Possessive Relative Pronouns. 258

Nonrestrictive Relative Clauses 260

Summary. 266

10. Count and Noncount Nouns   269

Count Nouns 270

Noncount Nouns. 273

Focus on Vocabulary: Common Noncount Nouns 275

Count and Noncount Nouns. 277

Summary. 283

11. Quantity Expressions and Articles.   285

General Quantity Expressions 286

Focus on Vocabulary: General Quantity Expressions 290

Specific Quantity Expressions 292

Indefinite and Definite Articles. 296

Summary. 310

12. Expressing Differences and Similarities: Comparatives, Superlatives, *As...As, The Same...As*   313

Comparative Adjectives and Adverbs. 314

Superlative Adjectives and Adverbs 318

As...As 323

Comparative Nouns, Superlative Nouns, *The Same...As* 325

So...That/Such (a)...That 332

Summary. 335

13. Expressing Unreal Situations: *Wish* Sentences and Imaginary *If* Sentences **339**

   Wish Sentences 340

   Imaginary *If* Sentences. 346

   Summary 353

14. Gerunds and Infinitives **355**

   Overview of Gerunds 356

   Subject Gerunds 357

   Object Gerunds. 359

   Focus on Vocabulary: Common Object Gerunds 360

   Preposition + Object Gerunds 365

   Focus on Vocabulary: Common Preposition + Object Gerunds . . . 366

   Overview of Infinitives 369

   Verb + Infinitive 371

   Focus on Vocabulary: Common Verbs + Infinitives 373

   Verb + Infinitive or Gerund 375

   It... + Infinitive 380

   In Order + Infinitive 383

   Summary 386

15. The Past Perfect and the Past Perfect Continuous, Past *Wish* Sentences, and Past Imaginary *If* Sentences **389**

   The Past Perfect. 390

   The Past Perfect Continuous 398

   Past *Wish* Sentences 403

   Past Imaginary *If* Sentences. 406

   Summary 411

16. Passive Sentences **415**

   Overview of Passive Sentences 416

   Simple Present and Simple Past Passives 420

   Simple Future Passives. 429

   Continuous and Perfect Passives. 431

   Future, Continuous, and Perfect Passives. 434

   Modal Passives 438

   Summary 444

17. Noun Clauses and Reported Speech **447**

Wh- Clauses 448

If/Whether Clauses 452

That Clauses 457

Overview of Reported Speech 461

Quoted Speech versus Reported Speech 462

Summary 474

Appendix

Two- and Three-Word Verbs 477

Spelling of Verbs and Nouns Ending in *-s* and *-es* 483

Pronunciation of Verbs and Nouns Ending in *-s* and *-es* 484

Spelling of Verbs Ending in *-ing* 485

Spelling of Verbs Ending in *-ed* 486

Pronunciation of Verbs Ending in *-ed* 487

Irregular Verbs 488

The Definite Article with Proper Nouns 492

Comparative and Superlative Adjectives and Adverbs 493

Gerunds and Infinitives 495

    Verb + Gerund 495

    Verb with Preposition + Gerund 495

    Be + Adjective + Preposition + Gerund 496

    Verb + Infinitive 497

    Verb + Infinitive or Gerund 497

Reporting Verbs 498

Glossary of Grammar Terms **499**

Index **511**

Acknowledgments

I would like to thank Deborah Campbell for her help with the exercises, her friendship, and her wonderful sense of humor; Dick Feldman, Ingrid Arnesen, Susan Lanzano, Eric Larsen, Randee Falk, and John Chapman for their help and support, especially at the beginning stages of this project; Patti Nardiello and Marietta Urban for their patient and scrupulous editorial assistance; and Jane Sturtevant for bringing it all together.

Finally, I would like to express my gratitude to Bob, Jenny, and Scott for helping to keep the balance between grammar and life.

This book is dedicated to my parents, Sam and Bess Kesner.

To the Student

As intermediate language learners, you and your classmates have a fairly wide range of English skills and knowledge. The important word here is *range*, because of the differences in listening, speaking, reading, and writing skills and knowledge of grammar that you each bring to class.

Although your skills may be different, all of you are learning to create with English. This means that you are beginning to express your own thoughts without relying on translation or memorization. You are beginning to talk about unfamiliar topics more successfully and to express your thoughts in more than one way. You are getting better at beginning conversations. You can respond to questions with longer answers, you can volunteer information, and you can ask questions of your own that keep the conversation going.

The practice exercises in this book cover the wide range of skills that you are developing. They will also help you learn what forms are appropriate in different situations. When you do the exercises, sometimes you will be thinking about grammatical forms, but more often you will be using your imagination, judgment, intelligence, and feelings to communicate something in English.

You may feel that you already know many of the structures in Chapters 1–4. But even if you are already familiar with their most basic meanings and uses, you will learn more about what the structures mean, as well as where, when, and why they are used. You will look at these structures from a more "intermediate" point of view, and will learn to use them in new ways.

You may have noticed that sometimes you feel quite successful using a certain grammatical structure, only to find that you have "forgotten" it a few days later. This is not unusual for intermediate students, and, in fact, I have written this book with this in mind. Short, authentic examples, clear charts and explanations, chapter summaries, a glossary of grammar terms, and an easy-to-use index will help you retrieve lost information and refresh your memory.

Intermediate Grammar can help you achieve more consistent and accurate use of grammatical structures that you need for communication.

Good luck with your study of English!

~~~~~

You will often find this "sound wave" symbol in spoken practice exercises. It means that now it is your turn to make up questions, provide examples, or invent situations for practice.

To the Teacher

Wouldn't it be nice if your students paid attention to the "grammar" all around them in daily life; if they noticed the language when they read directions on a package, paid a bill, looked at a newspaper, read a sign, or listened to a recorded message? Wouldn't it be nice if they knew how to generalize from these examples and apply their new understanding to their own speech and writing?

We use the same grammatical forms over and over again in predictable ways. For example, we use the present continuous not only for describing an activity in progress (*I'm writing my thesis this semester*), but also for complaining (*He's always smoking cigars*) and for describing a planned event in the future (*She's starting graduate school next semester*). *Intermediate Grammar* will help you draw students' attention to the systematic meanings and uses of grammatical forms in adult daily life. You will find clear explanations, authentic examples, and exercises that accommodate the wide range of student needs at the intermediate level. *Intermediate Grammar* will help you help your students to become more language-aware and to incorporate a wider range of grammatical forms into the language they use.

Parts of a chapter

Preview
- The first page of each chapter. Describes and gives examples of the meanings and uses of structures in the chapter.
- Assign it for before-class preview of structures or use it for presentation.

Form box
- Displays, describes, and explains the forms of a given structure.
- Use it with form exercises to confirm or revise students' conclusions about form.

  Students can use it as a reference for study and review.

Meaning and Use box
- Gives the *what*, *where*, *when*, and *why* of meaning and use.
- Use with meaning and use exercises to revise, confirm, and expand students' understanding of meaning and use.

  Students can use it as a reference for study and review.

Conversation Note	• Describes a special feature of pronunciation or usage. It often contrasts spoken and written language. (See, for example, pages 77 and 263.)
	• Use it as a springboard for discussion of the differences between spoken and written language and what "correctness" is.
Focus on Vocabulary	• Presents vocabulary associated with a specific structure. There are seven in the book (for example, pages 78 and 360).
	• Use it to focus instruction on grammar problems related to vocabulary.
	Students can use for study and review.
Summary	• A comprehensive, at-a-glance display of form, meaning, and use for each structure in the chapter.
	• Use it as a detailed table of contents for the chapter when planning lessons and writing tests.
	Students can use it for reference and review.
Exercises	• Early exercises for each structure are strictly on form and are quite controlled. Later exercises focus on meaning and use, and become more open-ended.
	• Each chapter has exercises appropriate for diagnostic use, interactive practice, dictation, homework, and review.

In the back of the book

Appendix	• Spelling and pronunciation rules, word lists, and explanations related to specific structures.
	• Use it to teach these grammar-related topics and to supplement basic vocabulary supplied in the chapters.
	Students can refer to it when writing or doing exercises.
Glossary	• Definitions and examples of all grammar terms used in the book.
	• Use it as a ready source of examples.
	Students can refer to it for study and review.
Index	• Lists structures, alternate terms, common language functions and uses, grammar terms, and words and phrases related to specific structures (for example, *haven't, how long, guess, generally*).
	• Find which structures in the book fulfill a given language function or use.
	Students can use almost any related word to look up a structure.

Assessing your students' needs

Assessment is an ongoing process and is most often done informally — even intuitively. However, you may sometimes want to give a quick diagnostic quiz to find out how well your students already control a given structure. The Teacher's Book provides assessment quizzes for each structure. If you do not have the Teacher's Book, the Student Book offers ready resources for assessment. The summary exercise at the end of each chapter is an error-correction exercise covering all the structures in the chapter. It can be used as a diagnostic instead of review. For a diagnostic quiz on a specific structure in the chapter, choose instead the first exercise following the form chart for that structure, or an appropriate meaning-and-use exercise.

Teaching with *Intermediate Grammar*

Chapters are independent of one another, so you can change the order or skip chapters or parts of chapters completely. You will probably want to vary your presentations according to the proficiency level of the class, the time available, and your own preferences and experience with the subject matter. The use of different presentation techniques will help meet the needs of students with different learning styles and abilities. What you do will no doubt be affected by your basic approach to teaching the material. Is it deductive, inductive, or some combination? For many of us, the answer is a pragmatic mix of deductive and inductive teaching.

With intermediate students, the structures themselves may have a bearing on your approach. For example, the present perfect has one basic form but three different meanings that are hard for students to conceptualize. With guidance and appropriate examples, most intermediate students can induce the rules for forming the present perfect, but they may not be able to induce rules for using it appropriately. Most teachers will probably get good results by teaching the form of the present perfect inductively, then teaching meaning and use deductively. Alternatively, teach the three meanings separately, providing examples of only one meaning at a time. In this way, students should be able to induce each rule.

By contrast, the comparative has several distinct forms, but only one meaning. With most intermediate students, I would begin with meaning and use, teaching that inductively, then use a deductive approach for the various forms. With more advanced or analytical students, I might teach the forms inductively too, but would still begin with the simpler concept of meaning and use.

Deductive teaching is quite straightforward. You might assign the preview page to be read before class, start in class with one of the form charts, move on to the associated exercises, and use the summary for follow-up and review. Inductive teaching is typically less linear. The following notes suggest ways that you might use *Intermediate Grammar* for inductive teaching.

Choose examples from the preview page to begin your presentation of a structure. Write your choices on the board and move from them to questions such as these:

- What structure do the examples have in common?
- What meaning does the structure have in these examples?
- What other examples of the same structure can the students think of? (Be ready to supply some if they can't.)
- How is this structure formed?

- Can the students express the same idea with other structures they know?
- How is this structure different in form or in meaning from another structure they know? (For example, how is the present perfect different from the simple past?)

You may choose to bring in authentic language samples (audio or video clips, newspaper headlines, advertisements, and so on) to supplement those in the book. Such examples will dramatize the grammar as living language, and can be very effective if used well.

At the initial presentation stage, your students' answers and the rules they induce may be incomplete or even wrong. You will have to decide how much to guide and correct them, and which misapprehensions can be left to clear up later. Your students' understanding of a structure will grow and strengthen as they work with the exercises, generalize rules, consult the charts, and continue to discuss the structure and compare it with others.

The Teacher's Book

I would like to recommend that you consider using the Teacher's Book for *Intermediate Grammar*. It contains no filler—just useful information:

- photocopiable diagnostic and achievement quizzes
- ideas for presentation
- extension activities
- an answer key to the Student Book

A final word

I hope you find *Intermediate Grammar* informative and helpful. I would like to have your comments and questions. You can write to me in care of the U.S. Publishing Group, ESL Department, Oxford University Press, 198 Madison Avenue, New York, New York 10016.

— *Susan Kesner Bland*

CHAPTER 1

Expressing the Present: The Simple Present, the Present Continuous, and Stative Verbs

Dominique :

Preview

Marie is getting ready to go to work. Her roommate, Karen, is watching the clock:

Karen: It's **getting** late. **Doesn't** your bus **come** at 8:10?
Marie: Don't worry. I never **miss** it. It **comes** late every day.

Marie is looking for something:

Karen: What **are** you **doing?**
Marie: **I'm looking** for my umbrella. It's **raining** hard right now, and I **don't have** a raincoat.

Marie sees her friend Chris on the bus:

Marie: Hi, Chris. How's everything? **Are** you **working** now?
Chris: No, but **I'm looking** for a job.

The simple present and the present continuous are often used in the same conversation. They both relate to the present, but in different ways. The simple present describes habits — things you do again and again — and routines and schedules — things you do regularly. The simple present is also used to state a general fact; for example, *Water freezes at 0° centigrade.* The present continuous describes an activity in progress or a situation that we expect to change.

This chapter compares the form, meaning, and use of the simple present and the present continuous. It also includes a special group of verbs called stative verbs, such as **have, be,** and **see,** that typically express states and conditions in the simple present.

The Simple Present: Form

Statements

I	**work**.	Marie	**works**.
You		She	
We		He	
They		It	

- To form the simple present, use the simple form of the verb for most forms. Add **-s** or **-es** only to the third-person singular.
- Look at pages 483–484 for spelling and pronunciation rules for third-person singular forms.
- Statements in the simple present do not usually have **do** or **does**, except for emphasis:

  You're wrong. I **do** like her!

Negative Statements | Contractions

I	**do**	**not**	**work**.	I	**don't**	**work**.
You				You		
We				We		
They				They		

Karen	**does**	**not**	**work**.	Karen	**doesn't**	**work**.
She				She		
He				He		
It				It		

- For negative statements, use **do** or **does** + **not**. The main verb is in the simple form.
- **Do** or **does** + **not** contract to form **don't** or **doesn't**.

Yes/No Questions | Short Answers | Contractions

Do	you	**drive**?	Yes, I **do**.	
			No, I **do not**.	No, I **don't**.
Does	she	**drive**?	Yes, she **does**.	
			No, she **does not**.	No, she **doesn't**.

- To form *yes/no* questions, use **do** or **does** before the subject and use the simple form of the verb.
- Short answers to *yes/no* questions have a subject pronoun + **do** or **does**.
- For negative short answers, use **do** or **does** + **not** or **-n't**.

Information Questions				Answers
When	**do**	you	**read**?	In the evening.
What	**does**	Peter	**read**?	Mystery stories.

- The *wh-* word is followed by **do** or **does**, the subject, and the main verb in the simple form.

Information Questions (Subject)			Answers
Who	**reads**	mysteries?	Peter **does**.
What	**happens**	in a mystery story?	A murder.

- If **who** or **what** is the subject, then **do** and **does** are not used in the question. **Who** and **what** are singular, so the verb takes **-s** or **-es**.

CONVERSATION NOTE

The contractions **don't** and **doesn't** are frequently used in speaking and informal writing, and especially in short answers:

Do you smoke?   No, **I don't.**

Does he smoke?   No, he **doesn't.**

⟹ Exercise 1: Working on Form

Work with a partner. Complete the conversations using the simple present and contractions wherever you can. Then practice the conversations.

1. Two students:

   A: My teacher ___gives___ (give) too much homework.

   B: Really? Mine ___doesn't give___ (give/not) any. What kind of homework ___do you get___ (you/get)?

2. Two acquaintances meet on a very cold day:

   A: My family ___lives___ (live) in Florida. Every winter I ___think___ (think) about moving there too.

   B: How often ___do they visit you___ (they/visit/you)?

   A: Not very often. They ___refuse___ (refuse) to come in the winter because it ___is snowing___ (snow) too much here. Sometimes they ___come___ (come) during the summer.

3. Two office friends:

A: Why ___does Ellen Watch___ (Ellen/watch) me so much?

B: What ___do you mean___ (you/mean)?

A: She ___watchs___ (watch) everything that I ___did___ (do) and it

___makes___ (make) me feel very uncomfortable.

4. Two classmates:

A: What ___does your brother do___ (your brother/do)?

B: He ___sells___ (sell) insurance. He ___work___ (work) for a large

company.

5. Two strangers at a bus stop:

A: When ___does the bus come___ (the bus/come)?

B: It usually ___arrive___ (arrive) at ten minutes after the hour, but not today.

A: ___Does this happen___ (this/happen) often?

B: No, it usually ___comes___ (come) on schedule, but the bus company

___has___ (have) a new driver on this route. He ___doesn't drive___

(drive/not) very fast.

6. Person A is admiring the roses in Person B's garden:

A: Roses ___doesn't grow___ (grow/not) in my garden. They don't get enough sun.

B: Why ___don't you try___ (you/try/not) begonias?

⫸ Exercise 2: Working on *Who* and *What* Questions

1. Match the occupations in Column A with the job descriptions in Column B. (Use a dictionary if you need one.) Then work with a partner. Take turns asking and answering questions with *who* in the simple present.

A: *Who defends people in trouble?*
B: *A lawyer does.*

Column A	Column B
a lawyer	serves people in a restaurant
a meteorologist	prepares drinks in a bar
a waiter	defends people in trouble
a bartender	studies weather patterns
a professor	teaches in a university
a mayor	treats heart patients
a cardiologist	runs a city government

Column A	Column B
a newscaster	cleans buildings
a janitor	fixes cars
a surgeon	runs the state government
a governor	investigates crimes
a mechanic	performs operations
a detective	reports the news

2. Think of some other <u>occupations.</u> Then with your partner, take turns asking and answering questions with *what* in the simple present.

    A: *What does a bus driver do?*
    B: *She drives a bus.*

The Simple Present: Meaning and Use

HABITS, ROUTINES, SCHEDULES, FACTS, DEFINITIONS

1. We use the simple present to make general statements about habitual or repeated activities (such as things we do every day, every week, every summer), and about permanent situations:

Habit:	Marie **runs** two miles every day.
Routine:	She **gets up** at 6:30 A.M. and **goes** to bed at 10:00 P.M.
Schedule:	The university **follows** a semester schedule. Classes **begin** at the end of August and **continue** until the first week of December. Classes **resume** the third week of January and **continue** until the first week of May.
Permanent Situation:	The university **is** on State Street.

2. The simple present is also used to express facts, generalizations, definitions, and newspaper headlines:

Fact:	Water **freezes** at 32° Fahrenheit, 0° centigrade.
Generalization:	Infants usually **take** two naps a day; toddlers **take** only one.
Definition:	Begonias **are** garden plants with brightly colored leaves and flowers. They **grow** in shade or partial sun.
Newspaper Headline:	PRICES **RISE** DURING JANUARY

▥➡ **Exercise 3: Expressing Facts**

Work with a partner. Take turns reading the following statements to each other. Tell whether the statement is true or false. If the statement is false, change it to a negative statement. Then write a true statement using the simple present.

1. Batteries change chemical energy into electrical energy. _True._

2. Water freezes at 0° Fahrenheit. _False. Water doesn't freeze at 0° Fahrenheit._
   It freezes at 0° centigrade.

3. The earth revolves around the moon. _The moon around the earth._

4. Water boils at 100° centigrade. _true_

5. Palm trees grow in cold climates. _Palm trees grow in warm climates._

6. Magnets attract pieces of glass. _____

7. Penguins live in the desert. _Penguins live in the South pole._

8. The sun rises in the north. _The Sun rises in the east._

9. Water conducts electricity. _true, but If the water is Purified, Water will not conduct electricity._

10. Birds spin webs. _Spiders spin webs._

11. Spiders make wax and honey. _bees make wax and honey._

12. Raisins come from grapes. _true,_

⟹ Exercise 4: Making Generalizations 提高能

Make generalizations about American life. Complete the following sentences with *most, many, some, few,* and a noun (for example, *people, Americans, children, teenagers, adults).* Then compare your generalizations and discuss the differences in meaning.

1. _____ *Many people* _____ watch too much television.
2. _____ Most americans _____ shop in supermarkets.
3. _____ ~~Many~~ most children use computers.
4. _____ watch TV four or more hours a day.
5. _____ skip breakfast.
6. _____ vote in elections.
7. _____ live in apartments.
8. _____ bring lunch to work.
9. _____ get a college education.
10. _____ jog two miles a day.
11. _____ eat sushi.
12. _____ graduate from high school.

⟹ Exercise 5: Making Generalizations

Write your own generalizations about American life. Complete the following sentences using the simple present. Read your sentences to the class and find out if your classmates agree.

1. Not many people _*retire before they are sixty.*_____

2. Most children _____

3. Many college students _____ Can drive car. _____

4. Not many adults _____ are entrepreneur. _____

5. Some teenagers_____

6. Many Americans _____

7. Most _____

8. Some _____

▓➤ **Exercise 6: Explaining Definitions**

1. Match each verb in Column A with a word in Column B that is similar in meaning. If necessary, use a dictionary.

Column A   **Column B**

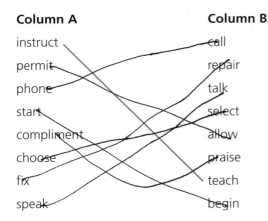

instruct   call

permit   repair

phone   talk

start   select

compliment   allow

choose   praise

fix   teach

speak   begin

2. Work with a partner. Take turns checking your work. Follow the example.

    A: *What does* instruct *mean?*
    B: Instruct *means* teach.

3. Working on your own, match each adjective in Column A with a word in Column B that is opposite in meaning.

Column A   **Column B**

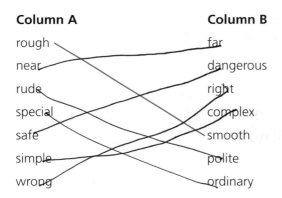

rough   far

near   dangerous

rude   right

special   complex

safe   smooth

simple   polite

wrong   ordinary

4. Work with a partner. Take turns checking your work. Follow the example.

    A: *What does* rough *mean?*
    B: Rough *means* not smooth.

The Present Continuous: Form

Statements			Contractions
I	**am**	**working**.	I**'m**
He She It	**is**	**working**.	He**'s** She**'s** It**'s**
We You They	**are**	**working**.	We**'re** You**'re** They**'re**

- To form the present continuous (also called the present progressive), use the simple present form of **be + verb + -ing**.
- Look at page 485 for spelling rules for verbs ending in **-ing**.

Negative Statements				Contractions
I	**am**	**not**	**working**.	**I'm not**
He	**is**	**not**	**working**.	He**'s not**/He **isn't**
We	**are**	**not**	**working**.	We**'re not**/We **aren't**

- To form negative statements, use a form of **be + not** or its contracted form **-n't**. The main verb is in the **-ing** form.
- Except for **I'm not**, there are two negative contracted forms for each person; for example, **he's not** and **he isn't**. The meaning is the same.

Yes/No Questions			Short Answers	Contractions
Am	I	**going**?	Yes, I **am**. No, I **am not**.	 No, I**'m not**.
Is	he	**going**?	Yes, he **is**. No, he **is not**.	 No, he **isn't**./No, he**'s not**.
Are	they	**going**?	Yes, they **are**. No, they **are not**.	 No, they **aren't**./No, they**'re not**.

- To form a *yes/no* question, use a form of **be** before the subject.
- Short answers have a subject + a form of **be**.
- Affirmative short answers do not have contracted forms. We never say, **Yes, I'm* or **Yes, he's*. (INCORRECT)

(continued)

Information Questions				Answers
Where	**are**	you	**going?**	To the store.
What	**are**	you	**looking for?**	My wallet.

- The *wh-* word comes before **be** and the subject.

Information Questions (Subject)			Answers	Contractions
Who	**is**	**calling?**	Karen.	Who**'s**
What	**is**	**happening?**	Nothing much.	What**'s**

- If **who** or **what** is the subject, then the word order is the same as for affirmative statements.

CONVERSATION NOTES

1. Forms of **be** can be contracted. With pronouns, contractions are often used both in speaking and in informal writing. However, when you write names and other nouns, contractions are usually avoided:

Written Form	Spoken Form
He**'s** cooking dinner.	"He**'s** cooking dinner."
Tom **is** cooking dinner.	"Tom**'s** cooking dinner."
The car **is** running well today.	"The car**'s** running well today."
The boys **are** practicing.	"The boys**'re** practicing." (SPOKEN ONLY)

2. Contractions with *wh-* words are also common in conversation. However, in writing, contractions with **is** and a *wh-* word are common, but contractions of **am** or **are** with *wh-* words are avoided:

Written Form	Spoken Form
Who**'s** coming to the party?	"Who**'s** coming to the party?"
What **am** I wearing?	"What**'m** I wearing?" (SPOKEN ONLY)
When **are** you going?	"When**'re** you going?" (SPOKEN ONLY)

⫸ Exercise 7: Working on Form

Make up sentences for the following situations using the words in parentheses in the present continuous. Use <u>contractions</u> if possible.

1. Two children walk into the house on a rainy day:

   Parent: Please take your boots off. (you/get/mud/on the floor) _You're getting mud on_ _the floor._

2. Sue is carrying her groceries into the house. She calls her daughter for help:

   Sue: Lisa, I need some help. (the bag/tear/and/I/drop/groceries/on the floor) _____

   _____

3. Joe walks into the living room. His roommate is taking everything out of the desk drawer:

   Joe: (what/you/do) _____

   Roommate: (I/look for/a pencil) _____

   Joe: But there are pencils in the kitchen. (why/you/make/such a mess) _____

   _____

4. Linda is walking to school. She calls out to her friend Julie on the street:

   Linda: (why/you/walk/so fast)_____

   Julie: I'm late for an appointment. (I/try/to hurry) _____

5. Lee sees Sam at the vending machine:

   Lee: (why/you/kick/the machine) _____

   Sam: (I/try/to get/my money back) _____

⫸ Exercise 8: Working on Questions and Short Answers

Work with a partner. Take turns asking and answering the following questions. Use short answers with the correct pronouns.

1. Are your relatives visiting you right now?

   A: *Are your relatives visiting you right now?*
   B: *No, they're not.*

2. Are you getting any exercise?

3. Are you sleeping well these days?

4. Are you feeling OK?

5. Are your expenses getting higher every month?

6. Is it raining today?

7. Is your car giving you any problems?

8. Are your friends studying English too?

9. Are you working hard this semester?

10. Are you having difficulty with any of your courses?

The Present Continuous: Meaning and Use

ACTIVITIES IN PROGRESS

1. The present continuous often focuses on an activity or process that is happening at the moment of speaking:

> Karen: What **are** you **doing**?
> Marie: **I'm looking** for my umbrella.

2. Adverbs and adverbial phrases such as **now, right now,** and **at this moment** frequently occur with the present continuous. They help emphasize that the event is in progress:

> Marie: It's **raining** hard **right now**.

3. The activity or process does not have to be happening precisely at the moment of speaking. You can use the continuous to describe activities that stop and start during longer time periods that include the present time, such as **these days, this semester, this year**:

> Mark: What **are** you **doing this semester**?
> Paul: **I'm writing** my thesis.

4. Notice that even the expressions **now** and **right now** do not always mean at the moment of speaking:

> *Marie runs into Chris on the bus:*
> Marie: **Are** you **working** now?
> Chris: No, but **I'm looking** for a job.

5. While the present continuous focuses on an activity in progress, the simple present describes the situation in general. Compare Paul's two sentences:

> Mark: Where's your brother today?
> Paul: He's **working** right now. He **works** at the pharmacy on Main Street.

6. Sometimes sentences in the present continuous and the simple present are close in meaning (but not exactly the same):

> Chris: Hi, Karen. Do you live near here?
> Karen: Yes, we're **living** on Eddy Street. We have a one-year lease.

Chris: Hi, Marie. Do you live near here?

Marie: Yes, we **live** on Eddy Street. We bought our house last year.

You can choose whether to use the present continuous or the simple present depending on the way that you are thinking about the particular situation. If you think the situation is temporary or changing, as Karen did, then you should choose the continuous. But if you think that the situation is more permanent or habitual, then you should choose the simple present, as Marie did.

7. Present continuous sentences with the adverb **always** (and with other adverbs that mean *all of the time*) often express complaints:

Chris: He's **always calling** me at two in the morning.

(This use of the continuous with adverbs of frequency is discussed further in Chapter 2.)

➠ Exercise 9: Asking and Answering Questions About Activities in Progress

Work with a partner. Make up questions for the following situations using the words in parentheses and the present continuous. Answer your partner's questions.

1. You are visiting your cousin. When you arrive, he's sitting in the middle of a big pile of clothing, boxes, and papers. The closet door is open:

   (what/do)   **A:** *What are you doing?*
                  B: *I'm cleaning out my closet.*
   (why/do/that) **A:** *Why are you doing that?*
                  B: *It was a mess!*

2. Something smells good in the kitchen. Your roommate is busy cooking:
   (what/make)

3. Your neighbor is walking down the street quickly:
   (where/go)
   (why/rush)

4. Someone is knocking on the door. Your roommate is laughing:
   (who/knock)
   (why/laugh)
   (what/go on)

5. Someone calls and asks for Sam. No one named Sam lives with you. You think it might be a wrong number:
   (what number/call/please)

6. A stranger calls and asks for your wife/husband. You want to know who it is:
   (who/call/please)

➠ **Exercise 10: Describing Current Activities**

Use the present continuous to write four sentences describing activities that are going on right now in your life. Use the phrases *this year, this semester, these days*.

1. I'm learning to swim this year and I'm also jogging a lot.

2. _____

3. _____

4. _____

5. _____

➠ **Exercise 11: Thinking About Meaning**

Read each sentence and answer the questions below it with one of these answers: *Yes, No, Probably, Probably not, It's not clear*. Then explain your answers in small groups.

1. I'm writing a book.

   (a) Is the speaker finished with the book yet? No.

   (b) Did the speaker start writing the book a few days ago?_____

   (c) Is the speaker writing at the moment of speaking? _____

2. The bus is stopping.

   (a) Is the bus speeding up? _____

   (b) Is the driver putting his foot on the brake? _____

   (c) Are the passengers getting off the bus yet? _____

3. I'm sleeping much better this week.

   (a) Is the speaker sleeping right now? _____

   (b) Did the speaker sleep well last week? _____

   (c) Will the speaker sleep well next week? _____

4. I'm taking a French course right now.

   (a) Is the speaker in the French class right now? _____

   (b) Has the course begun? _____

   (c) Is the course over? _____

➡ **Exercise 12: Thinking About Meaning**

Match each sentence in Column A with a sentence in Column B that provides an appropriate context for it. Discuss your choices in groups.

Column A

Tom lives on Dryden Road.

Peter is living on Dryden Road.

Alex wears a tie to school.

Matt is wearing a tie to school.

James works at the bank.

Andrew is working at the bank.

Column B

He usually wears jeans and a T-shirt, however.

He has worked there since 1980.

He has lived there for a long time.

He started the job a few days ago.

He's a very formal dresser.

He just moved there a few weeks ago.

Stative Verbs: Meaning

CONDITIONS AND STATES

1. Some verbs do not express actions. These verbs express conditions and states that we do not expect to change. They are called stative verbs:

My roommate's name **is** Peter. He's tall and **has** brown hair. He **resembles** his brother. He **likes** loud music and sports cars. He **hates** country music and bowling.

2. Stative verbs most commonly occur in the simple present and are used to express descriptions, possession, relationships, measurement, senses, physical sensations, emotions, attitudes, and ideas:

Descriptions

be, resemble, look like	Peter **is** a veterinarian.
look, seem, appear	He **seems** happy with his job.
sound, sound like	That **sounds** interesting.
include, involve	His book **includes** many home remedies.
consist of, contain	It **contains** many explanations.
lack	It **lacks** the latest medical discoveries.

Possession and Relationships

have, possess, own	Diane **has** a new baby.
belong to, owe, depend on	The baby **depends on** her mother.

(continued)

Measurements

weigh, measure	This bicycle **weighs** 25 pounds.
equal	One kilogram **equals** about 2.2 pounds.
cost	It **costs** too much.

Senses and Physical Sensations

feel, hear, see, taste, smell	I **feel** sick.
hurt, ache, tingle, itch	My throat **hurts** and my head **aches.**

Emotions and Attitudes

love, like, care for, adore	He **cares for** her very much.
appreciate, value	They **appreciate** our help.
hate, dislike, mind	She **dislikes** him intensely.
want, need, prefer, wish	I **prefer** tea to coffee.

Ideas

know, think, believe	They **know** the answer.
recognize, remember	I don't **recognize** anyone in that photo.
understand, mean	What do you **mean?**

CONVERSATION NOTE

In conversation, some stative verbs, especially verbs of emotion and attitude, may have a continuous form. Using the continuous shows a more intense or emotional situation. These verbs often occur with adverbs such as **just** or **really**, or with special intonation:

I'm just loving this novel!

He's really liking it here.

⯈ Exercise 13: Giving Physical Descriptions

1. Make up sentences on your own describing an adult male with the following physical characteristics. Use stative verbs such as *be*, *weigh*, and *have* in the simple present.

Example: *He is 5 feet 11 inches tall.*

height:	5 feet 11 inches	eyes:	brown
weight:	165 pounds	other:	mustache, beard, freckles
hair:	short, straight, brown		

2. Now write a description of a classmate, but do not identify him or her. Read your description to the class and let students guess who the person is.

⬛▶ Exercise 14: Complimenting

Work with a partner. Imagine this is the first time you are a dinner guest at your friend's apartment and you are having a great time. You especially like the large apartment, comfortable chairs and sofas, nice furniture, pictures on the walls, stereo, cassettes, CDs, and interesting books. The dinner is great, too. You are having soup, salad, chicken, rice, vegetables, dessert, and coffee.

Make up compliments using stative verbs *(be, like, love, taste, smell, look, have)* in the simple present. Use other verbs if you wish.

> **A:** *You have a nice apartment.*
> **B:** *Thank you.*
> **A:** *This chicken tastes delicious!*
> **B:** *Thank you. I'm glad you like it.*

⬛▶ Exercise 15: Criticizing

You are in a department store with your friend and you are in a very bad mood. Respond to all of your friend's comments and questions with a critical remark. Use stative verbs *(be, cost, like, smell, weigh, sound, taste, look, feel, seem)* and these adjectives: *awful, cheap, bad, strong, crowded, big, heavy, salty, sweet, strange, loud.*

1. Walking into the department store:

   Your friend: I like this department store. It always has everything I need.

   You: _I don't like it. It's too crowded._

2. In men's and women's fragrances:

   Your friend: I think I'll buy some of this cologne. I really like it.

   You: _____

3. In the clothing department:

   Your friend: These slacks are a great buy. I think I'll try them on.

   You: _____

   Your friend: How do you think they look on me?

   You: _____

4. In the luggage department:

   Your friend: I like this carry-on bag. What do you think?

   You: _____

5. In the music department:

Your friend: Listen to this music. It's my favorite group.

You: _____

Your friend: What do you think about this singer?

You: _____

6. In the cafeteria:

Your friend: The soup is good here.

You: _____

Your friend: The apple pie is just like mom's.

You: _____

7. In the sports department:

Your friend: I need a new tennis racket. I'm thinking about buying this one.

You: _____

8. In the furniture department:

Your friend: This is a nice-looking desk, and it's just the right size.

You: _____

Stative Verbs: Meaning and Use

STATE OR ACTION?

Stative verbs do not generally occur in the continuous; however, there are some common exceptions:

1. Stative verbs that express physical sensations (**feel, hurt, ache, tingle,** and **itch**) can be used with either the simple present or the present continuous, without changing the meaning. The sentences in each pair below have the same meaning:

Simple Present	**Present Continuous**
My foot **hurts.**	My foot **is hurting.**
I **feel** sick.	I**'m feeling** sick.

2. **Am being, is being,** or **are being** plus **adjective** expresses a more temporary meaning than **am, is,** or **are** plus **adjective.** Compare these examples:

Two mothers are describing their children:

The kids **are being** so good today! I'm really surprised. They don't usually behave in restaurants.

The kids **are** so good. We can take them anywhere without worrying about their behavior.

This continuous use of **be** requires a certain kind of adjective to follow **being**. Compare these examples:

He**'s being** foolish. I've never seen him act like this.
*He**'s being** sick. I've never seen him act like this. (INCORRECT)

These sentences show that the adjective must describe behavior that the subject can control such as good behavior or foolish behavior. For this reason, you can't say, for example, *He's being sick* or *He's being pale*. (INCORRECT)

3. Some stative verbs have both a stative meaning and an active meaning. With the stative meaning, the simple present tense is generally used when talking about the present. But with the active meaning, the present continuous is used. These verbs include **taste, smell, see, weigh,** and **have**. Notice that with actions you can ask the question *What are you doing?*, but with states you cannot:

State	**Action**
Tom: What's the matter?	Tom: What are you doing?
Ann: I **taste** something strange in this soup.	Ann: I**'m tasting** this soup to see if there is something wrong with it.
I **smell** something awful. What is it?	I**'m smelling** the milk to see if it is spoiled.
I **don't see** anyone in the hall.	I**'m seeing** Robert now. *(seeing = dating)*
I **weigh** 120 pounds on that scale.	I **am weighing** myself on that scale because mine is broken.
I **have** a computer at home.	I**'m having** trouble with my computer. It's not working today.

When **have** means *to possess*, it expresses a state and must be in the simple present. But when **have** means *to experience*, or *to eat* or *drink*, it has an active meaning and it is used in the continuous. Other examples of **have** in the continuous include: **having dinner, having a good time,** and **having a baby.**

⟹ **Exercise 16: Choosing the Simple Present or the Present Continuous**

Work with a partner. Complete the conversations using the appropriate simple present or present continuous forms of the verbs in parentheses. Use contractions wherever possible. Then practice the conversations. Discuss any cases where you think you can use both the present continuous and the simple present.

1. **A:** Zachary, Bob _____*is calling*_____ (call) you.

   B: I _____*know*_____ (know), but I ___*'m doing*___ (do) my homework right now.

2. **A:** What course ___*do you take*___ (you/take) with Professor Hale?

   B: Psych 101.

   A: ___*is it*___ (it/be) a good course?

   B: Well, that ___*depend*___ (depend) on my mood. I ___*guess.*___
   (guess) it ___*is*___ (be) okay, but it ___*gets*___ (get) more
   and more difficult. I ___*have*___ (have) trouble right now with our
   latest assignment.

3. **A:** Excuse me. I ___*hope*___ (hope) I ___*am not*___ (be/not) rude,
   but I ___*need*___ (need) some help.

   B: What ___*seem*___ (seem) to be the problem?

   A: My engine ___*is smoking / smokes*___ (smoke).

4. **A:** My sister ___*complains*___ (complain) a lot about her job.

   B: It ___*sounds*___ (sound) as if she ___*needs*___ (need) a change.

   A: I ___*think*___ (think) she ___*is looking for*___ (look for) a new job.
   At least I ___*hope*___ (hope) so. I ___*have gotten*___ (get) tired of
   her complaints.

5. **A:** Hello. I ___*am calling*___ (call) to make an appointment with Dr. Alden for my
   yearly checkup. My name ___*is*___ (be) Meryl Jensen.

   B: Dr. Alden ~~*hasn't*~~ *hasn't* (have) an opening on June 15 at 2:00 P.M.

6. **A:** What ___*do you do*___ (you/do)?

   B: I ___*am looking for*___ (look for) some receipts because I ___*am preparing*___
   (prepare) my income tax form.

   A: ___*Do you want*___ (you/want) any help?

⬛➡ Exercise 17: Thinking About Meaning

Work in small groups. Read the statement and the list of words below. Which words
can substitute for *they* in the sentence? Which cannot substitute for *they?* Why?

They're being quiet.

the children	the dogs
the birds	the guests
the flowers	the raindrops

⟫ Exercise 18: Thinking About Meaning

You've heard the following comments at work. Explain the use of *is being* or *is* by giving more details about each situation.

1. Walter is being so polite.

   Examples: *He is usually very rude.* OR
   He often insults people. OR
   His behavior is unusual.

2. Maria is very helpful.

3. The company is being generous.

4. The employees are being so quiet at staff meetings.

5. Mr. Johnson is unfair.

Summary

The Simple Present: Form

Statements:	Some students **study** all night for an exam.
Negative Statements:	I **don't drive** to school. I walk.
Yes/No Questions:	**Do** you **read** science fiction?
Short Answers:	Yes, I **do.** OR No, I **don't.**
Information Questions:	Where **do** you **buy** your books?
Information Questions (Subject):	Who **buys** books there?

The Simple Present: Meaning and Use

想，特别.   再三

The simple present expresses general statements, especially about habitual or repeated activities and permanent situations.

Habits:	She **bites** her nails.
Routines:	I **study** every evening at the library.
Schedules:	Classes **begin** at eight o'clock every morning.
Facts:	Only birds **have** feathers and a wishbone.
Generalizations:	Americans **spend** a lot on their pets.
Definitions:	The word *extravagant* /ɪkˈstrævəgənt/ **means** to spend much more than necessary.
Newspaper Headlines:	OLYMPIC GAMES OPEN

The Present Continuous: Form

Statements: I**'m calling** to make an appointment.

Negative Statements: He**'s not working** right now.

Yes/No Questions: **Is** it **raining** outside?

Short Answers: Yes, it **is.** OR No, it **isn't.**

Information Questions: What **are** you **bringing** to the party?

Information Questions (Subject):   Who**'s bringing** dessert?

The Present Continuous: Meaning and Use

The present continuous focuses on activities in progress or on temporary and changing situations.

Activities in Progress: We**'re waiting** for the mail now.

                               He**'s writing** a research paper this semester.

Temporary Situations: They**'re living** in an apartment right now, but they**'re looking for** a house to buy.

Stative Verbs: Meaning and Use

Stative verbs describe conditions or states that we do not expect to change. They are usually in the simple present tense. They express descriptions, possession, relationships, measurement, senses and physical sensations, emotions, attitudes, ideas, compliments, and criticism.

Descriptions: Tom **is** five feet eight and **has** curly hair.

Possessions and Relationships: He **has** a new stereo.
                                       She **has** many cousins.

Measurements: This package **weighs** almost two pounds.

Senses and Physical Sensations: I **see** two cars on the road right now.
                                       My throat **hurts.**

Emotions and Attitudes: I **love** you.
                                       I don't **care!**

Ideas: I **remember** my first day of school.

Compliments: This chicken **tastes** great.

Criticism: That music **sounds** awful.

Some verbs have both active and stative meanings. As active verbs, they are often used in the present continuous. Verbs in this category include **be** with certain adjectives and **weigh, taste, smell, see,** and **have.**

State: We **have** tropical fish at home.

Action: We**'re having** fish for dinner tonight.

⇢ Summary Exercise: Finding Errors

Each of the following sentences has an error in form or use. Find each error and correct it.

1. Look outside. ~~It snows!~~ It's snowing!

2. The baby is being very big now. The baby ~~has been~~ is weigh very big now.

3. What means this? What does this means? ✓

4. I have to look in the phone book. I'm not knowing his number. I don't know his number.

5. My father is a carpenter. What your father does? What does your father do?

6. That's a good restaurant. We're eating there all the time. We ~~had eaten~~ eat there all the time.

7. Do you know that water is freezing at 0° centigrade? Water freezes at the time.

8. Susan doesn't goes there anymore. Susan doesn't go there anymore.

9. We are take the bus every morning. We take the bus every morning.

10. Ron go to work every Sunday. Ron went to work every Sunday. goes

Adverbs of Frequency, *There Is* and *There Are*, and Imperatives

Preview

Two friends are discussing their weekend plans:

Mark: Do you **ever** eat out?
Paul: Yes, we **usually** eat out on Friday night. We **often** go to a Japanese restaurant.
Mark: Oh. **Is there** a Japanese restaurant nearby?
Paul: Yes, **there is. Go** straight ahead one block, **turn** right at the light, and it's the second building on the left. **Be** sure to get there early.
Mark: Thanks. We will. Anita **always** complains when we have to wait.

Adverbs of frequency (such as **always, usually, often**) tell how often something happens. **Ever** means *at any time*, **always** means *all of the time*, **usually** means *most of the time*, and **often** means *much of the time*. Adverbs of frequency are typically used with the simple present to express routines, habits, and generalizations.

There is and **there are** introduce a noun that the speaker hasn't mentioned yet (in this case, *a Japanese restaurant*). **There is** and **there are** introduce new information in announcements, descriptions, and facts.

Imperatives generally tell people to do something. In the conversation above, Paul is giving directions and advice to Mark.

Adverbs of Frequency: Meaning

HOW OFTEN?

1. Adverbs of frequency tell how often something happens. They range in meaning from *all of the time* (100%) to *none of the time* (0%):

Affirmative

100% always, constantly, continually, forever

almost always

frequently, usually, generally, normally, typically

often

sometimes, occasionally

Negative

hardly ever, rarely, seldom

almost never

0% never

> Paul **often** eats Japanese food.
> He **sometimes** eats raw fish.

2. Ever means *at any time*. It is typically used in questions, in negative sentences, and with **hardly**:

> Do you **ever** eat hot dogs?
> I **don't ever** eat hot dogs.
> I **hardly ever** eat hot dogs.

3. Affirmative adverbs of frequency are sometimes used with **not**. Negative adverbs of frequency do not occur with **not** because a negative idea is already included in their meaning:

> We **don't often** eat fast food.
> We **seldom** eat fast food.
> *We don't seldom eat fast food. (INCORRECT)

▥➡ Exercise 1: Working on Meaning

Read each sentence and write an adverb of frequency with the same meaning in the blank. Be prepared to explain your answers.

1. Nina eats cereal for breakfast every morning.

   Nina _____*always*_____ eats cereal for breakfast.

2. Once or twice a week she has some juice too.

   _____ she has some juice too.

3. She doesn't have coffee because most mornings she _____ has time to make it.

4. Most of the time, someone makes a fresh pot of coffee before she arrives at work.

   Someone _____ makes a fresh pot of coffee before she arrives at work.

5. Every morning, she fills up her cup on the way into her office.

   She _____ fills up her cup on the way into her office.

6. She tries not to drink more than two cups because she worries all the time about the negative effects of caffeine.

   She _____ drinks more than two cups because she _____ worries

   about the negative effects of caffeine.

Adverbs of Frequency: Form

POSITION OF ADVERBS OF FREQUENCY

1. Adverbs of frequency come before the main verb in statements and questions:

Statements:	Anita **always** eats breakfast.
Yes/No Questions:	Do you **always** eat breakfast?
Information Questions (Subject):	Who **always** eats breakfast?
Information Questions:	When do you **usually** eat breakfast?

2. Adverbs of frequency come between the auxiliary verb and the main verb:

Negative Statements:	We don't **always** eat breakfast.
With Modals:	You should **always** eat breakfast.

(continued)

3. Adverbs of frequency generally come after the main verb **be.** However, in *yes/no* questions with the main verb **be,** they follow the subject:

Statements:	She is **always** late.
Negative Statements:	He isn't **always** late.
Information Questions (Subject):	Who is **always** late?
Yes/No Questions:	Is he **always** late?

4. In short answers, adverbs of frequency come before forms of **do** and **be:**

With **do**:	Yes, I **always** do.
	No, I **never** do.
With **be**:	Yes, he **always** is.
	No, he **never** is.

5. Sometimes adverbs of frequency begin the sentence for contrast or special emphasis. These adverbs include some of the longer adverbs such as **frequently, generally, normally, ordinarily, usually, sometimes,** and **occasionally:**

The weather is very strange this winter. **Sometimes** it gets very warm, and **occasionally** we even have thunderstorms. **Usually,** it's much cooler.

⯈ Exercise 2: Working on Meaning and Form

Choose an adverb of frequency (*always, frequently, often, sometimes, hardly ever*) to substitute for each underlined time expression. More than one answer is possible. Then rewrite the sentence and put the adverb of frequency in the correct position.

Work with a partner and compare your answers. Be prepared to tell the class why you chose a particular adverb of frequency.

1. She listens to the morning news on the radio <u>every day</u>.

    She always listens to the morning news on the radio.

2. He remembers to send his aunt a birthday card <u>every year</u>.

    _____

3. We go to the movies <u>once a week</u>.

    _____

4. She watches television <u>one hour a week</u>.

    _____

5. He cooks dinner <u>once or twice a month</u>.

_____

6. He visits his girlfriend in another city <u>every other weekend</u>.

_____

7. We call each other <u>five times a week</u>.

_____

8. I see her about <u>once every two or three months</u>.

_____

Adverbs of Frequency: Use

ROUTINES, HABITS, GENERALIZATIONS, COMPLAINTS

1. Adverbs of frequency are used with many verb tenses, but they are especially common with the simple present tense to describe routines and habits and to make generalizations:

Routine: Bob **always** has a cigarette at 7:30 A.M.

Habit: He **usually** smokes a pack of cigarettes every day.

Generalization: Smokers **often** die of lung cancer.

2. With adverbs of frequency that mean *all of the time* (such as **always, constantly, forever,** and **continually**), you can use the present continuous to complain about things that people do:

Complaint: He's **constantly** smoking cigarettes.

3. Compare the use of the simple present and the present continuous in these sentences:

Simple Present	**Present Continuous**
They **always call** me early Sunday morning.	They**'re always calling** me early Sunday morning.
He **constantly smokes** cigarettes.	He**'s constantly smoking** cigarettes.

These sentences are close in meaning. However, the sentences in the simple present are only stating a fact, whereas the sentences in the continuous are clearly expressing a negative attitude as well.

⯈ Exercise 3: Describing Routines

Read the following situations. Then write new sentences putting each adverb of frequency (in parentheses) in an appropriate position.

1. (often) They eat dinner at six o'clock.

    They often eat dinner at six o'clock.

2. (usually) On Saturday morning, I sleep late. (sometimes) I sleep until eight or nine o'clock. (always) On weekdays, my alarm rings at 6:00 A.M. (rarely) I go to bed before midnight. (often) Therefore, I am very tired by lunchtime.

    _____

    _____

    _____

    _____

3. (normally) Jack is very slow in the morning. (always) He needs lots of time. (usually) He takes a shower after his alarm rings. (occasionally) He spends half an hour in the shower. (typically) He spends a lot of time getting dressed and eating breakfast. (often) As a result, he is late for work.

    _____

    _____

    _____

    _____

4. (usually) The baby sleeps through the night. (occasionally) She wakes up in the middle of the night. (frequently) This happens when she has a long nap during the day. (always) We try to wake her from her nap after two hours. (sometimes) But we can't wake her up.

    _____

    _____

    _____

    _____

➡ **Exercise 4: Finding Out About Study Habits**

Work with a partner. Take turns finding out about each other's study habits using the questions below. Choose an appropriate adverb of frequency to answer each question and put a checkmark (✓) in the box.

A: *Do you ever wake up early to study for an exam?*
B: *Yes, I sometimes do.* OR *No, I never do.*

Do you ever...	always	usually	sometimes	rarely	never
1. wake up early to study for an exam?	☐	☐	☐	☐	☐
2. study at night?	☐	☐	☐	☐	☐
3. delay studying as long as you can?	☐	☐	☐	☐	☐
4. eat while you're studying?	☐	☐	☐	☐	☐
5. listen to music while you're studying?	☐	☐	☐	☐	☐
6. call up a friend to ask questions?	☐	☐	☐	☐	☐
7. fall asleep while you're studying?	☐	☐	☐	☐	☐
8. study with a friend?	☐	☐	☐	☐	☐
9. study at a desk?	☐	☐	☐	☐	☐
10. study on Friday night?	☐	☐	☐	☐	☐

➡ **Exercise 5: Describing Study Habits**

Write five sentences about your partner's study habits. Use adverbs of frequency and the simple present. Be ready to read your sentences to the class.

1. *Anna never studies at night. Sometimes she wakes up early to study for an exam.*
2. _____
3. _____
4. _____
5. _____
6. _____

⟫ **Exercise 6: Complaining**

Work with a partner. What kind of behavior do you find annoying? Use *always, continually, forever,* and *constantly* with the present continuous to complain about people you know, politicians, or other famous people.

> Examples: *My father is always smoking a cigar.*
> *The mayor is constantly exaggerating.*
> *The governor is always losing his temper.*

⟫ **Exercise 7: Thinking About Meaning**

Work in small groups. Read the statements and answer the questions. Be ready to explain your answers to the class.

1. Think of a situation for the following sentence. What are some other ways of saying it?

   Joe is always talking on the phone.

2. Now describe the meaning of the sentence below. How is it different from the one above?

   Joe always talks on the phone.

There Is and *There Are*: Form

Statements			Contractions
There	**is**	a restaurant nearby.	**There's**
There	**are**	many restaurants nearby.	

- The verb **be** agrees with the noun that follows it.
- Contractions with **there + is** are acceptable in informal writing and in speaking.
- Contractions with **there + are** are generally avoided in writing.

Negative Statements				Contractions
There	**is**	**not**	a restaurant nearby.	**There isn't / There's not**
There	**is**	**no**	restaurant nearby.	**There's no**
There	**are**	**not any**	restaurants nearby.	**There aren't any**
There	**are**	**no**	restaurants nearby.	

- **Not, no,** and **not any** come before the noun.
- **Any** is used instead of **some** in negative statements.

Yes/No Questions	Short Answers	Contractions
Is **there** a restaurant nearby?	Yes, **there is**. No, **there is not**.	No, **there isn't**.
Are **there** any restaurants nearby?	Yes, **there are**. No, **there are not**.	No, **there aren't**.

- **Be** comes before **there**.
- Short answers include **there + be (+ not)**.

Information Questions (Subject)	Answers	Contractions
What **is** **there** for dinner?	Chicken salad.	**What's**

- The *wh-* word comes before **be** and **there**.

CONVERSATION NOTE

In conversation, you will hear the contraction **there's** with both singular and plural nouns. This is acceptable now in conversation, but not yet in written English:

Singular Nouns

There's an egg in the refrigerator.

Plural Nouns

"**There's two eggs** in the refrigerator." (SPOKEN ONLY)

➡ **Exercise 8: Working on Form**

Work with a partner. Choose a topic (time, weight, distance, or money) and take turns asking and answering questions with *how many* and *there are*.

   A: *How many days are there in a year?*
   B: *There are 365.*

Time	Weight	Distance	Money
days/year	ounces/pound	inches/foot	pennies/dollar
hours/day	pounds/ton	feet/yard	nickels/quarter
weeks/year	grams/kilogram	meters/kilometer	quarters/dollar
years/century	pounds/kilogram	kilometers/mile	nickels/dime
decades/century	milligrams/gram	centimeters/inch	dimes/dollar

⮞ Exercise 9: Working on Form

Work with a partner. Take turns asking and answering questions with *there is* and *there are*. Use the topics and information in Exercise 8. Try to trick your partner.

> **A:** *Are there six nickels in a quarter?*
> **B:** *No, there aren't. There's only five.* OR *There're only five.*

There Is and *There Are*: Meaning and Use

NEW INFORMATION

1. There in **there is** and **there are** has no meaning. It is used to fill the subject position in the sentence.

2. There is and **there are** introduce a topic that you haven't mentioned before:

There's a steak in the freezer. Should we have it tonight?

3. Since **there** introduces new information, it is often used to make announcements, describe things, and state facts:

Announcement:	Sue, **there's** someone at the door. Please get it.
Description:	In my apartment, **there are** two large windows in the living room.
Fact:	**There are** 365 days in a year.

⮞ Exercise 10: Making Announcements

Work with a partner. You are a secretary in a busy office. Take turns making announcements using *there is* and the person's name. Then write out the answers.

1. You took a phone message for Ms. Malik while she was out:

   Ms. Malik, there's a message for you.

2. A package has arrived for Ms. Stern:

   _____

3. A special delivery letter has arrived for Mr. Blake:

   _____

4. Mr. Blake has to attend an emergency meeting at two o'clock:

   _____

5. A phone call comes in for Ms. Stern from someone who won't give his name:

   _____

⫸ Exercise 11: Understanding Descriptions

Work with a partner. One person is an apartment hunter. The other person is a rental agent. The apartment hunter asks questions. The rental agent answers using *there is* or *there are* and the information below or *I don't know*. Then ask and answer your own questions (⁓).

```
111 Washington Street, Apartment #3.
Two bedrooms.

Bedrooms and living room are carpeted.
Three large closets. The bathroom has
a tub with a shower. Large eat-in
kitchen. Brand new appliances
including a dishwasher and a microwave
oven. Gas heat.

Quiet building. Four apartments.
Free tenant parking behind building.

Conveniently located. Supermarket is
one block west. The #5, #12, and #13
buses stop at the corner.
```

1. Does it have a lot of closets?

   Apartment hunter: *Does it have a lot of closets?*
   Rental agent: *Yes, there are three large closets.*

2. What about cabinets in the kitchen?

3. What kind of kitchen appliances does it have?

4. Does the bathroom have a bathtub?

5. What kind of heat does the apartment have?

6. How many apartments are there in the building?

7. Can I catch the bus nearby?

8. Is it near a grocery store?

9. Is there a park nearby?

10. ⁓

Imperatives: Form

Imperative

Open your books.

- The affirmative imperative form of the verb is the same as the simple form of the verb. The verb does not change form.
- The imperative addresses one or more people. *You* is implied, and does not have to be mentioned.
- **Please** comes at the beginning or at the end of the sentence:

  Please open your books.
  Open your books, **please**.

Negative Imperative	Contraction
Do not open your books.	**Don't**

- **Do not** or the contraction **don't** comes before the verb.

⇒ Exercise 12: Working on Form

Work with a partner. Write an affirmative or negative imperative sentence for each situation. Use *please* if you think it is appropriate.

1. Ask your friend to call you later. *Please call me later.*

2. Direct your friend to the post office. *Go three blocks and turn left.*

3. Ask your mother not to worry about you. _____

4. Ask your friends not to speak so fast. _____

5. Direct someone to the telephone, which is downstairs and straight ahead. _____

   _____

6. Warn your friend that she shouldn't drive over the speed limit. _____

   _____

7. Offer an old man your seat on a bus. _____

8. Tell your uncle not to work so hard. _____

9. Ask your roommate to wait for you after class. _____

10. Warn your cousin not to drink and drive. _____

Imperatives: Meaning and Use

COMMANDS, REQUESTS, DIRECTIONS

1. Imperatives generally tell someone to do something. They have many uses both in conversation and in writing:

Commands: **Wash** your hands before you sit down at the table.

Requests: Please **come** early.

Directions: **Go** straight ahead one block and **turn** right.

Instructions: **Preheat** the oven to 350°.

Warnings: **Be** careful. There's a slippery spot on the road.

Offers: Here. **Have** another piece of cake.

Signs: PLEASE **KEEP OFF** THE GRASS.

Advice: You're sick. **Go** to bed.

2. **Don't** is frequently used in conversation; **do not** is typically used in certain types of written material, such as signs:

A conversation:

> Ann: Please **don't leave** so soon.
> Sue: I'm sorry, but I have to go.

A sign:

> **DO NOT ENTER**

3. Imperatives can easily sound rude or angry, depending on the situation and your tone of voice. **Please** helps to soften a command. Using modals (such as **would** and **could**) is a more polite and indirect way to tell someone to do something. (These modals are discussed in detail in Chapter 7.)

CONVERSATION NOTE

You is generally omitted with imperatives, but you will sometimes hear it in conversation:

You wait here and I'll go and look for Tina.

Here. **You take** this one.

In the first example, **you** distinguishes the listener from the speaker; in the second example, **you** gets the attention of the listener.

⟱ Exercise 13: Giving Advice

Work with a partner. Take turns stating a problem and giving advice. Try to use both affirmative and negative imperatives. Then write out the answers.

1. My car won't start. _Check the battery._
2. The toast is stuck in the toaster. _Don't stick a fork in the toaster! Unplug it first._
3. The gas tank is empty. _____
4. I have a cold. _____
5. I can't fall asleep at night. _____
6. I don't have enough money. _____
7. My pen's out of ink. _____
8. I can't find his telephone number. _____

⟱ Exercise 14: Giving Instructions

You're leaving on a long vacation. A friend is going to stay in your apartment. Make a list of things for your friend to do. Use imperatives.

THINGS TO DO

Walk the dog every day at 7:00 a.m. and 7:00 p.m.

_____
_____
_____
_____
_____
_____
_____
_____
_____
_____

➧ **Exercise 15: Giving Advice**

Imagine you are writing a letter to your niece or nephew, who is visiting a big city for the first time. Because you are worried about your relative, give her or him some advice on how to cope in a big city. Use imperatives in your sentences.

December 5

Dear _____

   I have been worrying about your trip next week. You know that the city is very expensive, so ___figure out___

how much money you will need _____ *and* _____

_____

   Also, it can be very dangerous. The crime rate is very high. Please _____

_____

   And another thing—the weather is bad this time of year. There are frequent snowstorms and cold winds.

_____

   I know the city can be a lot of fun, too. _____

_____

_____

   Now remember, I'm going to worry about you so _____

_____

_____

          Love,

        _____

P.S. I almost forgot! _____

_____

Summary

Adverbs of Frequency: Form

Statements:	He **usually** cooks dinner.
	You should **always** eat breakfast.
	I'm **always** on time.
Negative Statements:	We don't **always** agree.
Yes/No Questions:	Do you **usually** leave on time?
Short Answers:	Yes, I **always** do. OR No, I **never** do.
Information Questions:	When do you **usually** leave for work?
Information Questions (Subject):	Who **always** eats breakfast?

Adverbs of Frequency: Meaning and Use

Adverbs of frequency tell how often something happens. They range in meaning from *all of the time* to *none of the time*.

Routines:	He **normally** arrives at work at nine o'clock.
Habits:	I **always** bite my nails before an exam.
Generalizations:	Children **generally** need more sleep than adults.
Complaints:	He's **forever** forgetting his keys.

There Is and *There Are*: Form

Statements:	**There's** a message on your desk.
Negative Statements:	**There's** no milk in the refrigerator.
	There isn't any cheese either.
Yes/No Questions:	**Are there** any messages for me?
Short Answers:	Yes, **there are.** OR No, **there aren't.**
Information Questions (Subject):	What **is there** for dinner?

There Is and *There Are*: Meaning and Use

There is and **there are** introduce new information in a sentence. They are often used to make announcements, describe things, and state facts.

Announcements:	**There's** someone at the door.
Descriptions:	**There's** a large closet in my bedroom.
Facts:	**There are** 365 days in a year.

Imperatives: Form

Imperative: **Check** your battery.

Negative Imperative: Please **don't be** late.

Imperatives: Meaning and Use

Imperatives tell someone to do something. They are used in commands, requests, directions, instructions, warnings, offers, signs, and advice. They can be softened by *please* and by the tone of voice.

Commands: **Don't be** late.

Requests: Please **leave** your boots outside.

Directions: **Walk** to the corner and then **turn** left.

Instructions: **Preheat** the oven to 350°.

Warnings: **Be** careful. There's a puddle here.

Offers: Here. **Have** another cookie.

Signs: **DO NOT ENTER**

Advice: If you feel sick, **go** to bed early.

⇒ **Summary Exercise: Finding Errors**

Each of the following sentences has an error in form or appropriate use. Find each error and correct it.

1. Suzanne, ~~it's~~ someone at the door. Please answer it for me.   *there's*

2. Always it arrives late.

3. Here. Take you this one, OK?

4. We take never a trip in August.

5. Look! A hole is in your shoe.

6. I don't seldom eat pizza.

7. I think there is nine people in line.

8. I'm angry at her! Forever she's waking me up in the morning.

9. Don't please smoke.

10. Mark, it's a message for you.

CHAPTER 3

Expressing Past Time: The Simple Past, *Used to*, and the Past Continuous

A riddle:

> Why **did** the man **throw** his clock out the window?
> He **wanted** to see time fly!

Talking about the past:

> I **used to** live in Atlanta. The spring **was** so beautiful. There **were** many dogwoods and native azaleas that **would** bloom in March.

The beginning of a story:

> It **was snowing** hard outside. The children **were playing** *Monopoly* in the living room. Aunt Dorothy **was knitting** a sweater. The cat **was sleeping** on the couch. Suddenly, there **was** a big crash on the front lawn. It **shook** the whole house.

The simple past describes actions and events that were completed at a definite time in the past. The situations and actions may be recent or a long time ago, habitual, short or long.

Used to is a special simple past verb that expresses a past habit or a situation that doesn't exist any longer. **Would** can also be used to describe a repeated action in the past.

The past continuous expresses an action or situation in progress at a specific time in the past. It emphasizes a longer action in the background in contrast with a shorter action in the simple past.

The Simple Past of Regular and Irregular Verbs: Form

Statements: Regular Verbs	Irregular Verbs
I **worked** yesterday.	I **left** yesterday.
You	You
She	She
He	He
It	It
We	We
They	They

- All regular simple past verbs end in **-ed**.
- Look at pages 486–487 for spelling and pronunciation rules for regular simple past verbs.
- Irregular verbs have special simple past forms. Look at pages 488–491 for a list of irregular verbs and their simple past forms.
- The simple past forms of regular and irregular verbs are the same for all subjects (*I, you, she*, and so on).

Negative Statements	Contraction
I **did not work** yesterday.	I **didn't** work.
You	You
She	She
He	He
It	It
We	We
They	They

- To form negative statements, use **did + not** or the contraction **didn't**. The main verb is in the simple form.

Yes/No Questions	Short Answers	Contraction
Did you **work** hard?	Yes, I **did**.	
	No, I **did not**.	No, I **didn't**.

- To form *yes/no* questions, use **did** before the subject. The main verb is in the simple form.
- Short answers to *yes/no* questions have a subject pronoun + **did**.
- For negative short answers, use **did + not** or the negative contraction **didn't**.

Information Questions	Answers
When **did** you **leave**?	The day before yesterday.
Where **did** you **go**?	To Chicago.

- The *wh-* word is followed by **did**, the subject, and the simple form of the main verb.

Information Questions (Subject)	Answers
Who **called?**	James **did**.
What **happened?**	He **twisted** his ankle.

- If **who** or **what** is the subject, then **did** is not used in the question. The main verb stays in the simple past with the same word order as for affirmative statements.

CONVERSATION NOTES

1. The negative contraction **didn't** is typically used in speaking and informal writing, and especially in short answers:

Did you eat yet?   No, I **didn't.**

2. In fast informal conversation, **did you** sounds more like *didja*:

Written Form	Spoken Form
Did you work yesterday?	"**Didja** work yesterday?" (SPOKEN ONLY)
Did you eat yet?	"**Didja** eat yet?" (SPOKEN ONLY)

3. **Did** contracts with *wh-* words in fast informal conversation:

Written Form	Spoken Form
What **did** he do?	"What**'d** he do?" (SPOKEN ONLY)
Where **did** she go?	"Where**'d** she go?" (SPOKEN ONLY)

➡ Exercise 1: Working on Pronunciation

1. Listen to your teacher pronounce the regular simple past verbs in each column. Write the number of syllables next to each verb.

Column 1	Column 2	Column 3
worked __1__	tried __1__	invited __3__
looked __1__	arrived __2__	started __2__
asked _____	sprained _____	rented _____
picked _____	closed _____	reported _____
dropped _____	allowed _____	waited _____
wished _____	traveled _____	needed _____
laughed _____	judged _____	added _____
sliced _____	robbed _____	decided _____
watched _____	stayed _____	attended _____

2. Work with a partner. Take turns pronouncing the verbs in each column. Then answer the questions.

How is *-ed* pronounced in Column 1? _____

How is *-ed* pronounced in Column 2? _____

In Column 3, what happened to the number of syllables each time the simple past verb ended in *-ted* or *-ded*? _____

➡ Exercise 2: Working on Pronunciation

Work with a partner. Take turns pronouncing these regular simple past verbs. Write the number of syllables next to each verb. Check (✓) the correct column according to how the *-ed* ending is pronounced.

Simple Past Verb	Column 1 /t/	Column 2 /d/	Column 3 /id/
walked __1__	✓	☐	☐
phoned _____	☐	☐	☐
bumped _____	☐	☐	☐
twisted _____	☐	☐	☐
pushed _____	☐	☐	☐
happened _____	☐	☐	☐
traded _____	☐	☐	☐

Simple Past Verb	Column 1 /t/	Column 2 /d/	Column 3 /id/
answered_____	☐	☐	☐
studied_____	☐	☐	☐
waved _____	☐	☐	☐
punched _____	☐	☐	☐
admitted _____	☐	☐	☐
wanted _____	☐	☐	☐
missed _____	☐	☐	☐
pretended _____	☐	☐	☐

⇒ Exercise 3: Working on Form

Work with a partner. Complete the conversations using the simple past form of the regular verbs in parentheses. Then practice each conversation with your partner. Pay attention to how *-ed* is pronounced.

1. Two friends are telling each other about their summer:

   A: We _____*rented*_____ (rent) a cabin on the lake for a week this summer.

   B: Really? We _____*decided*_____ (decide) to stay home this summer since we _____*traveled*_____ (travel) so much last year.

2. Two roommates:

   A: Sue, you _____ (drop) crumbs all over the carpet.

   B: I know. I _____ (try) to be careful, but I _____ (bump) into something.

3. Two classmates:

   A: I _____ (study) all morning in the library.

   B: Oh, so that's why nobody _____ (answer) the phone. We _____ (call) you three times because we _____ (want) to come over for a while.

4. Two students:

   A: You're late. What _____ (happen)?

   B: I _____ (miss) the bus, so I _____ (walk) to school instead.

5. Two friends:

   A: We _____ (watch) a funny movie on TV last night. I _____ (laugh) so loud that I _____ (frighten) the dog.

   B: Really? _____ (you/rent) it at the video store?

6. Two office friends:

   A: Karen _____ (stay) home from work this week because she _____ (injure) her back, _____ (sprain) her ankle, and _____ (bump) her head in a car accident.

   B: I know. I _____ (phone) her last night and _____ (ask) her how she was feeling.

⇒ Exercise 4: Working on Irregular Forms

Work with a partner. Write the simple past form of the irregular verb in parentheses. Complete each conversation with a short answer that shows Person B's agreement with Person A. Then practice the conversations.

1. **A:** She _____*came*_____ (come) too late for the show.
   B: ___*Yes, she did*___. She _____*had*_____ (have) a flat tire on the way.

2. **A:** You ___*didn't pay*___ (not/pay) last month's phone bill.
   B: ___*No, I didn't*___. The phone company _____*made*_____ (make) a mistake and overcharged us.

3. **A:** They _____ (leave) without saying good-bye.
   B: _____. They _____ (get) a call from their baby-sitter and _____ (run) out quickly.

4. **A:** You _____ (forget) your raincoat.
   B: _____. But I _____ (bring) an umbrella. I _____ (find) it in my car.

5. **A:** The teacher _____ (not/give) an assignment.
   B: _____. But she _____ (give) two last week.

6. **A:** You _____ (make) a lot of food.

    B: _____. I _____ (see) these recipes in the newspaper last night and I _____ (think) we should try something different.

7. **A:** I _____ (not/take out) the garbage this morning.

    B: _____. So I _____ (take it out) when I _____ (wake up).

8. **A:** I _____ (hear) that Emma _____ (break) her leg.

    B: _____. I _____ (speak) to her last night. She _____ (fall) off a ladder. She also _____ (hurt) her arm.

⇨ Exercise 5: Working on Information Questions

Work in small groups. Match the names of the famous works in Column A with the people in Column B. Then check your answers with another group by asking and answering questions. Use *who* or *what* and the verbs *write*, *paint*, *compose*, and *sculpt*.

    A: *Who wrote Macbeth?*
    B: *Shakespeare did.*
      OR
    A: *What did Shakespeare write?*
    B: *He wrote Macbeth.*

Column A	Column B
Macbeth	Dostoyevsky
Guernica	Frida Kahlo
The Ninth Symphony	Frédéric Bartholdi
Don Quixote	Gabriel García Márquez
Snow Country	Shakespeare
Crime and Punishment	Beethoven
One Hundred Years of Solitude	Dante
The Statue of Liberty	Pablo Picasso
Self-Portrait, 1926	Cervantes
The Divine Comedy	Yasunari Kawabata

The Simple Past of *Be:* Form

Statements

I	**was**	sick last week.	We	**were**	sick last week.
She			You		
He			They		
It					

- **Be** has two forms in the simple past: **was** and **were**.

Negative Statements   Contractions

I	**was**	**not**	there.	I	**wasn't**	there.
He				He		
She				She		
It				It		

We	**were**	**not**	there.	We	**weren't**	there.
You				You		
They				They		

- For negative statements, use **was** or **were** + **not**.
- **Was** or **were** + **not** contract to form **wasn't** or **weren't**.

Yes/No Questions   Short Answers   Contractions

Was	he	sick?	Yes, he **was**.	
			No, he **was not**.	No, he **wasn't**.

Were	they	sick?	Yes, they **were**.	
			No, they **were not**.	No, they **weren't**.

- To form *yes/no* questions, use **was** or **were** before the subject.
- Short answers to *yes/no* questions have a subject pronoun + **was** or **were**.
- For negative short answers, use **was** or **were** + **not** or **-n't**.

Information Questions   Answers

When	**was**	I	late?	Two days ago.
Why	**were**	you	late?	I missed the bus.

- The *wh-* word is followed by **was** or **were** and the subject.

Information Questions (Subject)	Answers
Who **was** late?	Tom **was**.
What **was** the problem?	He **had** a flat tire.

- If **who** or **what** is the subject, then the word order is the same as for affirmative statements.

CONVERSATION NOTE

The negative contractions **wasn't** and **weren't** are typically used in speaking and informal writing, and especially in short answers:

Were you there last week?	No, I **wasn't**.
Were they there last week?	No, they **weren't**.

⟹ **Exercise 6: Working on Form**

Work with a partner. Complete each question and answer with *was* or *were*. Read the conversation aloud. Then take turns asking and answering the same questions with true information about yourself.

1. **A:** Where _____*were*_____ you five years ago?

   B: I _____*was*_____ in Atlanta, Georgia.

2. **A:** What _____ your favorite books when you _____ a child?

   B: They _____ *The Secret Garden* and *Alice in Wonderland*.

3. **A:** How old _____ you when you graduated from high school?

   B: I _____ seventeen years old.

4. **A:** What _____ your favorite subjects in school?

   B: I guess they _____ mathematics and physics.

5. **A:** Who _____ your first boss?

   B: Let's see. His name _____ Dr. Trujillo. I worked in his dental office

   after school.

6. **A:** Where _____ you and your family three years ago?

   B: We _____ in Hong Kong.

7. **A:** What _____ your last meal?

   B: It _____ breakfast. I only ate some fruit, so now I'm starving.

8. **A:** When _____ the last time you saw your best friend?

   B: It _____ two weeks ago. That reminds me. I need to call her.

➥ Exercise 7: Asking Information Questions

Work with a partner. Write two questions with *who*, *what*, or *when* about each of the following statements. Then take turns asking and answering the questions.

1. Genghis Khan was the leader of the Mongols. He conquered Persia and much of China in the 1200s.

   A: Who was Genghis Khan? OR

   What happened in the 1200s? OR

   What did Genghis Khan do in the 1200s? OR

   When did Genghis Khan conquer Persia and much of China?

   B: Genghis Khan was the leader of the Mongols. OR

   Genghis Khan conquered Persia and much of China. OR

   He conquered Persia and much of China. OR

   In the 1200s.

2. Mahatma Gandhi led the movement against British rule in India in the 1940s.

   _____

   _____

3. The Pilgrims celebrated the first Thanksgiving in 1621.

   _____

   _____

4. Julius Caesar was one of the rulers of the Roman Empire. He established the 365-day calendar that we use today.

   _____

   _____

5. Charlemagne became emperor of the western Roman Empire in the year 800.

_____

_____

6. Archimedes was a Greek physicist, mathematician, and inventor. He calculated the value of *pi*.

_____

_____

7. In 1815, the British and the Prussians defeated Napoleon in the Battle of Waterloo.

_____

_____

8. Simón Bolívar was a hero of the South American wars of independence in the nineteenth century.

_____

_____

The Simple Past: Meaning and Use

DEFINITE COMPLETED ACTIONS

1. The simple past describes an action that began and ended at a definite time in the past. It can be recent or a long time ago:

> I **saw** her a minute ago.
> He just **called.**
> Amelia Earhart **flew** the first solo from Hawaii to the American mainland in 1935.

2. The action can last for a long time or for a very short time:

> I **lived** in California for fifteen years.
> The Great Earthquake of San Francisco **lasted** for thirty seconds.

3. The action can happen only once or many times:

> I **lost** my umbrella this morning.
> It **rained** every day last week.

(continued)

4. Some common uses of the simple past include correcting, reminding, making excuses, telling jokes or riddles, guessing, accusing, denying, agreeing, and disagreeing:

Correcting: Alexander Graham Bell **didn't invent** the light bulb. He **invented** the telephone.

Reminding: **Did** you **take** your raincoat?

Making Excuses: I'm sorry I'm late. I **had** a flat tire.

Telling Jokes: Why **didn't** the little boy **want** to use toothpaste? Because his teeth **weren't** loose!

Guessing: She probably **sprained** her ankle.

Accusing: **Did** you **leave** the TV **on?**

Denying: It **wasn't** me.

Agreeing: Sonya: She **came** too late for the show.
                   Tracy: Yes, she **did.** She **had** a flat tire on the way.

Disagreeing: The test **wasn't** easy. It **was** hard.

▶ Exercise 8: Reminding

Work with a partner. Take turns asking and answering questions in the simple past. Use the following verbs (*get, take, wash, water, brush, lock, do, pack, stop, take out, bring, sharpen, remember, finish*) and the words in parentheses. Then ask your own questions (⌒⌒).

1. Your friend is going to the beach:

   (bathing suit)

   A: *Did you get your bathing suit?*
   B: *Yes, I did.* OR *No, I didn't.*

2. Your friend is going on a trip. Before you take her to the airport, you try to make sure that she has everything that she needs:

   (toothbrush)
   (raincoat)
   (ticket)
   (glasses)
   (⌒⌒)

   Now remind your friend about all the things she needs to do before leaving:

   (plants)
   (garbage)
   (mail)
   (doors)
   (⌒⌒)

3. You stayed overnight with your nephew while his parents were on a business trip. Your nephew is getting ready to go to school. Before he leaves, you ask him if he has done everything that he was supposed to do:

(teeth)
(face)
(pencils)
(homework)
(‿‿‿‿)

Now remind him about everything that he needs to take:

(lunch money)
(gym shoes)
(backpack)
(jacket)
(‿‿‿‿)

⮕ Exercise 9: Making Excuses

Work in small groups. Imagine you are late for an important appointment for the second time. You are very embarrassed and keep thinking of excuses. Make up excuses using the words in parentheses and the simple past. Then make up your own creative excuse.

1. (miss/bus)

   Example: *I'm sorry I'm late. I missed the bus.*

2. (my watch/stop)

3. (I/get lost)

4. (I/oversleep)

5. (the electricity/go off/in my apartment)

6. (my goldfish/jump out of the tank)

7. (my cat/die)

8. (I/fall into a manhole)

9. (a mugger/take all my money)

10. (my cousin/call long distance/from Antarctica)

11. (aliens from outer space/kidnap me)

12. (‿‿‿‿)

⦿ Exercise 10: Telling Riddles

Here are some riddles that English-speaking children like to tell. Use the words in parentheses to write the questions in the simple past that go with each answer.

1. (why/not/the little boy/want to use toothpaste)

   Why didn't the little boy want to use toothpaste?

   Because his teeth weren't loose!

2. (why/the banana/go out with/the prune)

   _____

   Because he couldn't get a date!

3. (why/the house/seem empty)

   _____

   The fire went out, the steam escaped, and the milk evaporated!

4. (who/get up last night/when the baby cry)

   _____

   The whole neighborhood!

5. (what/the digital watch/say to its mother)

   _____

   Look, Ma, no hands!

6. (what/the Beatles/say/during a rockslide)

   _____

   Watch out for the Rolling Stones!

7. (what/cause/a lot of trouble/when it stop smoking)

   _____

   The chimney!

8. (why/the turkey/join the band)

_____

Because it had the drumsticks!

9. (what kind of chair/the geologist/like)

_____

A rock-ing chair!

10. why/the jogger/go to the veterinarian

_____

Because he hurt his calves!

➠ Exercise 11: Guessing

Work in small groups. Look at the following pictures and try to guess what happened. Make up several sentences about each picture with *probably* and the simple past.

1.

Example:
He probably had an accident or a fight.
He probably broke his arm.
He probably needed an X ray.

2.

3.

4.

5.

6.

7.

8.

9.

10.

11.

➠ Exercise 12: Accusing and Denying

Work in two large groups. In each group, start a question chain as follows: Person A selects a problem from the list below and asks Person B an accusing question in the simple past. Person B denies the accusation and blames Person C by saying, *It wasn't me. Maybe it was* _____, OR *I didn't do it. Maybe* _____ *did.* Continue until everyone in the group has had a turn. Then start again with a new accusation.

> **A:** *Sophie, did you leave the computer on?*
> **B:** *No, it wasn't me. Maybe it was Carlos.*
> **C:** *I didn't do it. Maybe Maria did.*

Problems

leave the computer on

call at 3:00 A.M.

write on the desk

drop crumbs all over the floor

spill soda on the desk

lose the car keys

leave the milk out

throw out the newspaper

tear the book

step on my coat

knock over the plant

➠ Exercise 13: Disagreeing

Work with a partner. Take turns disagreeing. Say the opposite of each sentence using a short answer with a form of *be*. Then add another sentence to explain why you disagree.

1. The exam was easy yesterday.

> **A:** *The exam was easy yesterday.*
> **B:** *No, it wasn't. It was hard.*

2. I wasn't very helpful yesterday.

> **A:** *I wasn't very helpful yesterday.*
> **B:** *Yes, you were. In fact, you were very helpful.*

3. It was too cold last night.

4. The pancakes weren't hot enough.

5. The homework assignment was too long.

6. I wasn't home on Tuesday evening.

7. My composition wasn't very good.

8. The textbook wasn't very helpful.

9. Sam wasn't in class today.

10. There weren't any visitors last night.

11. I was wrong about that.

12. You were angry at her in class.

Focus on Vocabulary

PREPOSITIONS OF TIME

Here are some common prepositions that help express a definite time in the past. They are often used with time phrases and the simple past to tell when an action or event took place.

in
in the twentieth century
in the sixties
in 1963
in the fall
in November

on
on Friday
on November 22, 1963

at
at 1:00 P.M.

⯈ Exercise 14: Correcting Misinformation

Work with a partner. Take turns reading the following statements to each other. Tell whether the statement is true or false. If the statement is false, change it to a negative statement. Then write a true statement using the simple past.

1. John F. Kennedy died in the seventeenth century. _False. John F. Kennedy didn't die in the seventeenth century. He died in the twentieth century._

2. Hawaii became part of the United States in the nineteenth century. _____

_____

_____

3. Marie and Pierre Curie discovered radioactivity. _____

_____

4. Alexander Graham Bell invented the piano. _____

_____

5. Charles Lindbergh flew across the Atlantic Ocean in the early twentieth century. _____

_____

6. Astronauts landed on Mars in 1969. _____

_____

7. Mozart wrote novels. _____

_____

8. Rembrandt painted the *Mona Lisa*. _____

_____

9. Mao Zedong established the Communist People's Republic of China in 1965. _____

_____

10. Albert Einstein proposed the Theory of Relativity. _____

_____

11. In *Romeo and Juliet*, Romeo and Juliet got married at the end of the story. _____

_____

12. *Time* magazine named the computer as *Man of the Year* in 1983. _____

_____

_____

⇒ Exercise 15: Asking Questions with *In, On, At*

Work in small groups. Start a question chain as follows: Person A asks a question using the phrase in parentheses in the simple past. Person B answers the question using a time phrase with *in*, *on*, or *at*. Person B then asks Person C a new question. Continue until everyone has had a turn.

1. (go to sleep last night)

   A: *When did you go to sleep last night?*
   B: *At midnight. When did you leave for school this morning?*
   C: *At 8:30. When did you...*

2. (have your last medical checkup)

3. (take a vacation)

4. (visit the dentist)

5. (speak to one of your relatives)

6. (see a good movie)

7. (do your homework)

8. (begin to learn English)

9. (go to the supermarket this week)

10. (leave your country)

Used to: Form

Statements

I	**used to**	**arrive**	late.
You			
She			
He			
It			
We			
They			

- **Used to** is a special simple past tense verb. It is followed by the main verb in the simple form.

Negative Statements   Contraction

I	**did**	**not**	**use to**	**leave**	early.	**didn't**
You						
She						
He						
It						
We						
They						

- **Did** is followed by **not** or **-n't** and **use to**.

- The contraction **didn't** is used with **use to** in conversation and informal writing:

  I **didn't use to like** classical music.

Yes/No Questions				Short Answers	Contraction
Did	**you**	**use to**	**eat** meat?	Yes, **I did.** No, I **did not.**	No, I **didn't.**

- **Used to** is written **use to** when it occurs with **did**. (The simple past is marked only once with **did**.)
- **Did** is followed by the subject, **use to**, and the simple form of the main verb.
- Short answers to *yes/no* questions have a subject + **did**.
- For negative short answers, use **did** + **not** or the negative contraction **didn't**.

Information Questions					Answers
Where	**did**	she	**use to**	**work**?	At a computer store.
What	**did**	she	**use to**	**do**?	Sell software.

- The *wh-* word is followed by **did**, the subject, **use to**, and the simple form of the main verb.

Information Questions (Subject)				Answers
Who	**used to**	**live**	there?	Matt **did**.
What	**used to**	**be**	there?	An old farmhouse.

- If **who** or **what** is the subject of the question, then **did** is not used. **Used to** follows the *wh-* word, with the same word order as an affirmative statement.

⇒ **Exercise 16: Working on Form**

Complete the following conversations on your own with the appropriate form of *used to*. Then work with a partner. Check your answers and practice the completed conversations.

1. **A:** What ___did you use to___ (you) eat before you started your diet?

   B: A lot more meat, butter, and cheese. I ___didn't use to___ (not) worry about eating fat.

2. **A:** Gayle Davis _____ drive me to school before I bought my car. Do you know her?

   B: Yes. _____ (she/not) work in the library?

3. **A:** Who _____ live next door?

   B: The guy who _____ be the manager at Johnson's before it closed.

4. **A:** _____ (you) shop at Miller's Supermarket? I think I _____ see you

there on Tuesdays.

  B: Yes. I _____ stop there on my way home from work, but I don't anymore.

I work late on Tuesdays.

5. **A:** This library is only a few years old. Where _____ (the library) be?

  B: It _____ be on Aurora Street in a much smaller building.

Used to: Meaning and Use

COMPARING THE PAST AND THE PRESENT

1. Used to expresses a comparison of the past with the present. It shows a past habit or a situation that was true in the past but doesn't exist anymore:

Past Habit:	Mark **used to bite** his nails. Now he just chews his pencil.
Past Situation:	He **used to be** overweight. Now he is very thin.

2. We use **used to** when we remember our past and when we compare how things were then with how they are now. When we talk about now, we use the simple present because we are describing a routine or habit related to the present time:

Memories:	We **used to play** checkers and chess in the evening. Now we rent a video.
Then and Now:	Stores **used to sell** records and record players. Now they sell CDs and CD players.

3. When **used to** shows a repeated action that is a past habit, **would** may also be used with the same meaning:

> I **used to spend** the summer at my grandmother's house in the country.
> I **would spend** the summer at my grandmother's house in the country.

4. In a story about the past, **used to** commonly appears in the more general opening sentence, and **would** is used for the details in the rest of the story:

> When I was a child, we **used to** spend the summer at my grandmother's house in the country. We **would** leave the city at the end of June, and we **wouldn't** return until the beginning of September.

▥➡ **Exercise 17: Remembering the Past**

Ellen and Peter are talking with their children about their childhoods. Here are some of the things they remember. Rewrite the sentences with *used to*.

1. I visited my grandmother every Sunday. *I used to visit my grandmother every Sunday.*

2. Every year my grandmother cooked a big dinner for the holidays. _____

_____

3. My father had a Ford station wagon. _____

_____

4. In the fifties, a candy bar cost ten cents and a quart of milk cost a quarter. _____

_____

5. My brother and I played a lot of *Monopoly.* _____

_____

6. I had a cat named Sylvester. _____

_____

7. My brother and I quarreled a lot. _____

_____

8. We spent summers in a cabin near Lake George. _____

_____

▥➡ **Exercise 18: Remembering Your Past**

Write five sentences with *used to* describing different situations, routines, likes, and dislikes from your past.

1. *I used to run a mile in four and a half minutes.*

2. _____

3. _____

4. _____

5. _____

6. _____

⫸ **Exercise 19: Comparing Then and Now**

Work with a partner. Talk about how the past and the present are different. Add *used to* to the first sentence. Use the words in parentheses and the simple present in the second sentence.

1. Offices had only typewriters.
   (now/computers)

   Example: *Offices used to have only typewriters. Now they have computers.*

2. Many Americans lived on farms.
   (now/in or near large cities)

3. A trip from Chicago to New York took two days.
   (now/one and a half hours by plane)

4. We had a small variety of fresh fruit and vegetables.
   (now/wide variety)

5. Businesses often closed in the summer because of the heat.
   (now/have air-conditioning)

6. House keys were almost four inches long.
   (now/only two inches long)

7. Mothers stayed home with their children.
   (now/many mothers work outside the home)

8. Most Americans went to work right after high school.
   (now/many Americans/college)

9. Americans had large families.
   (now/small ones)

10. Girls had to wear skirts or dresses to school.
    (now/jeans and sweatshirts)

⫸ **Exercise 20: Comparing Then and Now**

Work on your own. Write three comparisons between the past and present with *used to* in the first sentence and the simple present in the second sentence.

1. _Most drugstores used to have ice cream and soda counters. Now they don't._

2. _____

   _____

3. _____

   _____

4. _____

   _____

The Past Continuous: Form

Statements

I	**was**	**sleeping** at 6:15.	We	**were**	**sleeping** at 6:15.
She			You		
He			They		
It					

- To form the past continuous (also called the past progressive), use the simple past form of **be** + verb + **-ing**.
- Look at page 485 for spelling rules for verbs ending in **-ing**.

Negative Statements   Contractions

I	**was**	**not**	**sleeping**.	I	**wasn't**	sleeping.
We	**were**	**not**	**sleeping**.	We	**weren't**	sleeping.

- Use **was** or **were** + **not** + verb + **-ing**.

Yes/No Questions   Short Answers   Contractions

Was	I	**sleeping**?	Yes, you **were**.	
			No, you **were not**.	No, you **weren't**.
Were	you	**sleeping**?	Yes, I **was**.	
			No, I **was not**.	No, I **wasn't**.

- To form *yes/no* questions, use **was** or **were** before the subject.
- Short answers have a subject pronoun + **was** or **were**.
- For negative short answers, use **was** or **were** + **not** or **-n't**.

Information Questions   Answers

Why	**was**	she	**shouting**?	She **was** angry.
What	**were**	they	**doing**?	They **were laughing**.

- The *wh-* word comes before **was** or **were** and the subject.

(continued)

Information Questions (Subject)	Answers
Who **was** **shouting?**	She **was**.
What **was** **happening?**	They **were fighting**.

- If **who** or **what** is the subject, then the word order in the question is the same as for affirmative statements.

▶ Exercise 21: Working on Form

Work with a partner. Take turns asking and answering the following questions using the past continuous.

1. What were you doing…?

   (last night at ten o'clock)

   A: *What were you doing last night at ten o'clock?*
   B: *I was studying.*

   (last night at midnight)

   A: *What were you doing last night at midnight?*
   B: *I was sleeping.*

2. What were you doing…?

   (last night at 7:30 P.M.)

   (this morning at 6:00 A.M.)

   (this morning at 8:00 A.M.)

   (an hour ago)

3. Where were you living…?

   (last year)

   (five years ago)

   (ten years ago)

4. What were you thinking about…?

   (when you went to sleep last night)

   (when you woke up this morning)

   (when you were coming to class)

   (when the class started)

   (a minute ago)

The Past Continuous: Meaning and Use

ACTIVITIES IN PROGRESS IN THE PAST

1. The past continuous expresses an action in progress at a specific time in the past. The action began before the specific point in time and might also continue after that time:

> Ron: I saw you outside at six o'clock this morning. What **were** you **doing?**
> Joe: I **was walking** my dog.

2. The past continuous often describes background information in stories. It frequently expresses a number of events that are occurring simultaneously (at the same time). The past continuous emphasizes the duration of the background events in contrast to other events in the story that happen more quickly or for a shorter time. These events are expressed in the simple past:

> The day **was becoming** hot. Lawn sprinklers and air conditioners **were whirring** softly. Children **were running** down the street and then **stopping** because the heat **was exhausting** them. The air **was getting** thicker and thicker. The sky **was getting** darker. Finally, the storm hit. Rain fell slowly at first. Big drops bounced off the sidewalk. Suddenly lightning flashed....

3. Sometimes the past continuous and the simple past are close in meaning (but not exactly the same). The choice of the past continuous emphasizes the long duration of the action:

> It **was snowing** this afternoon.
> It **snowed** this afternoon.

4. The past continuous often occurs in complex sentences that have time clauses beginning with **when** and **while.** You will study this use of the past continuous in Chapter 5.

▸ **Exercise 22: Describing Simultaneous Events**

Write three past continuous sentences that describe activities that were happening at the same time as the events below.

1. My phone rang at 7:00 A.M.

   I was sleeping.

   My roommate was taking a shower.

   The cat was meowing in the kitchen.

2. The exam started at 2:00 P.M.

_____

_____

_____

3. I fell asleep at ten o'clock.

_____

_____

_____

4. I ate lunch in the cafeteria today.

_____

_____

_____

5. At noon, Jennifer cashed a check at the bank.

_____

_____

_____

⟹ Exercise 23: Describing Background Information

Work in small groups. Write sentences in the past continuous that add more background information to the beginning of each story.

1. Everyone was sitting at the dinner table:

   Soft music was playing.

   A warm breeze was blowing through the open windows.

   _____

   _____

   _____

   Suddenly, there was a strange sound from the garden…

2. The sun was rising over the city:

Shopkeepers were opening their stores.
_____

_____

_____

_____

Without any warning, the bombs began to fall…

Summary

The Simple Past of Regular and Irregular Verbs: Form

Statements:	We **saw** a movie.
Negative Statements:	She **didn't like** the movie.
Yes/No Questions:	**Did** you **leave** early?
Short Answers:	Yes, we **did.** OR No, we **didn't.**
Information Questions:	What movie **did** you **see?**
Information Questions (Subject):	Who **liked** it?

The Simple Past of *Be*: Form

Statements:	I **was** tired this morning.
Negative Statements:	They **weren't** hungry.
Yes/No Questions:	**Was** he angry?
Short Answers:	Yes, he **was.** OR No, he **wasn't.**
Information Questions:	Where **were** you?
Information Questions (Subject):	Who **was** there?

The Simple Past: Meaning and Use

The simple past tense describes completed actions or events that began and ended at a definite time in the past. The simple past is used for corrections, reminders, excuses, jokes and riddles, guesses, accusations, denials, agreement, and disagreement.

Corrections:	Astronauts **didn't land** on Mars. They **landed** on the moon.
Reminders:	**Did** you **take** your umbrella?
Excuses:	I'm sorry I'm late. I **got** a ticket.
Riddles:	Why **did** the man **throw** his clock out the window? He **wanted** to see time fly!

Guesses:	Carol: Why is she wearing a cast? Stephen: She probably **broke** her leg.
Accusations:	Isaac: Laurie, **did** you **scratch** my new car?
Denials:	Laurie: No, I **didn't do** it. Maybe Amy **did.** OR No, it **wasn't** me. Maybe it **was** Amy.
Agreement:	Karla: It **took** too long. Kathy: Yes, it **did.** It **took** forever!
Disagreement:	Jessie: That **was** easy. Michael: No, it **wasn't.**

Used to: Form

Statements:	They **used to be** friends.
Negative Statements:	I **didn't use to like** jazz.
Yes/No Questions:	**Did** you **use to play** the piano?
Short Answers:	Yes, I **did.** OR No, I **didn't.**
Information Questions:	Where **did** you **use to go** to school?
Information Questions (Subject):	Who **used to play** an instrument?

Used to: Meaning and Use

Used to compares the past with the present. It expresses a past habit or a situation that was true in the past but doesn't exist any longer. We use **used to** when we remember our past and when we compare then with now.

Memories:	We **used to play** checkers and chess in the evening. Now we rent a video.
Then and Now:	Stores **used to sell** records and record players. Now they sell CDs and CD players.

The Past Continuous: Form

Statements:	At midnight they **were sleeping.**
Negative Statements:	The TV **wasn't working** last night.
Yes/No Questions:	**Were** you **eating** dinner then?
Short Answers:	Yes, I **was.** OR No, I **wasn't.**
Information Questions:	Why **were** you **laughing?**
Information Questions (Subject):	What **was happening** at that moment?

The Past Continuous: Meaning and Use

The past continuous expresses an action or a situation in progress at a specific time in the past. It often describes background information in stories.

Simultaneous Events: Mike **was reading,** Tom **was studying,** and Joe **was listening** to music.

Story Backgrounds: We **were** all **sleeping** soundly. Suddenly, there was a big crash.

⟶ Summary Exercise: Finding Errors

Each of the following sentences has an error in form or use. Find each error and correct it.

1. Did you ~~found~~ the umbrella?   find
2. What she did last night?
3. When you called this morning?
4. He didn't went out.
5. She use to work at the library.
6. It was dark outside. The wind is howling. The temperature was falling quickly.
7. Did you used to live in an apartment?
8. Did they had any refreshments?
9. Did he went to class yesterday?
10. You weren't here at December 10.

Expressing Future Time: *Be Going to, Will*, the Present Continuous, and the Simple Present; Connecting Sentences

Preview

You're planning a business trip. You call the airlines. This is the recording you hear:

Please continue to hold. One of our customer service representatives **will take** your call as soon as possible.

You're on your business trip. You call your office to tell them your travel plans for that afternoon:

I'm taking the hotel van to the airport at 12:30. The flight **takes off** at 1:45 and **arrives** at 3:00. **I'll be** back in the office about 4:00.

Later you're telling your friend about your decision to quit your job:

You: **I'm going to quit** my job. I'm not happy there anymore and I travel too much. I never have any time for myself.
Friend: I know. **I don't either**. But how **are** you **going to pay** your rent?
You: **I'm going to use** the money that I've saved while I look for a new job. Maybe **I'll work** part-time for my uncle.
Friend: That's risky, but I think you're making the right decision.
You: **So do I.** I think everything **will turn out** OK, **and my uncle does too.**

There are four different forms for expressing future time in English: the **be going to** future, the **will** future, and the use of the present continuous and the simple present to describe future events. They are often used in the same conversation.

These verb forms can express intentions, choices, decisions, plans, schedules, promises, expectations, and predictions. In some sentences these forms are very close in meaning. Sometimes the future form you choose can make what you say sound more formal or less formal, more planned or less planned, more immediate or less immediate.

The present, past, and future tenses are reviewed through a look at attached statements with **but/and** (**...and my uncle does too**) and rejoinders (**I don't either** and **So do I**).

Be Going to: Form

Statements				Contractions
I	am	going to	move.	I**'m**
She He It	is	going to	move.	She**'s** He**'s** It**'s**
We You They	are	going to	move.	We**'re** You**'re** They**'re**

- To form the future with **be going to**, use the simple present of **be** + **going to** + the simple form of the main verb.

Negative Statements					Contractions
I	am	not	going to	wait.	I**'m not**
She He It	is	not	going to	wait.	She**'s not**/She **isn't** He**'s not**/He **isn't** It**'s not**/It **isn't**
We You They	are	not	going to	wait.	We**'re not**/We **aren't** You**'re not**/You **aren't** They**'re not**/They **aren't**

- To form negative statements, use a form of **be** + **not going to** + the main verb.
- Except for **I'm not**, there are two negative contractions for each person, for example, **he's not** and **he isn't**. The meaning is the same.

Yes/No Questions				Short Answers	Contractions
Am	I	going to	move?	Yes, I **am**. No, I **am not**.	 No, I**'m not**.
Is	Mei	going to	move?	Yes, she **is**. No, she **is not**.	 No, she**'s not**./No, she **isn't**.
Are	they	going to	move?	Yes, they **are**. No, they **are not**.	 No, they**'re not**./No, they **aren't**.

- To form a *yes/no* question, use a form of **be** before the subject.
- Short answers have a subject + a form of **be**.
- Affirmative short answers do not have contracted forms. We never say *Yes, I'm* or *Yes, she's*. (INCORRECT)

Information Questions				Answers
When	**are**	you	**going to** **move**?	Next month.
Where				Denver.

- The *wh-* word is followed by **be** and the subject.

Information Questions (Subject)				Answers	Contractions
What	**is**	**going to**	**happen?**	**I'll get** a new job.	**What's**
Who	**is**	**going to**	**hire you?**	My uncle **is**.	**Who's**

- If **who** or **what** is the subject, then the word order is the same as for affirmative statements.

CONVERSATION NOTES

1. Be going to is frequently used in conversation to express the future. Be is often contracted in speaking and informal writing:

I'm going to quit my job.

2. Going to is often pronounced as *gonna* in informal conversation:

Written Form	**Spoken Form**
I'm **going to** quit.	"I'm **gonna** quit." (SPOKEN ONLY)

➡ Exercise 1: Working on Form

Work with a partner. Complete the following conversations using a form of **be** plus **going to** and the words in parentheses. Use contractions whenever possible. Then practice the conversations.

1. **A:** What _____*are you going to do*_____ (you/do) after you graduate?

   B: I _____*'m going to look for*_____ (look for) a job.

2. **A:** _____ (you/apply) for a scholarship?

   B: Yes, but I _____ (not/send) in the form yet. It's too early.

3. **A:** Be careful. That bag _____ (break).

   B: I know, and everything _____ (fall) on the floor unless you

   help me.

4. **A:** Who _____ (help) you set up for the party?

   B: Jenny and Scott. They _____ (bring) all the food this

   afternoon.

5. **A:** What _____ (you/wear) to the party?

   B: I don't know. I _____ (buy) something new.

6. **A:** It looks like it _____ (rain).

   B: I know. That's why I _____ (not/walk) to work today.

   I _____ (ask) Brian for a ride.

Focus on Vocabulary

FUTURE TIME PHRASES

Here are some common phrases that express a definite time in the future. They answer the
question *When are you going to return?*

In + Quantity of Time

in	five minutes
	three days
	two weeks

This + Definite Time Period

this	afternoon	this	spring
	evening		summer
	Sunday		fall
	weekend		winter
	week		semester
	month		year
	August		

Next + Definite Time Period

next		next	
	Sunday		spring
	weekend		summer
	week		fall
	month		winter
	August		year
	semester		

The + Definite Time Period + *After Next*

the		
	weekend	after next
	week	
	month	
	semester	
	year	

Today/Tonight/Tomorrow

today	tomorrow	
tonight		morning
tomorrow		afternoon
the day after tomorrow		evening
		night

⮞ Exercise 2: Asking *When* Questions with Future Time Phrases

Work with a partner. Take turns asking and answering *when* questions with *going to* and the words in parentheses. Use future time phrases in your answers.

1. (take a vacation)

   A: *When are you going to take a vacation?*
   B: *This summer.*

2. (get a medical checkup)

3. (take the day off)

4. (clean your apartment)

5. (take a trip)

6. (go out to dinner)

7. (do the laundry)

8. (shop for groceries)

9. (read a novel)

10. (~~~~~~)

Be Going to: Meaning and Use

表示打算 脂做的事 也 即将 发生 或 肯定 要 发生的事

INTENTIONS, PLANS, EXPECTATIONS, PREDICTIONS

1. The **be going to** future often expresses a person's intentions or plans. The speaker has already thought about or planned the future event:

You're telling your friend that you are unhappy at work:

You: **I'm going to talk** to my boss. He's not treating me fairly.
Friend: So, what **are** you **going to say?**
You: **I'm going to tell** him I <u>deserve</u> a raise.

应受, 值得

2. Sometimes the speaker may know about someone else's plans:

You're talking to a friend about going to the movies after dinner:

You: Should I call Peter? Maybe he's free tonight.
Friend: No, don't bother. He told me that he has a lot of work to do. **He's going to study** all evening.

3. Be going to can also express expectations and predictions that are based on evidence or knowledge. In conversation, it often refers to the immediate future, especially when the speaker sees evidence that something is about to happen:

There are black clouds in the sky and the wind is starting to blow very hard:

Look! We're **going to have** a storm.

A newspaper article reports that your preferred candidate in the local election is much more popular than the other candidate:

I'm really glad that Smith **is going to win.**

⇒ Exercise 3: Expressing Intentions

l to do at the times shown in parentheses. Write your intentions
rase can go at the beginning or at the end of the sentence. Then
tions.

ernoon I'm going to play tennis. OR

this afternoon.

3. (tomorrow afternoon) _____

4. (in three months) _____

5. (the day after tomorrow) _____

6. (next semester) _____

⮕ Exercise 4: Talking About Plans

Work with a partner. Take turns asking and answering questions about your future plans.
Use time phrases such as *in two weeks, next spring, this winter, tomorrow night*, and so on.

    A: *What are you going to do this winter?*
    B: *Go skiing at Jackson Hole.*

⮕ Exercise 5: Making Predictions

Work in small groups. Look at the following pictures and predict what you think is going to
happen in each case. Use the *be going to* future.

1.

He's going to spill the milk.

2.

3.

4.

5.

6.

7.

8.

9.

Will: Form

Statements			Contractions
I	**will**	help.	I**'ll**
You			You**'ll**
She			She**'ll**
He			He**'ll**
It			It**'ll**
We			We**'ll**
They			They**'ll**

- **Will** is a modal auxiliary. It does not change form to agree with the subject. (Modals such as **can, could, would,** etc. are presented in Chapters 7 and 8.)

Negative Statements			Contraction	
I	**will**	**not**	**help**.	I	**won't**	help.

- Use **will** + **not** + the simple form of the main verb. The negative contraction is **won't**.

Yes/No Questions				Short Answers	Contraction
Will	Chris	**be**	there?	Yes, he **will**.	
				No, he **will not**.	No, he **won't**.

- To form a *yes/no* question, use **will** before the subject. The main verb is in the simple form.
- Short answers have a subject + **will** or **won't**. Affirmative short answers have no contracted forms.

Information Questions				Answers
When	**will**	Ann	**arrive**?	This Saturday.
How long	**will**	she	**stay**?	For a week.

- The *wh-* word comes before **will** and the subject.

Information Questions (Subject)				Answers
Who	**will**	**meet**	her at the airport?	Her brother **will**.
What	**will**	**happen**	if he's late?	She**'ll worry**.

- If **who** or **what** is the subject, the word order is the same as for affirmative statements.

CONVERSATION NOTES

1. The contracted form of **will** is common in informal conversation. However, it is difficult to hear and can sometimes be confused with the simple present. Listen to your teacher say these two sentences at a normal conversational rate. Can you hear the difference?

Simple Present   **Future**

They ride the bus.   They**'ll** ride the bus.

2. In conversation, you can use the contracted form 'll with both nouns and pronouns. In informal writing, you can use the contraction only with pronouns (except for *it*). With a noun or a person's name, use the full form **will**:

Written Form   **Spoken Form**

Bob **will** come later.   "Bob**'ll** come later." (SPOKEN ONLY)

He**'ll** come later.   "He**'ll** come later."

3. In conversation, the contracted form 'll is often used with *wh-* words:

Written Form   **Spoken Form**

What **will** happen to him?   "What**'ll** happen to him?" (SPOKEN ONLY)

⟹ Exercise 6: Working on Form

Work with a partner. Complete the following conversations using *will*. Use contractions whenever possible. Then practice the conversations.

1. **A:** Anna, the doorbell is ringing.

   B: OK, I __'ll get_____ (get) it.

2. **A:** Sue, _____ (you/help) me?

   B: Sure, I _____ (help) you now if you help me later.

3. **A:** Do you think that Bob _____ (be) late?

   B: No, I'm pretty sure he _____ (come) right after the game is over.

4. **A:** I think that Smith _____ (win) the election without any trouble.

   B: Really? I don't. If she wants my vote, she _____ (have to) talk more about the important issues.

5. **A:** The whole family _____ (be) in Florida next week, right?

   B: No, I doubt it. They _____ (be) at my uncle's house in the mountains

   until the fifteenth.

6. **A:** I _____ (lock) the doors if you put the suitcases in the car.

   B: OK, but hurry up. The plane leaves at nine and it _____ (take) us

   forty-five minutes to get to the airport. We don't have much time.

⏵ Exercise 7: Asking and Answering Questions with *Will*

There's a big exam soon, but your teacher has not discussed it very much. The whole
class is nervous about the exam and wants to find out more about it. Work in small groups.
Take turns asking and answering questions with *will* and the words in parentheses. Then make
up more questions.

1. (when)

   A: *When will the exam be?*
   B: *The day after tomorrow.*

2. (true/false questions)

   A: *Will there be true/false questions?*
   B: *Yes, there will.*

3. (fill-in-the-blank questions)

4. (how long)

5. (multiple-choice questions)

6. (difficult or easy)

7. (review session)

8. (essay questions)

9. (grades)

10. (～～～～)

Will: Meaning and Use

PROMISES, CHOICES, OFFERS TO HELP, DECISIONS, PREDICTIONS, REFUSALS

1. The **will** future is often used with promises. Since we usually make promises only about our own future behavior, **will** is commonly used in the first person:

A baby-sitter is speaking to the parents before they leave:

> Don't worry. I'll **watch** them carefully.

2. The **will** future is also used at the moment when the speaker is making a quick choice and when the speaker is offering to do something. In contrast to the **be going to** future, the speaker does not think about this much in advance:

A customer in a restaurant is asking about the soup of the day:

> Customer: What kind of soup do you have?
> Waiter: Tomato and chicken noodle.
> Customer: I'll **have** a bowl of tomato soup.

Two roommates are at home:

> David: Peter, someone's at the door.
> Peter: OK. I'll **get** it.

The party host is asking his friends for help:

> Host: Will someone help me with the dishes?
> Matt: I **will.**
> Todd: I **will** too.

3. The **will** future can also express the speaker's expectations and predictions about events that are uncertain. These sentences often include **maybe, probably, I think, I hope,** or **I guess:**

Your car is at the repair shop, but you're trying to make plans to go somewhere in a few days:

> I think I'll **have** my car back on Monday, but I'm not sure.

You are offering your opinion about the upcoming election:

> Harris **will probably win** the election.

4. To refuse someone, use the negative of the **will** future, wil

> Matt: Will you help us next week?
> Todd: I'm terribly sorry, but I **won't be able to.** I'm going t

5. Will is more formal than **be going to**. Choosing **will** instead of **be going to** depends on the situation and on the relationship between the speakers. **Will** frequently appears in books, newspapers, signs, and in more formal speech situations such as news broadcasts, weather forecasts, speeches, and announcements:

TV weather forecast:

> The temperature **will be** near freezing tonight, but it **will warm up** considerably tomorrow.

Sign:

> THE BANK **WILL BE** CLOSED UNTIL MONDAY

6. The same information in news broadcasts, weather forecasts, speeches, and announcements using **will** is usually restated in informal conversations with the more informal **be going to:**

You just heard the TV weather forecast and tell your friend:

> The temperature **is going to be** near freezing tonight, but it**'s going to** warm up tomorrow.

Your sister can't see the sign on the bank. You tell her what it says:

> The bank **is going to be closed** until Monday.

7. With the verb **be, will** often expresses future time only, rather than a promise, decision, or opinion:

Two friends are talking:

> Karen: Can you have dinner with us next weekend?
> Chris: No, I'm sorry, but **I'll be** in Ohio at a meeting.

▶ Exercise 8: Making Promises

Work in groups of three. Play the roles of parents and teenager. Parents, you're going away for the weekend. You're nervous about leaving your teenage son or daughter alone. Discuss your concerns with him or her, using *We hope* or *I hope* with *will* or *won't* and the words in parentheses. Teenager, answer using *I promise...* or sentences beginning with *I will* or *I won't.*

1. (be home on time)   **Parent:** *We hope you'll be home on time.*

   (break the rules)   **Teenager:** *I promise I won't break the rules.*

2. (make a mess)

   (clean up the house)

   (a wild party)

   (ore than two friends over)

4. (stay out late)

   (follow the rules)

5. (lock the doors)

   (open the door to strangers)

6. (drive carefully)

   (～～～)

7. (do your homework)

   (～～～)

8. (turn off the stove)

   (～～～)

⟹ Exercise 9: Making Choices

Work with a partner. Take turns making up sentences with *will* to express your choices in these two situations.

1. Give the waitress your order from the following dessert menu:

Example: *I'll have chocolate ice cream, please.*

Dessert Menu

ice cream (chocolate, vanilla, or strawberry)	$2.25
orange sherbet	$2.00
apple pie	$3.50
à la mode	$4.50
coconut cream pie	$3.50
lemon meringue pie	$3.50
cheese cake	$3.50
assorted fruit plate	$3.50
coffee, tea, or milk	$1.50

2. Tell a salesperson in a department store what you want to buy. There are five shirts and five pairs of pants in the following patterns and colors: striped, plaid, checked, yellow, blue, and gray.

Example: *I'll take the plaid shirt and the blue pants.*

➡ **Exercise 10: Volunteering**

1. Work in small groups and plan a class party. Each person volunteers to do or bring in something on the list. Have one person in your group write down the names of the volunteers next to each item on the list. Make up sentences with *I'll* and one of the following verbs (*buy, order, bring, pick up, make, bake, get, hang, blow up*). You can volunteer more than once.

Example: *I'll bring the tortilla chips.*

Snacks	Paper Goods	Decorations
tortilla chips	cups	balloons
salsa	plates	streamers
nuts	plastic utensils	
pretzels	napkins	
carrot sticks	tablecloth	
celery sticks		
dip	**Beverages**	**Music**
cake	soda	CDs
fruit	juice	cassettes
cheese	punch	CD player
crackers	seltzer	guitar

2. The group leader wants to check the list to make sure that everything has been taken care of. Take turns telling your group members who volunteered for each item on the list, using a form of *be* plus *going to*.

Examples: (tortilla chips) *Danilo is going to bring tortilla chips.*
(cake) *Anna is going to order a cake and Carlos is going to pick it up.*

➠ **Exercise 11: Expressing Expectations**

Work in small groups. Talk about some of the things you might do in the future. Use *maybe, probably, I think, I believe,* or *I hope* with the following future time expressions: *in a few minutes, tomorrow, in two days, on Sunday, next month, in three weeks, on New Year's Day, next year.*

Examples:
Maybe I'll call you on Sunday.
I'll probably sleep late tomorrow.
I think I'll work late tonight.

➠ **Exercise 12: Making Predictions**

In class, work in groups of three to predict endings for these unfinished stories. Use *will* or *be going to* in your predictions. For homework, choose one of the stories and write an ending for it, using tenses that are appropriate to the particular story.

1. This is the most important basketball game of the high school season. Kevin is a senior and he's never made an important play. This is his last chance to be a high school hero. The score is tied. Jenny is watching. Kevin has adored her for four years, but she doesn't even know he's alive. Oh, no! The ball is coming toward him. "Grab it and score!" he screams to himself.

   Examples:
   He's going to make the winning basket.
   He'll miss and have an unhappy life.
   He'll score and Jenny will run out onto the court and throw her arms around him.

2. The night is stormy. Tom is driving on a narrow, unfamiliar country road. As he realizes he's lost, the car suddenly runs out of gas. Tom curses himself because he had suspected that the gas gauge was not working properly. He sees a light from a house deep in the woods and begins to walk toward it. His flashlight begins to grow dimmer and dimmer, until finally Tom is alone in the dark woods. The thunder and lightning are constant now, and the light in the house has gone out.

3. On the first day of class, Janet sits down and looks at the textbook for the course. A guy in a wheelchair pulls up next to her and says, "Hello." She hesitates because she has always felt a little uncomfortable around people in wheelchairs. She doesn't want to seem rude, so she says, "Hello" and asks his name. They are still talking when the professor finally arrives. After class they meet in the cafeteria where they talk for a few hours.

4. Kyong Ho and Sun Hye came to the United States ten years ago. Since coming here, they have studied very hard to learn English and they have saved some money despite their low wages. But they still do not have enough money in the bank to fulfill their dream: to own a fine Korean restaurant decorated with brilliant white tablecloths and vases of red flowers. On a summer day they are sitting on a park bench talking about their dream when someone

behind them says, "Excuse me, but I couldn't help overhearing you." Kyong Ho and Sun Hye turn around. A man in a white suit is standing behind them in the bright afternoon sun. "Who are you?" they ask. The man replies, "My name doesn't matter. I heard you discussing your plans, and I would like to help you."

⫸ Exercise 13: Refusing

Work with a partner. Take turns using *won't* to express your refusals in each situation.

1. You are a teacher. You tell your students that all papers are due next Thursday. Announce that you refuse to make any exceptions because final grades are due two days later.

   Example: *I won't make any exceptions. All papers are due on Thursday.*

2. Tell your child that you refuse to clean up her room. She has to do it herself.

3. You are having lunch with your friend. Tell him that you refuse to let him pay for lunch because it's his birthday.

4. Your car makes a terrible noise when you start it. You took it to a garage in your neighborhood. They claimed that they needed to replace several parts and charged you $300. The car still makes the same noise. You refuse to pay the bill.

5. A friend has told you a secret. Your sister asks you to tell her about it. Tell your sister that you refuse to discuss it.

6. Your niece wants to ride her bicycle on a street that has lots of traffic. Tell her that you refuse to allow her to do that.

7. Last month, you paid your electric bill on the fifteenth of the month even though it was due on the twentieth. Your most recent bill charges you a five dollar late fee for last month's bill. You call the electric company and tell them that you refuse to pay this fee.

8. It's 97° Fahrenheit outside today. You return from your lunch hour and learn that the electricity has gone off in your office building, so the air-conditioning and the elevators are not working. Some of your co-workers decide to take the stairs. You refuse to climb up twenty-four flights of stairs in this heat.

➡ **Exercise 14: Restating Announcements**

Work with a partner. Decide where you might see or hear each sentence. Then restate each sentence in a more informal spoken form with *be going to*.

1. The weather will be cool tomorrow with a chance of rain.

    Situation: radio weather forecast

    Restatement: It's going to be cool tomorrow with a chance of rain.

2. The president will meet the Polish ambassador early tomorrow morning.

    Situation:

    Restatement:

3. Flight 276 will be delayed until 6:35.

    Situation:

    Restatement:

4. Smith's will close at nine o'clock tonight.

    Situation:

    Restatement:

5. Classes will resume on January 22.

    Situation:

    Restatement:

6. This chapter will summarize recent research on this problem.

    Situation:

    Restatement:

7. Tonight we will begin with a short poem.

    Situation:

    Restatement:

8. On April 1 the fare will increase to $1.25.

    Situation:

    Restatement:

➠ **Exercise 15: Comparing *Will* and *Be Going to***

Work with a partner. Complete each conversation using *will, won't,* or *be going to* with the verbs in parentheses. Then practice the conversations, using contractions wherever possible.

1. **Sue:** My mother wants to see our new apartment. She told me that she ___'s going to visit___ (visit) us soon.

   Ann: That's fine. ___Are you going to make___ (you/make) dinner for her?

2. **Guest:** Can I please have a drink of water?

   Host: Sure, I _____ (get) it for you.

3. **Wife:** Why are you turning on the oven?

   Husband: I _____ (bake) a cake.

4. **Natalia:** What are your plans for the summer?

   Kyoko: We _____ (rent) a house on the lake for two weeks.

5. **Answering machine:** No one can come to the phone right now. Please leave your name and number, and we _____ (get back to) you as soon as possible.

   Caller: Hi, Debbie, it's Sue. I wanted to know if you _____ (play) tennis tomorrow. Please call me.

6. **Customer:** I'd like to find out the price of that wallet, please.

   Salesperson: Sure. I _____ (be) with you in a moment.

7. **Alexander:** Josephine, I need to ask you an important question. _____ (you/marry) me?

   Josephine: I'm sorry, Alexander, but I _____ (marry) Nicholas. He proposed last night and I accepted.

8. **Paul:** What _____ (you/do) tonight?

   Matt: I don't know. Maybe I _____ (stay) home and watch TV.

⮞ Exercise 16: Thinking About Meaning

Work in small groups. Read each statement and discuss the questions. Be ready to explain your answers to the class.

1. I'll get a sponge.

   (a) What do you think happened?

   (b) When did the speaker say this?

   (c) Did the speaker think about the situation a lot in advance?

   (d) What happens if we begin the sentence with *maybe*?

2. Which of the following sentences could come before the statement *I'll have a bowl of soup*? Why?

   (a) Why did you turn on the stove?

   (b) I'm ready to take your order.

   (c) What are your plans for dinner?

3. Write either sentence (a) or (b) below as the answer to each of the following conversations.

   (a) I'll get it.

   (b) I'm going to get it.

   A: Joe, the phone is ringing and my hands are full of paint.
   B: OK, <u>I'll get it.</u>

   A: Who wants to get me the hammer over there?
   B: _____

   A: Who volunteered to pick up the pizza for the party tonight?
   B: I did. _____

   A: Are you going out? We need a quart of milk.
   B: Sure,_____ on my way home

> ➔ *for fixed plans*

The Present Continuous as a Future Form: Meaning and Use

PLANNED FUTURE EVENTS 表示按计划要发生的事

表示计划

1. The present continuous can refer to planned future events. In this case, some kind of arrangements have usually been made. The future time (tomorrow, next week, on Sunday) must be stated in the sentence or understood in the context:

Jeff: What are you going to do with your car?
Otto: Well, we spoke to a car dealer downtown, and we're **selling** it to him **next week**.

Pat: What are your plans for **next year**?
Ann: I'm **starting** graduate school.

2. The event cannot depend on chance or luck. It must be something that a person can plan. We cannot say: *It's raining tomorrow.* (INCORRECT)

3. To express the future, the verbs **go** and **come** are used more often with the present continuous than with **be going to**. The present continuous forms of **go** and **come** express both plans and intentions:

Plans: We're **going** fishing this weekend, and we're **coming** back on Monday morning.

Intentions: I'm **going** to Spain when I have enough money.

4. Certain verbs frequently combine with the present continuous as a future form. These include: **do, have breakfast, have lunch, have dinner, have a drink, stay, remain,** and travel verbs such as **go, come, leave, arrive, fly, land, take a bus, take a plane,** and so on:

Martha: What **are** you **having**?
Steve: Just a tuna sandwich. I'm not very hungry. What about you?
Martha: Well, I'm very hungry. I'm **having** a cup of chili and a roast beef sandwich.

Ted: When **is** Sam **leaving**?
Diane: On Tuesday. He's **driving** to New Orleans after he picks up Mary.

5. Look at Chapter 1, pages 9–10, for a review of present continuous verb forms.

...anned and Unplanned Events

...event, use the present continuous. If it is an unplanned
...these verbs in each sentence: *sign, win, stay, cut, have,*

...next week for his birthday.

...he game on Thursday.

...gton this weekend.

4. The temperature is dropping very quickly. It _____ tonight.

5. Hurry up. Our plane _____ in ten minutes.

6. _____ you _____ at the Hilton tomorrow night?

7. I _____ the contract tomorrow at 10:00 A.M.

8. I think that the senator _____ the election next week.

9. If you're not careful, you _____ your finger.

10. The students _____ from their vacation this Sunday.

➡ Exercise 18: Thinking About Meaning

Work in small groups. Read the statement and the list of words below. Which words can substitute for *one* in the sentence? Which cannot substitute for *one*? Why not?

We're having one tomorrow.

a party	an earthquake
a meeting	a barbecue
an exam	a fire
an accident	an election
a sale	a tornado

The Simple Present as a Future Form: Meaning and Use

PROGRAMS, SCHEDULES, ITINERARIES 表示按计划或时刻表要发生的事

旅程,路线

1. The simple present can refer to a future program, schedule, or itinerary. The speaker generally cannot change these arrangements:

Program: The conference **starts** on Tuesday evening and **ends** on Saturday afternoon.

Schedule: Flight 304 **departs** from Gate 6 at 7:05 P.M.

Itinerary: We **arrive** in Riyadh on Monday, March 5, at 6:00 A.M.

客观

2. The simple present form of the future is more impersonal than the present continuous future form or **be going to**. It is used more frequently in certain f...... radio, TV, and loudspeaker announcements:

Radio Announcement: Our new branch office **opens** this ......

3. In conversation, however, we use any one of the following to express about the same meaning:

The new branch office **opens** this Monday at the Cedar Mall.
The new branch office **is opening** this Monday at the Cedar Mall.
The new branch office **is going to open** this Monday at the Cedar Mall.

4. Look at Chapter 1, pages 2–3, for a review of simple present verb forms.

Ⅲ➤ Exercise 19: Discussing Schedules

Work with a partner. Read the fall-semester schedule from an American university calendar and then describe it to your partner. Use the simple present form of the future and the verbs *begin, start,* and *end.* Your partner will write down the schedule and then repeat it back to you, also using the simple present form of the future. Compare the schedules to see if they are the same.

Example: *Classes start on September 1.*

University Calendar

September 1	First day of classes
October 12–15	Fall vacation
November 22–25	Thanksgiving recess
December 6	Last day of classes
December 13–20	Final exams

Ⅲ➤ Exercise 20: Discussing Itineraries

1. Work with a partner. Play the roles of travel agent and client. Travel agent, call your client and read the trip itinerary. Use the simple present form of the future to describe the itinerary. Client, take notes and ask questions, if necessary. Then change roles for the second trip.

Travel Agent: *You leave New York at 7:00 P.M. on July 5.*
Client: *What airline do I take?*
Travel Agent: *French Airways.*

European Trip Itinerary

July 5	leave New York (French Airways 7:00 P.M.)
July 6	arrive in Paris
July 6–10	Paris
July 11	fly to London (Air Britain 11:00 A.M.)
July 11–14	London
July 15–22	car trip through Scotland
July 23	return to London
July 24	leave for New York

Washington, D.C./Georgia/Florida Trip Itinerary

August 19	fly from Newark Airport to Washington, D.C.
August 19–21	Washington, D.C.
August 22	fly to Atlanta
August 22–25	Atlanta
August 26	fly to Orlando
August 26–29	Orlando
August 30	drive to West Palm Beach
August 30–31	West Palm Beach
September 1	drive to Miami Beach
September 1–6	Miami Beach
September 7	leave for New York

2. For homework, write a conversation between a travel agent and a client, using one of the itineraries.

Travel Agent: *You spend six days in Miami Beach.*

Client: Six days? *And when do I leave for New York?*

Travel Agent: *You leave for New York on September 7.*

⟫ **Exercise 21: Thinking About Meaning**

Work in small groups. Read the sentence and the list of words below it. Which words can substitute for *it* in the sentence? Which cannot substitute for *it*? Why not?

It begins in two days.

winter vacation	a sale
a snowstorm	a hurricane
school	my new job
an explosion	spring

⟫ **Exercise 22: Thinking About Meaning**

Work in small groups. Read the sentence and answer the questions.

We leave on Friday.

1. Is there a definite plan?

2. What kind of plan could it be?

3. Do you expect the speaker to change the plan? Why or why not?

But: Form

Affirmative and Negative Sentences

I like oysters. + He doesn't like oysters. = I like oysters, **but he doesn't**.

I don't like sushi. + He likes sushi. = I don't like sushi, **but he does**.

- **But** introduces information that is different from the first sentence.
- When one sentence is affirmative and the other is negative, use **but** to connect the two sentences.
- If the sentences have the same verb and different subjects, use an auxiliary in the same tense to replace the second verb phrase.

⟫ **Exercise 23: Working on Form**

Work in small groups. Complete the following statements about yourself and your classmates using *but*.

1. I have a _____ backpack _____, but_ Jill doesn't. _____

2. I'm not wearing _____ a sweater _____, but_ Rosa is. _____

3. I never eat _____ meat _____, but _____ Abdul does. _____

4. I want a _____, but _____

5. I don't speak _____, but _____

6. Five years ago, I was _____, but _____

7. My apartment has _____, but _____

8. I didn't use to _____, but _____

9. I don't have _____, but _____

10. I hardly ever eat _____, but _____

11. I'm going to visit _____, but _____

12. I'm staying _____ tonight, but _____

And...Too/And...Either: Form

Affirmative Sentences

I like chocolate. + She likes chocolate. = I like chocolate, **and she does too**.

You like chocolate. + They like chocolate. = You like chocolate, **and they do too**.

- **And** adds information that is similar to the first sentence.
- When both sentences are affirmative and have different subjects, use **and...too** to connect the two sentences. Use an auxiliary in the same tense to replace the second verb phrase if the verbs are the same.

Negative Sentences

He doesn't like hot dogs. + I don't like hot dogs. = He doesn't like hot dogs, **and I don't either**.

He doesn't like hamburgers. + She doesn't like hamburgers. = He doesn't like hamburgers, **and she doesn't either**.

- When both sentences are negative and have different subjects, use **and...either** to connect the two sentences. Use an auxiliary in the same tense to replace the second verb phrase if the verbs are the same.

⟱➔ **Exercise 24: Working on Form**

Work with a partner. Take turns choosing a category that you are interested in. Have your partner read the statements to you. Respond to the statements by adding information about the person, place, or thing in parentheses. Use *and...too, and...either,* or *but* plus an auxiliary. When you complete a category, switch roles with your partner and continue.

> **A:** *Tokyo is in Japan. Jakarta.*
> **B:** *Tokyo is in Japan, but Jakarta isn't.*

Geography

1. Tokyo is in Japan. (Jakarta)

2. Bangkok is in Thailand. (Istanbul)

3. Egypt has a canal. (Panama)

4. Guam is an island. (Puerto Rico)

History

5. The Vikings were from Scandinavia. (Cleopatra)

6. Albert Einstein wasn't an American president. (Thomas Edison)

7. World War I occurred in the twentieth century. (World War II)

Music

8. The trumpet is not a string instrument. (the flute)

9. The sitar is a musical instrument from India. (the piano)

10. Beethoven wrote sonatas. (Mozart)

Food

11. Beets are root vegetables. (carrots)

12. Yogurt isn't made of bean curd. (tofu)

13. Strawberries are red. (bananas)

Animals

14. Horses are vertebrates. (humans)

15. Mice don't lay eggs. (raccoons)

16. Chickens don't live in the water. (fish)

Famous People

17. Charles de Gaulle was a French president. (Louis Pasteur)

18. Galileo was an astronomer. (Copernicus)

19. Mikhail Baryshnikov is a dancer. (Woody Allen)

Movies

20. Humphrey Bogart was in *Casablanca*. (Kevin Costner)

21. Pelé is not an actor. (Sylvester Stallone)

22. *Star Trek* isn't a cartoon. (*Star Wars*)

And So.../And Neither...: Form

Affirmative Sentences

You like chocolate. + My mother likes chocolate. = You like chocolate, **and so does my mother**.

You like chocolate. + My parents like chocolate. = You like chocolate, **and so do my parents**.

- **And so...** is an inverted form. The auxiliary comes before the subject.

Negative Sentences

He doesn't like it. + She doesn't like it. = He doesn't like it, **and neither does she**.

He doesn't like it. + They don't like it. = He doesn't like it, **and neither do they**.

- **And neither...** is an inverted form. The auxiliary comes before the subject.

➡ Exercise 25: Working on Form

Work with a partner and complete the sentences. Then make up two more sentences for your partner to complete.

1. Skiing is a winter sport, _and so is sledding._____

2. I don't have a pet, _and neither does my roommate._____

3. Water contains oxygen,_____

4. Food is getting more expensive,_____

5. The word *study* doesn't have three syllables,_____

6. I didn't get up late this morning, _____

7. _____ I resemble my mother _____, and so does my sister.

8. _____, and neither is North America.

9. _____, and so did I.

10. _____, and neither do you.

11. _____, and so should men.

12. _____, and so is tennis.

13. _____, _____

14. _____, _____

But/And: Meaning and Use

DIFFERENCES AND SIMILARITIES

1. But is used to connect sentences when the information in the second clause is different from the information in the first clause:

He will succeed. + His brother won't succeed. = He will succeed, **but his brother won't.**

2. And...too, and...either, and so..., and neither... add information that is the same as the first clause:

We live on Dunn Street, **and the Nelson family does too.**
I don't work on Saturday, **and she doesn't either.**
Paula has one child, **and so does Susan.**
They don't have a new car, **and neither do I.**

3. Sentence pairs with **and so..., and...too** have the same meaning. Likewise, sentence pairs with **and neither..., and...either** have the same meaning:

You like chocolate, **and so does my mother.**
You like chocolate, **and my mother does too.**

You don't like it, **and neither does she.**
You don't like it, **and she doesn't either.**

4. And...too, and...either are used more frequently in conversation than in writing. In conversation **and** is often omitted. These short conversational responses are called rejoinders:

Ann: I thought the movie was terrible.
Tom: **I did too.**

Ann: I won't see that movie again!
Tom: **I won't either.**

5. And so… and **and neither…** are also frequently used in conversation. **And** may be omitted, and the result is a rejoinder:

Karen: I loved that movie!
Marie: **So did I.**

Karen: I didn't have enough time.
Marie: **Neither did I.**

6. Me too and **me neither** are used as rejoinders in very informal conversation instead of the subject and auxiliary with **too** or **either:**

Ann: I thought the movie was terrible!
Tom: **Me too.**

Ann: I didn't like the movie.
Tom: **Me neither.**

⫸ Exercise 26: Expressing Similarities

Work with a partner. Take turns as Person A and Person B, responding to each statement by using *too* or *either* in an appropriate phrase. Then practice with *me too* or *me neither.*

1. I like the new cafeteria.

    A: *I like the new cafeteria.*
    B: *I do too.* OR *Me too.*

2. I don't want to study tonight.

    A: *I don't want to study tonight.*
    B: *I don't either.* OR *Me neither.*

3. I need a vacation.

4. I had a small breakfast this morning.

5. I don't think it's very fair.

6. I don't get enough sleep.

7. I thought we had no more assignments until next week.

8. I'm not getting any exercise.

⏩ Exercise 27: Expressing Similarities

Work with your partner. Take turns responding to the statements using *so* or *neither*. Then continue to practice using *me too* or *me neither*.

1. He's looking for a job.

    A: *He's looking for a job.*
    B: *So am I.* OR *Me too.*

2. They don't want to leave.

    A: *They don't want to leave.*
    B: *Neither do I.* OR *Me neither.*

3. I want a better apartment.

4. I never watch TV. (Hint: *Never* is negative.)

5. I don't have any free time.

6. I wasn't in class yesterday.

7. I'm busy right now.

8. They wanted to leave.

⏩ Exercise 28: Expressing Similarities and Differences

Fill out the following questionnaire about your own habits, personality traits, likes, and dislikes. Then compare your answers with a partner's. Make up sentences using *and so...*, *and neither...*, or *but...*, and write them on a separate piece of paper. Choose one category and report your comparisons to the class.

Examples:

Do you ever skip breakfast? (yes)
Maria often skips breakfast, and so do I.

Are you an early riser? (no)
Raoul isn't an early riser, and neither am I.

Are you right-handed? (yes)
Kazuo is right-handed, but I'm not.

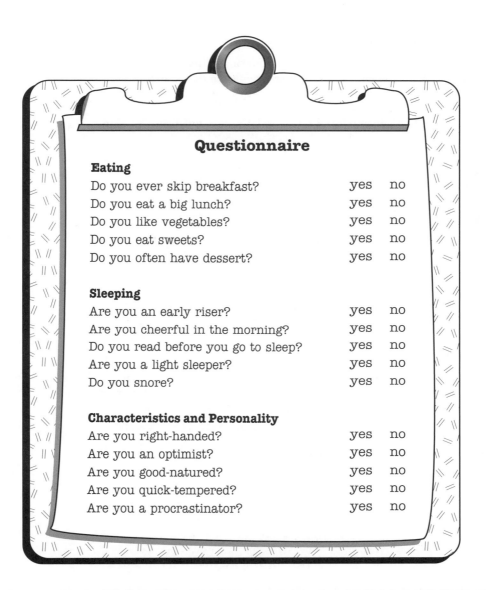

Questionnaire

Eating

Do you ever skip breakfast?	yes	no
Do you eat a big lunch?	yes	no
Do you like vegetables?	yes	no
Do you eat sweets?	yes	no
Do you often have dessert?	yes	no

Sleeping

Are you an early riser?	yes	no
Are you cheerful in the morning?	yes	no
Do you read before you go to sleep?	yes	no
Are you a light sleeper?	yes	no
Do you snore?	yes	no

Characteristics and Personality

Are you right-handed?	yes	no
Are you an optimist?	yes	no
Are you good-natured?	yes	no
Are you quick-tempered?	yes	no
Are you a procrastinator?	yes	no

Summary

***Be Going to*: Form**

Statements:	**I'm going to study** tonight.
Negative Statements:	We**'re not going to stay** home.
Yes/No Questions:	**Are** you **going to travel** this summer?
Short Answers:	Yes, I **am.** OR No, I**'m not.**
Information Questions:	When **are** you **going to leave?**
Information Questions (Subject):	Who **is going to** leave work early?

Be Going to: Meaning and Use

Be going to expresses a person's plans or intentions. It also expresses expectations and predictions, especially when the speaker sees evidence that something is about to happen.

Plans and Intentions:	I**'m going to clean** my apartment tomorrow.
Expectations and Predictions:	The sky is getting dark. It**'s going to rain.**

Will: Form

Statements:	I**'ll help** you later.
Negative Statements:	She **won't be** here tonight.
Yes/No Questions:	**Will** you **be** home tonight?
Short Answers:	Yes, I **will.** OR No, I **won't.**
Information Questions:	When **will** he **arrive?**
Information Questions (Subject):	What **will happen** to him?

Will: Meaning and Use

Will expresses future time. It is often used for promises, offers to help (volunteering), choices, expectations, predictions, refusals, and announcements. It is used in more formal situations that express the future.

Promises:	I**'ll be** home early. I promise.
Volunteering:	Fred: Who wants to help? Barney: I **will.**
Choices:	I**'ll have** a bowl of chili, please.
Expectations and Predictions:	I think he**'ll win** the election.
Refusals:	I **won't** do all this work. It's unfair.
Announcements:	An operator **will be** with you in a moment.

The Present Continuous as a Future Form: Form

Statements:	I**'m leaving** soon.
Negative Statements:	He**'s not coming** tonight.
Yes/No Questions:	**Is** she **working** tomorrow?

Short Answers:	Yes, she **is.** OR No, she **isn't.**
Information Questions:	Why **are** you **leaving** tomorrow?
Information Questions (Subject):	Who **is coming** tonight?

The Present Continuous as a Future Form: Meaning and Use

The present continuous can express future events that you have already planned. The event does not depend on chance.

| Plans: | I**'m taking** the train to New York tomorrow. |

The Simple Present as a Future Form: Form

Statements:	The show **begins** at eight o'clock.
Negative Statements:	The flight **doesn't take off** until 9:00 P.M.
Yes/No Questions:	**Do** classes **end** next Friday?
Short Answers:	Yes, they **do.** OR No, they **don't.**
Information Questions:	When **does** the next session **start?**
Information Questions (Subject):	Who **leaves** at nine o'clock tonight?

The Simple Present as a Future Form: Meaning and Use

The simple present expresses future arrangements in programs, schedules, itineraries, and announcements. The speaker generally cannot change these arrangements.

Programs:	The conference **begins** this Friday.
Schedules:	The flight **takes off** at 6:00 P.M.
Itineraries:	We **land** in London on Friday and **spend** two days there.
Announcements:	The new branch office **opens** this Monday.

But/And: Form

But:	They took the train, **but I didn't.**
And…too:	I love chocolate, **and she does too.**
And…either:	We don't have a car, **and you don't either.**
And so…:	She was born in Trinidad, **and so was he.**
And neither…:	I don't have any change, **and neither does the taxi driver.**

But/And: Meaning and Use

But/and are used to connect sentences with similar verb phrases. **But** adds information that is different from the first sentence. **And...too/and...either/and so.../and neither...** add information that is similar to the first sentence.

Similarities:	I stay up late, **and he does too.**
	I stay up late, **and so does he.**
	He's not happy, **and she's not either.**
	He's not happy, **and neither is she.**
	Bob: I'm tired.
	Ray: **Me too.**
	Joe: I don't understand.
	Dan: **Me neither.**
Differences:	They left early, **but we didn't.**
	They didn't like the movie, **but we did.**

⇒ Summary Exercise: Finding Errors

Each of the following sentences has an error in form or use. Find each error and correct it.

1. I promise ⅄ help you later.   I'll

2. I think it is raining tomorrow.

3. **A:** Why did you buy flour, sugar, and eggs?

    B: I will bake a cake.

4. You be in Santa Fe on Tuesday, won't you?

5. He finished early, and so I did.

6. I need a vacation, and he needs too.

7. **Parent:** Please help your brother.

    Child: No, I don't. He's not being nice to me.

8. **A:** They didn't understand.

    B: Neither I.

9. **A:** What are you doing next summer?

    B: I don't know. Maybe I work at the pharmacy again.

10. I think Taylor wins the election next week. What about you?

11. When are you going take a vacation?

12. The receptionist was talking on the phone, but the secretary didn't.

Complex Sentences: Past Time Clauses, Future Time Clauses, and Real *If* Sentences

Preview

A parent and teen:

> Parent: What was going on **when I called home this morning?** There was so much noise in the background!
>
> Teen: **While I was talking to you,** some workmen were repairing the street and the mail carrier delivered a package.
>
> Parent: OK. Well, you need to do your homework now.
>
> Teen: I'll do it **after I finish this game.**
>
> Parent: (*Warning in a stern voice*): **If** you **wait** too long, you**'ll be** too tired to do your homework.

Three different kinds of complex sentences are presented in this chapter: sentences with past time clauses, sentences with future time clauses, and sentences with real **if** clauses (as opposed to imaginary **if** clauses, which are presented in Chapter 13).

Time clauses (**when I called home this morning, while I was talking to you,** and **after I finish this game**) express the relationship in time between two different events in the same sentence.

If sentences express a real or possible situation in the **if** clause (**if you wait too long**) and the expected result in the main clause (**you'll be too tired to do your homework**).

These sentences are called complex sentences because they have a main (independent) clause and one or more dependent clauses. Dependent clauses begin with words such as **when, while, before, after, if, who, that,** and **which.**

In this chapter you will study complex sentences with dependent time clauses and with real **if** clauses. You will study other dependent clauses in later chapters.

Past Time Clauses: Form

Time Clause			Main Clause
While	**Larry**	**was talking,**	Billy interrupted him.
When	**Susan**	**was eating,**	Debby called.
Before	**the kids**	**went to bed,**	they watched a movie.
After	**Sarah**	**ate,**	she went out.

- Time clauses begin with a time word (**while, when, before,** and **after**) and have a subject and a verb. They are dependent clauses; they cannot stand alone. They depend on the main clause to complete their meaning and must be attached to it.
- The time clause can come before or after the main clause. The meaning is the same.
- If the time clause comes first, it is followed by a comma.

Main Clause	Time Clause		
Billy interrupted Larry	**while**	**he**	**was talking**.
Debby called	**when**	**Susan**	**was eating**.
The kids watched a movie	**before**	**they**	**went to bed**.
Sarah went out	**after**	**she**	**ate**.

- If the main clause comes at the beginning of the sentence and the time clause is last, there is no comma.

⇒ Exercise 1: Working on Form

Work with a partner. Combine the time words with the simple sentences to form as many complex sentences as you can. Are any combinations inappropriate because of their meanings?

1. (when)

   (I went home.)

   (I finished my work.)

   Examples: *When I went home, I finished my work.* OR
   When I finished my work, I went home. OR
   I went home when I finished my work. OR
   I finished my work when I went home.

2. (while)

   (He was reading.)

   (He was listening to music.)

3. (after)

   (He was sick for a long time.)

   (He died.)

4. (before)

   (She fell asleep.)

   (The doorbell rang.)

5. (when)

   (The fire started.)

   (We were sleeping.)

Past Time Clauses: Meaning and Use

ORDER OF PAST EVENTS

1. Time clauses with **while, when, before,** and **after** describe the relationship in time between two events or situations. The past time clause helps you understand which event happened or started first, and which event happened second.

2. If both verbs are in the simple past, the action in the **when** and **after** clauses happened first. Their order in the sentence does not change the meaning:

1st Action	2nd Action
When I went home,	I finished.
After I finished,	I went home.

2nd Action	1st Action
I finished	**when I went home.**
I went home	**after I finished.**

3. If both verbs are in the simple past, the action in the **before** clause happened second:

2nd Action	1st Action
Before I finished,	I went home.
Before I went home,	I finished.

1st Action	2nd Action
I went home	**before I finished.**
I finished	**before I went home.**

(continued)

4. In **while** or **when** sentences, if one verb is in the simple past, and one verb is in the past continuous, the action in the past continuous clause always starts first:

1st Action	2nd Action
I was reading	**when the phone rang.**
When I was reading,	the phone rang.

2nd Action	1st Action
The phone rang	**while I was reading.**

5. In **while** or **when** sentences, the past continuous event is longer than the simple past event. The simple past event happens during the past continuous event:

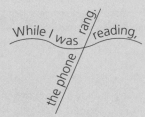

6. If both verbs are in the past continuous, then the activities are happening at the same time (simultaneously) in **while** or **when** sentences:

I was sitting down **while they were dancing.**
I was sitting down **when they were dancing.**

7. Both **while** and **when** can introduce a past continuous time clause to mean *during the time*. These sentences have the same meaning:

While I was dancing, I lost my necklace.
When I was dancing, I lost my necklace.

8. When can also introduce the shorter completed event to mean *at the time*, but **while** cannot:

I was dancing **when I lost my necklace.**

9. Sometimes a sentence with a time clause expresses a cause-and-effect relationship. The first action in the **when** clause caused the second action:

I tripped **when my heel broke.**

➠ Exercise 2: Deciding the Order of Events

Decide which event happened or started first, and underline it.

1. When <u>I went home</u>, I opened the mail.
2. After I played tennis, I took a shower.
3. I finished my work before I went home.
4. The phone rang while I was fixing the bathroom sink.
5. She came home before it started to rain.
6. While I was waiting for John, I saw Erica.
7. Before I ate breakfast, I took a walk.
8. After Jim got up, he called me.
9. When I shouted, she turned around.
10. The water ran out when I opened the drain.
11. After I called the operator, she connected me with Bogotá.
12. A few minutes after the election ended, the TV reporters declared a winner.

➠ Exercise 3: Talking About Two Events

In each of the following sentences, two events happened. Complete the sentences with the words in parentheses. Use the past continuous for the event that started first, and use the simple past for the shorter, completed event.

1. It _____was raining_____ (rain) when she _____arrived._____ (arrive)

2. When the library _____ (close), he _____ (read) an interesting article.

3. Lightning _____ (strike) when they _____ (watch) television.

4. When World War II _____ (begin), she _____ (live) in Paris.

5. When they _____ (talk) about their childhood, they suddenly _____ (remember) that their father's birthday was next week.

6. She _____ (study) biology when she _____ (decide) to become a science illustrator.

7. The police _____ (stop) her while she _____ (drive) 85 mph.

8. The copy machine _____ (break) when he _____ (copy) his paper.

9. She _____ (eat) lunch when she _____ (hear) the news.

10. I _____ (slip) on the ice while I _____ (climb) the stairs to the front entrance.

⮞ Exercise 4: Understanding Cause and Effect

Work with a partner. Read each pair of sentences and decide which is the cause (the first action) and which is the effect (the second action). Label the cause and effect. Then combine each pair of sentences, using a *when* clause to express the cause.

1. The temperature dropped below freezing. _____*cause*_____

   The roads became icy. _____*effect*_____

   _____*When the temperature dropped below freezing, the roads became icy.*_____

2. They painted their house bright pink. _____

   The neighbors refused to talk to them. _____

   _____

   _____

3. The lights went out. _____

   The lightning struck. _____

   _____

   _____

4. All work stopped. _____

   The computer system went down. _____

   _____

   _____

5. They had to call for help. _____

   They ran out of gas. _____

   _____

   _____

6. He went on a strict diet. _____

   His best suit didn't fit anymore. _____

   _____

   _____

7. He sneezed. _____

   Everyone jumped. _____

   _____

   _____

8. Her arm started to itch. _____

   A mosquito bit her. _____

   _____

   _____

9. The doorbell rang. _____

   He answered the door. _____

   _____

   _____

10. She found the lost jewelry. _____

    She got a reward. _____

    _____

    _____

⮞ **Exercise 5: Telling a Story**

Imagine that you had a terrible day. It's 9:00 P.M. and you are describing your terrible day to a friend. Complete the story by writing complex sentences with the words in parentheses. Use *while* and the past continuous in the first clause and the simple past in the second clause.

You wouldn't believe what a terrible day I had! (I try to sleep/the cat jump on my chest)
While I was trying to sleep, the cat jumped on my chest.

So I got up to let him go out, but (I go down the stairs/I trip on a shoe) _____

_____

By this time, I was fully awake even though it was just 5:15 in the morning. So I decided to

make breakfast. Would you believe that (I make coffee/I spill nearly a whole can of coffee on

the floor) _____

_____

_____? I tried to calm down, eat my breakfast, and get

washed. But (I take a shower/the phone ring) _____

_____ (I rush out of the shower/I slip on the wet floor)

_____

_____ Who was it, but an old friend who drives me crazy! He asked

to come and stay with me for two weeks. (I try to explain how busy I am/he hang up on me)

_____

_____

Well, I got to school all right. The most important thing that I had to do today was to type

a paper for my economics class. Well, guess what? (I type the paper/the computer system go

down) _____

_____ I had to go to class without my paper. On my way there, (elevator

go up/it suddenly stop and the alarm go off) _____

_____ I was thirty-five

minutes late, so I missed most of my class. Fortunately, my professor has a sense of humor.

(I explain what happened/he begin laughing) _____

_____

Now I'm safe at home and I'm not leaving here until tomorrow morning. Thanks for

listening to all of this nonsense! How was your day?

⫸ **Exercise 6: Describing Your Day**

Work with a partner. Can you remember a bad day that you had recently? Did anything unexpected happen while you were doing something else? Take turns telling your partner what happened. Use complex sentences with *while* and the past continuous in the first clause and the simple past in the second clause.

> Example: *Yesterday was a bad day for me. While I was pouring some milk, I dropped the glass. While I was cleaning up the mess, I stepped on a piece of broken glass and cut my foot!*

⫸ **Exercise 7: Describing Changes with *Before* and *After***

Work with a partner. Tell how the pictures relate to each situation using complex sentences with *before* and *after*. Use the simple past in both clauses or the simple past and the past continuous. After you discuss the pictures, write about one pair.

1. The doorbell rang.

Example:
Before the guests arrived, they were fighting.

2. He fell in love.

3. Realtors developed the land.

BEFORE

AFTER

Future Time Clauses: Form

Time Clause			Main Clause
After	**Jan**	**gets home,**	she will help you.
When	**you**	**pick me up,**	I'll give you my key.
Before	**they**	**arrive,**	he's going to call the airlines.

- When a time clause beginning with **before, after,** or **when** refers to the future, use the simple present, not the future. Future forms are used in the main clause if it is appropriate.
- The time clause can come before or after the main clause with no change in meaning.
- If the time clause comes first, it is followed by a comma.

Main Clause	Time Clause		
She will help you	**after**	**Jan**	**gets home.**
I'll give you my key	**when**	**you**	**pick me up.**
He's going to call the airlines	**before**	**they**	**arrive.**

- If the main clause comes at the beginning of the sentence and the time clause is last, there is no comma.

⟶ **Exercise 8: Working on Form**

Work with a partner. Combine the time words with the simple sentences to form as many complex sentences as you can. Use the simple present in the time clause and *will* or *be going to* in the main clause. Are any combinations inappropriate?

1. (when)

   (I go home.)

   (I finish my work.)

   Examples: *When I go home, I'll finish my work.* OR
   When I finish my work, I'll go home. OR
   I'll finish my work when I go home. OR
   I'll go home when I finish my work.

2. (before)

   (I go shopping.)

   (I call you.)

3. (after)

   (The mail arrives.)

   (I eat breakfast.)

4. (when)

   (He falls asleep.)

   (He reads the newspaper.)

5. (before)

   (He sets the table.)

   (He cooks dinner.)

Future Time Clauses: Meaning and Use

ORDER OF FUTURE EVENTS

1. Future time clauses with **before, after,** and **when** express the relationship in time between two future events in a complex sentence. They show the order of the future event in the main clause and the future event in the time clause:

Time Clause	Main Clause
Before I **get** on the plane,	I**'ll buy** a mystery novel.
When I **finish** the book,	we**'ll be** ready to land.
After we **land,**	I**'ll call** you.

(continued)

2. If **before** begins a future time clause, the action in the **before** clause will happen second:

1st Action	2nd Action
I'll read my mail	**before I call you.**
I'll call you	**before I read my mail.**

2nd Action	1st Action
Before I call you,	I'll read my mail.
Before I read my mail,	I'll call you.

3. If **when** or **after** begins a future time clause, the action in the **when** or **after** clause will happen first:

1st Action	2nd Action
When I go to the library,	I'll see you.
After I go to the library,	I'll see you.
When I see you,	I'll go to the library.
After I see you,	I'll go to the library.

2nd Action	1st Action
I'll go to the library	**when I see you.**
I'll go to the library	**after I see you.**
I'll see you	**when I go to the library.**
I'll see you	**after I go to the library.**

4. Future time clauses are especially useful when a person wants to procrastinate. Procrastinating is intentionally delaying doing something that a person does not want to do even though he or she should do it:

I'll study for the test **after I relax** for a while.

⟫ Exercise 9: Expressing Order of Future Events

Work in small groups. Describe the order of events that will probably happen in the following situations. Use the time words *before, when,* and *after* and the verbs *leave, arrive,* and *begin* in your sentences.

1. You're going to the movies:

Examples: *Before I leave home, I'll eat dinner.*
When I arrive, I'll buy a ticket and some popcorn.
After the movie begins, I'll eat my popcorn.

2. You're going to a concert:

3. You're going to class:

4. You're going to take an exam:

5. You have a job interview:

6. You are going to have dinner with your boyfriend's or girlfriend's parents for the first time:

7. You're going to play in a piano recital:

8. You're going to give a lecture to 100 people about your research:

➡ Exercise 10: Procrastinating

Work with a partner and take turns completing the conversations. Person A is reminding Person B to do something that he or she doesn't really want to do. Person B procrastinates by finding other things to do first. Use future time clauses with *before, after,* and *when* to say when you are going to do what your partner is asking.

1. **Parent:** Please take out the garbage.

   Child: OK, but not now. (before) _I'll take out the garbage before I go to bed._

2. **Husband:** Don't forget to call your aunt.

   Wife: Yes. (before) _____

   _____

3. **Parent:** Weren't you going to mow the lawn today?

   Teenager: Well, yes…. (after) _____

   _____

4. **Secretary:** I need your signature on all of these letters.

   Boss: I'm too busy right now. (when)_____

   _____

5. **Roommate A:** Weren't you going to call the landlord to complain about the furnace?

   Roommate B: Oh yeah. I said I was going to do that, didn't I? (before)_____

   _____

6. **Wife:** It's your turn to make dinner tonight.

   Husband: Right. (when)_____

   _____

7. **Friend A:** Did you apply for the job that I told you about?

   Friend B: Not yet. (after) _____

   _____

8. **Co-worker A:** Weren't you going to tell the boss that you are going to resign?

   Co-worker B: Yes, but I'm kind of scared. (when) _____

   _____

Real *If* Sentences: Form

Real *If* Clause	Expected Result
If you **press** the red button,	**(then)** the door **will lock**.
If you **press** the green one,	**(then)** the door **is going to open**.

- Real **if** sentences have a dependent **if** clause and an independent result clause.
- The **if** clause is in the simple present. The result clause has **will** or **be going to** + the main verb.
- **Then** is optional in the result clause.

Real *If* Clause	Expected Result
If it **doesn't rain** tonight,	**(then)** I'**ll go** to the baseball game.

- **If** clauses can go before or after the result clause. The meaning is the same.
- When the **if** clause comes first, it is followed by a comma. **Then** is optional in the result clause. It is not necessary, but it is always implied.

Expected Result	Real *If* Clause
I'**ll go** to the baseball game	**if** it **doesn't rain** tonight.

- When the result clause comes first, there is no comma and **then** is not used.

⫸ **Exercise 11: Working on Form**

1. Work in small groups and take turns practicing real *if* clauses with the simple present and result clauses with *will* or *be going to*. Start a chain as follows: Person A begins with an *if* clause, and Person B responds with a result. Person C uses that result as a new *if* clause and Person D responds with a new result. Continue until everyone in the group has a turn.

   A: *If the teacher cancels class tomorrow,...*
   B: *...I'm going to go shopping.*
   C: *If you go shopping,...*
   D: *...you'll spend a lot of money.*

2. Work with a partner and write down on a separate sheet of paper as many of the real *if* sentences from the chain as you can remember.

If the teacher cancels class tomorrow, I'm going to go shopping.

If you go shopping, you'll spend a lot of money.

If you spend a lot of money, you'll need a second job.

Real *If* Sentences: Meaning and Use

POSSIBLE CONDITIONS AND RESULTS

1. Real **if** sentences express real or possible situations that can happen in the present or in the future. They are also called real conditional sentences because the expected result in the main clause depends on the real or possible condition in the dependent **if** clause.

2. The real or possible condition is expressed with **if** and the simple present, even when the situation refers to the future. The expected result is expressed with **will** or the **be going to** future:

   If Joe **calls** me tonight, **I'll tell** him my plans.

3. Real **if** sentences are frequently used to give warnings, to make threats, to offer advice, to make promises, and to state advantages and disadvantages:

Warning: If you smoke, you'll damage your lungs.

Threat: 威胁   If you don't stop, I'm going to call the police.

Advice: If you drink hot tea with honey, you'll feel better.

Promise: If I win the election, I won't raise taxes.

Advantages: If you buy a smaller car, you will get better gas mileage.

Disadvantages: If you buy a small car, you won't have as much room.

(continued)

4. Threats expressed in real **if** sentences announce a person's negative intentions. Threats are stronger than warnings. Threats with **be going to** or **will** are very similar, but a threat with **be going to** is often stronger because it expresses a person's immediate intentions. A threat with **will** may sound more like a vague promise about the future. Compare these examples:

If you don't help me, **I'll call** the manager.
If you don't help me, **I'm going to call** the manager.

⇒ Exercise 12: Expressing Conditions and Results

Work in small groups and write five real *if* clauses. They can be as funny or creative as you wish. Then exchange the clauses with another group and write result clauses for them. Finally, read the complete sentences aloud to the class.

1. If you help me learn English...
   If you help me learn English, I'll teach you to dance the lambada.

2. _____

3. _____

4. _____

5. _____

6. _____

⇒ Exercise 13: Giving Warnings

Work on your own to complete the following warnings about your health. Use *will* or *won't* in the result clause.

1. If you don't eat vegetables, you won't have a balanced diet.

2. If you don't brush your teeth, _____

_____

3. If you eat too much fat, _____

_____

4. If you drink too much alcohol, _____

_____

5. If you don't get enough calcium, _____

_____

6. If you don't exercise, _____

_____

7. If you don't get enough rest, _____

_____

8. If you eat too many sweets, _____

_____

⮞ Exercise 14: Giving Warnings

Complete the following warnings by adding conditions in the *if* clauses that lead to these negative results.

1. If _____ you don't pay your taxes _____, you'll get into trouble.

2. If _____, your car won't work properly.

3. If _____, you'll have to pay a fine.

4. If _____, you'll get arrested.

5. If _____, you won't have enough money for rent.

6. If _____, you'll slip.

7. If _____, you'll get an electric shock.

8. If _____, you'll start a fire.

➠ Exercise 15: Making Threats

Work in small groups. Read these situations where the speaker is annoyed and is going to threaten the listener. Make up appropriate threats for each situation using real *if* sentences with *be going to* in the result clause.

1. Your neighbors are having a very loud party. You didn't mind the noise between the hours of 8:00 P.M. and midnight, but it's now 1:30 A.M. You've called several times and asked politely if they could lower the music, but they didn't. Now you're tired and angry. You have to go to work tomorrow at 8:00 A.M.

   Example: *If the music doesn't stop immediately, I'm going to call the police.*

2. You're in a restaurant for lunch. The restaurant isn't busy, but you have been waiting forty-five minutes for your sandwich. You're very hungry and you have to go back to work soon. You've already asked the waiter twice about your order.

3. When you come out of your apartment building, you find a car parked in an illegal spot and it's blocking your car. You need to go to work. The car belongs to your neighbor's friend, and you've already told him several times to park properly when he stops by.

4. You teach a history class. You have assigned a paper that everyone has turned in except for one student who turns in every paper late.

5. It's been raining a lot lately and your eight-year-old child has been wearing his muddy shoes into the house. You have white wall-to-wall carpeting.

6. You have a friend who has been telling lies about you behind your back. This has happened before and, once again, this is causing you great embarrassment.

➠ Exercise 16: Giving Advice

Work with a partner. Read these statements of advice and rewrite them as real *if* sentences with *if* clauses in the simple present and result clauses with *will*. Notice that the meaning is the same.

1. Turn down your thermostat at night and you won't use so much fuel.

   If you turn down your thermostat at night, you won't use so much fuel.

2. Take my advice and your troubles will be over.

3. Go to sleep early and you'll feel better in the morning.

4. Call at night and your telephone bill won't be so high.

5. Don't eat so much and you won't get indigestion.

_____

6. Read for a while and you'll fall asleep easily.

_____

7. Pick the baby up and he'll stop crying.

_____

8. Don't yell at her and she won't yell back.

_____

9. Take a break every few hours and you won't get so tired.

_____

10. Call the doctor and she'll tell you what to do.

_____

⟹ Exercise 17: Making Promises

Work with a partner. Imagine you are a political candidate running for the office of mayor, governor, or president. In your campaign speeches, you often make promises. Give promises using the words in parentheses and be prepared to tell them to the class.

1. (create jobs)

   Examples: *If I am elected mayor, I will create jobs.* OR
              If I am governor, I will create jobs. OR
              If I become president, I will create jobs.

2. (give money for education/health care)
3. (build new schools/hospitals/day-care centers/airports)
4. (help the poor)
5. (work for peace)
6. (clean up the environment)
7. (raise/lower taxes)
8. (solve the drug/crime/unemployment/pollution problem)
9. (hire more police/firefighters/women/minorities)
10. (⌇⌇⌇⌇)

⮞ Exercise 18: Stating Advantages and Disadvantages

Work with a partner. Imagine you want to move. You are trying to decide between two apartments. One is the first floor of a house on Oak Street; the other is on the third floor of a large apartment building on Elm Street. Take turns making up real *if* sentences that describe the advantages and disadvantages of each location.

Examples: *If I move to Oak Street, I'll have a garage.*
If you live on Elm Street, you won't have a garden.

Oak Street — 1st floor of a house

	Advantages	Disadvantages
Location	on a quiet street garage close to a park	bus stop far away far from stores far from school
Rent/Utilities	lower rent	higher utilities
Inside Space	two floors big closets large bedrooms thick walls large windows	tiny, dark kitchen small refrigerator no dishwasher worn carpeting old furnace
Outside Space	place for a garden	a lawn to mow

Elm Street — 3rd floor of an apartment building

	Advantages	Disadvantages
Location	near a bus stop near a supermarket near schools	on a busy street poor parking no park nearby
Rent/Utilities	lower utilities	higher rent
Inside Space	big kitchen big refrigerator dishwasher	small rooms little closet space thin walls
Outside Space	a balcony	no place for a garden

Summary

Past Time Clauses: Form

Time Clause	Main Clause
While I was sleeping,	the phone rang.
When I was sleeping,	the phone rang.
Before I called,	they left.
After I called,	they left.

Main Clause	Time Clause
The phone rang	**while I was sleeping.**
The phone rang	**when I was sleeping.**
They left	**before I called.**
They left	**after I called.**

Past Time Clauses: Meaning and Use

Past time clauses describe the relationship in time between two past events or situations. They tell which event happened or started first and which event happened second.

Order of Events:	**Before Tom left,** he fed the cat.
Simultaneous Events:	Pat was laughing **while I was singing.**
Cause and Effect:	His fever dropped **when he took** some aspirin.
Storytelling:	This morning, **while I was trying to sleep,** the cat jumped on my chest.

Future Time Clauses: Form

Time Clause	Main Clause
After she gets home,	she'll take a shower.
When she gets home,	she'll take a shower.
Before I go to bed,	I'm going to lock the door.

Main Clause	Time Clause
She'll take a shower	**after she gets home.**
She'll take a shower	**when she gets home.**
I'm going to lock the door	**before I go to bed.**

Future Time Clauses: Meaning and Use

Future time clauses express a relationship in time between the future event in the time clause and the future event in the main clause.

Order of Events: She'll brush her teeth **after she gets up.**

Procrastinating: Parent: Please take out the garbage.
                    Teen: Not now. I'll take out the garbage **before I go to bed.**

Real *If* Sentences: Form

Real *If* Clause	Expected Result
If you **help** me,	**(then)** I'll **help** you.

Expected Result	Real *If* Clause
I'll **help** you	**if** you **help** me.

Real *If* Sentences: Meaning and Use

Real **if** sentences describe possible present or future conditions and their expected future results.

Warnings: If you smoke, you'll damage your lungs.

Threats: If you don't stop, I'm going to call the police.

Advice: If you drink hot tea with honey, you'll feel better.

Promises: If I win the election, I won't raise taxes.

Advantages: If you move to that apartment, you'll have a garage.

Disadvantages: If you move to that house, you'll have higher utility bills.

⫸ Summary Exercise: Finding Errors

Most of the sentences have an error in form, meaning, or use. Find each error and correct it. (Hint: four sentences are correct.)

1. When ~~he'll get~~ a letter, he'll be happy.   *he gets*

2. When I was taking a shower, the phone rang.

3. If I will press the button, the machine will start.

4. I was talking on the phone while I dropped the glass.

5. You'll get a speeding ticket, if you drive too fast.

6. After he fell asleep, he was reading a book.

7. Before she's going to leave the house, she's going to call you.

8. While you were talking, I was finishing my work.

9. I dialed again, after I heard the dial tone.

10. What were you doing when I came in?

11. I'll call you before I left.

12. If I remove the price tag, the store won't take back the item.

13. He jumped up when I call.

14. **A:** Please clean up this mess.
    B: Not now. I clean it up after I'll take a nap.

CHAPTER

Connecting the Past and the Present: The Present Perfect and the Present Perfect Continuous

Preview

A telephone recording:

> The number you **have reached** is not a working number. Please check the number and dial again….

A job interview:

> Manager: **Have** you ever **worked** with a computer?
> Interviewee: Yes, I **have**. I'**ve done** word processing and spreadsheets.

A news broadcast:

> We **have** just **learned** that the mayor **has resigned**. A few moments ago, Mayor John Wells announced his resignation due to a serious health condition. The mayor stated that he **has known** about this condition for only a few days.

A telephone conversation:

> Peter: Where **have** you **been**? I'**ve been trying** to reach you since yesterday.
> Alex: I'**ve been studying** at the library. I have finals next week.

The present perfect is used to express past time that is related to the present in some way. Sometimes the past action is very recent, or it is still continuing at the present moment, or we don't know exactly when the past action happened. We only know that it happened sometime before the present.

All of these connections to the present distinguish the present perfect from the simple past tense that you studied in Chapter 3. Unlike the present perfect, the simple past is used to talk about events that happened at specific past times. The simple past does not express any relationship between present and past time.

The present perfect continuous typically focuses on the duration of actions that began in the past and continue into the present moment, much like the present continuous. The present perfect continuous can also be used to emphasize the recency of a past action.

The Present Perfect: Form

Statements / Contractions

Statements			Contractions
I	**have**	**finished**.	I**'ve**
You			You**'ve**
We			We**'ve**
They			They**'ve**
He	**has**	**finished**.	He**'s**
She			She**'s**
It			It**'s**

- To form the present perfect, use the simple present form of **have** + the past participle of the main verb.
- The past participle of regular verbs is the same form as the simple past form (verb + **-ed**).
- Look at pages 486–487 for spelling and pronunciation rules for regular past participles.
- Irregular verbs have special past participle forms. Look at pages 488–491 for a list of irregular verbs and their past participles.

Negative Statements / Contractions

Negative Statements				Contractions	
I	**have**	**not**	**finished**.	I	**haven't**
He	**has**	**not**	**finished**.	He	**hasn't**

- To form negative statements, use **have** or **has** + **not** or the contraction **-n't** and the past participle of the main verb.

Yes/No Questions / Short Answers / Contractions

Yes/No Questions			Short Answers	Contractions
Have	you	**finished**?	Yes, I **have**.	
			No, I **have not**.	No, I **haven't**.
Has	he	**finished**?	Yes, he **has**.	
			No, he **has not**.	No, he **hasn't**.

- To form *yes/no* questions, use **have** or **has** before the subject. The past participle of the main verb follows the subject.
- Short answers to *yes/no* questions have a subject + **have** or **has**.
- Affirmative short answers do not have contracted forms. We never say, *Yes, I've* or *Yes, he's*. (INCORRECT)

Information Questions				Answers
What	**have**	you	**done**?	Nothing.
Where	**has**	he	**gone**?	To New York.

- The *wh-* word is followed by **have** or **has,** the subject, and the past participle of the main verb.

Information Questions (Subject)			Answers	Contractions
Who	**has**	**finished?**	I **have**.	**Who's**
What	**has**	**happened?**	He broke his arm.	**What's**

- If **who** or **what** is the subject of the question, the word order is the same as for affirmative statements.

CONVERSATION NOTES

1. Have and **has** are often contracted. With pronouns, contractions are frequently used both in speaking and in informal writing. However, when you write names and other nouns, contractions are usually avoided:

Written Form	Spoken Form
Dan **has** won.	"Dan**'s** won."
The cars **have** stopped.	"The cars**'ve** stopped." (SPOKEN ONLY)

2. Contractions with *wh-* words are also common in conversation. In writing, contractions with **has** and a *wh-* word are common, but contractions of **have** with *wh-* words are avoided:

Written Form	Spoken Form
Who**'s** finished?	"Who**'s** finished?"
What **have** you done?	"What**'ve** you done?" (SPOKEN ONLY)

➠ **Exercise 1: Working on Form**

Work with a partner. Complete the following conversations with the present perfect.
Then take turns reading the conversations aloud, using contractions as much as possible.

1. **A:** I _____*haven't eaten*_____ (not/eat) at the new cafeteria yet.

   _____*Have you tried*_____ (you/try) it?

   B: No, but I _____ (hear) that it's very good and very fast.

   It seems that the management _____ (finally/begin) to

   understand that most students don't have time for long lunch breaks.

2. **A:** _____ (you/find) a job yet?

   B: No, so far I _____ (have/not) any luck.

   I _____ (look) in the classified ads,

   I _____ (check) at the employment office,

   and I _____ (apply) for a job at the telephone company.

   I don't understand it. Everyone else _____ (get) jobs without

   any problems.

   A: It sounds like you _____ (think) of everything

   except you _____ (not/call) my uncle yet.

   He _____ (be) the manager of the electric

   company downtown for fifteen years. A lot of my friends

   _____ (work) for him during summer vacations.

   I'll give you his number.

3. **A:** How long _____ (Tom/be) married?

   B: He _____ (be) married for only a year, but

   he _____ (know) his wife since he was ten.

4. **A:** I _____ (not/write) to my parents for two weeks. They

   probably think that something terrible _____ (happen)

   to me.

   B: I'm surprised that they _____ (not/call) or sent a telegram.

   _____ (you/ever/use) electronic mail? You could contact

   your father at work right now.

5. **A:** The weather _____ (be) awful this summer.

   I _____ (not/go) swimming since the beginning

   of July. I _____ (not/play) tennis either.

   B: I know. I _____ (not/spend) much time outside at all

   since summer began. I _____ (not/take) any long walks,

   and I _____ (not/ride) my new bike yet.

6. **A:** I _____ (see) your long list of things to do.

   What _____ (you/do) so far?

   B: I _____ (do) the laundry,

   I _____ (sweep) the kitchen,

   I _____ (make) some phone calls, and

   I _____ (write) some letters. But

   I still _____ (not/take) the clothes to the cleaners

   or paid my bills yet.

The Present Perfect: Meaning and Use

INDEFINITE TIME

1. The present perfect often expresses indefinite past time. This means that the specific time of the past event is not important. The experience itself is far more important:

   I've read that book. It's fascinating.

2. The event may be repeated several times in the past. Again, the exact time is unimportant:

   He's seen that movie many times.

3. Questions with **ever** and their answers also express the indefinite meaning of the present perfect:

   Paul: **Have** you ever **ridden** a motorcycle?
   Mark: **I've sat** on one, but I've never actually **taken** a ride.

In this conversation, the specific time is not expressed. The only information that you know is that Mark has sat on a motorcycle at least one time in his life. That time can be any time in his life up to the present moment.

(continued)

4. The adverbs **ever, never, already, yet, still, so far, once, twice, three times, many times,** and so on frequently express the indefinite meaning of the present perfect. They are grouped below by their position in the sentence:

Before the Past Participle

ever	at any time up to now	Have you **ever** had sushi?
		I haven't **ever** had sushi.
never	at no time up to now	He's **never** had sushi.
already	at some time sooner than expected	Have you **already** eaten?

End of Sentence

already	at some time sooner than expected	I've eaten **already.**
yet	expected at some time before now	Have you eaten **yet?**
		I haven't eaten **yet.**
once, twice, three times	exact number of times up to now	We've eaten there **once.**
a few times, many times	indefinite number of times up to now	I've eaten there **a few times.**
so far	at any time up to now	What have you done **so far?**
		He hasn't answered **so far.**

Beginning of Sentence

so far	at any time up to now	**So far,** he hasn't answered.

Before *Have* or *Has*

still	expected at some time before now	They **still** haven't finished.

⇒ Exercise 2: Talking About Life Experiences

Work with a partner. Take turns asking and answering questions about your life experiences. Use the present perfect with *ever* and the expressions in parentheses. Respond with a short answer in the present perfect and add another sentence of explanation. If your answer is affirmative, tell how many times you have done it. If your answer is negative, use *never* in your sentence. Then make up several questions of your own.

1. (have a flat tire)

    A: *Have you ever had a flat tire?*
    B: *Yes, I have. I've had a flat tire once.* OR
        No, I haven't. I've never had a flat tire.

2. (ski in the Rockies)

3. (bounce a check)

4. (lose your wallet)

5. (run out of gas)

6. (tell a lie)

7. (write a poem)

8. (meet a movie star)

9. (eat raw fish)

10. (take a bus trip)

11. (see a shooting star)

12. (～～～)

➡ Exercise 3: Telling About Personal Accomplishments

Work on your own. Write sentences about some of your own accomplishments using the present perfect and the suggested adverbs. Choose one sentence to tell the class.

1. Name three things that you've done this semester. Use *so far* or *already* in each sentence.

   So far, I've read two novels. OR

   I've already read two novels.

   _____

   _____

   _____

   _____

2. Name three things you are supposed to do this semester but haven't done yet. Use *still* or *yet*.

   I still haven't looked for a job. OR

   I haven't looked for a job yet.

   _____

   _____

   _____

   _____

⟫ Exercise 4: Describing Progress

Work in small groups. Imagine you are having a surprise birthday party for your friend at your apartment tomorrow night. You've made a long list of things you need to do and have checked each item that you've done. Various friends call to find out about your progress and to offer help. Take turns asking questions in the present perfect with *already, yet,* and *so far.* Answer the questions with *already, yet,* or *still.*

A: *Have you gone shopping yet?*
B: *Yes, I have, but I haven't bought everything yet.*
A: *Have you bought the soda?*
B: *Yes, I've already bought it.*

To Do

1. Buy:
   soda ✓
   juice
   beer
   pretzels
   fresh veggies
   dip
   nachos
   cups
   napkins
   paper plates
   crackers (2 boxes)
   cheese (2 kinds)

2. Order birthday cake

3. Borrow:
   chairs
   folding table
   CD player
   CDs

4. Clean apartment

5. Move furniture

6. Decorate

⮞ Exercise 5: Reminding

Work with a partner. Take turns making up reminders. Ask questions using the words in parentheses and the present perfect. Then ask your own questions.

1. Your sister is going to the beach with you. She is very pale:

   (take sunscreen)

   Example: *Have you taken the sunscreen?*

2. Your friend has his first job interview tomorrow. He's trying to prepare for it, but he's worried that he's forgotten something. He's called you for reminders:

   (get a haircut)
   (shine your shoes)
   (pick up your suit at the cleaners)
   (choose a matching shirt and tie)
   (∼∼∼∼)

3. Your friend has just picked out a used car to buy. You've just bought one and you know how complicated it can be:

   (check the mileage)
   (take it to a mechanic)
   (drive it)
   (talk to your bank about a car loan)
   (∼∼∼∼)

4. Your roommate is going to mail the telephone bill to the phone company instead of paying it at the bank. He notices a list of reminders on the back of the envelope:

   (enclose a check or money order)
   (write your account number on the front of your check or money order)
   (sign your check)
   (include the top portion of your bill)
   (place a stamp on the envelope)
   (∼∼∼∼)

⮞ Exercise 6: Refusing

Work with a partner. Use the present perfect and the adverbs in parentheses to refuse the offers in the following conversations. Then take turns practicing the conversations.

1. **A:** Would you like to go out to lunch with us?

   B: Thanks for the offer, but ___I've already eaten.___ (already)
   Maybe another time.

2. **A:** Would you like to borrow this book after I finish it?

   B: It's nice of you to offer, but _____ (already).

3. **A:** Would you like a ride home?

   B: Thanks, but _____ (already). He should be here
   in a few minutes.

4. **A:** Do you want to see *Gone With the Wind* with us?

   B: Thanks, but _____ (already). It was great.

5. **A:** Come over to my house. I have a good video and I'm making some popcorn.
   You've studied enough already.

   B: Thanks, but _____ (still).

6. **A:** Look at this advertisement for a trip up the Alaskan coast. Would you like to go
   with me?

   B: It sounds great, but _____ (yet).

The Present Perfect: Meaning and Use

RECENT TIME

1. In conversation, letters, and news reports, the present perfect often describes recent past actions and experiences, especially when their results are important in the present. Adverbs like **recently** and **just** frequently emphasize this meaning of recency. Even if they're not used, they are still implied:

A conversation:

   Jan: Where's your sister **been** lately? I **haven't seen** her at all.
   Sue: She's **recently moved** to Boston. She's looking for a job there.

News broadcast:

   We've **just learned** that the mayor **has resigned.**

Telephone recording:

   The number you **have (just) dialed** is not a working number…

Notice that **recently** and **just** come before the past participle. **Recently** can also come at the beginning or end of a sentence.

2. The present perfect is often used to draw conclusions about recent actions based on present results:

Result: The doorbell is ringing.

Conclusion: I think the guests **have (just) arrived.**

⫸ **Exercise 7: Understanding News Headlines**

Read each newspaper headline. Then complete the first line of each news article. Use the information in the newspaper headline and the present perfect to express recent time.

1. GOVERNOR RAISES GASOLINE AND CIGARETTE TAXES

   For the second time in less than a year, Governor Deborah Davis *has raised gasoline and cigarette taxes* by 5 percent.

2. MAYOR SIGNS ANTI-POLLUTION LEGISLATION

   Mayor Alex Powell _____

   that promises to reduce the amount of carbon monoxide in the air we breathe.

3. SCIENTISTS DISCOVER TWO NEW CANCER DRUGS

   Scientists _____

   that appear to be effective against certain forms of bone cancer.

4. GEOLOGIST FINDS RARE FOSSILS

   A geologist _____

   in the William Robb State Forest, twenty miles west of the city.

5. SOYBEAN PRICES FALL RAPIDLY

   According to the Agriculture Department, soybean prices_____

   _____ since June.

6. MURDER TRIAL COSTS TAXPAYERS $1 MILLION

   The nine-week-old Smith murder trial _____

   _____so far.

7. GROCER WINS $2 MILLION IN LOTTERY

   Douglas Lake, owner of Lake Grocery Store, _____

   _____ in the state lottery.

8. TOWN COUNCIL SELECTS SITE FOR RECYCLING CENTER

   The Fulton Town Council _____a site for a recycling center

   on the north side of town.

⏩ **Exercise 8: Drawing Conclusions**

Look at the following pictures. Write your own sentences to describe what you think has just happened. Use the present perfect and *just*.

1. <u>(I think) she has just won a contest.</u>
_____
_____

2. _____
_____
_____

3. _____
_____
_____

4. _____
_____
_____

5._____ 6._____

_____ _____

_____ _____

⫸ Exercise 9: Drawing Conclusions

Find a busy place where you can observe a lot of people, for example, a shopping mall, a bus station, an airport, or the student cafeteria. Write down what various people are doing, using the present continuous. Then write another sentence that tells what you think has just happened, using the present perfect with *just*.

1. A little boy is walking with a woman and eating an ice-cream cone.

   His mother has just bought it for him.

2. _____

   _____

3. _____

   _____

4. _____

   _____

5. _____

   _____

6. _____

   _____

The Present Perfect: Meaning and Use

CONTINUING TIME UP TO NOW

1. The present perfect also expresses actions and situations that began in the past and continue at the present time. **For** tells how long and **since** tells the beginning of the time period:

for a minute	**since** three o'clock
four hours	dinner
a few days	Thursday
two weeks	yesterday
six months	May 17
a year	school began
a while	I saw you
years	he was a young child

I've **lived** here **for ten years**. (I still live here.)
We've **lived** here **since 1989**. (We still live here.)

2. For and **since** are not used with expressions beginning with **all** (all day, all morning, all week, all my life, all winter):

He's **worked** on this assignment **all day**.
I've lived here **all my life**.

⟶ **Exercise 10: Telling *How Long***

Work in groups of three. Person A asks a question with *how long* and the phrases below. Person B answers the question using *for* plus a time phrase, and Person C answers the question with *since* plus a time phrase. Then switch roles for the next item.

1. (be in this room)

 A: *How long have you been in this room?*
 B: *I've been in this room for ten minutes.*
 C: *I've been in this room since ten o'clock.*

2. (know how to speak English)

3. (have your driver's license)

4. (own this book)

5. (be a student)

6. (live in your apartment/dorm)

7. (know the students in this class)

8. (be able to understand English)

9. (own your car/bicycle)

10. (know how to use a computer)

11. (have your student ID)

12. (be in this country)

The Present Perfect versus the Simple Past: Meaning and Use

1. While the present perfect can express situations that continue at the present time, the simple past can only express situations that no longer exist. Compare these sentences:

Present Perfect	**Simple Past**
She **has been** lucky all her life.	She **was** lucky all her life.
(She is still alive.)	(She is dead.)
I**'ve worked** there for ten years.	I **worked** there for ten years.
(I still work there.)	(I don't work there anymore.)

2. The simple past is used to talk about historical events that are not connected to the present. The present perfect cannot be used to describe these events:

Alexander Graham Bell **invented** the telephone.
Shakespeare **wrote** many plays.

3. The present perfect does not indicate the precise time of an event. The simple past is used for this:

Present Perfect	**Simple Past**
I**'ve visited** her two times.	I **visited** her two times **last year**.

4. The present perfect and simple past can both express how many times something has happened, but only the simple past can tell when something happened. Use the simple past to ask and answer **when** questions:

Maria: **When did** you **visit** your grandmother?
Pablo: I **visited** her **in January and in August**.

(continued)

5. Time expressions with **ago** and **from...to...** are used with the simple past, but not with the present perfect:

> I **worked** there **three years ago.**
> They **lived** here **from 1990 to 1994.**

6. The present perfect is often used at the beginning of a conversation or a written text to introduce a general idea with indefinite past time. The conversation or text often continues with the simple past to give more specific details about this general idea:

A conversation:

> Linda: **Have** you ever **been** to Japan?
> Kathy: Yes, I'**ve been** there twice. I **stayed** for two weeks in 1987, and last year I **stayed** for a month.

A newspaper article:

> For the second time in two weeks, an inmate **has escaped** from the local prison. Last night at 2:00 A.M., several guards **heard** strange noises coming from an underground tunnel. An investigation **revealed**...

7. It is common, especially in American English, to use the simple past with **just, already,** and **yet** instead of the present perfect. These simple past sentences have the same meanings as similar sentences in the present perfect:

Simple Past	Present Perfect
Pat: **Did** you **eat yet?**	**Have** you **eaten yet?**
Ann: No, not yet.	No, not yet.
Ann: You should call Mary.	You should call Mary.
Pat: I **just called** her.	I'**ve just called** her.
Ann: Don't forget to buy some milk.	Don't forget to buy some milk.
Pat: I **already bought** some.	I'**ve already bought** some.

⫸ **Exercise 11: Asking for Information**

Work with a partner. Imagine today is the town festival in the park. You are working at the information booth answering questions and giving directions. Take turns asking questions in the present perfect using the words in parentheses. Answer with the present perfect, the simple past, or the simple present future based on the time of the question.

1. 1:30 (the juggler/perform)

   A: *Has the juggler already performed?*
   B: *Yes, he has. He finished two and a half hours ago.*

2. 10:00 (the jazz band/play)

   A: *Has the jazz band played yet?*
   B: *No, they haven't. They play this afternoon at four.*

3. 10:00 (the mayor/speak)

4. 5:00 (the picnic/start)

5. 8:00 (the fireworks/begin)

6. 3:00 (the three-legged race/occur)

7. 3:45 (the pie-eating contest/end)

8. 2:00 (The Melodians/sing)

9. 6:00 (the sing-along/take place)

10. 4:10 (The Harem/dance)

⯈ Exercise 12: Adding Specific Examples in the Simple Past

Work on your own. Read the present perfect sentence that expresses a general idea. Then write a sentence in the simple past that describes when the particular experience happened.

1. Computers have helped me a lot with my school work. For example, _I did all my_ _assignments on a word processor last semester._

2. There have been several disasters in recent years. For example, _____

_____

3. I've made many mistakes in my life. For example, _____

_____

4. There have been many changes in my country (hometown, family) lately. For example,

_____

5. I've learned a lot of important things in recent years. For example, _____

_____

6. A: Have you ever taken a long trip by car?

   B: Yes, many times. For example, _____

_____

The Present Perfect Continuous: Form

Statements				Contractions
I	**have**	**been**	**working**.	I**'ve**
You				You**'ve**
We				We**'ve**
They				They**'ve**
She	**has**	**been**	**working**.	She**'s**
He				He**'s**
It				It**'s**

- To form the present perfect continuous, use the present perfect form of the verb **be** + the main verb + **-ing**.
- Look at page 485 for spelling rules for verbs ending in **-ing**.

Negative Statements | Contractions

I	**have**	**not**	**been**	**working**.	I **haven't**
She	**has**	**not**	**been**	**working**.	She **hasn't**

- To form negative statements, use **not** after **have** or **has**.

Yes/No Questions | Short Answers | Contractions

Have	you	**been**	**working**?	Yes, I **have**.	
				No, I **have not**.	No, I **haven't**.
Has	she	**been**	**working**?	Yes, she **has**.	
				No, she **has not**.	No, she **hasn't**.

- To form a *yes/no* question, use **have** or **has** before the subject.

Information Questions | Answers | Contractions

What	**have**	you	**been**	**doing**?	Sleeping.	
Who	**has**	he	**been**	**calling**?	Sheila.	**Who's**

- The *wh-* word is followed by **have** or **has**, the subject, **been**, and the main verb + **-ing**.

Information Questions (Subject) | Answers | Contractions

Who	**has**	**been**	**working?**	Joe **has**.	**Who's**
What	**has**	**been**	**happening?**	A lot.	**What's**

- If **who** or **what** is the subject of the question, then the word order is the same as for affirmative statements.

⫸ Exercise 13: Working on Form

Work with a partner. Complete the following conversations using the present perfect continuous forms of the verbs in parentheses. Use contractions when appropriate.

1. **A:** What's wrong?

   B: I ___'ve been trying_____ (try) to call the doctor for over an hour, but the line

   is still busy.

   A: It's not an emergency, is it?

   B: No, but I _____ (not/feel) well for a few weeks and I'm

   starting to worry.

   A: You do look tired. _____ (you/get) enough sleep?

   Maybe you _____ (work) too hard. I

   _____ (think) about going away for a few days.

   Would you like to come?

2. **A:** I _____ (not/go) to the movies this semester.

   B: Why not?

   A: I _____ (go) home every weekend.

   I _____ (help) my mother because

   she _____ (not/feel) well.

3. **A:** We normally don't get any homework in this course, but lately the instructor

   _____ (give) us an hour or two each night. I don't understand it.

   B: Maybe you _____ (not/make) enough progress, or maybe the

   material _____ (get) more difficult.

4. **A:** You look wonderful. What _____ (you/do)?

   B: I _____ (exercise) a lot at the gym and

   I _____ (not/eat) junk food.

▹ **Exercise 14: Unscrambling Sentences**

Work with a partner. Reorder the words in each group to make a question in the present perfect continuous. Make sure you use every word. Then take turns asking and answering the questions. Respond to each question and ask *What about you?*

1. (you/how/been/have/lately/feeling)

    A: *How have you been feeling lately?*
    B: *I've been feeling fine. What about you?*
    A: *I've been feeling great.*

2. (who/you/writing to/have/lately/been)

3. (lately/sleeping/you/well/have/been)

4. (been/you/working/semester/hard/this/have)

5. (anything/lately/you/learning/been/have)

6. (time/what/recently/getting up/have/you/been)

7. (doing/you/what/in/the/been/have/evening)

The Present Perfect Continuous: Meaning and Use

FOCUS ON CONTINUING OR RECENT ACTIONS

1. The present perfect continuous describes actions that began in the past and are continuing at the present time. To emphasize that an action is continuing up to the present, **for** and **since** are often used with the present perfect continuous:

She **has been reading** that novel **for a week.** (She's still reading it.)
I've **been writing** a letter **since four o'clock.** (I'm still writing it.)

2. The present perfect continuous also describes recent actions that have just ended. To emphasize recent time, **recently, just,** and **lately** often occur with the present perfect continuous:

I've **been thinking** about you **recently.**
I **have just been reading** the most wonderful book.

An apology:

Rosa: Why haven't you called me for so long?
Maria: I'm sorry. I **haven't been feeling** well **lately.**

(continued)

3. Like the present perfect, the present perfect continuous is often used to draw conclusions about recent actions, based on present results:

Result: Half of this cake is gone.

Conclusion: Somebody **has been eating** it.

4. The meanings of certain common verbs used with **for** and **since** are very similar in the present perfect continuous and the present perfect. These verbs include **live, work, study, teach, stay, feel,** and **wear**:

Present Perfect	**Present Perfect Continuous**
I**'ve lived** here since 1980.	I**'ve been living** here since 1980.
I**'ve taught English** for ten years.	I**'ve been teaching** English for ten years.
He**'s worn** the same jacket for years.	He**'s been wearing** the same jacket for years.

5. The present perfect continuous suggests that an action is continuing up to the present, while the present perfect expresses a completed activity or situation that may or may not have been recent:

  I've been reading a book about astronomy. (I'm not finished.)
  I've read a book about astronomy. (I finished it at some indefinite time in the past.)

6. Although the meaning of the present perfect continuous and the present perfect are similar, sometimes the focus on the continuing situation is stronger in the present perfect continuous. To emphasize the length of time or to show that the activity has not stopped throughout the time period, you can choose the present perfect continuous instead of the present perfect:

  I've been waiting for an hour and the doctor hasn't come.
  I've been thinking about this for three days.

7. Because the present perfect continuous can express an action that continues without stopping, it usually isn't used to tell how many times an action is repeated. The present perfect is used instead:

  I've read the report three times this week.
  *I've been reading the report three times this week. (INCORRECT)

8. With stative verbs (**have, own, know,** etc.), use the present perfect with **for** or **since** to show that the state began in the past and continues into the present. The present perfect continuous is not used with stative verbs:

  I've known him for ten years.
  *I have been knowing him for ten years. (INCORRECT)

  I've had this book since I was a child.
  *I have been having this book since I was a child. (INCORRECT)

➡ **Exercise 15: Comparing the Present Perfect and the Present Perfect Continuous**

Complete the following letter with the present perfect or the present perfect continuous. In some sentences, either one is acceptable.

Dear Ellen,   March 20th

How are you and how's your family?_____Has your father_____

_____been feeling_____(your father/feel) better? I hope so.

I_____ (not/receive) a letter from you since last month. I_____(think) about you a lot and _____(wonder) if everything is OK.

I_____ (read) the book that you sent me for my birthday, but I_____(not/finish) it yet. So far, I_____(read) about a hundred pages and I'm really enjoying it. I_____(be) so busy lately that I_____ (not/have) much time to read, but hope to finish it soon.

Right now, I'm writing a paper for one of my courses. I_____(write) it for two weeks. It's going to be long. So far, I_____ (change) the topic four times, but now I'm finally pleased with it.

What_____(you/do) during the past few weeks?_____(you/work) hard?_____(you/have) any exams yet? I_____(have) two so far, and I did pretty well on them. I_____ (work) very hard.

_____(you/decide) what you're going to do this summer? We really need to make plans soon! Please write!

Love,
Pat

▥➡ **Exercise 16: Apologizing**

Work with a partner. Use the present perfect continuous to apologize for the problems that
your partner has noticed. Then take turns practicing the conversations.

1. **Spouse A:** What's the matter? You're not listening to me.

   Spouse B: _I'm sorry. I've been thinking about something else._

   _____

2. **Friend A:** You're really late. What took you so long?

   Friend B: _____

   _____

3. **Teacher:** Where's the assignment you were supposed to finish yesterday?

   Student: _____

   _____

4. **Friend A:** I thought we were going to the movies sometime this week.

   Friend B: _____

   _____

5. **Spouse A:** You never come home in the evenings anymore. What's going on?

   Spouse B: _____

   _____

6. **Friend A:** Is something wrong? You keep looking out the window.

   Friend B: _____

   _____

7. **Downstairs Neighbor:** You're making an awful lot of noise up there. What's going on?

   Upstairs Neighbor: _____

   _____

8. **Roommate A:** Where's the phone book? Did you take it out of the kitchen?

   Roommate B: _____

   _____

▸ **Exercise 17: Drawing Conclusions**

Work in small groups. Read the evidence for each situation and offer as many conclusions as you can. Use the present perfect continuous.

1. Your friend seems very upset about something. Her eyes are all red.
   It appears that __she has been crying._____

2. Your thirteen-year-old nephew is staying with you. When you enter his room
   you smell cigarette smoke and you see him putting something away.
   You think that _____

3. Stephen was failing the course during the first month, but now he is doing very well.
   You think that _____

4. When you meet Samantha on the street, she's wearing a running suit and running shoes.
   She is breathing heavily. You assume that _____

5. When you enter your friend's apartment building, there's a very strong smell of garlic.
   It smells like _____

6. It's late but you really need to talk to your friend. When she answers the phone,
   she is polite, but she sounds very tired. You think that _____

   _____

⇛ Exercise 18: Advertising

Work in small groups. Imagine you're reading the bulletin board in the Student Union. Here are some of the advertisements posted on it. Read each ad and write one or more appropriate questions with the present perfect continuous.

*Come to **Diet Helpers**.
We'll help you lose
weight easily and healthfully.
For more information
call 124-2323*

Try our Computerized
Dating Service. It's
confidential, reliable,
and inexpensive.
Call 214-9040
for more information.

1. Have you been trying to lose weight
   without success? Have you been
   starving yourself ?

2. _____
   _____
   _____

Don't pay high prices anymore.

**Shop at *Discount Market* for
all your basic needs.
Open 7 days from
9A.M.–9P.M.**

YOU NEED MORE EXERCISE!
Join the
Aurora Health & Fitness Club.
Reasonable rates. Friendly staff.
Stop by for information about a
free trial membership.
298 Ridgewood Road · 213-0908

3. _____
   _____
   _____

4. _____
   _____
   _____

5._____   6._____

_____   _____

_____   _____

▐▶ **Exercise 19: Writing Advertisements**

With your group, write an advertisement like the ones above for a local laundromat, take-out restaurant, photocopy center, ice-cream shop, or smoker's help group. Be prepared to read your advertisement to the class.

Have you been spending hours washing your clothes every week?

Why don't you let us do it for you? We offer fast and reasonable service and free

pickup and delivery of your laundry. Try Paragon Wash and Dry at 234-1234.

▐▶ **Exercise 20: Thinking About Meaning**

Work with a partner. Read each sentence and decide whether the statements below are true (T), false (F), or (?) if you do not have enough information to decide. Then explain your answers in small groups.

1. I've been reading for several hours.

    ___T___ (a) I'm still reading.

    ___?___ (b) I expect to finish soon.

2. I've studied Russian.

    _____ (a) I'm still studying Russian.

    ___T___ (b) I studied Russian at some time in the past.

3. I haven't eaten breakfast this morning.

_____ (a) It's still morning.

___7___ (b) I'm going to eat breakfast.

4. I've worked there for many years.

_____ (a) I don't work there anymore.

_____ (b) I'm changing jobs next week.

5. I've been writing a report.

_____ (a) I'm still working on it.

_____ (b) I started it a few moments ago.

6. I still haven't visited the exhibit.

_____ (a) I didn't visit the exhibit.

_____ (b) I expect to visit the exhibit.

7. I've owned a house.

_____ (a) I still own a house.

_____ (b) I bought a house some time ago.

8. I've had this cold for two weeks already.

_____ (a) I don't have this cold anymore.

_____ (b) I caught this cold two weeks ago.

9. I lived there for two years.

_____ (a) I still live there.

_____ (b) I moved two years ago.

10. I've already finished my work.

_____ (a) I finished sooner than expected.

_____ (b) I finished it a few minutes ago.

Summary

The Present Perfect: Form

Statements:	I**'ve worked** here for ten years.
Negative Statements:	She **has not been** here for months.
Yes/No Questions:	**Have** you ever **used** a computer?
Short Answers:	Yes, I **have.** OR No, I **haven't.**
Information Questions:	What **have** you **done** this morning?
Information Questions (Subject):	Who **hasn't arrived** yet?

The Present Perfect: Meaning and Use

The present perfect expresses a connection between the past and the present. It indicates indefinite time, recent time, or continuing time.

Accomplishments:	I**'ve** already **finished** all my work.
Reminders:	**Have** you **enclosed** a check or money order?
Refusals:	Thank you, but I**'ve** already **eaten** lunch.
News:	We**'ve** just **learned** that the mayor **has resigned.**
Conclusions:	I think he**'s** just **won** the lottery.
Schedules:	The juggler **has** already **performed.**
General Ideas:	Computers **have helped** me a lot with my schoolwork.

The Present Perfect Continuous: Form

Statements:	I**'ve been reading** an interesting book.
Negative Statements:	He **hasn't been coming** to work lately.
Yes/No Questions:	**Have** you **been working** hard?
Short Answers:	Yes, I **have.** OR No, I **haven't.**
Information Questions:	How **have** you **been feeling?**
Information Questions (Subject):	Who **has been calling** you?

The Present Perfect Continuous: Meaning and Use

The present perfect continuous focuses on situations that began in the past and are continuing at the present time or that have just ended.

Apologies: I'm sorry. I **haven't been paying** attention.

Conclusions: It appears that he**'s been working** very hard.

Advertisements: **Have** you **been looking** for a used car?

⮞ Summary Exercise: Finding Errors

Most of the sentences have an error in form, meaning, or use. Find each error and correct it. (Hint: Four sentences are correct.)

1. Marie Curie ~~has~~ discovered radium.   *Marie Curie discovered radium.*

2. Have you ever driven a truck?

3. When I was a child, I have been very sick.

4. I live in this house since 1989.

5. How long you have been married?

6. He's been working there since ten years.

7. Someone has taken my coat.

8. I've been typing this page five times.

9. I've seen her two days ago.

10. Have you been owning your car for a long time?

11. Already he has gone shopping.

12. I have never saw a flying saucer.

13. I've been feeling sick for a long time.

14. He's known about the problem for all week.

15. Have you yet eaten?

16. I haven't taken a vacation since I was a student.

Social Modals: Requests, Permission, Suggestions, Advice, Opinions, Obligations, Necessity, Lack of Necessity, and Prohibition

Preview

Two students:

Pablo: **Can** I borrow your notes after class?
Abdul: Sure, but **could** you please return them before dinner? I think I'll need them for the homework assignment.

Two strangers in an elevator:

Woman: **Would** you please hold the door for me?
Man: Certainly.

Two friends:

Paul: What **should** I buy my father for his birthday? He really doesn't need anything, but I **have to** do something.
Teresa: Well, you **could** take him out to dinner or you **could** take him to the theater.

Driver's manual:

Bicyclists **must** obey the rules of the road, just as vehicle drivers do. They **must** signal turns and stops with hand signals. Bicyclists **may not** carry a passenger unless the bicycle has a passenger seat.

Modals (also called modal auxiliaries) change the meaning of the main verb in many ways. Modals are used to make requests, ask for permission, ask for advice, and offer suggestions. They also express what is necessary or not necessary, and what is not allowed. Social modals express politeness, formality, and authority in different kinds of social situations. (Modals also have other meanings that you will study in Chapter 8.)

Often there are several modals you can use in a particular situation. The modal you choose can make what you say sound more polite or less polite, more formal or less formal. Your situation and your relationship to the listener may help you decide which modal to choose. Consider, for example, how well you know the listener. Is there a difference in your ages? Is one of you in a position of greater authority or power? Is one of you the boss?

In this chapter you will also study **have to, have got to, ought to,** and **had better.** These forms are not true modals, but they are very close in meaning to **must** and **should.** All the modals in this chapter relate to the present or the future. Past modals will be discussed in Chapter 8.

Social Modals: Form

Statements

I	**should**	buy a present for him.
You		
He		
She		
We		
They		

- **Should, can, could, will, would, may, might,** and **must** are modal auxiliaries.
- To form a statement, use the modal + the simple form of the main verb.
- Modals do not change form to agree with the subject. There is no final **-s** or **-es** after a modal.

Negative Statements / Contractions

I	**should not**	worry.	I **shouldn't**
You	**must not**	drink and drive.	You **mustn't**
He	**cannot**	borrow my car.	He **can't**
She	**may not**	borrow it either.	

- To form negative statements, use the modal + **not** or **-n't** plus the simple form of the main verb.
- **Can** + **not** is written as one word.
- **May not** has no contracted form.

Yes/No Questions / Short Answers / Contractions

Can	I	go with you?	Yes, you **can**.	
			No, you **cannot**.	No, you **can't**.

- In *yes/no* questions, modals come before the subject.
- Short answers have a subject + a modal.

Information Questions				Answers
What	**should**	I	buy for him?	Something unusual.
Where	**could**	we	go to celebrate?	To the theater.

- The *wh-* word comes before the modal and the subject.

Information Questions (Subject)		Answers
Who	**may**	apply for the job?	Anyone 21 or older.

- If **who** or **what** is the subject of the question, then the word order is the same as for affirmative statements.

⇒ **Exercise 1: Working on Form**

Work with a partner. Complete the following conversations using the words in parentheses. Use contractions wherever possible. Then practice the conversations.

1. **A:** _____ Can I park _____ (I/park/can) here overnight?

   B: No, I'm sorry. _____ (you/park/can/not) here after midnight.

2. **Salesperson:** _____ (I/help/may) you?

   Customer: Yes. I'm looking for a birthday gift for my aunt.

   _____ (you/suggest/could) something?

   Salesperson: Well, _____ (you/buy/could) her a scarf or

   a pair of gloves, or if you really can't decide, _____ (you/want

   to/might) purchase a gift certificate.

3. **A:** _____ (you/use/should/not) so much salt.

   It's not good for you.

   B: I didn't realize this was too much. _____ (I/use/should/

   how much)?

4. **A:** Madam, the sign says _____ (visitors/take/may/not)

   pictures inside the museum.

   B: Oh, I didn't see it. _____ (I/check/may) my camera

   in the lobby?

5. **A:** _____ (you/answer/can) the phone, please?

   My hands are full of paint.

   B: So are mine. _____ (you/buy/should) an answering machine.

6. **A:** _____ (you/read/will) the instructions to me?

   I don't have my glasses.

   B: Sure. It says _____ (you/take/should) one tablet every four

   hours, and _____ (you/take/must/not) more than six per day.

Social Modals: Meaning and Use

REQUESTS

1. The modals **can, will, could,** and **would** are all used to ask someone to do something. The meaning is the same:

> **Can** you please do me a favor?
> **Will**
> **Could**
> **Would**

2. Although these modals all have the same meaning, **could** and **would** are more formal than **can** and **will:**

↓ Less Formal   can, will

  More Formal   could, would

3. Could and **would** are used especially with strangers, people in authority, or older people. **Can** and **will** are used more often among friends.

4. Please can be used with any of these modals. However, since **please** makes a request more polite, it is used especially in requests with **could** or **would**. **Please** usually comes after the subject or at the end of the sentence:

> **Could** you **please** tell me the time?
> **Would** you open the door, **please?**

⫸ Exercise 2: Choosing Formal or Informal Requests

Work with a partner. Complete the requests with *can, will, could,* or *would.* (More than one answer is possible for each situation.) Then practice the conversations and decide which request you prefer for each situation. Be prepared to explain your choices to the class.

1. You are speaking to your neighbor:

   You: _____Can_____ you take in our mail while we're away?

   Neighbor: Sure, no problem.

2. You are speaking to a stranger:

   You: Excuse me, sir. _____ you please help me?

   Stranger: Certainly. What seems to be the problem?

3. You are speaking to your brother on the telephone:

   You: I'm busy right now. _____ you call me back later?

   Brother: I'm going out soon. I'll talk to you tomorrow.

4. You are speaking to the doctor:

   You: _____ you give me a medical excuse for my employer?

   Doctor: Yes, of course. You can pick it up from my secretary on your way out.

5. You are speaking to your child:

   You: _____ you help me for a minute?

   Child: OK.

6. You are speaking to a salesperson at a department store:

   You: _____ you put that in a box?

   Salesperson: I'm sorry. I don't have any boxes.

7. You are speaking to your spouse at the dinner table:

   You: _____ you pass the salad dressing?

   Spouse: Sure. Just a second.

8. You are speaking to a classmate:

   You: _____ you lend me your lecture notes tonight?

   Classmate: Sure. Do you want the lab notes too?

9. You are speaking to your boss:

   You: When you get a chance, _____ you please show me how to use this

   new computer program?

   Boss: OK. How about right now?

10. You are speaking to a bank teller:

    You: _____ you give me a roll of quarters, please?

    Bank Teller: Sure. Do you need anything else?

⫸ Exercise 3: Making Formal and Informal Requests

With the same partner as in Exercise 2, take turns making requests with *can, could, will,*
and *would*. In each situation, more than one type of request is appropriate.

1. Ask a friend to

   (a) meet you after class

   A: *Will you meet me after class?* OR
   B: *Can you meet me after class?*

   (b) go shopping with you

2. Ask a stranger to

   (a) open the door

   (b) hold the elevator

   (c) press 6 (the sixth floor)

3. Ask your roommate to

   (a) answer the phone

   (b) get the mail

   (c) cook dinner tonight

4. Ask your husband or wife to

   (a) take out the trash

   (b) turn off the television

   (c) answer the doorbell

5. Ask a travel agent to

   (a) reserve a hotel for you

   (b) call the airlines

   (c) check the schedule

6. Ask a grandparent to

   (a) watch the children

   (b) close the window

   (c) call you later

⯁ **Exercise 4: Thinking About Requests**

Work in small groups. Identify a situation, a speaker, and a listener for each of the requests below. There are several possible answers for each one. Then, on your own, make up two more requests. Ask the class to name a possible situation, speaker, and listener for your requests.

1. Could you open the window, please?

   Situation: *Two strangers on a bus*

   Speaker: *Passenger A*

   Listener: *Passenger B*

2. Will you hold this for me?

   Situation:

   Speaker:

   Listener:

3. Could you bring some water, please?

   Situation:

   Speaker:

   Listener:

4. Will you get me a cup of coffee?

   Situation:

   Speaker:

   Listener:

5. Could you sign this, please?

   Situation:

   Speaker:

   Listener:

6. Can you pick those up?

   Situation:

   Speaker:

   Listener:

7. Would you please come with me?

   Situation:

   Speaker:

   Listener:

8. Can you come here a minute?

   Situation:

   Speaker:

   Listener:

9. ~~~~~

   Situation:

   Speaker:

   Listener:

10. ~~~~~

   Situation:

   Speaker:

   Listener:

Social Modals: Meaning and Use

PERMISSION

1. The modals **can, could,** and **may** are all used in asking for permission. The meaning is the same:

> **Can** I take one of these forms, please?
> **Could**
> **May**

2. The choice of modal does not affect meaning, but it does affect formality:

Less Formal	can
	could
More Formal	may

3. **Can** and **could** are used much more often than **may. Can** is especially common with friends and family. **Could** is more neutral. It sounds softer and more polite than **can.** If you're not sure which modal to use when asking for permission, **could** is always appropriate.

4. **May** is quite formal. It is used especially with strangers, people in authority, and older people.

5. In the examples below, all three modals are acceptable, but the situation determines the most natural choice:

A bank customer asks a teller:

> **Can** I take one of these forms, (please)?
> **Could**
> **May**

After class, one student asks another:

> **Can** I (please) borrow your notes?
> **Could**
> **May**

The conversation at the bank is more formal than the conversation between classmates, so **could** is probably the most natural choice. Between classmates, the situation is less formal, so **can** and **could** are the most natural.

(continued)

6. Requests for permission, like all *yes/no* questions, can be answered with *yes* or *no* plus a short answer. The modal you choose to give or deny permission usually depends on the modal used in the question. However, only **may** and **can** are used to give or deny permission; **could** is not used:

At the library:

    Woman: **May** I renew this book?
    Librarian: Yes, you **may**. OR No, you **may not.**

After class, one student asks another:

    Ryan: **Could** I borrow your book?
    Matt: Yes, you **can**. OR No, you **can't.**

7. When someone asks you for permission, you can give many other answers without modals besides a simple *yes* or *no*. Here are some of them:

Less Formal		More Formal	
Affirmative	**Negative**	**Affirmative**	**Negative**
Uh huh.	Unh uh.	Yes.	No.
Yeah.	Nope.	Go right ahead.	I'm sorry, but…
OK.	No way.	Certainly.	Certainly not.
Sure.	Sorry, but…	Yes, certainly.	Absolutely not.

8. Longer statements with modals are also used to give or deny permission. Again, **can** is used more often than **may**. However, because **may** is formal, it is frequently used in public announcements, in signs, and in other forms of written English. In these cases, **could** is not used:

Parent to child:

    You **can't** go out until you finish dinner.

Flight attendant to passenger:

    You **can** only carry on two pieces of luggage.

Sign:

    VISITORS **MAY** PARK IN LOTS A AND B.

⫸ Exercise 5: Using the Telephone for Requests and Permission

Work with a partner. Begin a telephone conversation by matching a phrase from Person A with one from Person B. Some combinations are not appropriate. Can you explain why?

Person A

1. Hi. This is Ann.
   Is Joe there?

2. Could I please speak to
   Professor Sharwick?

3. Good morning, doctor's office.
   May I help you?

4. History Department.

5. My name is Thomas Greenfield.
   Can I please speak to Michael?

Person B

a. May I ask who's calling?

b. Sure, hold on a minute.

c. Is Ms. Sloan there, please?

d. Could you spell that, please?

e. He's not here right now. Can I take a message?

f. One moment, please.

g. Yes, I'd like to make an appointment.

h. May I please speak to Robert Jenning?

i. Could you hold, please?

⫸ Exercise 6: Asking for and Giving Permission

Work with a partner. Make and respond to requests for permission according to each situation. To make requests, use *can*, *could*, or *may*. To respond, use appropriate phrases from the list on page 172.

1. Dentist's office:

   Patient: _____May_____ I use the phone?

   Receptionist: ___Certainly.___

2. Your best friend's apartment:

   You: _____ I make a phone call?

   Your friend: _____

3. A friend's party:

   Guest: _____ I use your bathroom?

   Hostess: _____

4. Supermarket checkout counter:

   Customer: _____ I borrow your pen?

   Cashier: _____

5. School:

   Student: _____ I hand in my homework tomorrow?

   Teacher: _____

6. Home:

   Child: _____ I stay up late tonight?

   Parent: _____

7. Your sister's apartment:

   You: _____ I borrow your umbrella?

   Your sister: _____

8. A job interview:

   You: _____ I think it over for a few days?

   Employer: _____

⯈ Exercise 7: Asking for and Giving Permission

Work with a partner. Take turns asking for and giving (or denying) permission in each of the situations below. Use *can, may,* or *could* in your questions, and appropriate responses from those listed on page 172.

1. You ask a classmate for a pencil:

   You: *Can I use your pencil for a minute?*
   Classmate: *Yeah, sure.*

2. You are at school. You want to leave a scholarship application with the department secretary:

3. You want to rent an apartment. The landlord shows you the living room. You want to see the rest of the apartment:

4. You want to borrow your roommate's dictionary:

5. You are at a job interview. You want to see a copy of the employee handbook:

6. You are with a friend at work. You want to call him later for some advice:

7. You are at a friend's house. You want a drink of water:

8. You are talking to one of your professors after class. You want to make an appointment with her:

9. You are buying gas. You want to pay by check:

10. You are on the telephone with a friend. You have to leave for an appointment:

11. You want to borrow your roommate's car for the weekend:

⟫ Exercise 8: Understanding Signs

Work in small groups. Explain the meaning of the signs below using *can* or *cannot*.
Then consider where you might see each sign and describe the situation.

1. CREDIT CARDS ACCEPTED

   Meaning: You can pay with a credit card.

   Situation: Getting gas at a service station

2. ENTER HERE

   Meaning: _____

   Situation: _____

3. NO CHECKS

   Meaning: _____

   Situation: _____

4. SWIMMING PERMITTED WHEN LIFEGUARD IS ON DUTY

   Meaning: _____

   Situation: _____

5. NO EXIT

   Meaning: _____

   Situation: _____

6. FINAL SALE, NO EXCHANGES, NO RETURNS

   Meaning: _____

   Situation: _____

7. SMOKING SECTION

   Meaning: _____

   Situation: _____

8. NO TURN ON RED

   Meaning: _____

   Situation: _____

Social Modals: Meaning and Use

SUGGESTIONS, ADVICE, WARNINGS, INSTRUCTIONS

1. The modals **could** and **might** are used to make suggestions; **should** and **ought to** are used for advice; **had better** is used to give warnings; **have to, have got to,** and **must** are used for strong advice; **should** and **must** are also used for explaining instructions:

Suggestions:	You **could** call the doctor.
	You **might** call the doctor.
Advice:	You **should** call the doctor.
	You **ought to** call the doctor.
Warnings:	You **had better** call the doctor or you'll get pneumonia.
Strong Advice:	You **have to** call the doctor.
	You **have got to** call the doctor.
	You **must** call the doctor.
Instructions:	You **should** take one tablet after each meal. You **must not** exceed the recommended dosage.

2. The modal you choose will affect the strength and meaning of what you say:

You **could** call the doctor.
You **must** call the doctor.

Weaker	could, might
	should, ought to
	had better
	have to, have got to
Stronger	must

3. Could is used for making casual suggestions, especially when there is a choice:

Tom: My back still hurts. What should I do?
Bob: You **could** call the doctor now, or you **could** wait until tomorrow.

4. Might is also used for making casual or tentative suggestions:

Kate: I don't know what to do about my car. I'm having a lot of trouble with it.
Sonya: You **might** ask Diane about her mechanic. I think she just found a good one.

5. The modal **shall** is rare in American English. It is typically used in questions with **I** or **we** to make a suggestion and at the same time to ask if the suggestion is OK:

Shall I turn on the radio? (Is that OK with you?)
Shall we leave early? (Is that OK with you?)

6. Should and **ought to** make advice sound stronger. **Should** is much more common than **ought to. Should** can be used in questions and negative statements, but **ought to** cannot:

Joan: What **should** I do? I feel awful.
Alice: You **ought to** call the doctor. You **shouldn't** go to work.

7. Had better is stronger than **should** and **ought to.** It is used to give warnings and to mention bad consequences. These consequences are often stated in clauses beginning with **or. Had better** is used in affirmative and negative statements and in negative questions:

Ann: I've been sick for two weeks.
Pat: You **had better** go to the doctor, **or** your cold will get much worse.

8. Have to and **have got to** are used for strong advice:

Joe: Where should I take my parents tonight?
Anna: You **have to** take them to that new Thai restaurant. OR
You **have got to** take them to that new Thai restaurant.

9. Must is the strongest modal for advice and is used for emphasis when the advice is certain or when the situation is serious:

Joe: Where should I take my parents tonight?
Anna: You **must** take them to that new Thai restaurant. They'll love it.

Ann: I've been sick for two weeks.
Pat: You **must** see the doctor. Your cough sounds very bad.

CONVERSATION NOTES

1. In informal conversation, **ought to** is often pronounced *oughtta*, **have to** is often pronounced *hafta*, **has to** is pronounced *hasta*, and **have got to** is frequently pronounced *gotta*.

Written Form	Spoken Form
You **ought to** go to the doctor.	"You **oughtta** go to the doctor." (SPOKEN ONLY)
You **have to** go to the doctor.	"You **hafta** go to the doctor." (SPOKEN ONLY)
He **has to** go to the doctor.	"He **hasta** go to the doctor." (SPOKEN ONLY)
You **have got to** go to the doctor.	"You **gotta** go to the doctor." (SPOKEN ONLY)

2. Had better is often contracted to **'d better** in conversation and informal writing. In negative statements, **not** is not contracted:

Statements: You**'d better** call the doctor.

Negative Statements: You**'d better not** go to work.

Negative Questions: **Hadn't** you **better** call the doctor?

3. In very informal conversation, you will sometimes hear only **better** or **better not**. The contracted form of **had** is dropped completely:

"You **better** call the doctor." (SPOKEN ONLY)

"You **better not** wait any longer." (SPOKEN ONLY)

⟹ Exercise 9: Offering Suggestions and Giving Advice

Complete the conversations using *could, might, should, ought to, had better, have to, have got to,* and *must*. More than one answer may be possible.

1. **Your father:** I feel dizzy.
   You: You _'d better_____ lie down.

2. **Your spouse:** What should I make for dinner?
   You: I don't know. You _____ make fish chowder or maybe chicken.

3. **A friend:** I often lock my keys in my car. I don't know what to do about it.
   You: You _____ carry an extra key in your wallet.

4. **You:** My throat hurts and I have a headache.
   Doctor: It looks like the flu. You _____ drink plenty of liquids and stay in bed for a couple of days.

5. **A co-worker:** I don't think the manager likes me very much. I don't want to lose my job.
   You: You _____ try to get to work on time. He gets very angry when you're late.

6. **Your brother:** What should I get Mom for her birthday?
   You: Well, you _____ give her a plant, or some flowers, or maybe a wallet.

7. **Your roommate:** What movie should I see tonight?

   You: You really _____ see the new one on campus. I know you'll like it.

8. **A co-worker:** I'm not getting any work done in my office. There are too many interruptions.

   You: Maybe you _____ close your door.

⟱ ### Exercise 10: Giving Friendly Advice

Work with a partner. Take turns giving advice using *could*, *should*, *ought to*, or *had better* and the words in parentheses.

1. **A:** I don't have enough money to buy Christmas presents next month.

   B: (part-time job) _Maybe you ought to get a part-time job._

2. **A:** My books are due at the library, but I still need them.

   B: (renew) _____

3. **A:** My cold is better, but I cough a lot when I go to sleep.

   B: (cough medicine) _____

4. **A:** I need a baby-sitter every afternoon. I don't know how to find one.

   B: (newspaper) _____

5. **A:** My dog jumps on people when they come to visit. I'm afraid he'll knock someone over.

   B: (tie up) _____

6. **A:** My computer makes strange noises when I use it.

   B: (repair service) _____

7. **A:** I have a headache, but aspirin gives me a stomachache.

   B: (something else) _____

8. **A:** I'm failing my history course.

   B: (professor) _____

9. **A:** I lost my gloves.

   B: (lost and found) _____

10. **A:** I'd like to eat out tonight.

    B: (reservation) _____

➤ **Exercise 11: Asking for Permission, Advice, and Instructions**

Work in small groups. For each problem, make up questions to ask at the doctor's office. Use *can, could, may,* or *should* and the words in parentheses.

1. You have stomach pains:

   (drink coffee) *Can I drink coffee?*

   (eat special food) *Should I eat special food?*

   (take an antacid) *Should I take an antacid?*

2. You have a backache:

   (go back to work)

   (jog)

   (take aspirin)

3. You have an ear infection:

   (stay home from work)

   (go swimming)

   (take an airplane trip)

4. You have a cough:

   (take cough medicine)

   (smoke)

   (go on vacation)

5. You have a broken leg:

   (take a shower)

   (drive my car)

   (walk around)

➠ **Exercise 12: Understanding Instruction Labels**

Work in small groups. Read the label for each drugstore product. Then complete the sentences below it.

1. Adults should _take 2 teaspoonfuls every 4 hours._

   They must not _exceed 12 teaspoonfuls in 24 hours._

   Children ages 2 through 5 can _take 1/2 teaspoonful every 4 hours._

   You must not _use the cough medicine if the plastic ring is broken._

2. When you are in the sun, you should _____

   When you need it, you can _____

   Most important, you must not_____

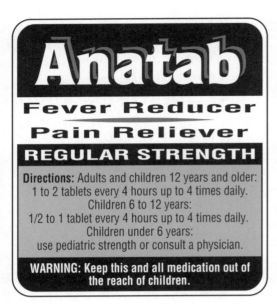

3. Adults can_____

   Children under 6 can_____

   Children 6 to 12 should _____

   You must_____

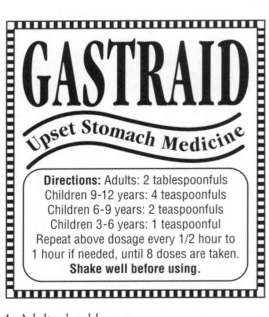

4. Adults should _____

   Children 3–6 years can _____

   Before you use this medicine, you should_____

5. When you put on the ointment, you should_____

For *external use only* means that you must not_____

It is not necessary to refrigerate the ointment, but you should _____

_____

⏩ Exercise 13: Explaining Instruction Labels

Bring in an instruction label from a product that you use at home. Write three sentences with modals explaining the correct use of the product. Be prepared to present them to the class.

⏩ Exercise 14: Giving Warnings

Write warnings in each of the situations below. Use *you'd better* or *you'd better not*.

1. Your roommate is making toast. A lot of smoke is coming out of the toaster:
   You'd better pull out the plug. OR
   You'd better not use the toaster anymore.

2. You're looking at your friend's car. The left rear tire is low:

   _____

3. Your roommate has a job interview. He's usually late for appointments:

   _____

4. Your brother wants to phone your aunt and uncle. It's 11:00 P.M. and they don't like to be disturbed after 10:00 P.M.:

   _____

5. It looks like rain. Your friend has left her car windows open:

_____

6. Your classmate has been working at the computer for several hours. She hasn't saved her work yet:

_____

7. Your upstairs neighbor has a broken pipe in his bathroom. Water is starting to leak into your apartment:

_____

8. Your cousin is driving you to the airport. He has just noticed that he forgot his wallet with his driver's license:

_____

Social Modals: Meaning and Use

OPINIONS, OBLIGATIONS, NECESSITY, REQUIREMENTS, RULES, LAWS

1. Should and **ought to** are used to express personal opinions and obligations. **Have to, have got to,** and **must** are all used to express necessity. When necessity is in the form of requirements, rules, and laws, **must** is used:

Opinions:	People **shouldn't** smoke in public buildings.
Obligations:	I **should** call my aunt soon.
Necessity:	I **have to** get up early tomorrow.
Requirements:	You **must** write a term paper for this course.
Rules:	You **must** be quiet in a hospital.
Laws:	You **must** be 16 to get a driver's license.

2. Obligations, requirements, and laws are stronger than opinions:

Obligations:	My friend is in the hospital. I **should** visit her.
Requirements:	Job applicants **must** have a high school diploma.
Laws:	You **have to** be 21 to buy beer in this state.

Weaker	should, ought to
	have to, have got to
Stronger	must

3. Should and **ought to** often express personal opinions about what is right or wrong:

You **shouldn't** phone people at dinnertime.

4. Have to, have got to, and **must** express necessity. They are very similar in meaning, but they are often used in different types of situations. **Have to** and **have got to** are used especially in conversation to avoid using the more formal **must. Have to** is used instead of **must** to ask questions about necessity. **Do** occurs in questions with **have to:**

Kate: I **have got to** leave now.
Peter: Do you **have to** leave right away?

5. Have to and **have got to** have a different form for the third person singular:

It **has to** be ready on Monday.
He **has got to** be ready on Monday.

6. Must is especially strong. It is used to express requirements, rules, and laws:

Professor and student:

You **must** take the final exam if you want to pass the course. I can't make any exceptions.

School handbook for parents:

If it is necessary for a child to receive medication in school, the parent **must** send a written, dated request.

Driver's manual:

Bicyclists **must** signal turns and stops with hand signals.

7. Note, however, that **should, have to,** and **have got to** are often used instead of **must** to restate rules and laws in less formal English:

Matt: Do cyclists **have to** use hand signals for turning?
Sam: The driver's manual says that cyclists **should** signal turns and stops with hand signals.

8. In the first person, **must** expresses a strong personal obligation, something that the speaker feels is necessary to do:

I **must** call my parents tonight. I haven't spoken to them all week.

9. Must has a special meaning in questions. It often expresses complaints or disapproval:

Must you make that awful noise?
Must we have spinach again?

CONVERSATION NOTES

1. Have or **has** in **have got to** is usually contracted to **'ve** or **'s**:

I**'ve got to** go.

She**'s got to** go.

2. **Have to** and **has to** are not contracted:

I **have to** go.

She **has to** go.

⯈ **Exercise 15: Expressing Your Opinion**

With your classmates, take turns asking and answering questions using *should* or *shouldn't*, *because*, and the phrases in parentheses below. Be sure to give your opinion.

1. (people/smoke in restaurants)

    A: *Should people smoke in restaurants?*
    B: *No, they shouldn't, because it bothers other customers.*
    A: *I agree. They shouldn't smoke because it's annoying.*

2. (women with small children/work)

3. (buses/have seatbelts)

4. (men/do housework)

5. (women/invite men to go out)

6. (married couples/live with their parents)

7. (women/fight in wars)

8. (you/phone your friends at dinnertime)

9. (students/ ⌇⌇⌇⌇)

10. (⌇⌇⌇⌇ / ⌇⌇⌇⌇)

➠ **Exercise 16: Expressing Complaints or Disapproval**

Work in small groups. Read the questions with *must*. Describe possible situations that explain the complaints or disapproval in each question. More than one situation may be possible. Then, working alone, make up two more questions using *must* to express disapproval. Ask the class to think of possible situations for your questions.

1. Must you pour salt all over your food?

   Situation: *You are eating dinner with your brother and you disapprove of his unhealthy eating habits.*

2. Must we do this again?

   Situation:

3. Must you leave so early?

   Situation:

4. Must you wear those pants with that shirt?

   Situation:

5. Must you drive so fast?

   Situation:

6. Must we go there tonight?

   Situation:

7. ～～～～

   Situation:

8. ～～～～

   Situation:

⇒ **Exercise 17: Expressing Obligations and Requirements**

Complete the following sentences. Use an appropriate modal in numbers 9–13.

1. I never have to ___get up early on the weekend._____

2. This weekend I should _____, but I probably won't.

3. For survival, plants must _____

4. I have to _____ every day.

5. In order to vote in the United States, you must _____

   _____

6. I've got to _____

   tonight, even though I don't want to do it.

7. In order to get a driver's license, you must_____

   _____

8. I ought to _____ as soon as I have the time.

9. To buy beer in this state, you _____

   _____

10. When you enter a foreign country, you_____

   _____

11. Before surgery, you _____

   _____

12. When this course ends, I_____

   _____

13. If you live far away from your family, you_____

   _____

⇢ **Exercise 18: Explaining Recommendations and Requirements**

Work with a partner. Take turns explaining the meaning of the following signs, using *should* or *have to*. Then tell where you might see each sign.

1. SPEED LIMIT 55 MPH means that _you have to drive 55 mph or less._

   Situation: _____a highway_____

2. ADMISSION $4.00 means that _____

   _____

   Situation: _____

3. ADULT SUPERVISION RECOMMENDED means that_____

   _____

   Situation: _____

4. I.D. REQUIRED means that _____

   _____

   Situation: _____

5. LATE REGISTRATION FEE $5.00 means that _____

   _____

   Situation: _____

6. EXACT CHANGE LANE means that _____

   _____

   Situation: _____

7. RESERVATIONS SUGGESTED means that _____

   _____

   Situation: _____

8. CASH ONLY means that _____

   _____

   Situation: _____

9. BRIDGE TOLL $1.00 means that_____

_____

Situation: _____

10. EXPRESS AISLE: 12 ITEMS MAXIMUM means that _____

_____

Situation: _____

➧ Exercise 19: Explaining Registration and Course Requirements

Work with a partner. Read the registration and course information from the college catalog below. Change the written information with *must* to a spoken form with *have to* or *have got to*.

Example: Read: Students must pay all fees before registering for courses.
         Say: *Students have to pay all fees before registering for courses.*

UNIVERSITY

Registration Information

1. Students must pay all fees before registering for courses.
2. Before registration, all students must present proof of immunization against diphtheria, tetanus, rubella, measles, mumps, and polio.
3. Students must register before attending courses.
4. New students must attend an orientation session during registration week.

Course Requirements

1. All students must complete two semesters of physical education.
2. All new students must take a swim test.
   Students who do not pass must enroll in a swim course.
   Nonswimmers must register in a beginning swim course.
3. All students must take an English placement exam.

⫸ **Exercise 20: Writing Course Requirements**

Working alone, write sentences with *must* about course requirements, registration, student responsibilities, and student behavior that you might find in a course catalog.

1. <u>Students must pick up current parking permits for their cars.</u>

2. _____

3. _____

4. _____

5. _____

6. _____

Social Modals: Meaning and Use

LACK OF NECESSITY AND PROHIBITION

1. Have to and **must** have almost the same meaning in affirmative statements. However, in negative statements, the meaning of **must not** is very different from **don't have to**:

You **don't have to** plant these seeds early. (You can choose whether to plant them early or later — it doesn't matter.)

You **must not** plant these seeds early. (If you plant them early, they won't survive — you don't have a choice.)

2. Don't have to means that something is not necessary — there is a choice of whether to do it or not:

In the United States, voting is optional. You **don't have to** vote if you don't want to.

Parent to child:

There's no school tomorrow. You **don't have to** go to bed early tonight.

3. Must not means that something is not allowed. It is prohibited — there is no choice at all. Like **must, must not** is used to express rules and laws:

Driver's manual:

Vehicles **must not** cross railroad tracks when red lights are flashing.

➠ **Exercise 21: Explaining Signs**

Explain the signs by filling in the blanks with *have to*, *don't have to*, or *must not*.

1. NO PETS ALLOWED means that you _____*must not*_____ bring your pet into this building.

2. NO BARE FEET means that you _____ wear shoes in this restaurant.

3. CHILDREN UNDER 12 FREE means that you _____ pay admission for children under 12.

4. NO APPOINTMENT NECESSARY means that you _____ make an appointment.

5. NO PARKING 4–7 P.M. means that you _____ park in this area between the hours of 4:00 P.M. and 7:00 P.M.

6. NO STANDING means that you _____ wait in your car in this place.

7. NO ENTRANCE means that you _____ enter here. You _____ find the proper place to enter.

8. NO CHECKS means that you _____ pay with cash, or perhaps with a credit card.

9. DIVING PROHIBITED means that you _____ dive into this swimming pool.

10. WATER SERVED ON REQUEST means that you _____ ask for water at this restaurant. The server does not automatically bring it to your table.

➡ **Exercise 22: Understanding Job Requirements**

Work in small groups. Read the following classified ads from the newspaper and complete the sentences. Then on your own, find an employment ad in the classified section of the newspaper and write three sentences with modals about the job requirements.

> **Receptionist** needed in travel agency. Must have secretarial skills. Energetic and willing to learn the travel business. Apply in person with resume: Wilson's Travel Agency, 200 West Main Street.

1. For this job you have to _____ *have secretarial skills.* _____ You should
   be energetic and willing to learn the travel business. _____

> **Part-time inventory takers** in local department stores. Flexible day hours, no weekends, no experience necessary. Car needed. Call G.A. Lambert, Inc., Department 5, 1-800-119-1141, 9 A.M.–5 P.M.

2. For this job, you don't have to _____ and you don't have to
   _____ However,
   you have to _____

> **Legal secretary** to work in busy local law office. Must be able to work with clients in person and over the telephone. Some bookkeeping and word-processing skills helpful. Must be able to take charge. Salary depends on experience. Send resume to P.O. Box 389, c/o this newspaper

3. For this job, you have to _____, but you don't
   have to _____

Host, part-time, some evenings.
The Baker Hotel is seeking a friendly,
responsible person who enjoys working
with people. No experience required.
Apply in person, 2310 North Lowry St.

4. For this job, you have to _____ and you

should also _____ You don't

have to_____

Fast-food cook
Full time, 4 P.M.–midnight
Must be 18 years old and able to work
weekends. Experience preferred. Apply
in person, 14 Jefferson Boulevard.

5. For this job, you have to_____ and you have

to _____ You don't have to

_____, but it's better if you do.

You should _____

Child care for one-year-old twins.
3–4 days, no weekends.
Nonsmoker, experienced, reliable.
Need car. References required.
Call 217-9859.

6. For this job, you have to _____, but you don't

have to _____ You must not

_____

You should _____ and you should

_____ You also

have to_____

⇒ **Exercise 23: Expressing Personal Obligation**

Write sentences about your next day off using *should, must,* and *don't have to.* Give reasons for each sentence.

1. Write three things you should do, but probably won't be able to.

   I should clean out my closets, but I probably won't be able to because I have to go

   to the dentist.

2. Write three things you absolutely must do.

3. Write three things you don't have to do, but would like to do if possible.

Summary

Social Modals: Form

Statements:	Participants **must** be 18 years old.
Negative Statements:	You **should not** water your plants every day.
Yes/No Questions:	**Could** you do me a favor?
Short Answers:	Yes, I **can.** OR No, I **can't.**
Information Questions:	Where **can** people smoke?
Information Questions (Subject):	Who **should** take the exam?

Social Modals: Meaning and Use

Social modals express politeness, formality, and authority when you make requests, ask permission, make suggestions, offer advice, give warnings and instructions, and talk about obligations, necessity, requirements, rules, and laws.

■ Requests: *Can, Will, Could, Would*

Less Formal:	**Can** you (please) do me a favor?
	Will you (please) do me a favor?
More Formal:	**Could** you (please) do me a favor?
	Would you (please) do me a favor?

■ Permission: *Can, Could, May*

Less Formal:	**Can** I (please) take one of these forms?
	Yes, you **can.** OR No, you **can't.**
	Could I (please) take one of these forms?
	Yes, you **can.** OR No, you **can't.**
More Formal:	**May** I (please) take one of these forms?
	Yes, you **may.** OR No, you **may not.**

■ Suggestions, Advice, Warnings, and Instructions: *Could, Might, Should, Ought to, Had Better, Have to, Have Got to, Must*

Suggestions:	You **could** call the doctor.
	You **might** call the doctor.
Advice:	You **should** call the doctor.
	You **ought to** call the doctor.
Warnings:	You **had better** call the doctor or you'll get pneumonia.
Strong Advice:	You **have to** call the doctor.
	You **have got to** call the doctor.
	You **must** call the doctor.
Instructions:	According to the label, you **should** take one tablet after each meal.
	You **must not** exceed the recommended dosage.

■ Opinions, Obligations, Necessity, Requirements, Rules, and Laws: *Should, Ought to, Have to, Have Got to, Must*

Opinions:	I think buses **should** have seatbelts.
	New students **should not** take more than three courses.
Obligations:	I **should** visit my friend in the hospital.
	I **ought to** visit my friend in the hospital.
	I**'ve got to** clean my apartment this afternoon.
Necessity:	I **have to** get up early tomorrow.
Requirements:	Applicants **must** have a high school diploma.
	All students **have to** take the final exam. No exceptions.
Rules:	You **must** be quiet in a hospital.
Laws:	You **must** be a U.S. citizen to vote.
Complaints:	**Must** you make so much noise?
Disapproval:	**Must** you pour salt all over your food?

■ Lack of Necessity and Prohibition: *Don't Have to, Must Not*

Lack of Necessity:	You **don't have to** drink orange juice every day.
Prohibition:	You **must not** drink and drive.

➠ **Summary Exercise: Finding Errors**

Most of the sentences have an error in form, meaning, or use. Find each error and correct it. (Hint: three sentences are correct.)

1. This course is optional. You ~~mustn't~~ take it, but you can if you want to.   *don't have to*

2. Could I speak to the manager, please?

3. May you please hold this for me?

4. She can takes this one. I don't mind.

5. NO SMOKING means that you don't have to smoke.

6. Students may take four courses per semester.

7. You must to stop at a red light.

8. Does she have got to go?

9. He's bleeding badly. You could call an ambulance. Hurry up!

10. Do you must take a driving test?

11. I really ought study tonight.

12. **Secretary:** Good morning. Cliff Plumbing. Should I help you?
    Customer: Yes, I'm looking for a plumber to fix my kitchen sink.

13. You don't can enter here. It's closed.

14. Could you please to open the door for me?

15. Must you leave so early? I didn't have much time to talk to you.

CHAPTER 8

Modals of Ability and Belief; Past Modals

Preview

A highway sign:

SEATBELTS **CAN** SAVE LIVES. BUCKLE UP!

At work:

Monica: Does anyone know where Anna is? She's not in her office and I have to see her now. I won't **be able to** see her later today.

Jessica: I don't know, but she **could** be at a meeting or she **might** be downstairs.

Nicole: Why don't you check the lounge? She **may** be there. She often has lunch there around this time.

Karen: I don't know where she is now, but I'm certain she**'ll** be in her office at one o'clock. I have a meeting with her then.

Peter arrives home at 5:40 P.M.:

Peter: Is Edward home yet?

Mark: No, but he **should** be here soon. He leaves work at 5:30 and it only takes him ten minutes to get here…. Wait a minute, I hear someone at the door. That **must** be him now.

Modals of ability and belief have different meanings from the social modals you studied in Chapter 7. **Can** expresses ability and opportunity; **could** expresses past ability; **could, might, may, should, must,** and **will** express beliefs and expectations that range from weak possibility to strong probability. The modal you choose to express your beliefs can make what you say sound more certain or less certain in particular situations.

You will also study **be able to, ought to, have to,** and **have got to.** These forms are not true modals, but they are close in meaning to **can, should,** and **must.**

Past modals are also discussed in this chapter. You will learn to use both the social modals from Chapter 7 and the modals from this chapter in past situations.

Present Ability: Form

Statements

I	**can**	swim.
You		
He		
She		
It		
We		
They		

- **Can** of ability has the same features as the social modal **can** in Chapter 7 (pages 164–165).
- It does not change form to agree with the subject.

Negative Statements · Contraction

I	**cannot**	dive.	I **can't**

- **Can** + **not** is written as one word.

Yes/No Questions · Short Answers · Contraction

Can	he	swim?	Yes, he **can**.	
			No, he **cannot**.	No, he **can't**.

- In *yes/no* questions, modals come before the subject.
- Short answers have a subject + a modal.

Information Questions · Answers

What	**can**	you	see?	Not much.

- The *wh-* word comes before the modal and the subject.

Information Questions (Subject) · Answers

Who	**can**	drive?	Julie **can**.

- If **who** or **what** is the subject of the question, then the word order is the same as for affirmative statements.

CONVERSATION NOTE

Did you say *can* or *can't*? Sometimes it's very difficult to hear the difference between **can** and **can't** in conversation. The main difference is stress: **can't** has strong stress, but **can** does not.

Listen to your teacher say these sentences:

We **can't** go. (*Can't* is stressed here.)

We can **go**. (*Go* is stressed here.)

▪▶ **Exercise 1: Distinguishing Between *Can* and *Can't***

Listen to your teacher say each sentence with either *can* or *can't*. Listen for the word with the strongest stress in each sentence. If the main verb gets the strongest stress, circle *can*. If *can't* gets the strongest stress, circle *can't*.

1. John can/can't swim.
2. I can/can't hear you very well.
3. If you can/can't come, call us.
4. She can/can't accept it.
5. They can/can't use that machine.
6. Can/can't you see the chalkboard?
7. We can/can't try it.
8. He can/can't speak Chinese.
9. She can/can't play the piano.
10. The baby can/can't walk.

Past Ability: Form

Statements

I	**could**	swim when I was five.
You		
He		
She		
It		
We		
They		

- **Could** of past ability has the same features as **can** and the social modals in Chapter 7 (pages 164–165).
- **Could** does not change form to agree with the subject.

(continued)

Negative Statements	Contraction
I **could** **not** dive.	I **couldn't**

- To form negative statements, use the modal + **not** or **-n't** + the simple form of the main verb.

Yes/No Questions	Short Answers	Contraction
Could he swim?	Yes, he **could**.	
	No, he **could not**.	No, he **couldn't**.

- In *yes/no* questions, modals come before the subject.
- Short answers have a subject + a modal.

Information Questions	Answers
What **could** you do?	Not much.

- The *wh-* word comes before the modal and the subject.

Information Questions (Subject)	Answers
Who **could** play an instrument?	Anton **could**.

- If **who** or **what** is the subject of the question, then the word order is the same as for affirmative statements.

➠ Exercise 2: Talking About Past Ability

Work with a partner. Take turns asking questions with *At what age could you…?* and the words in parentheses. Answer with a sentence using *could*. Then make up your own question.

1. (walk)

   A: *At what age could you walk?*
   B: *I could walk when I was about a year old.*

2. (talk)

3. (read)

4. (write your name)

5. (say something in a foreign language)

6. (multiply two numbers)

7. (tie a bow)

8. (swim)

9. (drive a car)

10. (~~~~~~)

Present, Past, and Future Ability: Meaning and Use

KNOWLEDGE, SKILLS, OPPORTUNITY, CAPABILITY

1. Can has the meaning of present ability. **Can** shows that something is possible now, in general, or in the future because the knowledge, skill, opportunity or capability exists at the present time:

Knowledge: He **can** speak Chinese and English.

Skill: She **can** play tennis very well.

Opportunity: The storm is over. We **can** leave.

Capability: SEATBELTS **CAN** SAVE LIVES

2. Can doesn't usually express future ability if the speaker doesn't have the ability right now. **Be able to,** which has the same meaning of ability as **can,** combines with **will** to express future ability:

Next year, **I'll be able to** speak English more fluently.
*Next year, I can speak English more fluently. (INCORRECT)

3. You can, however, use **can** when you are making a present decision about future ability:

I'm busy right now, but I **can** help you tomorrow.
I'm busy right now, but **I'll be able to** help you tomorrow.

4. Be able to also frequently combines with belief modals:

They **may be able to** finish their work.
      might be able to
      should be able to
      will be able to

5. Can and **can't** often combine with impersonal **you** as subject. Impersonal **you** refers to people in general instead of a particular person. **You can...** often means *It is possible to...*:

Nowadays, **you can** do almost all of your shopping at the supermarket.
You can even rent videos there.

(continued)

6. Could, as the past form of **can,** means that the general ability or opportunity existed for a long period of time in the past:

> He **could** walk when he was nine months old.
> Ten years ago, you **could** buy that for a quarter.

7. Could usually isn't used for a single event. The past form of **be able to** (**was** or **were able to**) expresses past ability both for a single event and in general for a long time period:

Single Event

Yesterday, I **was able to** run ten miles.

*Yesterday, I **could** run ten miles. (INCORRECT)

Long Time Period

When I was younger, I **was able to** run ten miles.

When I was younger, I **could** run ten miles.

8. Note, however, that **could** can be used for a single event with stative verbs of perception: **see, hear, feel, smell, taste, remember,** and **understand.** After these verbs, it has the same meaning and use as **was able to:**

> Yesterday, the sky was so clear I **could** see for miles.
> Yesterday, the sky was so clear I **was able to** see for miles.

9. In negative statements, **could** and **was** or **were able to** have the same meaning and use. They express lack of ability both for a single event and in general for a long time period:

Single Event

Yesterday, I **wasn't able to** run ten miles.

Yesterday, I **couldn't** run ten miles.

Long Time Period

When I was younger, I **wasn't able to** run ten miles.

When I was younger, I **couldn't** run ten miles.

⇒ Exercise 3: Expressing Abilities

Work with a partner. Take turns asking your partner questions about the abilities in parentheses. Use *can* in your questions and *can* or *can't* in your short answers.

1. (say the alphabet backwards)

   A: *Can you say the alphabet backwards?*
   B: *Yes, I can.* OR *No, I can't.*

2. (wiggle your nose)

3. (read in a car without getting sick)

4. (touch the end of your nose with your eyes closed)

5. (recite your phone number backwards)

6. (curl your tongue)

7. (stand on your head)

8. (remember your first teacher's name)

9. (raise one eyebrow without raising the other)

10. (cross your eyes)

11. (pull your fingers backwards to your wrist)

12. (～～～～)

⇒ Exercise 4: Describing Abilities

Use your partner's answers from Exercise 3 to write four sentences about his or her abilities.

1. ___Anna can wiggle her nose, but she can't touch the end of her nose___
   ___with her eyes closed.___

2. _____

3. _____

4. _____

5. _____

⇒ Exercise 5: Comparing Abilities

Compare the abilities of the people, animals, insects, or things in parentheses using sentences with *can* and *can't*. Then write your own comparison for number 12.

1. (infants/toddlers) __Infants can't walk, but toddlers can.__

2. (eighteen-year-olds/twelve-year-olds) _____

3. (spiders/ants) _____

4. (judges/lawyers) _____

5. (jets/helicopters) _____

6. (mice/bats) _____

7. (men/women) _____

8. (computers/typewriters) _____

9. (cats/dogs) _____

10 (ducks/chickens) _____

11. (glass/metal) _____

12. _____

⇒ Exercise 6: Expressing Opportunities

Work with a partner. Take turns asking and answering questions using impersonal *you* and *can*. Use the words in parentheses in your questions.

1. (what/buy/with a quarter)

   A: *What can you buy with a quarter?*
   B: *You can buy a piece of gum.*

2. (where/get/a driver's license)

3. (where/buy/a hammer)

4. (where/find out about/recycling trash)

5. (what number/call/in an emergency)

6. (what/do/with a broken wristwatch)

7. (where/buy/a magazine)

8. (what/do/for free in this town)

9. (what/buy/at a department store)

10. (where/get/ten dollars in quarters)

11. (where/read/newspapers from other cities)

12. (when/go swimming/around here)

▓▶ **Exercise 7: Comparing Present and Future Abilities and Opportunities**

Work on your own. Write five things you can do now but won't be able to do in five or ten years. Then write a sentence explaining why.

1. Right now, I can take courses during the day. In five years, I won't be able to be a student. I'll have to find a full-time job.

2. _____

3. _____

4. _____

5. _____

6. _____

▓▶ **Exercise 8: Comparing Present and Future Abilities and Opportunities**

Now write five things you can't do now, but will be able to do in five or ten years. Then write a sentence explaining why.

1. Right now, I can't afford a car, but I'll be able to afford one in five years. I'll have a job then.

2. _____

3. _____

_____

4. _____

_____

5. _____

_____

6. _____

_____

⇒ Exercise 9: Comparing Long Time Periods and Single Events

Work with a partner. Use *could* instead of *was* or *were able to* whenever possible. Discuss your answers.

1. For many years, we were able to take our vacations whenever we wanted.

   Example: *For many years, we could take our vacations whenever we wanted. Could is also possible because of the long time period* for many years.

2. I was able to get a lot of work done yesterday.

   Example: Could *is not possible because* yesterday *means it is a single event.*

3. When she was in college, she was able to read the newspapers and magazines from her country all the time in the library. Now she lives in a town where they're not available.

4. I was able to buy groceries easily when I lived in that apartment. The grocery store was right downstairs.

5. She was able to hear the marching band coming from a distance, and so she ran out to watch the parade.

6. On Monday, I was able to finish all of my work on time.

7. Before she injured her knee, she was able to run five miles a day.

8. The morning after the storm, I was able to go skiing.

9. I was able to see Central Park when I flew over New York.

10. When the doorbell rang, I was able to answer the door immediately.

11. Was she able to remember what happened after the accident?

12. She was able to register for the class this morning. There were three more spaces.

⟱▶ **Exercise 10: Comparing Present and Past Opportunities**

Read each situation and write statements using *could, couldn't, can,* or *can't.*

1. You've just won a million dollars in the lottery. Name three things that you can do now but couldn't do before:

   Now I can afford a larger apartment, but I couldn't before.

   _____

   _____

   _____

2. You've had a car for a while, but your car just broke down and the mechanic said it can't be fixed. Name three things that you could do when you had a car but you can't do now:

   _____

   _____

   _____

Modals of Belief: Form

Statements

I	**must**	be late.
You		
He		
She		
It		
We		
They		

- Modals of belief (**could, might, may, should, must,** and **will**) have the same features as the social modals in Chapter 7 (pages 164–165).

Negative Statements				Contraction
It	**should**	**not**	be difficult.	It **shouldn't**
	may	**not**		
	might	**not**		
	must	**not**		

- **May not** and **might not** have no contracted forms.
- **Must not** is not contracted to express belief. (However, it can be contracted to express prohibition. Look at Chapter 7, page 164.)

(continued)

Yes/No Questions	Short Answers	Contraction
Could it rain?	Yes, it **could**.	
	No, it **could not**.	No, it **couldn't**.

- **Could** is used instead of **might** to ask questions about possibility. **May** is never used in questions about possibility.
- **Must** is not used in *yes/no* questions to express certainty. (*Yes/no* questions with **must** often express disapproval. Look at Chapter 7, page 185.)

Information Questions				Answers
When	**should**	it	arrive?	Next week.
Where	**could**	they	be?	At the mall.

- The *wh-* word comes before the modal and the subject.

Information Questions (Subject)			Answers
Who	**might**	come?	Sharon **might**.
What	**could**	happen?	Who knows?

- If **who** or **what** is the subject of the question, then the word order is the same as for affirmative statements.

⟹ Exercise 11: Working on Form

Work with a partner. Complete the conversations using the words in parentheses.
Use contractions whenever possible. Then practice the conversations.

1. **A:** _____That may not be_____ (that/be/may/not) right. I haven't checked it.

   B: Don't worry. _____ (it/be/can/not) wrong. The computer

   doesn't make mistakes!

2. **A:** _____ (they/arrive/could) before we get home?

   B: I doubt it. _____ (they/arrive/might/not) until after dinner.

3. **A:** _____ (Lee/come/may/not). His car isn't ready yet.

   B: Really? _____ (He/be/must/not) very happy right now.

   But _____ (that/be/should/not) a problem.

   _____ (I/be able to/will) pick him up.

4. **A:** My brother could call soon, but then again _____

   (he/might/not).

   B: I know. _____ (He/have/may/not) a chance to call at all.

5. **A:** _____ (we/arrive/should) earlier than we expected.

   B: That's good. Then _____ (we/miss/might) the

   rush hour traffic.

Modals of Belief: Meaning and Use

CERTAINTY ABOUT THE PRESENT

1. Could, might, may, should, ought to, have to, have got to, and **must** express different degrees of certainty about the present:

> Tina: Where's Emily?
> Anna: I'm not sure. She **could** be upstairs, or she **could** be outside.
> Jan: Oh, she **must** be upstairs. I saw her go up there ten minutes ago.

2. The modal you choose shows how strongly you believe that something is true at the present time:

Less Certain	(Less than 50% sure)	could, might
		may
	(About 90% sure)	should, ought to
More Certain	(About 95% sure)	must, have to, have got to

3. Could, might, and **may** have similar meanings for making assumptions, but **could** and **might** sometimes show less certainty, especially when they are used with more than one possibility:

> Anna: She **could** be upstairs or she **could** be outside.

(continued)

4. Should and **ought to** express stronger certainty than **could, might,** or **may.** They are used when you are fairly certain about the present situation:

Jan: She **should** be upstairs.

5. Should be plus adjective and **ought to be** plus adjective aren't used with an adjective that is unpleasant or disagreeable for the subject of the sentence:

Mark: I wonder why Sue is absent. She **should** be well by now.
*She should be sick. (INCORRECT)

(**Should** is acceptable with the adjective *well*, but not with *sick*.)

6. Must, have to, and **have got to** express probability when you have a clear reason and you are drawing conclusions and making deductions based on it. Usually there is only one logical possibility:

Jan: She **must** be upstairs. I saw her go up there ten minutes ago.
She **has to** be upstairs.
She **has got to** be upstairs.

7. In conversations, **must be** plus adjective often shows the speaker's understanding of the listener's feelings:

Dave: I hardly slept last night. My neighbors were having a loud party.
Rosa: You **must be** very angry at them.

8. Maybe (one word) is not a modal. It is an adverb that begins a sentence. It is often used instead of **could, may,** or **might** to express possibility. Compare the use of **maybe** (adverb) and **may be** (belief modal plus verb):

Adverb	**Modal + Verb**
Maybe John is at home.	John **may be** at home.

9. The present continuous can be used with belief modals to show how sure you are that an action is in progress at the present time:

Tom: What's John doing right now?
Pat: He **must be studying.** I saw him go into the library ten minutes ago.

⇒ **Exercise 12: Expressing Certainty**

Work with a partner. Read each conversation and consider the information in parentheses. Then complete the conversation with a belief modal that expresses the appropriate degree of certainty.

1. **A:** What's bothering Alice? She's been looking strange ever since the class ended.

   B: She _____*might*_____ be depressed. (I don't think she did very well on the exam.)

   C: She _____*must*_____ be depressed. (I saw her exam. She got a very low grade.)

2. **A:** Are the clothes in the dryer ready yet?

   B: They _____ be dry now. (They usually take forty-five minutes to dry, and it's been almost forty minutes since we put them in.)

   C: They _____ be dry now. (They usually take forty-five minutes, and they've been in the dryer for almost an hour.)

3. **A:** Do you think they've finished repairing your car by now?

   B: It _____ be ready now. (It's now 2:00 P.M., and they said it'd be ready at noon.)

   C: It's noon. It _____ be ready. (They said they would probably finish by noon.)

4. **A:** Whose black jacket is this? Someone forgot to take it after the party.

   B: It _____ be Diane's. (I saw her wearing a black jacket when she arrived.)

   C: It _____ be Diane's. (She wears a lot of black.)

5. **A:** (The phone rings at 10:30 P.M.) Who could be calling so late?

   B: It _____ be Chris. (She looked very worried today and said she wanted to talk to me sometime.)

   C: It _____ be Chris. (She said she was going to call after ten o'clock.)

➡ **Exercise 13: Making Assumptions**

Work on your own. Make up your own assumptions about the following situations. Use belief modals to express the appropriate amount of certainty. Discuss your answers.

1. The teacher is absent today:

   She must be sick. OR

   She could be out of town.

2. The fire alarm is ringing:

3. Your new neighbor never smiles:

4. Your friend hasn't written you in several months:

5. You've been sneezing all morning:

6. The teacher looks angry:

7. Shhh! I hear noises in the next room:

8. Your sister's just received one dozen long-stemmed roses with no card:

9. Every time I pick up the phone I hear a loud, whining noise:

_____

_____

10. My neighbor's baby has been screaming all day:

_____

_____

⫸ Exercise 14: Expressing Understanding

Work with a partner and take turns reacting to the following statements. Answer with *you must be* plus an adjective to show your understanding.

1. **A:** I studied all night for my exam.
   B: You must be exhausted. _____

2. **A:** I didn't eat breakfast or lunch today.
   B: _____

3. **A:** Tomorrow is my first job interview.
   B: _____

4. **A:** My English teacher canceled our midterm exam.
   B: _____

5. **A:** My parents are going to visit me next week. I haven't seen them for six months.
   B: _____

6. **A:** My car broke down again. I just spent $300 on it last week.
   B: _____

7. **A:** I didn't get accepted to graduate school.
   B: _____

8. **A:** My family hasn't written for two months.
   B: _____

9. **A:** I'm going to get a scholarship next year.

   B: _____

10. **A:** My parents are going to get a divorce.

    B: _____

⫸ Exercise 15: Drawing Conclusions

Work with a partner. Terry's a nurse and works the day shift from 6:45 A.M. to 3:00 P.M. Read her work schedule. Complete each sentence using *must* or *should* to give your conclusion based on her schedule.

```
 DAY  SHIFT  SCHEDULE

 6:45   meet with night nurses
 7:15   check vital signs of patients
        (temperature, pulse, blood pressure)
 7:45   meet with doctors
 8:30   give patients medicine
 10:00  write notes on charts
 11:00  discharge patients
 12:30  give patients medicine
 1:00   admit new patients
 2:45   meet with evening nurses
```

1. If it's 7:30, Terry must be checking the patients' vital signs. OR
   Terry should be checking the patients' vital signs.

2. If Terry is meeting with the doctors, it must be 7:45. OR
   it should be 7:45.

3. If it's 1:10,_____

4. If it's 6:50,_____

5. If it's 11:00, _____

6. If it's 8:30,_____

7. If Terry is meeting with the evening nurses, _____

8. If Terry is writing notes on charts,_____

⟱ **Exercise 16: Drawing Conclusions**

Work on your own. Think about what one of your relatives living in another country is probably doing at different times during the day. Write five sentences using *should* or *must*.

1. _If it's 4:00 p.m., my mother must be working._

2. _____

3. _____

4. _____

5. _____

6. _____

⟱ **Exercise 17: Expressing Certainty**

Rephrase the following sentences, using a belief modal or *ought to, have to,* and *have got to* in order to express the appropriate degree of certainty. Use more than one alternative if you can.

1. Maybe he has a cold.

    He might have a cold. OR

    He may have a cold. OR

    He could have a cold.

2. There's a 30 percent chance of rain today.

    _____

3. I'm almost certain that he's at home.

    _____

4. I expect her to be working.

    _____

5. Maybe she needs help.

    _____

6. I'm quite certain that this is the meeting place.

_____

7. It's possible that he's sleeping.

_____

8. I'm almost sure that my keys are on the table.

_____

9. He's probably in his office.

_____

10. There's a very small chance that I need a new tire.

_____

Modals of Belief: Meaning and Use

CERTAINTY ABOUT THE PRESENT (NEGATIVE)

1. Negative belief modals express different degrees of certainty about a situation. However, negative belief modals tell whether you are more or less certain about the impossibility of the situation. They can also express belief or disbelief:

Jill: I'm worried. Joe doesn't answer his phone.
Mark: Well, he **may not** be at home.
Dave: He **can't** be home. I just saw him drive by.

2. The modal you choose shows how strongly you believe that something is not true at the present time:

Less Certain	(Less than 50% sure)	may not, might not
	(About 95% sure)	must not
More Certain	(99% sure)	can't, couldn't

3. The major differences between affirmative and negative belief modals concern the use of **can't** and **couldn't**. **Can't** and **couldn't** express strong certainty that something is impossible. They may also express surprise and disbelief:

Julie: I heard that you're going to get a big raise.
Susan: Oh, that **can't** be true. I heard that no one's getting a raise this year.

4. Can and **could**, however, do not have the same meaning as **can't** or **couldn't**. **Can** and **could** both express weak certainty that something is possible.

➠ Exercise 18: Guessing

Work in small groups. Make guesses about the following situations using *may not* and *might not*. Offer two possibilities in each sentence. Think up as many sentences as you can for each situation.

1. Maria never raises her hand in class.

   Examples: *She may not understand the questions, or she might not know the answers.*
   She might not study enough, or she might not like to speak in class.

2. Ellen has suddenly decided not to marry her boyfriend. Everyone's confused.

3. Everyone's eating chocolate cake for dessert except Tina.

4. Jenny doesn't answer the telephone.

5. Sam never goes with us to the movies.

6. No one answers when I ring Nora's doorbell, but some lights are on in the house.

7. He always looks tired.

8. Maria doesn't want to come to the class party.

➠ Exercise 19: Expressing Belief and Disbelief

Work in small groups. Take turns reading the statements. Comment on the statements as follows:

   (a) If you believe the statement is true, say *I agree.*
   (b) If you're not sure, but you think that there's a possibility, say *It may be true.* OR
      It might be true. OR *It could be true.*
   (c) If you're convinced it's false or if you're really surprised, say *It can't be true.*
      It must be _____ OR *It couldn't be true. It must be _____* (and try to guess
      the correct answer).

1. The literacy rate of Sweden is 99 percent.

   A: *I agree.*
   B: *It might be true.*
   C: *It can't be true. It must be about 90 percent.*

2. Japan's population is 500 million.

3. North America is composed of two countries.

4. Ethiopia has more citizens who are Christians than citizens who are Muslims.

5. The universe began about one billion years ago.

6. Italy exports more rice than India.

7. The butterfly is the name of a swim stroke.

8. The population density (people per square mile) in Japan is 6, whereas the population density in Australia is 857.

9. A tornado warning means that the storms in your area could produce tornadoes.

10. China has the highest population in the world.

11. According to the U.S. Bureau of Census, the world's population will be about 8 billion by the year 2020.

12. The life expectancy for North American women is 80, and the life expectancy for North American men is 73.

⏭ Exercise 20: Expressing Present Certainty

Work with a partner. Decide which sentence is the most certain for each situation and circle it.

1. The key is missing:
   - (a) It may be on the table.
   - (b) It must be on the table.
   - (c) It ought to be on the table.

2. Joe is eating lunch with an older woman:
   - (a) She might be his mother.
   - (b) She could be his mother.
   - (c) She's got to be his mother.

3. A letter has just arrived:
   - (a) It can't be from Mary.
   - (b) It must not be from Mary.
   - (c) It might not be from Mary.

4. Thomas is doing his homework:
   - (a) He might finish soon.
   - (b) He could finish soon.
   - (c) He can't finish soon.

5. The answer is twenty-five:
   - (a) That may not be right.
   - (b) That couldn't be right.
   - (c) That must not be right.

6. The doorbell is ringing:

    (a) It has to be the mail carrier.

    (b) It should be the mail carrier.

    (c) It ought to be the mail carrier.

7. I'm worried about Jeanne:

    (a) She might be ill.

    (b) She must be ill.

    (c) She could be ill.

8. My car is at the service station:

    (a) It ought to be ready now.

    (b) It could be ready now.

    (c) It may not be ready now.

Modals of Belief: Meaning and Use

CERTAINTY ABOUT THE FUTURE

1. **Could, might, may, should, ought to,** and **will** express different degrees of certainty about the future, ranging from possibility to strong certainty:

> Ryan: When is Tony going to arrive tonight?
> Matt: Well, he **could** arrive at 7:30, or maybe later.
> Anna: Oh, I'm sure he'**ll** arrive at 7:30. He called a few minutes ago and said
>   he's on schedule.

2. The modal you choose to predict the future can make your sentence sound more certain or less certain:

Less Certain	(Less than 50% sure)	could, might
		may
	(About 90% sure)	should, ought to
More Certain	(99–100% sure)	will

(continued)

3. Could, might, and **may** have similar meanings for expressing possibility about the future, but **could** and **might** show less certainty, especially when they are used with more than one possibility:

Matt: He **might** arrive at 7:30, or maybe later.

4. Should and **ought to** indicate future expectations more frequently than present expectations:

Peter: He **should** arrive at 7:30. That's what he told me yesterday.

5. Will usually expresses strong certainty about the future. However, **will** is often weakened with adverbs of possibility such as **maybe, perhaps,** and **probably:**

Adverb of Possibility	Meaning
Maybe he'**ll** come at 7:30.	He **might** come at 7:30.
Perhaps he'**ll** come at 7:30.	He **might** come at 7:30.
He'**ll probably** come at 7:30.	He **should** come at 7:30.

6. Must, have to, and **have got to** do not express beliefs about the future. They only express strong certainty about the present.

⮚ Exercise 21: Expressing Future Certainty

Rewrite each sentence using *could, might, may, should,* or *will* to express different degrees of certainty about the future.

1. I expect the exam to be easy.
   The exam should be easy.

2. Maybe we'll come later.

3. There's a small chance of rain this afternoon.

4. It's possible that the plane will be on time tonight.

5. Perhaps he's taking the express train this evening.

_____

6. The flight definitely arrives at 8:10.

_____

7. I don't expect it to be cold today.

_____

8. There's a good possibility that he'll get the job.

_____

⟱ **Exercise 22: Making Predictions**

Complete each sentence with an affirmative or negative belief modal to make a prediction about your lifetime. Then write five predictions that *could, might, may, should,* or *will* happen in your lifetime.

1. More people _____ will _____ live to the age of 100.
2. I _____ might not _____ visit another planet.
3. Researchers _____ find a cure for cancer.
4. Astronomers _____ solve the mysteries of the universe.
5. Governments _____ eliminate poverty.
6. I _____ ride in a spaceship.
7. Robots _____ do all of our housework.
8. Countries _____ stop producing nuclear weapons.
9. We _____ run out of landfill space to dump our trash.
10. There _____ be another world war.
11. _____
12. _____
13. _____
14. _____
15. _____

Past Modals: Form

Statements

I	**should**	**have**	**gone**.
You			
He			
She			
It			
We			
They			

- To form past modals (also called perfect modals), use the modal auxiliary + **have** + the past participle of the main verb.

Negative Statements / Contraction

I	**could**	**not**	**have**	**come**.	I **couldn't**

- In negative sentences, **not** is placed between the modal and **have**.

Yes/No Questions / Short Answers / Contraction

Should	she	**have**	**waited**?	Yes, she **should have**.	
				No, she **should not have**.	**shouldn't**

- In *yes/no* questions, the modal comes before the subject.
- Affirmative short answers have a subject + a modal + **have**.
- Negative short answers have a subject + a modal + **not** + **have**.

Information Questions / Answers

Where	**could**	they	**have**	**gone**?	I'm not sure.

- The question word is followed by the modal and then the subject.

Information Questions (Subject) / Answers

What	**could**	**have**	**happened?**	I have no idea.

- If **who** or **what** is the subject, the word order is the same as for affirmative statements.

CONVERSATION NOTES

1. In fast conversation, past modals are often shortened. When **have** follows a modal, it sounds like *of*:

Written Form	**Spoken Form**
I **could have** come.	"I **could-of** come." (SPOKEN ONLY)
She **might have** come.	"She **might-of** come." (SPOKEN ONLY)
He **may have** come.	"He **may-of** come." (SPOKEN ONLY)
We **should have** come.	"We **should-of** come." (SPOKEN ONLY)
They **must have** come.	"They **must-of** come." (SPOKEN ONLY)

2. The negative forms are also shortened in the same way:

Written Form	**Spoken Form**
I **could not have** come.	"I **couldn't-of** come." (SPOKEN ONLY)
She **might not have** come.	"She **might not-of** come." (SPOKEN ONLY)
He **may not have** come.	"He **may not-of** come." (SPOKEN ONLY)
We **should not have** come.	"We **shouldn't-of** come." (SPOKEN ONLY)
They **must not have** come.	"They **must not-of** come." (SPOKEN ONLY)

⏭ Exercise 23: Working on Past Modal Forms

Work with a partner. Complete the following conversations using the appropriate past forms of the modals and the verbs in parentheses. Then practice the conversations, switching roles.

1. **A:** I _____ *could have gone* _____ (could/go) to the movies with you, but I decided to

   study instead.

   B: You didn't miss anything. You _____ (might/not/like) it

   anyway. There _____ (must/be) ten different violent scenes!

2. **A:** I _____ (should/not/drive) to work this morning. There was

   so much traffic.

   B: You _____ (should/take) the bus. It was empty.

3. **A:** She _____ (could/not/leave) yet. It's only eight o'clock.

   B: But she _____ (might/forget) to wait for us. Let's call her

   at home.

4. **A:** You _____ (must/have) a great time last night. I heard you

come in at 2:00 A.M.

B: It was great. You _____ (should/stop by) after the library.

You _____ (could/hear) the new band. They played until 1:30.

5. **A:** I lost my keys last night. I _____ (might/leave) them at

your house.

B: No, you _____ (could/not). You drove home with them,

didn't you?

A: That's right. Then I _____ (must/drop) them after I parked

the car. I didn't use them to get into my apartment. The door was open.

B: You _____ (could/put) them in your pocket, or you

_____ (might/lock) them in the car. Have you checked?

Past Modals: Meaning and Use

ABILITY AND BELIEF MODALS

1. The past forms of modals don't express all of the same meanings as the simple forms of the modals that you've learned in this chapter and in Chapter 7. While most of the ability and belief modals express the same meanings in the past, only a few of the social modals do.

2. Could have, the past form of **could,** means that you had the ability or opportunity to do something in the past, but you didn't do it:

Past Ability: I **could have** passed the placement test, but I didn't take it. I didn't know about it.

Past Opportunity: I **could have** taken the bus, but I walked instead.

3. In the past, affirmative belief modals tell how sure you are that something happened:

Tina: Where was Emily?
Anna: I'm not sure. She **could have** been upstairs or outside.
Jan: Oh, she **must have** been upstairs. I saw her go up there some time ago.

Less Certain	(Less than 50% sure)	could have, might have
		may have
More Certain	(About 95% sure)	must have, have to have

4. When **could have** expresses past possibility, it is uncertain whether the event actually happened or not:

Past Possibility: He **could have** called while we were out. (It's possible, but we really don't know if he did or not.)

5. In the past, negative belief modals tell how sure you are that something didn't happen:

Tim: I'm looking for today's mail. Have you seen it?
Scott: It **might not have** arrived. I really don't know.
Mark: It **must not have** arrived. There's no mail in any of the boxes.
Ivan: It **couldn't have** arrived. It's too early. It's never here this early.

⇒ Exercise 24: Talking About Career Opportunities

Work with a partner. Make up sentences using *could have* and the expressions in parentheses to express the different opportunities that were available in each situation. Then add your own.

1. John went to college. He majored in biology and education. He became a teacher, but here are the other possibilities that he considered:

   (a) (work in a lab) _He could have worked in a lab._

   (b) (go to medical school) _____

   _____

   (c) (enter a Ph.D. program) _____

   _____

   (d) _____

   _____

2. Lee went to cooking school. He became a chef on a cruise ship after he considered the following careers:

   (a) (become a cook in a restaurant) _____

   _____

   (b) (open a restaurant) _____

   _____

   (c) (work in a hotel) _____

   _____

   (d) _____

   _____

3. Ella majored in English. She became an editor after she considered the following choices:

(a) (teach English in a high school) _____

_____

(b) (go to law school) _____

_____

(c) (work for a newspaper) _____

_____

(d) _____

_____

4. Ed majored in art. He thought about the following careers before he decided to paint on his own:

(a) (become an art teacher) _____

_____

(b) (get a job in advertising) _____

_____

(c) (do graphic design) _____

_____

(d) _____

_____

⫸ Exercise 25: Talking About Career Choices

Work on your own. What are some career choices that you have made? What did you decide to do? Write three sentences with *could have*.

1. I could have worked as a sales representative, but I decided to become a gardener instead.

2. _____

_____

3. _____

_____

4. _____

_____

➠ **Exercise 26: Expressing Disbelief and Impossibility**

Work with a partner. The following statements are probably not true. Take turns reading each statement and expressing disbelief with *couldn't have* and a reason.

1. You just won the lottery.

   A: *You just won the lottery.*
   B: *I couldn't have won the lottery because I didn't even buy a ticket.*

2. Your great-great-grandfather sent you a letter.

3. Your Rolls Royce ran out of gas.

4. You grew three inches taller this week.

5. Your hair has turned green.

6. You've memorized all of Shakespeare's plays.

7. You lost a million dollars yesterday.

8. You swam the English Channel last week.

9. You robbed a bank last night.

10. You've solved a famous mathematical problem.

Past Modals: Meaning and Use

SOCIAL MODALS

1. Should (not) have and **ought to have** also express a high degree of certainty about the past. However, their meaning is a combination of past obligation (social modal) and strong certainty (belief modal):

Where was Emily? She **should have** been downstairs. (I expected her to be there. That's where she was supposed to be.)

The mail **ought to have** arrived by now. (It was supposed to and I expected it to.)

2. As social modals, **could have** and **should have** mean that something was a good idea but you didn't do it, or you were supposed to do something but you didn't:

Past Suggestion:	You **could have** taken aspirin for your headache. (Taking aspirin was a possible choice, but you didn't do it.)
Good Idea:	You **should have** asked for help. (Asking for help was a good idea, but you didn't do it.)
Past Obligation:	You **should have** registered on Monday. (You were supposed to register on Monday, but you didn't.)

(continued)

3. In the first person, **should have** shows regret:

I **should have** accepted the job offer. (I'm sorry that I didn't; now I regret it.)

4. Social modals **may** (for expressing permission) and **must** (for expressing requirements) do not have past modal forms. **Was** or **were permitted to** and **had to** are used instead:

Present

At the present time, students **may** take four courses.

Today, all visitors **must** register at the front desk.

Past

Last year, students **were permitted to** take four courses.

Yesterday, all visitors **had to** register at the front desk.

⟫ Exercise 27: Making Past Suggestions

Work in small groups. Ask questions about each situation using *should have* and the words in parentheses. Give short answers with *could have, should have,* and *shouldn't have.*

1. Ko is a foreign student who recently arrived in the United States. Last night he was invited to an American friend's house for dinner. He didn't know what to bring:

   (an expensive gift)

   A: *Should he have brought an expensive gift?*
   B: *No, he shouldn't have.*

   (flowers)

   (a bottle of wine)

   (his visiting relatives)

   (〰〰〰)

2. Ko wanted to speak to the waiter last week in a restaurant. He didn't know what to do:

   (whistle)

   (snap his fingers)

   (clap loudly)

   (raise his hand when the waiter was looking at him)

   (〰〰〰)

3. There was a $4.00 mistake on Ko's bill at the restaurant. He didn't know what to do:

(ignore it)

(tell the waiter)

(call the manager immediately)

(shout at the waiter)

(~~~~~~)

➡ **Exercise 28: Expressing Regret**

Imagine that you made the following mistakes. Use *should have* and *shouldn't have* to express regret.

1. You didn't go to the party. Everyone had a great time:

   I should have gone to the party.

   I shouldn't have stayed home last night.

2. You cooked the rice too long. It burned:

3. You left your car windows open during a rainstorm:

4. You didn't study for your English quiz:

5. You decided not to buy household fire insurance. There was a fire in your apartment building, and many of your belongings were damaged:

6. You didn't apply for a summer job. Now it's too late:

7. You drove 55 mph in a 40 mph zone. You got a traffic ticket:

_____

_____

8. You spent all of your money. You won't get another paycheck for two weeks:

_____

_____

9. You gained twenty-five pounds last semester. Nothing fits you:

_____

_____

10. You didn't accept a job offer because you didn't like the boss. Now you can't find another job:

_____

_____

▶ Exercise 29: Thinking About Meaning

Work with a partner. Read each sentence and decide whether the statements below are true (T), false (F), or (?) if you do not have enough information to decide. Then explain your answers in small groups.

1. I shouldn't have gone to the movies.

_____F_____ (a) I didn't go to the movies.

_____T_____ (b) I am sorry that I went to the movies.

2. You must be tired!

_____ (a) The speaker is tired.

_____ (b) The speaker thinks the listener is tired.

3. Eva might be home.

_____ (a) Maybe she is home.

_____ (b) She is home.

4. She must have taken my notebook.

_____ (a) It was necessary for her to take my notebook.

_____ (b) She probably took my notebook.

5. That can't be John.

_____ (a) I'm certain that it's not John.

_____ (b) It must be his brother.

6. I should have called you.

_____ (a) I called you.

_____ (b) I'm sorry that I didn't call you.

7. The machine must be broken.

_____ (a) It has to be broken. That's the only explanation.

_____ (b) I'm quite sure that it's broken.

8. They might have left.

_____ (a) I'm not sure if they left.

_____ (b) They left.

9. You could have lost it in the park. Did you look?

_____ (a) Maybe you lost it in the park.

_____ (b) You might have lost it in the park.

10. The plane should arrive in an hour.

_____ (a) I expect the plane to arrive in an hour.

_____ (b) The plane hasn't arrived yet.

Summary

Present Ability: Form

Statements:	He **can** type.
Negative Statements:	She **can't** come on Sunday.
Yes/No Questions:	**Can** they see anything?
Short Answers:	Yes, they **can.** OR No, they **can't.**
Information Questions:	When **can** he help us?
Information Questions (Subject):	Who **can** work on Sunday?

Past Ability: Form

Statements:	I **could** walk when I was eleven months old.
Negative Statements:	He **couldn't** ski when he was young.
Yes/No Questions:	**Could** you swim when you were a child?
Short Answers:	Yes, I **could.** OR No, I **couldn't.**
Information Questions:	What **could** you see at sunset?
Information Questions (Subject):	Who **could** hear the music last night?

Present, Past, and Future Ability: Meaning and Use

Can expresses the idea that a situation is possible because the subject has the necessary knowledge, skills, opportunities, or capability at the present time. **Could** means that the general ability or opportunity to do something existed for a long time in the past.

Present Ability:	He **can** swim, but he **can't** water ski.
Present Decision About Future Ability:	I'm busy right now, but I **can** help you tomorrow.
Present Opportunity:	The storm is over. We **can** leave in an hour.
Future Ability:	Next year he**'ll be able to** drive.
Past Ability:	He **couldn't** walk until he was eighteen months old.
Past Opportunity:	Twenty years ago, you **could** swim in that lake. Now it's polluted.

Modals of Belief: Form

Statements:	He **must** be sick.
Negative Statements:	She **may not** be there.
Yes/No Questions:	**Could** that be right?
Short Answers:	Yes, it **could.** OR No, it **couldn't.**
Information Questions:	When **should** the plane arrive?
Information Questions (Subject):	What **might** happen?

Modals of Belief: Meaning and Use

Belief modals express various degrees of certainty about the present, ranging from possibility and expectation to strong probability. They tell how certain you are that a particular situation is true. Negative belief modals tell how certain you are that a situation is not true. Belief modals also express certainty about the future.

■ Certainty About the Present: *Could, Might, May, Should, Ought to, Have to, Have Got to, Must*

Assumptions:	My car **could** be ready now.
	My car **might** be ready now.
	My car **may** be ready now.
Conclusions:	If it's 9:15, she **should** be working.
Certainty:	He **must** be upstairs.
Understanding:	You **must** be exhausted.

■ Certainty About the Present (Negative): *May Not, Might Not, Must Not, Can't, Couldn't*

Guesses:	She **may not** be home.
	She **might not** be home.
Near Certainty:	He **must not** be home. No one answers the doorbell.
Disbelief:	That **can't** be true.
	That **couldn't** be true.
Impossibility:	The letter **can't** be from Mary.

■ Certainty About the Future: *Could, Might, May, Should, Ought to, Will*

Possibility:	She **could** call this evening.
	She **might** call this evening.
Stronger Possibility:	She **may** call this evening.
Expectations:	They **should** come soon.
	They **ought to** come soon.
Certainty:	He **will** arrive at 7:30. I'm certain.
Predictions:	In my lifetime, I **could/might/may** travel in a spaceship.
	In my lifetime, I **should** travel in a spaceship.
	In my lifetime, I **will** travel in a spaceship.

Past Modals: Form

Statements:	He **must have** left.
Negative Statements:	He **might not have** understood.
Yes/No Questions:	**Should** she **have** waited?
Short Answers:	Yes, she **should have.** OR No, she **shouldn't have.**
Information Questions:	Where **could** they **have** gone?
Information Questions (Subject):	What **could have** happened?

Past Modals: Meaning and Use

The past forms of belief modals express different degrees of certainty about the past. **Could have** and **should have** also express past abilities, opportunities, and obligations that did not actually happen.

Opportunities:	He **could have** worked in a lab, but he decided not to.
Possibility:	They **could have** called while we were out.
	They **might have** called while we were out.
	They **may have** called while we were out.
Expectations:	The mail **should have** arrived by now.
Conclusions:	He **must have** left. His car isn't here.
Impossibility:	I **couldn't have** won the lottery. I didn't even buy a ticket.
Suggestions:	You **could have** brought some flowers.
Obligations:	You **should have** registered this morning.
Regret:	I **should have** visited him in the hospital.
	I **shouldn't have** lost my temper.

⇒ Summary Exercise: Finding Errors

Most of the sentences contain an error in form, meaning, or use. Find each error and correct it. (Hint: Three sentences are correct.)

1. He ~~may working~~ today.   *He may be working today.*

2. That couldn't be Joe, but I'm really not sure.

3. When I was young, I could swim a mile.

4. The letter could arrived this afternoon.

5. He might have been late.

6. She must had a cold yesterday.

7. Yesterday, I could take a walk at noon.

8. I should have asked him. I'm sorry that I did.

9. It maybe too late.

10. He should have taking the exam.

11. You could of called me. I was home.

12. That must have been the new teacher.

13. There ought be some more in the kitchen.

14. **A:** I hope the weather is nice tomorrow.
    B: Don't worry. It must be. I heard the latest weather report. It will be warm and sunny.

Relative Clauses

Preview

Summary:

This story is about an African-American woman **who refused to give up her seat to a white passenger on a city bus.** Her refusal, **which occurred in 1955,** helped start the civil rights movement in the United States.

The woman, **whose name was Rosa Parks,** was arrested. However, Martin Luther King, Jr., led a year-long boycott of the bus system. The boycott was successful, and led to mass protests **that demanded civil rights for African-Americans.**

Definition:

Passive resistance is the nonviolent dissent **that Martin Luther King, Jr., encouraged in the 1960s.**

Giving directions:

Turn left onto State Street. The memorial, **which is next to the library,** is on your right.

Relative clauses are adjective clauses that generally begin with the relative pronouns **who, whom, that, which,** and **whose.** Like adjectives, relative clauses modify nouns. Unlike adjectives, they are dependent clauses that immediately follow the nouns they modify.

The two main types of relative clauses — restrictive and nonrestrictive — have distinct meanings and uses. The difference depends on the kind of information that the relative clause tells about the noun in the main clause. A restrictive relative clause gives information that helps to uniquely identify the noun that it describes:

My brother **who attends college** is very shy. (I have two brothers. This particular brother attends college and he's very shy. My other brother doesn't attend college.)

A nonrestrictive relative clause, on the other hand, adds extra information about the noun it modifies. This information is not necessary to identify the noun:

John, **who attends college,** is very shy. (John is very shy. He also attends college.)

In this chapter you will study different uses of restrictive and nonrestrictive relative clauses.

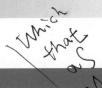

Restrictive Relative Clauses: Form

Noun in Main Clause	Relative Clause	Rest of Main Clause
The man	**who called**	is an old friend.
The men	**who called**	are old friends.
The woman	**whom I met**	lives near me.
The women	**whom I met**	live near me.
The letter	**that I received**	is very important.
The letters	**that I received**	are very important.
The book	**which we discussed**	was a best-seller.
The books	**which we discussed**	were best-sellers.
The writer	**whose book we read**	will speak at the college tonight.
The writers	**whose book we read**	will speak at the college tonight.

- A restrictive relative clause begins with the relative pronoun **who, whom, that, which,** or **whose**. The relative pronoun refers to the noun in the main clause that it immediately follows.
- **Who, whom,** and **that** are used for people. **Which** and **that** are used for animals, things, and events.
- **Who, whom, which,** and **that** can refer to either singular or plural nouns. The relative pronoun does not change form.
- Commas are not used with restrictive relative clauses. If commas are added, the meaning of the relative clause changes.
- A restrictive relative clause can occur anywhere in the sentence, but it must immediately follow the noun that it modifies:

  The letter **that I received** is very important.
  I showed you the letter **that I received.**

➤ Exercise 1: Working on Form

Work with a partner. Identify the relative clauses in the conversation below. Underline them and circle the nouns that they modify. Then read the conversation aloud.

1. **A:** What should I wear to my job interview?

   B: How about the shirt that you wore Saturday night?

2. **A:** You mean the one that has food all over it?

   B: Oh. Well, what about the shirt that you got for your birthday?

3. **A:** The one that you gave me or the one that my sister gave me?

   B: Wear the one that your sister gave you with the suit that you bought last month. What time is the interview?

4. **A:** The secretary that I spoke to last week said 10:15, but a letter that I received a few days later said 10:30. I'd better be there at 10:15.

   B: Was the book that I gave you helpful?

5. **A:** Yes, especially the part that talked about staying calm.

   B: Is the position that you're applying for a new position?

6. **A:** No. In fact, I know a man whose wife had this job a few years ago, and I also know the person who has it now. She's leaving to work at the new office that they recently opened in Boston.

Restrictive Relative Clauses: Meaning and Use

IDENTIFYING, DEFINING, SUMMARIZING

1. Restrictive relative clauses are also called identifying or defining relative clauses because they distinguish a particular person or thing from other similar people or things. They provide an explanation that answers the question *Which one(s)?*

You're discussing two neighbors:

> You: One of my neighbors is always borrowing things from me. Another neighbor always calls me at dinnertime.
> Friend: Which one is that?
> You: The man **who lives next door** is always borrowing things. The woman **who lives across the street** always calls me at dinnertime.

The relative clauses **who lives next door** and **who lives across the street** tell which neighbor we are talking about in each sentence. These relative clauses add necessary information to identify the neighbor to the listener.

2. A restrictive relative clause can combine two sentences that refer to the same noun phrase:

A summary:

> This movie is about a man. He traveled around the world.
> This movie is about a man **who traveled around the world.**

(continued)

3. Restrictive relative clauses can clearly identify the noun being discussed at the beginning of a conversation. A relative clause can also save time and space by combining two ideas. Compare these two ways of introducing new information into a conversation:

New information:

Guess what? A guy just won the lottery. He works with me.
Guess what? A guy **who works with me** just won the lottery.

The relative clause **who works with me** immediately identifies the noun *a guy* in this conversation. Without the relative clause, the listener has to wait until the next sentence in order to understand who the speaker is talking about.

4. Restrictive relative clauses often contain information that the speaker and the listener already share. This shared information helps the listener to easily identify the noun the speaker is introducing into the conversation:

The book **that Victor bought** is on the table.

In this situation, both the speaker and the listener already know that Victor bought a book. The speaker uses this information to help the listener identify the particular book.

5. Restrictive relative clauses often identify and classify nouns in definitions:

A spider is a small, eight-legged creature **that spins a web.**

6. That is the most frequently used relative pronoun for restrictive relative clauses. In informal conversation, **that** is often used in place of **who, whom,** and **which:**

The man **that called** is an old friend.
The woman **that I met** lives near me.
The book **that we discussed** was a best-seller.

7. In more formal situations, **which** is often used in place of **that:**

A news broadcast:

The storm **which blanketed the area today** has caused airports, businesses, and schools to shut down.

8. Whom is used in formal written and spoken English:

The woman **whom the president will appoint** is a judge.

➠ **Exercise 2: Identifying Things**

Work with a partner. Imagine someone is trying to help you find something that you own. Create a conversation for each situation. Take turns asking which one is yours, and provide a description with a relative clause. Then practice the conversations.

1. You're at the airport and you're looking for your luggage. There are five black suitcases that are similar to your black one:

   A: _Which suitcase is yours?_____

   B: _Mine is the one that has a green luggage tag._____

2. You can't seem to find your car in the parking lot. There are several red cars in the parking lot just like yours:

   A: _____

   B: _____

3. You took off your boots when you entered the doctor's office. When you're ready to leave, you notice that there are four other pairs of gray boots similar to yours:

   A: _____

   B: _____

4. You hung up a tan raincoat on the coat rack at the restaurant. So did several other people:

   A: _____

   B: _____

5. All the students left their backpacks on the bench outside the language lab. Several students have black ones just like yours:

   A: _____

   B: _____

6. You left your umbrella by the door before you entered your cousin's house. So did several other guests:

   A: _____

   B: _____

7. You've lost your car keys in a department store. When you go to the lost and found, the clerk says that there are several sets of keys:

   A: _____

   B: _____

8. You brought a cake to a potluck dinner. Two other people brought cakes too. Your friend wants to taste your cake:

A: _____

B: _____

⮞ Exercise 3: Combining Sentences with *Who, That*, or *Which*

Work on your own. Combine each pair of sentences using the information in the second sentence to make a relative clause with *who*, *that*, or *which*.

1. We walked down the steps. They led to the basement.

   We walked down the steps that led to the basement. OR

   We walked down the steps which led to the basement.

2. The professor called me. He speaks Russian.

   The professor who speaks Russian called me. OR

   The professor that speaks Russian called me.

3. My sister has a cat. It has three kittens.

   _____

4. The little girl was crying. She hurt her knee.

   _____

5. They gave us an exam. It lasted an hour.

   _____

6. I spoke to two women. They saw the accident.

   _____

7. My friend went on a diet. She was overweight.

   _____

8. I called my aunt. She lives in Albany.

   _____

9. She bought the sweater. It cost thirty dollars.

   _____

10. Did you buy the socks? They were on sale.

_____

11. The child went home. He was sick.

_____

12. I took the notebooks. They were lying on the desk.

_____

⫸ Exercise 4: Defining Words

Work with a partner. Here are the names of different types of medical specialists. Describe each specialist, using a relative clause with *who*. If necessary, use a dictionary.

1. (a dermatologist) _A dermatologist is a doctor who treats skin problems._

2. (an orthopedist) _____

_____

3. (an obstetrician) _____

_____

4. (an optometrist) _____

_____

5. (a cardiologist) _____

_____

6. (a pediatrician) _____

_____

7. (a podiatrist) _____

_____

8. (an orthodontist) _____

_____

⟫ **Exercise 5: Summarizing Stories**

Work in small groups. Complete the following sentences with a relative clause that briefly summarizes each story.

1. *E.T.* is about a creature _that visits from outer space._

2. *Jurassic Park* is about a group of people _____

_____

3. *Aladdin* is about a poor young man _____

_____

4. *Star Trek* is about a group of people _____

_____

5. *Home Alone II* is about a boy _____

_____

6. _____ is about _____

_____

_____

Subject Relative Pronouns: Form and Use

Noun	Subject	Verb	(...)	Rest of Main Clause
The woman	**who**	**lives**	**next door**	died suddenly.
The women	**that**	**live**	**upstairs**	are noisy.
The letter	**that**	**fell**	**on the floor**	is mine.
The letters	**which**	**came**	**today**	are late.

- When the relative pronoun **who, that,** or **which** comes before the verb in the relative clause, the relative pronoun acts as the subject of the relative clause. It is a subject relative pronoun.
- The verb that follows **who, that,** or **which** agrees with the noun in the main clause.
- **That** is used more often for things and animals than **which**.

⫸ Exercise 6: Working on Form

Work with a partner. Write the correct form of the verb in parentheses. Then practice the conversations.

1. **A:** Who is the person who _____*sits*_____ (sit) next to you at the Monday lecture?

   B: I don't know her name, but she's the woman who always _____ (ask) a lot of questions in chemistry class.

2. **A:** Where are the papers that _____ (be) lying on the table when I left?

   B: I don't know, but there's something over there that _____ (look) like it's yours.

3. **A:** The children who _____ (live) there play with my daughter.

   B: Really? I thought that the people who _____ (own) that house didn't have any children.

4. **A:** The students who _____ (be) absent last Friday have to listen to a tape in the lab. The lab assistant will help you.

   B: Is he the guy that _____ (have) long hair and a beard?

5. **A:** The men who _____ (be) going to move the furniture are coming at noon.

   B: Are they the ones who _____ (have) a blue van?

   A: No, they're the guys who _____ (drive) a gray pickup truck.

6. **A:** I need to see a doctor who _____ (treat) skin problems. How can I find one?

   B: Someone who _____ (do) that is called a dermatologist. Look up *dermatologist* in the Yellow Pages.

7. **A:** Let's divide the class into the same two groups as yesterday. The group that _____ (finish) first can start working on the story.

   B: But what about the people that _____ (be) absent yesterday?

8. **A:** Did you call all the volunteers that _____ (be) on the list?

   B: Yes. I reached everyone who _____ (want) to help us.

> ## Exercise 7: Identifying and Defining with Subject Relative Pronouns

Work with a partner. Read each passage and use the information to answer the questions. Write sentences with subject relative pronouns.

1. Georgia O'Keeffe was a twentieth-century American artist. She continued painting well into her eighties. She died at the age of ninety-eight.

   Who was Georgia O'Keeffe?

   Georgia O'Keeffe was a twentieth-century American artist who continued painting well into her eighties.

2. Gene therapy is a new branch of genetic engineering. It may someday prevent diseases such as cancer. This disease affects people of all countries and races.

   (a) What is gene therapy?

   _____

   _____

   (b) What is cancer?

   _____

   _____

3. Rosa Parks is an African-American. She refused to give up her seat to a white passenger on a city bus. She is sometimes called the mother of the civil rights movement.

   Who is Rosa Parks?

   _____

   _____

4. Martin Luther King, Jr., was an African-American. He led the civil rights movement in the 1960s. He believed in fighting for equal rights through passive resistance. This nonviolent method was previously used by Mahatma Gandhi in the 1940s.

   (a) Who was Martin Luther King, Jr.?

   _____

   _____

   (b) What is passive resistance?

   _____

   _____

5. SATs are college entrance exams. They help colleges decide whether or not to admit a student. High school students take SATs during their junior or senior year. These students are preparing to apply to college.

(a) What are SATs?

_____

_____

(b) Who takes SATs?

_____

_____

6. Throughout history, eagles have been important symbols. They represent strength and power to governments around the world. The bald eagle is a large North American bird. It is the national emblem of the United States.

(a) What type of symbol have eagles been?

_____

_____

(b) What is the bald eagle?

_____

_____

7. Phobias are exaggerated fears. These fears can sometimes prevent a person from leading a normal life. Some people suffer from agoraphobia. This is a fear of being in open places. Others suffer from claustrophobia. This is a fear of being in closed places.

(a) What is a phobia?

_____

_____

(b) Which people have agoraphobia?

_____

_____

(c) Which people have claustrophobia?

_____

_____

Object Relative Pronouns: Form and Use

Noun	Object	Subject	Verb	Rest of Main Clause
The lady	**whom**	I	**saw**	smiled.
	who	I	**saw**	
	that	I	**saw**	
		I	**saw**	
The road	**which**	Dave	**took**	was a shortcut.
	that	Dave	**took**	
		Dave	**took**	

- When the relative pronoun **whom, who, that** or **which** is followed by a noun or pronoun, the relative pronoun acts as the object of the relative clause. It is an object relative pronoun.

- An object relative pronoun takes the place of the object of the relative clause. The object is not repeated after the verb. We cannot say, **The lady who I saw her smiled.* (INCORRECT)

- Object relative pronouns are often omitted, but subject relative pronouns are not omitted in most cases:

    The lady **I saw** smiled.
    The lady **who saw me** smiled.

- In object relative clauses, **that** is used more often than **who, whom,** and **which:**

    The lady **that I saw** smiled.
    The road **that we took** was a shortcut.

- The form with the object relative pronoun omitted is the most common of all:

    The lady **I saw** smiled.
    The road **we took** was a shortcut.

- **Whom** is used in formal written and spoken English.

⇒ Exercise 8: Working on Object Relative Pronouns

Work in small groups. Imagine you're visiting your eighty-year-old aunt who is showing you family photos and souvenirs. Combine the two sentences with a restrictive relative clause. Give all possible forms by using *who, that, which,* or omitting the object relative pronoun.

1. Let's look at some things. I've saved them for a long time.

    Example: *Let's look at some things that I've saved for a long time.*
    Let's look at some things which I've saved for a long time.
    Let's look at some things I've saved for a long time.

2. This is a trunk. Your grandmother used it when she traveled.

3. Here's the dress. I wore it to my wedding.

4. I'll never forget the guests. I invited them to my wedding.

5. A cousin spilled wine all over my wedding dress. I didn't even know him.

6. A trophy is on the shelf. Your father won it in high school.

7. A picture is in this box. I drew it seventy years ago.

8. I remember a high school teacher. I liked her very much.

9. Here is a poem. I wrote it in her class.

10. A dog is in the picture. I loved the dog so much.

11. A lot of letters are in this envelope. Your father wrote them in college.

12. Here are some gold coins. My father gave them to me seventy-five years ago.

⏭ Exercise 9: Asking and Answering Questions with Object Relative Pronouns

Work with a partner. Take turns asking and answering *what* or *who* questions. Use relative clauses with object relative pronouns and the words in parentheses.

1. (the person/you call most often)

   A: *Who is the person that you call most often?*
   B: *My sister is the person that I call most often.* OR
   The person that I call most often is my sister.

2. (a game/you liked to play as a child)

   A: *What is a game that you liked to play as a child?*
   B: *Hide and Seek is a game that I liked to play as a child.*

3. (the relative/you resemble most)

4. (a friend/you will never forget)

5. (the person/you call when you're in trouble)

6. (a possession/you can't live without)

7. (a restaurant/you recommend)

8. (a teacher/you will always remember)

9. (a book/you like to read over and over again)

10. (a food/you have never tasted)

➡ Exercise 10: Adding Necessary Information

Work on your own. Add a restrictive relative clause that has necessary information to complete the meaning of each sentence. Use subject or object relative pronouns, or no relative pronoun wherever appropriate.

1. I know a man _who owns three horses._

2. My neighbor is a person _whom I can trust._ OR
   who I can trust. OR
   I can trust.

3. I once had a teacher_____

4. I'm taking a course _____

5. I'd like a job _____

6. Some day I'm going to live in a house_____
   _____

7. I shop in stores _____

8. I have a friend _____

9. I live in a neighborhood _____

10. My father is someone _____

➡ Exercise 11: Explaining Your Ideas

Write two sentences that give your opinion about the items in parentheses. Begin one sentence with *I like…* and the other sentence with *I don't like….* Use restrictive relative clauses with subject or object relative pronouns in each sentence.

1. (cars) _I like cars that are dependable in the winter._
   I don't like cars that you have to fix frequently.

2. (teachers)_____
   _____

3. (clothes)_____
   _____

4. (newspapers)_____

_____

5. (friends) _____

_____

6. (TV shows) _____

_____

7. (meals) _____

_____

8. (music) _____

_____

⫸ Exercise 12: Giving Explanations

Work in small groups. Use the words in parentheses to make predictions about life fifty years from now. Use a restrictive relative clause with a subject or object relative pronoun to explain your prediction.

1. (houses)

   Example: *There will be many houses that use only solar energy.*

2. (computers)

   Example: *We'll have powerful computers that we can carry in our pockets.*

3. (robots)

4. (airplanes)

5. (space stations)

6. (medicines)

7. (telephones)

8. (televisions)

9. (cars)

10. (⌇⌇⌇⌇)

Object Relative Pronouns with Prepositions: Form and Use

Noun	Object	Subject	Verb	Preposition	Rest of Main Clause
The girl	**whom**	I	**spoke**	**to**	is my sister.
	who	I	**spoke**	**to**	
	that	I	**spoke**	**to**	
		I	**spoke**	**to**	
The car	**which**	we	**rode**	**in**	is old.
	that	we	**rode**	**in**	
		we	**rode**	**in**	

- **Whom, who, that,** or **which** can be the object of a restrictive relative clause that ends in a preposition. These object relative pronouns can be omitted.
- In informal English, the preposition is at the end of the object relative clause.

Noun	Preposition	Object	Subject	Verb	Rest of Main Clause
The girl	**to**	**whom**	**I**	**spoke**	is my sister.
The car	**in**	**which**	**we**	**rode**	is old.

- In more formal English, a preposition can begin a relative clause. The preposition is followed by either **whom** for people or **which** for things, but it cannot be followed by **that. Whom** and **which** are never omitted after prepositions.

An award ceremony:

Ladies and gentlemen, the person **to whom I'm going to award this honor** has been working here for many years.

⟩ ## Exercise 13: Working on Object Relative Pronouns with Prepositions

Work in small groups. Read the following situations in which you have to distinguish between similar people or things. Use restrictive relative clauses with prepositions to make the appropriate distinction.

1. Bill is friends with two of his neighbors. He needs to ask one of them to water his plants while he's away. He works with one of them, but he doesn't work with the other one:

   He decides to ask the person ___that he works with.___ OR

   He decides to ask the person ___he works with.___

2. Your friend borrowed two cassettes from the library. She listened to one of them last night and she listened to the other one this morning:

   She decided to return the one _which she listened to last night._

3. Martha and John are in a store looking for a new desk chair. Martha is sitting on one of them and John is sitting on another one.

   A salesman recommends the one _which Martha is sitting on_

4. Anna has called her doctor's office twice this week. She spoke to one nurse on Tuesday and another nurse on Wednesday.

   Today she asked for the nurse _whom she spoke on Tuesday._

5. Two movies are playing nearby. Martin has heard about one of them, but he hasn't heard about the other one. He decides to see the movie _which he has heard_

   _____

6. You know that your friend was born in one small town but that she grew up in a different small town. You ask her the name of the town _which she grew up_

   _____

▶ **Exercise 14: Introducing New Information**

Work in small groups. The following sentences are not appropriate for introducing a new topic into a conversation because they don't have enough specific information about the noun that is introduced. Use the information in parentheses to add a relative clause with a preposition to each sentence.

1. A man called me last night.

   (My sister works with him.)

   Examples: *A man who my sister works with called me last night.* OR
   A man that my sister works with called me last night. OR
   A man my sister works with called me last night.

   (I always talk to him at the supermarket.)

   (I went to high school with him.)

   (I used to live next door to him.)

2. The movie was great.

   (We went to the movie last night.)

   (You told us about the movie.)

   (Many people have disapproved of it.)

   (You reported on it in class.)

3. Do you know the doctor?

   (John lives across from him.)

   (Eva fell in love with him.)

   (Joan is married to him.)

   (I was waiting for him.)

4. Have you read the book?

   (The whole class is interested in it.)

   (The teacher looked for it last week.)

   (Julie wrote about it.)

   (I brought in the book.)

5. Today we're going to read the story.

   (We heard a lot about it.)

   (You listened to it in the lab.)

   (I was working on it.)

   (Many people argue over it.)

⮕ Exercise 15: Asking Questions About Shared Information

Work on your own. Imagine you're a detective who is trying to find out more about a woman named Anna. You're interviewing her maid, who knows a lot about her. Using the information from the notes below, make up questions with *Do you know...?* and a relative clause with a preposition.

Notes About Anna

1. writes to someone every day
2. listens to music every evening
3. interested in sports
4. speaks to someone at midnight
5. was born in a small town
6. grew up in a big city
7. talks about a man a lot
8. waiting for someone right now
9. goes to a doctor once a week
10. works with someone occasionally

1. Do you know the person she writes to every day?

2. _____

3. _____

4. _____

5. _____

6. _____

7. _____

8. _____

9. _____

10. _____

Possessive Relative Pronouns: Form and Use

Noun	Possessive	Subject	Verb	Rest of Main Clause
The man	**whose**	**daughter**	**left**	called me.

- The relative pronoun **whose** shows possession. **Whose** is always followed by a noun that is the subject or object of the restrictive relative clause.

Noun	Possessive	Object	Subject	Verb	Rest of Main Clause
The man	**whose**	**book**	I	**borrowed**	is here.
The man	**whose**	**sister**	I	**spoke to**	is here.

- Like other relative pronouns, **whose** follows a noun in the main clause.
- The noun after **whose** belongs to or is related to the person in the main clause.
- **Whose** cannot be omitted.
- Relative clauses with **whose** usually refer back to people or animals, but sometimes they refer to things:

  The car **whose gas tank leaks** is at the repair shop.

⊪➡ Exercise 16: Working on Possessive Relative Pronoun Forms

Work on your own. Imagine your cousin has come to visit you for the first time. You are walking around town and pointing out all of the different people and things that you've told your cousin about. Combine each sentence pair by adding a possessive relative clause that explains the noun that you've introduced in the first sentence.

1. There's the man. His wife knows your mother.

   There's the man whose wife knows your mother.

2. The doctor lives there. His daughter wants to meet you.

   _____

3. A woman owns this store. I work with her son.

   _____

4. I know the family. Their house burned down right here.

   _____

5. This is the factory. Its furnace exploded.

_____

6. That's the man. My family rented his house last summer.

_____

7. You're looking at an apartment building. Its residents are all rich and famous.

_____

8. The man helped me find my apartment. His beard is white.

_____

9. The guy is crossing the street. I saved his life.

_____

10. That's the school. Its teachers are on strike.

_____

⟹ Exercise 17: Identifying People with *Who* and *Whose*

1. Bring in a picture of your family. Work with a partner. Identify the people in the picture for your partner. Use relative clauses with subject, object, object with preposition, or possessive relative pronouns.

> Examples: *The person who is wearing glasses is my father.*
> *The person who I'm standing next to is my mother.*
> *The person whose front teeth are missing is my little sister.*

2. Imagine that it's a special holiday and many of your relatives are celebrating together at dinner. Write a description that identifies everyone, using relative clauses. Begin your essay with:

Imagine that many of my relatives have gathered together to celebrate.

The man who.... The woman whose....

⟹ Exercise 18: Comparing Relative Pronouns

Work with a partner. Complete the following sentences with *who, whom, that, which, whose* or no relative pronoun where appropriate. If more than one answer is possible, list all of the possibilities.

1. The man _____*who*_____ I spoke to is in the next room. OR

   The man _____*that*_____ I spoke to is in the next room. OR

   The man _____ I spoke to is in the next room.

2. People _____ birthdays are between June 1 and July 30 may register on Monday.

3. Applications _____ are received after the deadline will be returned.

4. The individual _____ is responsible for this crime will be punished.

5. Please show me the book in _____ you found this material.

6. Anyone _____ wants to leave early needs permission.

7. Software _____ translates from Arabic to English is available.

8. The man _____ she is engaged to works here.

9. Do you know the person _____ wallet I found?

10. Please contact anyone with _____ she spoke.

11. People _____ need assistance should call 555-0909.

12. There are several problems _____ continue to trouble us at this time.

13. The student _____ she went out with left his coat.

14. Anyone _____ checks haven't cleared the bank should notify us immediately.

Nonrestrictive Relative Clauses: Form

Noun	Subject	Verb	(...)	Rest of Main Clause
My mother,	who	lives	next door,	is a widow.
Her ring,	which	fell	on the floor,	got scratched.

Noun	Object	Subject	Verb	Preposition	Rest of Main Clause
Lee,	whom	I	remembered,		didn't remember me.
Paris,	which	we	drove	through,	is beautiful.

Noun	Preposition	Object	Subject	Verb	Rest of Main Clause
Paris,	through	which	we	drove,	is beautiful.

Noun	Possessive	Subject	Verb	(...)	Rest of Main Clause
Julia,	**whose**	**husband**	**is**	**a teacher,**	is an architect.

Noun	Possessive	Object	Subject	Verb	Rest of Main Clause
My dad,	**whose**	**car**	**I**	**borrowed,**	is out of town.

- Nonrestrictive relative clauses begin with the relative pronouns **who, whom, which,** or **whose.** The relative pronoun immediately follows the noun in the main clause that it refers to.
- Commas are used before and after a nonrestrictive relative clause.
- **Who, whom, which,** and **whose + noun** function as subjects and objects of nonrestrictive relative clauses. **That** is not used in nonrestrictive relative clauses.
- Relative pronouns are never omitted in nonrestrictive relative clauses.
- Prepositions can go before **whom** and **which** in nonrestrictive relative clauses, but this is much more formal.

⮞ **Exercise 19: Working on Form**

Work with a partner. Add a nonrestrictive relative clause that gives extra information about the topic of each sentence.

1. Shakespeare, _who lived in the sixteenth century_____,

   is considered to be the world's greatest playwright.

2. Plato, _____,

   was the author of *The Republic*.

3. Indonesia, _____,

   is actually a group of islands.

4. Paris,_____,

   has a population of over two million.

5. Abraham Lincoln,_____,

   freed the slaves.

6. The Himalayas,_____,

   are the highest mountains in the world.

7. The Taj Mahal, _____,

   is a famous example of Islamic architecture.

8. Galileo,_____,

   built the first astronomical telescope.

9. Pagodas,_____,

   are used as Buddhist shrines and tombs.

10. Saturn, _____,

   has rings around it.

⇒ Exercise 20: Adding Information

Work with a partner. Write a sentence about specific persons, places, or things. Ask your partner to add a nonrestrictive relative clause to it.

1. **A:** _Calcium is necessary for strong teeth and bones._

   B: _Calcium, which is a mineral, is necessary for strong teeth and bones._

2. **A:** _____

   B: _____

   _____

3. **A:** _____

   B: _____

   _____

Nonrestrictive Relative Clauses: Meaning and Use

ADDING EXTRA INFORMATION

1. A nonrestrictive relative clause adds extra information about the noun that it modifies. This information can be omitted because it doesn't restrict or limit the identity of the noun, and it isn't necessary to the meaning of the sentence. Compare these sentences:

My son Scott, **who is three,** gets into a lot of mischief.
My son Scott gets into a lot of mischief.

The relative clause **who is three** is extra information about Scott. Without this information, the sentence is still meaningful.

2. Nonrestrictive relative clauses often modify nouns that name people and places and add extra information about these nouns that are already unique. (Restrictive relative clauses never modify names of people and places):

Boston, **which is in Massachusetts,** has many colleges and universities.
Jenny, **who is almost ten,** is in the fourth grade.

3. Nonrestrictive relative clauses are more common in writing than in speaking. In writing, there is more time to go back and combine sentences. When nonrestrictive relative clauses are used in speaking, there are pauses before and after them, since commas cannot be used.

CONVERSATION NOTE

In informal conversation, you often don't have the time to plan ahead to form a nonrestrictive relative clause. There are other ways to add extra information to a sentence. For example, pronouns are frequently repeated instead of using a relative clause:

A mother is talking about her son:

My son Scott — **he's three** — **he** gets into a lot of mischief.

➡ Exercise 21: Adding Extra Information

Work on your own to complete each sentence. For numbers 1–6, complete each main clause and then add more information with a nonrestrictive relative clause at the end of the sentence. For numbers 7–12, first add a nonrestrictive relative clause and then complete the main clause.

1. I've read about _____ the trash problem _____ , which ___ is not going ___
   ___ to be solved soon. ___

2. I come from _____ , which _____

3. I once visited _____ , which_____

4. I've never met _____ , who _____

5. I'd like to meet _____ , who _____

6. I'm worried about _____ , who_____

7. My mother, who lives in Florida, retired a few years ago.

8. My best friend, who _____,

   _____

9. My birthday, which _____,

   _____

10. My home, which _____,

    _____

11. My parents, whose _____,

    _____

12. My relatives, who _____,

    _____

➠ **Exercise 22: Choosing Restrictive or Nonrestrictive Relative Clauses**

Work with a partner. Read each situation and the following sentence with a relative clause. Decide whether the relative clause should be restrictive or nonrestrictive. Write *restrictive* or *nonrestrictive* and add commas for nonrestrictive relative clauses.

1. My parents moved to Florida a few years ago. They used to live in New York City:

   My parents **,** who used to live in New York City **,** moved to Florida a few years ago.
   nonrestrictive

2. I have two aunts on my mother's side. I visited one of them last year. I visited the other one recently. One of them came to stay with me:

   My aunt who I visited last year came to stay with me. _____

3. We live in the south. It's very warm and humid here:

   We live in the south which is very warm and humid. _____

4. My father retired from his job five years ago. His favorite sport is golf:

   My father whose favorite sport is golf retired from his job five years ago. _____

5. My dentist has several dental hygienists. I can't remember their names. The same one always cleans my teeth. A different one cleans my daughter's teeth:

   The dental hygienist who cleans my teeth doesn't clean my daughter's teeth. _____

6. My neighbor is talking about her three sons. One of her sons is in the second grade, one is in the fourth grade, and one is a sophomore in high school:

   Her son who is in the second grade really loves school this year. _____

7. You've invited your friend Jane to dinner. You've also invited your friend Tina. Jane and Tina met a long time ago. You tell this to Tina:

   I've invited my friend Jane Welch who you met a long time ago. _____

8. A newspaper article describes pollution:

   Pollution which is still a major problem was a political issue in the last presidential

   election. _____

▮▶ **Exercise 23: Thinking About Meaning**

Work on your own. Read each sentence and the statements below it. Mark each statement true (T) or false (F). Be prepared to discuss your answers.

1. My brother, who I resemble, lives in Dallas.

   __F__ (a) I live in Dallas.

   __T__ (b) I resemble my brother.

2. The man whose son is ill called the doctor.

   _____ (a) The man is ill.

   _____ (b) The man has a son.

3. The man my sister works with owns a Mercedes.

   _____ (a) My sister owns a Mercedes.

   _____ (b) My sister works with a Mercedes.

4. I spoke to my brother, who is very worried about something.

   _____ (a) I have a brother.

   _____ (b) I am very worried about something.

5. The explosion, which injured twenty people, happened at about 11:00 P.M.

   _____ (a) There were many explosions last night.

   _____ (b) The explosion injured twenty people.

6. My son who talked to Mary resembles John.

   _____ (a) I have more than one son.

   _____ (b) Mary resembles John.

7. The person whose wallet is missing should report to the office.

    _____ (a) Several people have lost their wallets.

    _____ (b) A wallet is missing.

8. The man who looked at my car was very old.

    _____ (a) My car was very old.

    _____ (b) A man looked at my car.

Summary

Restrictive Relative Clauses: Form

Subject Relative Pronouns:	I saw the girl **who left.**
	I saw the girl **that left.**
	I saw the car **which was blue.**
	I saw the car **that was blue.**
Object Relative Pronouns:	I know the man **who you called.**
	I know the man **whom you called.**
	I know the man **that you called.**
	I know the man **you called.**
	I ate the fruit **which we bought.**
	I ate the fruit **that we bought.**
	I ate the fruit **we bought.**
Object Relative Pronouns with Prepositions:	I know the man **whom you spoke to.**
	I know the man **who you spoke to.**
	I know the man **that you spoke to.**
	I know the man **you spoke to.**
	Those are the chairs **which they sat on.**
	Those are the chairs **that they sat on.**
	Those are the chairs **they sat on.**
Possessive Relative Pronouns:	I saw the girl **whose dog is lost.**
	I know the man **whose wallet I found.**
	I called the woman **whose house I looked at.**

Restrictive Relative Clauses: Meaning and Use

A restrictive relative clause restricts the meaning of the main clause noun that it modifies by giving necessary information to identify that noun.

Combining Sentences:	We walked down the steps **that led to the basement.**
Identification:	Isaac Newton was the scientist **who discovered the law of gravity.**
Definitions:	A tax is a sum of money **that people and businesses pay to a government.**
Summaries:	This story is about a child **whose dreams came true.**
Classification:	My father is someone **who likes to read mysteries.**
Explanations:	In the future, there will be many houses **that will use only solar energy.**
New Information:	A guy **I work with** won the lottery.
Shared Information:	The cheese **you bought yesterday** is spoiled.

Nonrestrictive Relative Clauses: Form

Subject Relative Pronouns:	My son, **who is three,** loves milk.
	The car, **which is broken,** is very old.
Object Relative Pronouns:	Helen, **who I took home,** was sick.
	Helen, **whom I took home,** was sick.
	Ohio, **which I visited last year,** is flat.
Object Relative Pronouns with Prepositions:	My mother, **whom I talk to on Saturdays,** lives in Florida.
	My mother, **who I talk to on Saturdays,** lives in Florida.
Possessive Relative Pronouns:	Sam, **whose car broke down,** wanted a ride.
	Bill, **whose apartment I stayed in,** is also a student.

Nonrestrictive Relative Clauses: Meaning and Use

A nonrestrictive relative clause gives extra information about the main clause noun that it modifies. This information does not restrict or limit the identity of the noun, and can be omitted.

Extra Information:	Paris, **which is the capital of France,** has a population of two million.

⟹ **Summary Exercise: Finding Errors**

Most of the sentences below have an error in form, meaning, or use. Find each error and correct it.

1. I know the man ~~who his~~ daughter is blind.   *whose*

2. Here's the receipt they gave me at the supermarket.

3. The book which I took it doesn't have the answer.

4. The people who is waiting should leave first.

5. The building in which she works in is very new.

6. There's the man whose I know his mother.

7. I don't remember the people who they came late.

8. Can you remember the story that I told you last week?

9. I spoke to the man he is very friendly.

10. My friend, which I met in college, called me yesterday.

11. This is the only thing what he could do.

12. Kim who is thirteen years old swims very well.

13. We can probably replace the key who is lost.

14. The house, which I lived in it for two years, was really beautiful.

15. The students with that I work are very friendly.

16. I'd like to own the car which is parked over there.

CHAPTER

Count and Noncount Nouns

Preview

Signs:

> BEWARE OF **THE DOG**
>
> PLEASE TAKE **A TICKET**
>
> CLOSED UNTIL **AUGUST** 15

An ad:

> FOR SALE: **1 bicycle, 2 pairs of skis, gardening equipment.** For **information,**
> call **Jane** at 231-9080.

There are different kinds of nouns in English. Nouns such as **August** and **Jane** are called proper nouns. Proper nouns are names and they always begin with capital letters. They usually don't occur with the articles **a** or **an, the,** or with such words as **some, several, my,** or **this.** These words are called determiners. (Look at page 492 for a list of proper nouns that are used with **the.**)

Nouns such as **dog, ticket, bicycle, equipment,** and **information** are called common nouns. Unlike proper nouns, common nouns may occur with articles and other determiners that are used to identify, classify, and quantify common nouns (for example, **the dog, a ticket, some information**).

Do you know why we can say a *ticket,* but we can't say *an information* in English? The reason is that common nouns are generally classified according to whether we can count them or not. **Ticket** is a count noun because we can count tickets (**one ticket, two tickets**); **information** is a noncount noun because we cannot count it in this way.

In this chapter you will learn about the features and uses of count and noncount nouns to help you understand how they are used in English sentences.

Count Nouns: Form

FEATURES OF COUNT NOUNS

Singular	Plural
an onion **a** man	onion**s** **men**
one onion **one** man	**two** onions **two men**
	a few onions **a few men**
	several onions **several men**
	some onions **some men**

- Count nouns have both singular and plural forms. They can occur with **a** or **an**, or a number (**one, two, three...**) because we can count them.
- Plural count nouns are used with plural verbs and they can be replaced with plural pronouns:

  Your **ideas are** very interesting. Why don't you write **them** down?

- Plural count nouns can occur alone without a determiner, or with certain plural determiners such as **a few** and **several**:

  Onions are cheap.
  I bought **a few onions**.

- **Some** can precede plural count nouns:

  I bought **some onions**.
  I bought **several onions**.

- There are both regular and irregular plural count nouns.

REGULAR COUNT NOUNS

Singular	Plural
lemon	lemon**s**
egg	egg**s**
list	list**s**
cake	cake**s**
orange	orange**s**
idea	idea**s**
glass	glass**es**
dish	dish**es**
sandwich	sandwich**es**
box	box**es**

- Count nouns that add **-s** or **-es** to the singular form are regular plural nouns.
- The spelling and pronunciation rules for these plural endings are the same as the rules for adding **-s** and **-es** to third-person singular verbs in the simple present. Look at pages 483–484 for spelling and pronunciation rules for nouns ending in **-s** and **-es**.
- Do you know the plural forms for **tomato, piano, leaf, wife, city,** and **monkey?** (Look at page 483 for the spelling rules for adding **-s** or **-es** to nouns ending in **o, f** or **fe,** and **y.**)

IRREGULAR COUNT NOUNS

Singular	Plural
man	**men**
woman	**women**
child	**children**
person	**people**
foot	**feet**
tooth	**teeth**
mouse	**mice**
goose	**geese**
ox	**oxen**

- Count nouns that have special plural forms are irregular plural nouns:

  The goose is flying south. **The geese** are flying south.

Singular	Plural
deer	**deer**
fish	**fish**
sheep	**sheep**
series	**series**
species	**species**

- Some irregular nouns have the same singular and plural forms:

  A sheep is eating grass. **Two sheep** are eating grass.
  This species is interesting. **These species** are interesting.

Singular	Plural
(no forms)	**police** **cattle**

- Some irregular nouns don't have singular forms and always take plural verbs:

  The **police** are on the way.
  The **cattle** are in the barn.

(continued)

Singular	Plural
(no forms)	**clothes** **belongings** **congratulations** **goods** **groceries** **tropics**

- Some nouns ending in **-s** or **-es** are always plural. They have no singular forms at all:

  Could you please pick up your **clothes** and put **them** away?

Singular	Plural
(no forms)	**jeans** **pants** **shorts** **trousers** **pajamas** **glasses** **scissors** **tongs**

- Some irregular plural nouns ending in **-s** or **-es** are the names of things that only come in pairs:

  The **scissors** are missing. Who took **them**?

CONVERSATION NOTE

When pronouncing the word **women,** the first syllable rhymes with *swim.*

⫘➡ **Exercise 1: Working on Form**

Work in a large group. Start a plural chain as follows: Person A starts with a sentence and completes it with a plural count noun beginning with the letter *a*. Person B repeats the sentence, adding a plural count noun beginning with the letter *b*. Person C continues by adding a plural count noun that starts with *c*, and so on. Continue until the sentence gets too long to remember, or you reach the end of the alphabet.

1. I went grocery shopping and I bought…

    A: *I went grocery shopping and I bought apples.*
    B: *I went grocery shopping and I bought apples and bananas.*
    C: *I went grocery shopping and I bought apples, bananas, and carrots….*

2. I went to the zoo and I saw….

3. I went to the doctor and I saw….

4. I went to a department store and I bought….

Noncount Nouns: Form

Singular	No Plural Form
pollution	
information	
patience	

- Noncount nouns cannot be counted. Therefore, they cannot occur with **a** or **an** or a number. We can't say, *a pollution* or *two pollutions*. (INCORRECT)

- Noncount nouns can occur without a determiner:

  Pollution is a serious problem.

- Noncount nouns don't have plural forms. They're always singular. They only occur with singular verbs:

  All of the **information is** helpful.

- Noncount nouns occur alone or with certain expressions of quantity such as **a little, little, a great deal of, a lot of, not…much, how much**:

  I **don't** have **much time** and I have very **little patience** left.

- Some noncount nouns end in **-s**, such as **news, athletics, gymnastics, politics, linguistics, mathematics,** and **physics.** They are always singular and take singular verbs:

  Mathematics is my favorite subject.

⇒ Exercise 2: Choosing Singular or Plural Forms

Work with a partner. Underline the appropriate singular or plural verb form, noun, or pronoun in parentheses.

May 3

Dear Johanna,

I'm writing to tell you about Lynn's condition so you can decide whether or not you should come while she is still in the hospital. Frankly, the news (is/are) not good. I'm afraid that her health (is/are) not improving very much. Her progress (is/are) very slow, but fortunately her spirits (is/are) still high. She is very friendly with the women who (is/are) in the room next to hers. She spends a lot of time talking to (her/them), and she reads a lot too. She broke her glasses on Friday, but she's managing well without (it/them). I ordered an extra pair for her, and (it/they) should be ready soon.

If you come, you'll probably want to go directly to the hospital. Don't worry about your belongings—you can leave (it/them) in my car until the evening. To save time, don't check your luggage. Take (it/them) with you on the plane and store (it/them) under your seat. Most of your stuff will probably fit by your (foot/feet), but if (it/they) (doesn't/don't), you can use the overhead compartment. After your plane arrives, if the traffic (is/are) light, it'll only take fifteen minutes to get to the hospital from the airport by taxi.

If you want more information about Lynn's condition, you can probably get (it/them) from the doctor when you come. He doesn't offer a lot of details unless you ask for (it/them). His advice (is/are) usually helpful, however. Most important, I appreciate his honesty. I'm sure you'll appreciate (it/them) too, even if the information (is/are) not always optimistic.

Call to let me know about your plans. Take care.

Love,
Maria

P.S. Bring your jeans. You'll need (it/them) when I take you for a long, refreshing hike in the woods. You'll need the fresh air after a day or two in the hospital!

Focus on Vocabulary

COMMON NONCOUNT NOUNS

The common noncount nouns in English tend to fall into these groups based on their meaning:

Solids

bread, meat, spaghetti, pasta, butter, margarine, cheese, ice cream, cotton, wool, silk, nylon, polyester, iron, coal, copper, glass, wood, chalk, soap, detergent, thread, string, rope

Liquids

gasoline, oil, vinegar, water, milk, juice, honey, cream, shampoo, lotion, blood

Gases

air, oxygen, hydrogen, smoke, pollution, smog, steam

Grains and Powders

rice, cereal, flour, wheat, corn, sugar, salt, pepper, dust

Category Names (general classes of objects)

mail, jewelry, money, furniture, food, fruit, clothing, luggage, baggage, transportation, junk, stuff, trash

Abstract Nouns

love, hate, honesty, patience, crime, beauty, unemployment, health, information, advice, help, behavior, permission, work, fun, experience, news, homework, insurance, progress

Fields of Study and Languages

biology, linguistics, engineering, mathematics, physics, Spanish, Indonesian, Turkish

Weather

weather, rain, snow, sleet, hail, ice, wind, fog, thunder, lightning, sunshine, humidity

Gerunds

shopping, camping, walking, jogging, running, skating, skiing, swimming
(Gerunds are discussed in Chapter 14.)

➥ Exercise 3: Distinguishing Count and Noncount Nouns

Work with a partner. Read these student announcements on a bulletin board. Underline all the common nouns. Then look at how each noun is used in the sentence and mark it as count (C) or noncount (NC).

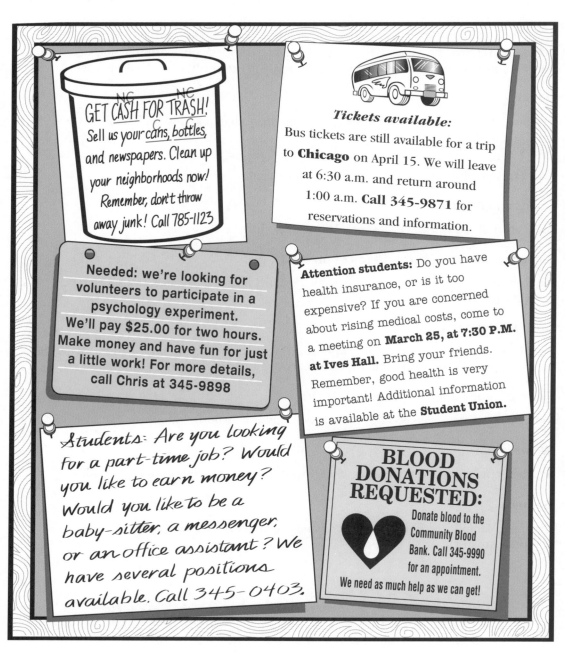

GET CASH FOR TRASH!
NC   NC
Sell us your cans, bottles,
                C
and newspapers. Clean up
your neighborhoods now!
Remember, don't throw
away junk! Call 785-1123

Tickets available:
Bus tickets are still available for a trip
to **Chicago** on April 15. We will leave
at 6:30 a.m. and return around
1:00 a.m. **Call 345-9871** for
reservations and information.

Needed: we're looking for
volunteers to participate in a
psychology experiment.
We'll pay $25.00 for two hours.
Make money and have fun for just
a little work! For more details,
call Chris at 345-9898

Attention students: Do you have
health insurance, or is it too
expensive? If you are concerned
about rising medical costs, come to
a meeting on **March 25, at 7:30 P.M.
at Ives Hall.** Bring your friends.
Remember, good health is very
important! Additional information
is available at the **Student Union.**

Students: Are you looking
for a part-time job? Would
you like to earn money?
Would you like to be a
baby-sitter, a messenger,
or an office assistant? We
have several positions
available. Call 345-0403.

**BLOOD
DONATIONS
REQUESTED:**
Donate blood to the
Community Blood
Bank. Call 345-9990
for an appointment.
We need as much help as we can get!

Count and Noncount Nouns: Meaning and Use

COUNT OR NONCOUNT?

1. When you say that a noun is used as a count noun or as a noncount noun, this means that you know something about the form of that noun in a sentence:

Plural Form: Does the noun have a plural form?

Verb Form: Is the noun used with a singular or a plural verb?

Determiners: Which determiners can be used with the noun?

No Determiner: Can the noun be used with no determiner?

2. Singular count nouns are always used with some type of determiner. But noncount nouns and plural count nouns can sometimes occur in sentences with no determiner at all:

Two roommates are making a shopping list:

Tom: What should I buy at the store?
Matt: We need **milk, eggs, bread, trash bags,** and **a mop.**

You can tell that **eggs** and **trash bags** are count nouns because they are plural nouns. If you know that **milk** and **bread** are singular nouns, then you know that they are noncount nouns, since they can occur without determiners.

3. Many nouns can be used as either count or noncount nouns, depending on the meaning that you want to express:

Noncount	Count
democracy	a democracy, democracies
wine	a wine, wines
cereal	a cereal, cereals
aspirin	an aspirin, aspirins
cake	a cake, cakes
coffee	a coffee, coffees
lamb	a lamb, lambs
Korean	a Korean, Koreans

(continued)

4. The noncount and count nouns above have different but related meanings. The noncount noun usually expresses a concept or a substance in general, while the count noun usually gives particular examples or types:

Concept and Example:	He left his country because he believes in **democracy** (a form of government). He wants to live in **a democracy**. (a specific country with a democratic government)
Substance and Variety:	We'd like to have **wine** (a type of drink) with dinner. Can you suggest **a wine**? (a specific variety of that drink)
Substance and Type:	We all eat **cereal** (a grain) for breakfast, but each one of us likes **a different cereal**. (a specific type or brand of cereal)
Substance and Dosage:	When you take **aspirin**, (a type of medicine) follow the recommended dosage. For example, if you are an adult, take **2 aspirins** (2 tablets of aspirin) every 4 hours.
Substance and Type:	I hope everyone likes **cake** (the dessert in general). I baked **two cakes** (two types of cake) for dessert.
Substance and Serving:	Customer: Where do I order **coffee**? (the drink) Cashier: Over there, by the counter. Customer: **Two coffees**, (two cups of coffee) please. Black. No sugar.
Substance and Source:	**Lamb** (the meat) comes from an animal called **a lamb**. (a specific animal)
Nationality and Language:	I know **a Korean** (a specific person) who speaks five languages in addition to **Korean**. (the language)

5. Sometimes the form of a noun in a sentence doesn't tell you whether the noun is count or noncount:

Please put **the equipment** on the table.

It's not clear from this sentence whether the noun **equipment** is count or noncount. This is because determiners like **some** or **the** can occur with both count and noncount nouns. Therefore, in these sentences, there are no clues to tell you if the noun is count or noncount. It's often helpful to consult a dictionary to find out whether a noun is generally considered to be count or noncount. (**Equipment** is listed as a noncount noun in the dictionary.)

Remember that a noun may be count in one situation *(I'll have a beer)* and noncount in another situation *(I like beer)*. Therefore, it's helpful to study the dictionary examples carefully to find out which use of the noun expresses a particular meaning.

⇒ Exercise 4: Distinguishing Count and Noncount Uses of Nouns

Each sentence below distinguishes between count and noncount uses of the same noun. Choose the correct answer from the words in parentheses. Use each answer once.

1. (wine, a wine) If you drink _____wine_____, you should try _____a wine_____ that comes from the local winery.

2. (hair, hairs) I have a few gray _____, but my _____ isn't gray.

3. (chocolate, chocolates) I don't know why I ate all of those _____. I really don't like _____ that much.

4. **A:** (beer, beers) Do you serve _____ here?
   B: Yes, in fact, we have several local _____.

5. (cheese, cheeses) Don't buy too much _____. The kids only eat certain _____, like Swiss cheese and cottage cheese.

6. (lamb, lambs) My daughter won't eat _____ because she says that it makes her think of all of the cute _____ in the pasture. I wonder if she's going to be a vegetarian.

7. (crime, a crime) Many of us never think seriously about _____ until _____ is committed in our neighborhood.

8. (coffee, coffees) We only ordered two _____ because he doesn't drink _____. He drinks tea.

9. (light, lights) There isn't enough _____ in this room. Let's hang up a few more _____.

10. (Indonesian, Indonesians) If you want to learn _____, I know some _____ who can probably help you.

➠ **Exercise 5: Understanding Ads**

1. Work on your own. Here are some items that are going to appear in an ad in the newspaper. Add *-s* or *-es* or the number *1* to the count nouns. Don't change the noncount nouns.

For Sale:

1 tricycle , plant s, lamp , farm equipment , computer game , book ,

magazine , furniture , clothing , toy , stroller , jewelry , dish ,

mattress , carpeting , bookshelf , computer , double bed

Call 455-1223 after 6 P.M.

2. Work with a partner. Do you have any belongings that you no longer need? Is there anything in your home that you would like to sell? Imagine that you and your partner are going to place an ad in the newspaper with five to ten items for sale. Write an ad, using the above ad as a model. Pay attention to the plural forms of the count nouns. Use a dictionary if necessary.

➠ **Exercise 6: Listing Items**

Work with a partner. List the items that you need to bring with you in the following situations. Use *a* or *an* with singular count nouns, and *some* or no determiner with plural count nouns and noncount nouns.

1. You're going to the grocery store. You need to bring _a shopping list, money, coupons, recycled plastic bags._

2. You're going to spend the day at the beach. You need to bring _____

3. You're going on an overnight camping trip. You need to bring _____

4. You're going to get a passport. You need to bring _____

5. You're going to play soccer (or another sport). You need to bring _____

6. You're going to spend the weekend at a friend's house. You need to bring _____

⵲⭢ **Exercise 7: Describing Concepts**

1. Work on your own. The passage below first describes the concept *smog* and then it gives two specific examples of smog. As you read the passage, underline the word *smog* along with any articles and adjectives that come before it. Then work with a partner to answer the questions.

> Smog is a form of air pollution. The term was first used in 1905 to describe the combination of *smoke* and *fog (sm + og)* that occasionally hung over London and other British cities.
>
> Today, smog also refers to a condition caused by the interaction of sunlight with exhaust gases from cars and factories. Heavy concentrations of smog are poisonous. In 1948, 20 people died and nearly 6,000 became ill from a photochemical smog in Pennsylvania. About 4,000 Londoners died as a result of a thick smog in 1952. Smog also destroys plant life and causes building material to deteriorate faster than usual.

1. How does the word *smog* appear when the concept is described in general?

   _____

2. Is it count or noncount?_____

3. How does the word *smog* appear when the specific examples are given? _____

   _____

4. Is it count or noncount?_____

5. How do you know?_____

   _____

2. This passage describes the concept *slang*. Underline the word *slang* each time it appears, along with any articles or adjectives that may come before it. Then answer the questions with your partner.

> Slang is an informal kind of language in which words and phrases are used in new and unusual ways. People use slang more often in speaking than in writing. They use it more often with friends than with strangers. Slang has a wide variety of uses. Many people use it because they want to seem fashionable and modern. Others use slang because it is frank and informal, it expresses friendliness, and it puts people at ease.

1. Write the different way(s) that *slang* is written here: _____

2. Is *slang* count or noncount?_____

3. How do you know?_____

_____

⬛➡ **Exercise 8: Categorizing Nouns**

Work with a partner. Read each group of related nouns in the chart on the next page and choose a general category from the list below. Write the category on the line. For items 7–10, write some examples of the general categories.

Categories

clothing

fruit

livestock

luggage

mail

money

Categories	Examples
1. _____mail_____	packages, letters, postcards
2. _____	dresses, shirts, blouses, ties, pants
3. _____	apples, oranges, bananas, grapes
4. _____	cows, horses, pigs, chickens
5. _____	suitcases, garment bags, duffel bags
6. _____	coins, bills, dollars
7. furniture:	sofas, chairs, _____tables_____, _____
8. transportation:	cars, buses, _____, _____
9. jewelry:	rings, bracelets, _____, _____
10. trash:	old newspapers, used bottles, _____,
	_____, _____

Summary

Count Nouns: Form

Singular:	**an apple, a banana, a box**
Regular Plural:	**apples, bananas, boxes**
	three apples, three bananas, three boxes
	several apples, several bananas, several boxes
Irregular Plural:	**women**
	sheep
	police
	clothes
	pants

Noncount Nouns: Form

Singular:	**patience**
	a little patience
	a lot of patience

Count and Noncount Nouns: Meaning and Use

Count nouns are items that can be counted. This means that they have a plural form. Noncount nouns are items that cannot be counted. They have no plural forms. Some nouns are used both as noncount nouns to indicate a concept or substance in general, and as count nouns to indicate particular examples or types.

Ads:	For sale: **three bicycles, two lawnmowers,** outdoor **furniture.**
Lists:	You'll need to bring **a bathing suit, a towel, sunscreen,** and **sunglasses.**
Concepts:	**Smog** is a combination of **smoke** and **fog.**
Substance:	We'd like to have **wine** with dinner.
Variety:	Could you suggest **a wine?**
Categories and Examples:	**Letters, postcards,** and **packages** are examples of **mail.**

⤷ Summary Exercise: Finding Errors

Most of the following sentences have an error in form, meaning, or appropriate use. Find each error and correct it.

1. In many families, husbands and ~~wifes~~ both work and share the child care responsibilities.   *wives*

2. There is a pollution in many cities around the world.

3. He's drinking coffee.

4. She gave me a good advice.

5. She brought notebook, pencils, and a pen.

6. His teeth is loose.

7. Oak tree fell down during the storm.

8. My glasses are missing. Did you see it in the living room?

9. Would you like to be computer programmer or engineer when you graduate?

10. He has a few blond hairs.

Quantity Expressions and Articles

A husband and wife are talking on the telephone:

> Wife: On your way home, could you pick up **a few onions** and **a pound of ground meat**?
> Husband: Sure. Anything else? How about **a loaf of bread** and **a quart of milk?**

Two students:

> Joe: Victor never locks his apartment.
> Mark: That's because he has **a dog.** If someone comes to **the door, the dog** barks.

Two co-workers:

> Linda: What's on **the menu** in **the cafeteria** today?
> Teresa: **Fish, rice,** and **vegetables. The fish** is overcooked, and so are **the rice**
>   and **the vegetables.**

General statement:

> **The giant panda** is endangered.

Definition:

> **A giant panda** is a black and white bear that lives in China.

Quantity expressions indicate a quantity or amount of the nouns they modify. Some quantity expressions such as **a few** are called general quantity expressions because they don't tell an exact amount. They only indicate whether the amount is large or small. Other quantity expressions, such as **a pound of, a quart of, a loaf of,** are called specific quantity expressions because they indicate a specific or exact amount.

Articles in English can be indefinite (**a/an** or no article) or definite (**the**). Indefinite articles classify a noun by introducing it as a member of a class or set of items (**fish, rice, vegetables, a dog**), not as one that has already been identified. Definite articles, on the other hand, identify nouns (**the fish, the rice, the vegetables**) based on assumptions about what information the speaker and listener share about the noun.

Both indefinite and definite articles are also used in general statements or definitions that generalize about a whole class or group of nouns.

General Quantity Expressions: Form

Count Nouns (Plural)		Noncount Nouns		Count and Noncount	
(not) many	books	**not much**	rain	**a lot of**	books/rain
too many		**too much**		**lots of**	
so many		**so much**		**plenty of**	
several		**a great deal of**		**some**	
quite a few		**quite a bit of**		**any**	
a few		**a little**		**not any**	
few		**little**		**no**	
very few		**very little**			

- Some general quantity expressions occur only with count nouns; others occur only with noncount nouns; and others can be used with both count and noncount nouns.

- **Many** is used with count nouns and **much** is used with noncount nouns to express a general quantity. **Many** and **much** are usually in phrases such as **how many, how much, too many, too much, so many, so much**:

  How many eggs did you use in this recipe? **How much salt?**
  There's **too much pepper** in it. Next time, don't use **so much pepper**.

- **Many** and **much** are also commonly used in negative sentences to express a general quantity:

  There is**n't much clothing** in the closets and there are**n't many books** on the shelves. We can pack everything up in a couple of hours.

- **Much** is common in questions and in negative sentences to express a general quantity, but it isn't used in affirmative statements. Use **a lot of** or **a great deal of** instead:

  I had **a lot of work** yesterday.
  *I had much work yesterday. (INCORRECT)

⟶ **Exercise 1: Working on Form**

Work with a partner. Take turns asking and answering questions about your hometown. In your questions, use *many* or *much* and the words in parentheses. In your answers, use *a lot of* or *a great deal of* for large quantities, *not many* or *not much* for small quantities, and *not any* or *no* for none.

1. (pollution)

    A: *Is there much pollution in Mexico City?*
    B: *Yes, there is. There's a great deal of pollution.* OR
    No, there isn't. There's not much pollution. OR
    No, there isn't. There's no pollution. OR
    No, there isn't. There is not any pollution at all.

2. (traffic)

3. (subways)

4. (taxicabs)

5. (crime)

6. (police)

7. (hospitals)

8. (cold weather)

9. (hurricanes)

10. (sunshine)

▶ Exercise 2: Asking and Answering Questions with *How Many?* and *How Much?*

Work with a partner. Imagine your partner took an advanced English course last semester. Take turns asking questions about the course with *how many* and *how much* and the words in parentheses. Check your verb agreement. Respond with appropriate short answers.

1. (classes per week)

   A: *How many classes per week are there?*
   B: *Five.*

2. (hours per class)

3. (weeks per semester)

4. (homework)

5. (students per class)

6. (exams)

7. (textbooks)

8. (writing)

9. (computer lab work)

10. (‿‿‿‿)

General Quantity Expressions: Meaning and Use

LARGE OR SMALL QUANTITIES

1. General quantity expressions are commonly used to indicate general quantities that are large or small:

Description: There are **several** movie theaters and **a few** good restaurants in this neighborhood.

Opinion: People spend **too little** time with their families these days.

2. **A few** and **few** are both used before plural count nouns to express small quantities. However, they don't have the same meaning. Their focus is different and depends on the point of view of the speaker. Compare these sentences:

> This machine is easy to use. You'll see when you read the directions. There are **a few** suggestions about how to use it.
> This machine is hard to use. You'll see when you read the directions. There are **few** suggestions about how to use it.

In the first sentence, **a few** refers to a small number of suggestions. The focus is on what exists. In the second one, **few** means that there are not enough suggestions. It expresses the idea that something is missing or there isn't enough. The focus is on what is absent.

3. Notice how the precise meaning of the general quantity expressions **few** and **a few** depends on the words they occur with. For example, if you are talking about having few problems, you usually don't mean that problems are missing or that there aren't enough. Rather, you just mean that the problems don't exist:

> We're lucky. We have **few** problems.
> We're unlucky. We have **a few** problems.

4. **A little** and **little** express the same differences in meaning as **a few** and **few**, but **a little** and **little** occur with noncount nouns:

> They're happy. They have **a little** money left.
> They're unhappy. They have **little** money left.

5. The general quantity expressions **very few** and **very little** are more common than **few** or **little**. **Not much** is often more idiomatic than **little**:

> He has **very little** money and **very few** friends.
> He **doesn't have much** money. (This is more common than *He has little money.*)

CONVERSATION NOTE

Lots of is more informal than **a lot of** or **a great deal of** to express a general quantity. It is used mostly in conversation:

If I had **lots of time,** I'd probably take piano lessons again.

⟹ **Exercise 3: Talking About Small General Quantities**

Work with a partner. Consider the meaning of each sentence and complete it with *a few, very few, a little,* or *very little.*

1. The students thought that the exam was too difficult. They complained that
   _____*very few*_____ people got high grades.

2. According to the police, this neighborhood is relatively safe. Fortunately, there are
   _____ crimes here.

3. Amy wants to do volunteer work. She's trying to fit it into her schedule on Thursday
   afternoon. She thinks she can probably work on Thursdays because she has
   _____ time in the afternoon.

4. You've interviewed a person for a job in your office. You want to hire him. You think that
   one of his previous jobs was good experience. You point this out to your colleagues:
   "He does have _____ experience."

5. **A:** I need _____ advice. Which refrigerator should I buy?
   B: I'd buy the one with the higher efficiency rating. I'm sure it uses _____
   electricity.

6. You're trying to teach your friend to drive. You think that he's not doing very well at all.
   He's making _____ progress. He needs much more help.

7. Your computer isn't working properly. You decide to call the help number listed in your
   manual. You call and say, "I'm having _____ problems with my computer.
   Can you help me?"

8. You're looking for an apartment. You find one that you like but it's quite small.
   There's _____ space for your belongings.

9. **A:** Why don't you come over sometime? It takes _____ time to get to my house on your way home from work. It's really very close.

   B: Sounds like a good idea to come after work. On the weekend, it's difficult because there are _____ buses. I think there are only one or two buses a day on Saturday and Sunday.

10. **A:** Do you like your car? We've been thinking of buying one like it.

    B: Yes. We like it a lot. We've really had _____ trouble with it. It has only needed a few minor adjustments, and it's been very dependable, even in the cold weather.

Focus on Vocabulary

GENERAL QUANTITY EXPRESSIONS

General quantity expressions describe large quantities, small quantities, or none at all.

Large Quantities	Small Quantities	None
a great deal of	not (too) much	not any
a lot of	not (too) many	no
quite a bit of	(only) a little	
quite a few	(only) a few	
plenty of	very little	
several	very few	

⟩ Exercise 4: Writing a Description

Complete this description of an ideal city. Choose from the general quantity expressions above.

In my ideal city, there are ___*not too many*___ people and there is _____ crime. There is _____ unemployment and there are _____ available jobs.

There is _____ public transportation; for example, _____ buses and _____ trains. Actually, there is _____ traffic because there are _____ taxicabs and there are _____ private automobiles in the downtown area.

My ideal city has _____ parks and museums, _____ restaurants, and _____ hotels. It has _____ tourists.

As for the climate, it has _____ sunshine, _____ rain, _____ snow, and _____ cold weather. It has _____ pollution.

My ideal city has _____ shopping malls. There are _____ department stores and _____ smaller shops. It has _____ skyscrapers, _____ apartment buildings, and _____ private homes.

My ideal city is a nice place to live and work. People have _____ fun there.

⇒ Exercise 5: Expressing Opinions

1. Work on your own. Choose one of the topics below and decide what you like and dislike about both items. Use *too many, not much, not many, so many, so much, very few, very little,* and *a lot of.* Make a chart like the one below, on a separate sheet of paper, of five to ten advantages and disadvantages of your topic.

Topics

big cities/small towns

big universities/small universities

warm climate/cool climate

apartment building/private home

BIG CITIES	
Advantages	**Disadvantages**
1. a lot of entertainment	1. too much noise
2. so many restaurants	2. too many people
SMALL TOWNS	
Advantages	**Disadvantages**
1. very little noise	1. very few theaters
2. not much traffic	2. not many restaurants

2. Exchange charts with a partner. Create eight to ten sentences from your partner's list of advantages and disadvantages of the topic.

Examples: *Big cities have a lot of entertainment.*
In small towns, there are very few theaters.

Specific Quantity Expressions: Form

Count	Noncount
a cup of beans	**a cup of** coffee
3 quarts of blueberries	**3 quarts of** oil
a pound of grapes	**a pound of** meat
2 containers of raisins	**2 containers of** yogurt
a bag of oranges	**a bag of** rice
1 box of paper clips	**1 box of** cereal
a package of mushrooms	**a package of** paper
a jar of olives	**a jar of** mustard
a can of beans	**a can of** soup
a carton of eggs	**a carton of** milk
a piece of a cookie	**a piece of** information
a bottle of pills	**a bottle of** olive oil
	a tube of toothpaste

- Noncount nouns cannot be counted, but they can be divided and measured. Both count and noncount nouns can be divided into different amounts with specific quantity expressions.
- Specific quantity expressions are followed by **of**.
- Containers (**a can, a box…**) and expressions of measurement (**a pound, an ounce…**) can be counted in expressions of quantity:

  1 **can of** soup
  2 **pounds of** rice

⟹ **Exercise 6: Working on Form**

Work with a partner. Look at the shopping list below and take turns telling your partner how much you're going to buy of each item. Use these specific quantity words: *box, package, bag, tube, container, jar, carton, pound, bottle, can, quart, roll.*

Example: *I'm going to buy a bag of apples, two cartons of eggs,…*

SHOPPING LIST

apples	spaghetti
eggs	cereal
peanut butter	napkins
orange juice	toilet paper
toothpaste	shampoo
crackers	tissues
yogurt	light bulbs
potatoes	vitamins
trash bags	tomato sauce
rice	salsa
flour	tortilla chips

Specific Quantity Expressions: Meaning and Use

MEASUREMENTS AND CONTAINERS

1. Specific quantity expressions indicate a certain amount of something. They are different from general quantity expressions such as *a great deal of*, which only tell whether the amount is large or small.

2. Certain nouns require special quantity expressions that are used only with that particular noun:

a loaf of bread (**2 loaves of** bread)
a head of lettuce
a bunch of carrots
        grapes
        celery
        bananas
a bar of soap

(continued)

3. A piece of is commonly used to express specific quantities of different kinds of nouns. **A piece of** is used with food nouns, objects and materials, and with abstract nouns:

Food:	**a piece of** cake
	meat
	bread
Objects and Materials:	**a piece of** wood
	furniture
	clothing
Abstract Nouns:	**a piece of** information
	advice
	news

4. To tell the specific price of an item, we say the price plus **a** plus the quantity:

$1.69 **a loaf**
49¢ **a pound**

Bread is a dollar sixty-nine **a loaf.**
Onions are forty-nine cents **a pound.**

⟹ **Exercise 7: Telling the Price**

Work with a partner. Read the ad from a local supermarket. Take turns asking and answering questions about the prices of the items. Use measurement and container expressions in your answers.

1. (milk) **A:** *How much is milk?*
    B: *It's ninety-nine cents a quart.*

2. (bananas) **A:** *How much are bananas?*
    B: *They're fifty-nine cents a pound.*

3. (grapes)

4. (lettuce)

5. (carrots)

6. (broccoli)

7. (tomatoes)

8. (ground beef)

9. (chicken)

10. (steak)

11. (crackers)

12. (soap)

13. (chocolate chip cookies)

14. (detergent)

15. (toilet paper)

16. (toothpaste)

17. (batteries)

18. (rice)

19. (spaghetti)

20. (salsa)

MILK 99¢/quart	**SWISS CHEESE** $4.89/lb.	**BANANAS** 59¢/lb.	**BROCCOLI** $1.59/lb.	**GRAPES** $1.69/lb.
YOGURT 79¢/container	8 oz. container	**CARROTS** 39¢/lb.	**LETTUCE** 99¢ head	**TOMATOES** $1.29/lb.
STEAK $4.29/lb.	**GROUND BEEF** $1.89/lb.	**POTATOES** 49¢/lb.	**SPAGHETTI** 79¢ box 12 oz. box	**CRACKERS** $1.99 box 16 oz. box
CHICKEN 99¢/lb.	**RICE** 69¢/lb.	**KIDNEY BEANS** 49¢/lb. 16 oz. can	**SALSA** $1.29 jar 12 oz. jar	**TORTILLA CHIPS** $1.98 bag 14 oz. bag
TOOTHPASTE $2.29 tube 8.2 oz. tube	**DISPOSABLE DIAPERS** $10.29 box 48 count	**DETERGENT** $4.49 bottle 128 oz.	**BATTERIES** $2.09 package 2 count	**ICE CREAM** $2.99 half gallon
TOILET PAPER $1.29 package 4 roll package	**SOAP** 79¢ bar bath size	**TISSUES** $1.69 box 250 count	**CHOCOLATE CHIP COOKIES** $2.19 package 12 oz.	

Indefinite and Definite Articles: Form

Singular Count	Plural Count	Noncount
a banana	bananas	water
an orange	oranges	
an hour	hours	
a hotel	hotels	

- The singular indefinite article is **a** or **an**.
- **An** is used before words that begin with a vowel sound; **a** occurs before all others.
- If a word begins with an *h,* the choice of **a** or **an** depends on whether or not the *h* is pronounced. **An** is used if the *h* is not pronounced. **A** is used if the initial *h* is pronounced:

an hour	**a** house
honor	hospital
honest person	human

- There is no article before indefinite plural count nouns or indefinite noncount nouns.

Singular Count	Plural Count	Noncount
the banana	**the** bananas	**the** water
the orange	**the** oranges	

- The definite article **the** is used before singular and plural count nouns and noncount nouns.
- Articles occur before nouns (**the orange**) or before an adjective + noun (**a large orange**).

⫸ **Exercise 8: Working on Form**

Read the passage and underline all of the common nouns with their articles and adjectives. Then classify the nouns as definite (D) or indefinite (I).

I

Have you ever eaten <u>coconut</u>? You probably have, but you may not be very familiar with coco palms. Coconuts come from coco palms, which are trees that grow in tropical regions. Coco palms are very unusual because all of the parts of the tree have a commercial value. For example, coconuts are an important food in tropical regions, and coconut milk, which comes from inside the coconut, is a nutritious drink. Coconut oil, the most valuable product of all, also comes from coconuts. Some of the other parts of the tree that are eaten include the buds and the young stems. Besides food, the tree is also used for manufacturing commercial products. The leaves are used for making fans and baskets, and the fibers from the husks and trunks are made into mats, cord, and rope. The hard shells and the husks are used to make fuel, and the trunks are used for timber. Finally, even the roots are used. They are chewed as a narcotic.

Indefinite and Definite Articles: Meaning and Use

INTRODUCING AND IDENTIFYING NOUNS

Articles are used to introduce and identify nouns. The choice of **a** or **an,** or **the** depends on whether the noun is count or noncount, and whether the listener knows which specific noun the speaker is talking about.

Indefinite Articles

1. The indefinite article **a** or **an** is used to introduce a noun that may be specific for the speaker, but not specific for the listener. The noun is new information for the listener:

Two friends are talking:

> Ann: What did you do last night?
> Bob: I watched **a movie.**

(Ann doesn't know which movie Bob watched. This is new information for her.)

2. Sometimes the noun isn't specific for the speaker and it isn't specific for the listener either:

A woman is talking to her husband about their son:

> Bobby needs **a new coat.**

(The woman can't identify a specific coat, and the husband can't either.)

Definite Articles

1. The use of the definite article **the** depends on how familiar the speaker thinks the listener is with the noun. Definite articles identify nouns based on assumptions about what information the speaker and listener share about these nouns.

(continued)

2. The listener can identify the noun if the noun was already mentioned in the conversation or the text. It is mentioned again with **the:**

A man is telling a friend about his lunch:

I ordered **a steak** and **a salad**. **The steak** was great but **the salad** was awful.

3. Notice that the exact words do not have to be repeated:

A woman is telling her friend about an accident:

A dog was hit by a car near my apartment. **The poor creature** howled in pain.

4. The listener can identify the noun if he or she can see the noun:

A family is eating dinner:

Mother: Watch out! Don't bump **the table**. You'll spill **the milk**.
Son: OK. Could you please pass **the rice?**

5. The listener can identify the noun from the situation or from general knowledge about objects and events:

A sign:

BEWARE OF **THE DOG**

(A person reading this sign makes an inference that a particular dog is behind the fence.)

Two friends are talking:

I went to an unusual wedding. **The bride** and **the groom** wore jogging clothes.

(The listener knows that a wedding has a bride and a groom.)

6. The listener can identify the noun if the listener and the speaker share general knowledge about their geographic location and social environment:

The mayor is going to be on television tonight.

(The listener assumes that this refers to the mayor of the speaker's particular city.)

Two co-workers in a law firm are at lunch:

Do you think that **the secretaries** make enough money?

(The listener assumes that this means the secretaries who work with them.)

7. Certain names of places and things that are very familiar to the speaker almost always take the definite article **the.** The listener may not know the specific identity of the noun but assumes that the speaker would tell which one if asked. Some examples are: **the store, the dentist, the doctor, the hospital, the movies, the post office, the bank, the park, the radio, the TV:**

> If you go to **the store,** could you buy some milk? And don't forget to turn off **the TV** before you go.

8. The listener can identify the noun if the noun is unique (there is only one):

> I took them to **the best restaurant** in town, and they chose **the most expensive wine** on the menu.
> **The earth** revolves around **the sun** every twenty-four hours.
> **The capital** of Italy is Rome.
> Please look at **the top** of the page.

9. The listener can identify the noun if the information in the noun phrase itself identifies the specific noun:

> **The book** that's on sale is on the counter.

(The relative clause tells which book — the one on sale.)

⯈ Exercise 9: Choosing Definite or Indefinite Articles

Work with a partner. Read each situation and decide whether to use *a, an,* or *the.*

1. My desk has _____*a*_____ drawer that's stuck.

2. If there are no chairs left in this classroom, you'll have to sit on _____ floor. Or maybe you should go next door and ask if you can borrow _____ chair from that classroom.

3. I like _____ person who sold me my car. She's not at all like her partner.
   He's _____ very aggressive salesman.

4. _____ apartment that I live in now is too small. I have to start looking for _____ new one. I'd really like to find _____ apartment with _____ garden.

5. There's _____ interesting exercise in your textbook. Please look at _____ bottom of page ten.

6. Last night we went to _____ movies. All of a sudden _____ electricity went off. _____ manager came out and said there was _____ blackout. He told us to come back another time to see _____ end of _____ movie, and he returned our tickets to us.

7. Did you read _____ article that I sent you last week? It had _____ interesting story about _____ mayor of Philadelphia.

8. Would you answer _____ telephone, please? I'm trying to diaper _____ baby.

9. I want to build _____ bookcase for my office. It has to have _____ shelf that is twelve inches high for my new textbooks.

10. Have you ever read _____ book about prehistoric times? I'd like to find _____ good one for my brother. I don't know of any.

⟹ Exercise 10: Identifying People and Objects

Work with a partner. Person A introduces a new subject with an indefinite article. Person B asks a question about it using the words in parentheses and the definite article *the*. Be sure to use the appropriate tense in your question.

1. **A:** I bought a shirt and a pair of pants.

   B: (what color/be/shirt)

   A: *I bought a shirt and a pair of pants.*
   B: *What color is the shirt?*

2. **A:** Who watches your children when you go out?

   B: We have a very nice baby-sitter.

   A: (how/much/you/pay/baby-sitter)

3. **A:** There's always a cat or a dog on my lawn in the morning. The cat belongs to the Smiths.

   B: (who/own/dog)

4. **A:** I take my child to a park every afternoon.

   B: (be/park/nearby)

5. **A:** There's a football game and a concert on Sunday. Which one do you want to go to?

   B: Well, (what time/football game/start)

6. **A:** There are several packages in the car. I need some help.

   B: I'll take this one. (can/you/carry/others)

7. **A:** I bought a jacket and a pair of jeans.

   B: (How much/jacket/cost)

8. **A:** I'd like to buy a birthday gift for my brother.

   B: Well, I'd suggest a shirt or maybe a wallet.

   A: (be/wallets/on sale)

9. **A:** This looks like a letter from home. Yes, very interesting....

   B: Well, (what/letter/say)

10. **A:** You probably need a raincoat and an umbrella today.

    B: (where/you/put/umbrella)

➠ Exercise 11: Making Assumptions About Shared Information

Work in small groups. Imagine you're sitting in a restaurant booth and you overhear various conversations. In these conversations, the definite article is used because the people involved share certain information.

Think about each situation and try to figure out what information they share. Explain different assumptions about each situation based on the use of the underlined definite noun.

1. You hear two women talking. One of them says, "Did you order the flowers yet?"

   Assumptions: _The women are sisters. They're sending a gift to their mother._ OR
   The women are friends. One of them is getting married soon.
   They're discussing the wedding.

2. Two young men are talking. One says, "The book costs $30.00." The other says, "I don't know how I'll be able to afford it."

   Assumptions: _____
   _____
   _____

3. A man is joined by a woman who says, "I got the money."

Assumptions: _____

_____

_____

4. Three women are talking. One asks, "Did you bring the photographs?"

Assumptions: _____

_____

_____

5. A woman is talking to a man. The woman says, "How could you forget to pay the bill?"

Assumptions: _____

_____

_____

6. Two men are talking. One says, "Oh, by the way, I got the tickets."

Assumptions: _____

_____

_____

7. Two women are talking. A third woman comes in, sits down, and says, "Well, did we get the contract?"

Assumptions: _____

_____

_____

8. A student is joined by a friend who says, "I had to argue with them, but the ad will appear in tomorrow morning's newspaper."

Assumptions: _____

_____

_____

➠ Exercise 12: Writing Assumptions About Shared Information

Choose a situation from Exercise 11 and write several sentences about it that give more details.

The woman says, "How could you forget to pay the bill?" The woman is angry because

the man usually pays bills late and he promised to start paying the bills on time.

Today, their phone service was cut off. The woman discovered that the man hadn't

paid the telephone bill.

➠ Exercise 13: Making Inferences

Work on your own. In each situation, a definite noun is missing. Select a noun from the following list that is appropriate to each situation: *computers, teacher, waiter, engine, star, drawers, driver, mechanic.*

1. Last summer I took a bus ride that was a nightmare. _____The driver_____ threatened to kick a passenger off the bus.

2. I had lunch at the Pinewood Restaurant yesterday. _____ almost charged us the dinner prices.

3. My car began vibrating, so I took it to a garage. _____ told me that I had probably gotten cheap gasoline.

4. I went to deposit some money at the bank this morning. I had to wait a long time because _____ were down.

5. I watched an awful TV program last night. _____ did the worst job of acting that I've ever seen.

6. Last semester I took a statistics course. _____ wasn't able to explain the concepts very well to the students.

7. I have a desk that I don't need anymore. Sometimes _____ stick, but otherwise it's in great condition.

8. My friend is buying a car for only $500. It doesn't have any rust, but _____ needs some work.

➠ **Exercise 14: Using Old and New Information in Recipes**

Work with a partner. Read the recipes and underline all the nouns that you find in the directions below the list of ingredients. Decide if the noun is count or noncount and if it has been mentioned before or inferred from the context. Insert articles where they are needed in each paragraph.

Check your work by reading each recipe aloud. Listen carefully. (Hint: Have the nouns with definite articles been mentioned before or inferred? Are the nouns with indefinite articles count nouns? Are the indefinite nouns without an article noncount nouns or plural count nouns?)

Grandma's Chicken Soup

1 chicken, cut up
1 large onion
1 carrot
1 stalk celery

2 cloves garlic, crushed
6 sprigs parsley, chopped
1 teaspoon salt
1/4 teaspoon pepper

Put *the* chicken in *a* large pot. Cover chicken with water. Cut up onion, carrot, and celery. Add vegetables to water. Also add garlic, parsley, salt, and pepper. Boil ingredients for 10 minutes. Lower heat and simmer ingredients slowly for 1 hour. Skim fat occasionally. Remove chicken from pot. When it has cooled, remove skin and cut chicken from bones. Strain soup and discard vegetables. Put chicken back into liquid. Reheat and serve. You may add pasta if you like.

Old-Fashioned Chocolate Chip Cookies

2 1/4 cups flour
1 teaspoon baking soda
1/2 teaspoon salt
1 cup (2 sticks) butter, softened
3/4 cup sugar

3/4 cup firmly packed brown sugar
1 teaspoon vanilla extract
2 eggs
2 cups chocolate chips
1 cup chopped nuts

Preheat oven to 375° Fahrenheit. In small bowl, combine flour, baking soda, and salt. Set these aside. In large mixing bowl, combine butter, sugar, brown sugar, and vanilla extract. Beat until creamy. Beat in eggs. Gradually add flour mixture. Stir in chocolate chips and nuts. Drop tablespoonfuls of batter onto ungreased cookie sheets. Bake for 10–12 minutes. Remove cookies from cookie sheets with spatula while still warm. Recipe makes about 5 dozen cookies.

➠ Exercise 15: Thinking About Meaning

Work with a partner. Number the sentences to make an organized paragraph. Pay attention to articles, tenses, and pronouns to help you decide on the best order. Read the story aloud to see if it sounds right.

_____ He cut the wire and jumped from the window into a creek.

_____ No one knows exactly where he found the ladder.

___1___ Another prisoner has escaped from the local prison.

_____ He was able to reach a high window in the dining hall, covered with wire.

_____ He swam across the creek, climbed over a wall, stole a car, and drove away.

_____ Sometime during the night, the prisoner climbed up a ladder.

➠ Exercise 16: Thinking About Meaning

Work with a partner. In sentences 1–5, identify each underlined noun for your partner by explaining more about it. Then discuss your answers to questions 6–8.

1. I went to the supermarket last night.

   I went to the supermarket — the A & P near my house.

2. I went to the bank before I came to class.

3. I bought the newspaper before I came to class.

4. The mayor is going to speak on television tonight.

5. I didn't feel well yesterday, so I went to the doctor.

6. If your father (or mother, grandmother, uncle) said sentences 1–5 above, would his or her explanation be the same as yours?

7. When you hear these sentences, do you need to know the exact supermarket, bank, newspaper, or doctor in order to understand the sentences?

8. Compare the following answers to the question *Where did you go this morning?*

   (a) I went to a bank to ask about a loan.

   (b) I went to the bank to ask about a loan.

   How does *the* change your interpretation of the sentence?

Indefinite and Definite Articles: Meaning and Use

GENERAL STATEMENTS

1. We don't always use a noun to refer to a specific object, event, or concept. Sometimes we use the noun to make a general statement about a whole class or group of objects, events, or nouns. The noun represents all other nouns of its class or group:

> **Spiders** are insects.
> I like **rice**.
> **A bird** can fly.
> **The bald eagle** is threatened.

2. Plural count nouns (**spiders**) and noncount nouns (**rice**) are used to make general statements. These nouns refer to all spiders and all rice. No articles are used with them:

> **Spiders** are insects.
> I like **rice**.

3. A singular count noun and the articles **a** or **an** and **the** (**a bird, the bald eagle**) are also used to make general statements. The singular count noun refers to all members of its class:

> **A bird** can fly.
> **The bald eagle** is threatened.

4. General statements made with plural count nouns without articles or noncount nouns can express opinions, likes, and dislikes:

Opinions: **Dogs** make good pets.

Likes: I like **spiders.**

Dislikes: I don't like **rice.**

5. Generalizations with **a** or **an** plus a singular count noun often take the form of definitions. They are used to classify people, animals, and things:

> **A locksmith** is a person who makes and repairs locks and keys.
> **A penguin** is a black and white bird that lives in the Antarctic.
> **A tulip** is a flower that grows from a bulb.

6. General statements with **the** are less common than other types of generalizations. They are used mainly in scientific and technical writing. These generalizations usually refer to plants, animals, and mechanical objects:

> **The tulip** blooms in early spring.
> **The giant panda** is extremely endangered.
> **The computer** has changed our lives in recent years.

7. General statements with **the** are also frequently used to refer to musical instruments:

I used to play **the piano,** but now I only play **the violin.**

8. The with a plural noun does not express general meaning. It refers instead to specific nouns:

The computers that we bought last year have completely changed our business.

⫸ Exercise 17: Expressing Your Opinion

Write a general statement that expresses your opinion about each of the nouns in parentheses. Use any of the following phrases: *I like, I don't like, I don't mind, I have no opinion about, I'm against, I'm in favor of, I love, I really hate.*

1. (homework) __I don't mind homework.__

2. (exams) _____

3. (jogging) _____

4. (politics) _____

5. (computers)_____

6. (house pets)_____

7. (solar power) _____

8. (museums)_____

9. (classical music) _____

10. (hard rock) _____

11. (snow) _____

12. (marriage) _____

13. (cooking)_____

14. (housework) _____

15. (sports cars) _____

⫸ Exercise 18: Writing Your Opinion

Write a short paragraph about one of the nouns above. Use your general statement as the first sentence of your paragraph.

I don't like sports cars. First of all, they are expensive to buy and to repair.

Second, if I had a sports car, I would need a garage to put it in...

⬛➡ Exercise 19: Defining Nouns

Work with a partner. Make up simple general statements that define or classify the nouns in parentheses. Use the indefinite article. You may use a dictionary if necessary.

1. (begonia)

    Example: *A begonia is a flower.*

2. (spatula)

    Example: *A spatula is a cooking utensil.*

3. (elm)

4. (mango)

5. (screwdriver)

6. (shark)

7. (crib)

8. (penny)

9. (herb)

10. (square)

11. (bibliography)

12. (moth)

13. (calculator)

14. (astronomer)

⬛➡ Exercise 20: Explaining Generalizations

Work with a partner. Read each general statement. Write a sentence that gives details about the noun to explain the generalization. Use the definite or indefinite article in your sentences.

1. I don't like cats. <u>My neighbor has a cat that always digs up my flower garden.</u>

2. Vacations aren't always relaxing. _____

   _____

3. I don't usually like dinner parties. _____

   _____

4. Supermarkets sell everything nowadays. _____

_____

5. Teachers have to be patient. _____

_____

6. I don't know much about cars. _____

_____

➡ Exercise 21: Making Generalizations

Make up generalizations about ten of the following definite nouns: *the computer, the dishwasher, the unicorn, the chimpanzee, the VCR, the piano, the willow tree, the elephant, the common cold, the atom bomb, the abacus, the microwave oven, the human heart, the motorcycle, the rose, the kangaroo, the gypsy moth.* Your generalization should be appropriate to use as the first sentence of a paragraph about that noun.

Examples: *The gypsy moth destroys trees.*
The computer has changed the way we do business.

➡ Exercise 22: Choosing Between General and Specific Nouns

In the following sentences, some nouns are used with no article to express a general meaning, and others are used with articles to refer to a specific thing. Distinguish between these general and specific uses by writing *a* or *an, the,* or *nothing*.

1. I don't really like _____ dogs, but my neighbor has ____*a*____ dog that I'm very
   fond of.

2. Many people don't care about _____ food they eat. They don't think there's any
   difference between _____ healthy food and _____ junk food.

3. _____ cars have gotten very expensive. I'm hoping to find _____ cheap used car.

4. It's hard to find _____ inexpensive clothing. _____ clothing in the stores is so
   expensive these days.

5. I eat _____ rice at almost every meal. _____ rice that I buy is usually on sale
   downtown. It's _____ very flavorful kind of rice.

6. If you like _____ fish, you should try to buy _____ fresh fish. If _____ fish at the market doesn't look very good, go next door and buy _____ meat instead. Smith's has _____ best meat in town. It's much better than _____ meat at Goodrich's.

7. _____ camels are animals with long necks and humps on their back. In desert countries, people ride on _____ camels and use them for transport.

8. He's allergic to _____ cats. When he goes near _____ cat, he starts to sneeze.

Summary

General Quantity Expressions: Form

Count:	Julie bought **a few** books.
Noncount:	She has **very little** money.
Count and Noncount:	I have **a lot of** photographs.
	I have **a lot of** work.

General Quantity Expressions: Meaning and Use

General quantity expressions indicate general quantities that are large or small.

Descriptions:	There are **a lot of** parks in this town.
Opinions:	Big cities have **too much** noise.

Specific Quantity Expressions: Form

Count:	**a box of** crackers
	a pound of carrots
Noncount:	**a can of** soup
	a piece of cheese

Specific Quantity Expressions: Meaning and Use

Specific quantity expressions indicate precise amounts. They are either measurements or containers.

Measurements:	I need **a pound of** carrots.
Containers:	I bought **a jar of** olives.
Prices:	Carrots are fifty-nine cents **a pound.**
	Celery is ninety-nine cents **a bunch.**

Indefinite Articles: Form

Singular Count:	I found **a new recipe** for potatoes.
Plural Count:	We're having **potatoes** for dinner.
Noncount:	We're having **ice cream** for dessert.

Definite Articles: Form

Singular Count:	**The recipe** I found sounds delicious.
Plural Count:	**The potatoes** on the stove are ready.
Noncount:	Please pass **the pepper.**

Indefinite and Definite Articles: Meaning and Use

The choice of **a** or **an, the,** or no article depends on three important factors: whether the noun is count or noncount, whether the listener knows which specific noun the speaker is talking about, and whether the speaker is making a general statement about the noun.

Indefinite articles classify nouns by introducing them as a member of a class of items. Definite articles identify nouns based on assumptions about what information the speaker and listener share about the noun. Both definite and indefinite articles are also used with nouns for making generalizations about a whole class or group of nouns.

Identification:	I bought a shirt and a vest. **The shirt** is white and **the vest** is blue.
Shared Information:	Have you bought **the flowers** yet?
	When you walk into my apartment, **the kitchen** is on the left.
Old and New Information:	In this recipe, first you put **the chicken** in **a large pot.**
Opinions, Likes, Dislikes:	I like **tea.**
Definitions:	**A spatula** is a cooking utensil.
Generalizations:	**The gypsy moth** destroys trees.
	Tulips bloom in early spring.

⫸ Summary Exercise: Finding Errors

Most of the following sentences have an error in form, meaning, or use. Find each error and correct it.

1. How ~~much~~ pencils do you need?   *many*

2. Please buy bag potatoes at the supermarket.

3. I have a piece of information that you might want to know.

4. Much water spilled on the floor. Please help me wipe it up.

5. I'd like two pound of ground beef, please.

6. The life is not always easy.

7. Calcium is mineral.

8. Please pass the rice and the salt.

9. The book I bought was on sale.

10. I spoke to bank manager about my problem.

11. She began to love mathematics in college. Eventually, she graduated with a major in mathematics and physics.

12. I need new coat. Please help me find one.

13. I'll buy three package of crackers.

14. When you get to my house, you don't have to ring doorbell. Just walk in.

CHAPTER 12

Expressing Differences and Similarities:
Comparatives, Superlatives,
As...As, The Same...As

Preview

A new student is asking for some recommendations:

Abdul: Where do you buy your groceries?
Pedro: Logan's.
Abdul: It's **cheaper than** Super?
Pedro: Yes, it's **the cheapest** store in town. I find that fruit and vegetables are much
more expensive at Super, so I don't shop there.
Abdul: I'm glad I asked you. I thought Super was **the most inexpensive** store in the area.

At a bakery:

Customer: Will my order be ready by noon?
Clerk: I think so. We're working **as fast as** we can.

Two friends are talking:

Jan: You look **thinner**. Are you losing weight?
Anna: No. Actually, I'm sure I'm **the same weight as** I was the last time you saw me.

There are many different ways to make comparisons using adjectives, adverbs, and nouns. For example, the differences between two items are expressed using the comparative forms of adjectives and adverbs (**-er** and **more**), and the comparative forms of nouns (**more, less,** and **fewer**). The similarities between two items are expressed using adjectives and adverbs with **as...as** and nouns with **the same...as.**

To rank an item as first or last in a group of three or more, the superlative forms of adjectives and adverbs (**-est** and **most**) are used, and nouns are used with **the most, the least,** and **the fewest.**

In this chapter you will study the various uses of the patterns of comparison in different situations. You will also study expressions of degree using adjectives, adverbs, and nouns with **so...that,** and **such (a)...that.**

313

Comparative Adjectives and Adverbs: Form

Adjective + *-er*	*More* + Adjective
My sister is **taller than** I.	She is **more patient than** I.
My sister is **taller than** I am.	She is **more patient than** I am.
My sister is **taller than** me.	She is **more patient than** me.

- **Than** often follows comparative adjectives. If **than** is not used, it is still implied:

  I'm **older than** my sister. I'm also **taller,** and my hair is **straighter.**

- **Than** can be followed by a subject noun or pronoun + an optional verb:

  I'm older than **my sister (is).**
  I'm older than **she (is).**

- If the verb in the **than** clause is omitted, an object pronoun can replace the subject pronoun:

  I'm older than **her.**

- **Less** is also used before an adjective:

  I am **less patient than** my sister.

- Look at pages 493–494 for spelling rules for adjectives ending in **-er**, for irregular forms, and for when to use **-er** or **more**.

Adverb + *-er*	*More* + Adverb
I run **faster than** he.	He speaks **more clearly than** I.
I run **faster than** he does.	He speaks **more clearly than** I do.
I run **faster than** him.	He speaks **more clearly than** me.

- An auxiliary verb can replace the final verb, or the first verb can be repeated:

  I run faster than he **does.**
  I run faster than he **runs.**

- Look at pages 493–494 for irregular forms and for when to use **-er** or **more**.

⟹ Exercise 1: Working on Form

Work with a partner. Complete the conversations using the appropriate comparative forms of the adjectives and adverbs in parentheses. Then practice the conversations.

1. **A:** Should we buy this plant or that one?

   B: Well, this one's _____*cheaper*_____ (cheap), but that one looks
   _____*healthier*_____ (healthy).

2. **A:** You look like your sister.

B: Yes, I know. But actually, I'm _____ (tall) and _____ (thin) and my hair is much _____ (curly).

A: Isn't your hair _____ (light) than hers too?

3. **A:** Which do you prefer, tennis or swimming?

B: Well, it's hard to say. Tennis is _____ (challenging), but swimming is _____ (refreshing) on a hot day. They are both _____ (strenuous) than golf, which is really my favorite sport.

4. **A:** You haven't solved your problem yet, have you? You seem _____ (annoyed) today than yesterday.

B: You're right. I'm _____ (angry) today because I've had more time to think. I'm still trying to find a _____ (simple) solution than the one I mentioned yesterday.

5. **A:** May I help you?

B: Yes, I understand there's an 8:45 flight to Boston tomorrow morning. Is there anything _____ (early)?

A: Yes, there are two flights. One leaves at 7:05 and the other leaves a little bit _____ (late), at 7:25, but these two flights are _____ (expensive) than the 8:45.

6. **Relative:** How is my aunt today?

Doctor: Well, actually, she's a little _____ (bad) than yesterday. I'm afraid that her condition is _____ (serious) than we thought.

Relative: But is she going to get _____ (well)?

Doctor: Yes, she will, but she might have to stay in the hospital _____ (long) than we expected. Let's wait and see the results of today's tests. They should be _____ (accurate) than yesterday's. Now, how are you feeling? You look _____ (tired) than your aunt does.

Comparative Adjectives and Adverbs: Meaning and Use

DIFFERENCES BETWEEN TWO ITEMS

1. Comparative forms of adjectives and adverbs express the differences between two items or situations. Therefore, comparatives are often used to express preferences and opinions:

Preference: A bath is **more relaxing than** a shower.

Opinion: Travelers checks are **safer than** cash.

                Last year they worked **harder than** this year.

2. Comparatives are also frequently used to give compliments:

You look **much healthier** now **than** before your vacation.

3. More and **-er** are used in comparisons to express a higher degree:

A diamond is **more expensive than** a piece of glass.
A rabbit is **faster than** a turtle.

4. Less expresses a lower degree:

The old computer program is **less useful than** the new one.

5. Less sounds especially awkward with one-syllable adjectives whose opposites are short common words:

He is **shorter than** his father.
He **isn't as tall as** his father.
*He is less tall than his father. (INCORRECT)

6. Some comparative forms sound more formal than others. For example, if you use a subject pronoun after **than** with no verb, the sentence sounds formal:

More Formal   He's **much taller than I.**

                He's **much taller than I am.**

Less Formal   He's **much taller than me.**

⏩ Exercise 2: Stating Preferences and Opinions

Work with a partner. Take turns asking about preferences and opinions using the words in parentheses. Answer each question with a reason, using the comparative.

1. (a bath/a shower)

    A: *Which is better, a bath or a shower?*
    B: *A bath, because it's more relaxing.*

2. (a headache/toothache)

    A: *Which is worse, a headache or a toothache?*
    B: *A toothache, because it's usually more painful.*

3. (classical music/jazz)

4. (soccer/American football)

5. (coffee/tea)

6. (rain/snow)

7. (a romance novel/a mystery)

8. (a written exam/an oral exam)

9. (a hurricane/a tornado)

10. (poverty/loneliness)

11. (the chicken pox/pneumonia)

12. (a broken arm/a broken leg)

⏩ Exercise 3: Complimenting

Work with a partner. Make positive comments about changes in the appearance of the people in the situations below using the comparative form of the suggested adjectives.

1. Your friend looked pale and tired when she was sick. She's not sick now:

    (good/energetic) _You look much better now. You look more energetic._

2. Your nephew was four years old when you saw him last. He's five now:

    (tall/grown-up) _____

3. Your grandmother was in the hospital and she was very weak. She's home now:

    (healthy/strong) _____

4. Your friend was tired from driving for several hours. He's not tired after a cup of coffee:

   (wide awake/alert) _____

5. Your friend was unhappy for a few weeks. She's smiling today:

   (happy/cheerful) _____

6. Your co-worker was very tense before his vacation. He's not tense after his return:

   (relaxed/calm)_____

⇒ Exercise 4: Describing Differences

Work with a partner. Make up two sentences with the comparative that describe differences between two types of each item in parentheses.

1. (types of bicycles)

   Example: *One-speed bicycles are usually less expensive than ten-speeds.*
   Ten-speeds go much faster than one-speeds do.

2. (brands of soap)

3. (brands of toothpaste)

4. (types of cars)

5. (brands or types of computers)

6. (brands of athletic shoes)

7. (clothing in your country and clothing in the United States)

Superlative Adjectives and Adverbs: Form

The + Adjective + *-est*	*The Most* + Adjective
It's **the hardest** game of all.	It's **the most difficult** game of all.

- Look at pages 493–494 for spelling rules for adjectives ending in **-est**, for irregular forms, and for when to use **-est** or **most**.
- **The least** is also used before an adjective:

  It's **the least expensive** game of all.

The + Adverb + *-est*	*The Most* + Adverb
He works **the hardest** of all.	He works **the most quickly** of all.

- The definite article **the** comes before superlative adjectives or adverbs:

  That's **the best** restaurant in town.
  He talks **the loudest** of all.

- Possessives can also come before superlatives:

  my happiest moment
  John's funniest story
  the world's deepest lake

- **The least** is also used before an adverb:

  He works **the least efficiently** of all.

- Look at pages 493–494 for irregular forms and for when to use **-est** or **most**.

⬛➡ Exercise 5: Working on Form

Work with a partner. Complete the conversations using the appropriate superlative forms of the adjectives and adverbs in parentheses. Then practice the conversations.

1. **A:** I'm _____ the slowest _____ (slow) reader in my family, but I'm also
   _____ the most careful _____ (careful).

   B: Really? Who's _____ (fast) reader?

2. **A:** This is _____ (popular) restaurant in this area, probably

   because it's _____ (cheap).

   B: What about Joe's? Isn't that supposed to have _____ (good)

   pizza?

3. **A:** Yesterday I had _____ (painful) toothache of my life.

   It's better today.

   B: You should try my dentist. He's _____ (competent) dentist

   I've ever had.

4. **A:** I don't know which pair of slippers would be _____

(suitable) for my father.

B: How about these slippers? I think they have _____ (nice)

leather and they look _____ (comfortable).

5. **A:** Gray's is supposed to be _____ (reliable) car dealer around.

Do you know anything about them?

B: Not too much. Just that they're _____ (near) dealer that sells

compact cars. Just remember to stay away from Thompson's. They have

_____ (bad) reputation in town.

Superlative Adjectives and Adverbs: Meaning and Use

RANKING THREE OR MORE ITEMS

1. The superlative form of adjectives and adverbs is used to compare three or more items. The superlative selects one of these items and ranks it first or last in comparison with the other items in the group. Therefore, superlatives are often used to give opinions and recommendations:

Opinion: We visited four cities. I thought Paris was **the most beautiful of all.**

Recommendation: There are several good restaurants around here, but Carmine's
                        is **the best.**

2. **Most** and **-est** in superlatives indicate the highest degree:

Mt. Everest is **the highest** mountain in the world.
He's **the most intelligent** person I know.

3. **Least** in superlatives indicates the lowest degree:

Wyoming is **the least populated** state in the United States.

4. **Least** sounds awkward with one-syllable adjectives whose opposites are short common words:

He is **the shortest** person in his family.
*He is the least tall in his family. (INCORRECT)

5. The preposition **in** often follows superlatives. **In** is typically used with locations (the world, continents, countries, cities, buildings, etc.) and with nouns such as **the class, the group, the government, the club**:

> The cheetah is the fastest land animal **in the world.**
> Chez Pierre is the best restaurant **in Los Angeles.**
> Paul is the tallest student **in the class.**

6. Of is used with expressions of time and quantity, and with plural nouns:

> the hottest day **of the year**
> the biggest surprise **of all**
> the smallest **of the oil producers**

7. Other prepositions such as **on** and **at** are also possible with certain nouns:

> the biggest crater **on the moon**
> the youngest person **at the party**

8. One of plus a superlative weakens the superlative meaning. For example, **one of my happiest moments** suggests that there may be more than one very happy moment. **My happiest moment** suggests only one.

9. If you are not sure if something is first or last, the use of **one of** can keep your statement correct:

> The giant panda is **one of the most endangered animals** in the world.

⬛▶ Exercise 6: Recommending Places

Work with a partner. Imagine your cousin has just moved into your neighborhood. Give her or him recommendations for supermarkets, laundromats, restaurants, movie theaters, shopping malls, transportation, parks, and so on. Use the superlative form of the adjectives in parentheses.

1. (beautiful) _The most beautiful park is Memorial Park._

2. (expensive) _The least expensive supermarket is Joe's._

3. (good) _____

4. (near) _____

5. (nice) _____

6. (crowded) _____

7. (popular) _____

8. (interesting) _____

9. (bad) _____

10. (cheap) _____

⯈ Exercise 7: Stating Your Opinion

Work with a partner. State your opinion about people and things you know using *one of* with the superlative form of the adjectives in parentheses.

1. (beautiful)

   Example: *San Francisco is one of the most beautiful cities I know.*

2. (funny)

3. (talented)

4. (boring)

5. (expensive)

6. (unusual)

7. (exciting)

8. (thrifty)

9. (crowded)

10. (smart)

⯈ Exercise 8: Ranking

Work in small groups. Make up a list of ten famous people (movie stars, politicians, athletes, authors, scientists, artists). Use the superlatives in parentheses to rank the people on your list.

1. (oldest/youngest)

   Example: *Patrick Stewart is the oldest. Macaulay Culkin is the youngest.*

2. (most/least intelligent)

3. (funniest/least funny)

4. (most/least talented)

5. (richest/poorest)

6. (most/least successful)

As...As: Form

As + Adjective + *As*	*As* + Adverb + *As*
Sue is **as tall as** I.	Joe runs **as fast as** Mark.
Sue is **as tall as** I am.	Joe runs **as fast as** Mark does.
Sue is **as tall as** me.	Joe runs **as fast as** him.

- **As...as** can be used with adjectives and adverbs.
- A subject noun or pronoun follows the final **as.** The verb can be omitted.
- If the verb is omitted, an object pronoun can replace the subject pronoun after the final **as:**

  Sue is as tall as **me.**

- An auxiliary verb can replace the final verb, or the first verb can be repeated:

  Joe runs as fast as Mark **does.**
  Joe runs as fast as Mark **runs.**

⟶ **Exercise 9: Working on Form**

Work with a partner. Take turns comparing the person, place, or thing to something very similar. Use *about* plus *as...as.*

1. How much is a pound of apples?

   A: *How much is a pound of apples?*
   B: *About as much as a pound of pears.*

2. How big is your hometown?

3. How much is a computer?

4. How tall is your father?

5. How large is a pumpkin?

6. How heavy is a quart of milk?

7. How high is your house?

8. How strong are you?

As...As: Meaning and Use

SIMILARITIES AND DIFFERENCES

1. Another way to make comparisons is to talk about similarities instead of differences. To compare two similar items, you can use **as...as** to give an approximation:

My office is almost **as big as** this room.

2. The negative form of **as...as** does not express similarity. It expresses differences and is very similar to the comparative. The first item in the comparison is less than the second item:

This letter is **not as important as** that one.
This letter is **less important than** that one.

3. The negative form of **as...as** is often used instead of the comparative with **less**. This is because **less** sounds awkward with certain adjectives, especially if their opposite is a short common word:

Sharon is **not as tall as** George.
Sharon is **shorter than** George.
*Sharon is less tall than George. (INCORRECT)

4. Sometimes it may be better to use **not as...as** instead of the comparative because **not as...as** is more indirect and polite. Compare these two sentences. The first sentence is not as strong as the second one:

Joe isn't **as fast as** Chris.
Joe is **slower than** Chris.

5. As...as is also used in making promises:

I'll be there **as soon as** I can.

⟱➡ **Exercise 10: Making Promises**

Work with a partner. Make promises using *as...as.*

1. Your boss needs you to finish a report immediately. Promise to work very fast:

Example: *I'll work as fast as I can.*

2. Your friend wants to go out with you tomorrow, but you have a lot of work to do. Promise to work very hard:

3. You need to help your roommate clean the apartment, but you also need to go out for a while. Promise to come home very early:

4. It's raining very hard. Your family doesn't want you to drive on the wet roads. Promise to drive very carefully:

5. You and your friend are expecting six dinner guests in a few minutes. You need to go and buy some ice. Promise to return very soon:

6. Your friend who is moving needs empty boxes for packing. You know that there are many empty boxes at work. Promise to bring a lot of these boxes:

➭ Exercise 11: Expressing Similarities and Differences

Work on your own. Compare yourself today with the way you used to be five or ten years ago. Use the phrases in parentheses in affirmative and negative sentences with *as...as*.

1. (work hard)   I still work as hard as I did ten years ago.

2. (be poor)   I'm not as poor as I was ten years ago.

3. (get up early) _____

4. (be energetic) _____

5. (be happy)_____

6. (eat out frequently) _____

7. (feel healthy)_____

Comparative Nouns, Superlative Nouns, *The Same...As:* Form

Comparative Nouns

This course has **more students than** that one does.
This course has **more homework than** that one does.

This course has **fewer students than** that one does.
This course has **less homework than** that one does.

- **More** is used with comparative count and noncount nouns.
- **Fewer** is used with count nouns; **less** is used with noncount nouns.
- **Than** can be followed by a subject noun or pronoun + an optional verb. If the verb is omitted, an object pronoun can replace the subject pronoun:

  Matt has more homework than **Lisa (does).**
  Matt has more homework than **she (does).**
  Matt has more homework than **her.**

- An auxiliary can replace the final verb, or the first verb can be repeated:

  He reads more books than I **do.**
  He reads more books than I **read.**

  (continued)

Superlative Nouns

This course has **the most students**.
This course has **the most homework**.

This course has **the fewest students**.
This course has **the least homework**.

- **The most** is used with superlative count and noncount nouns.
- **The fewest** is used with count nouns; **the least** is used with noncount nouns.

The Same...As

This course has **the same students as** that one.
This course has **the same homework as** that one.

- **The same...as** is used with count and noncount nouns.
- The final **as** can be followed by a subject noun or pronoun + an optional verb. If the verb is omitted, an object pronoun can replace the subject pronoun:

  Scott is the same height as **Mary (is)**.
  Scott is the same height as **she (is)**.
  Scott is the same height as **her**.

- An auxiliary can replace the final verb, or the first verb can be repeated:

  I wear the same perfume as she **does**.
  I wear the same perfume as she **wears**.

➡️ **Exercise 12: Working on Comparative Nouns**

Work with a partner. Complete the following sentences with the comparative forms of the nouns in parentheses. Use *more*, *fewer*, or *less*.

1. (pollution) Small towns have _____ less pollution than _____ big cities.

2. (calories) A stalk of celery has _____ a piece of cake.

3. (money) A billionaire has _____ a millionaire.

4. (value) A penny has _____ a quarter.

5. (people) China has _____ Canada.

⫸ Exercise 13: Working on Superlative Nouns

Work with a partner. Complete the following sentences with the superlative forms of the nouns in parentheses. Use *the most, the fewest,* or *the least*. Note: The plus sign (+) indicates the highest degree; the minus sign (−) indicates the lowest degree.

1. (+ people) California *is the state with the most people.*

2. (− land area) Rhode Island *is the state with the least land area.*

3. (+ lakes) Minnesota _____

4. (− income) Mississippi _____

5. (+ islands) Hawaii _____

6. (− rainfall) Nevada _____

7. (− people) Wyoming _____

8. (+ land area) Alaska _____

⫸ Exercise 14: Working on *The Same...As*

Work with a partner. Restate each pair of sentences using *the same...as* and a noun (*weight, price,* and so on) to express the appropriate relationships.

1. John weighs 158 pounds. So does Tom.
   John is the same weight as Tom.

2. The book costs twenty dollars. So does the videocassette.

   _____

3. My office building is three stories high. So is yours.

   _____

4. This paper is eight inches wide. So is that one.

   _____

5. The pool is twelve feet deep. So is the lake.

   _____

6. This book is 400 pages long. So is my math book.

   _____

Comparative Nouns, Superlative Nouns, *The Same...As*: Meaning and Use

DIFFERENCES AND SIMILARITIES

1. Comparative forms of nouns are used with **more, fewer,** and **less** to compare the different quantities of two nouns:

I get **more mail than** my assistant.
My assistant gets **less mail than** I do.
My assistant gets **fewer letters than** I do.

2. Superlative forms of nouns with **the most, the fewest,** and **the least** are used to rank the different quantities of three or more nouns. The superlative noun selects the largest or smallest quantity in the group:

My boss gets **the most mail** in our office.

3. **The same...as** is used to express the equality of two nouns that are being compared. Sometimes the noun can be omitted if it is understood in the situation:

This shirt is **the same style as** that one.
This shirt is **the same as** that one.

4. Since comparative and superlative nouns express differences, they are often used for describing problems, and for making choices:

Problem: There is **more industrial waste** today **than** there was a few years ago.

Choice: I'm going to buy this overnight bag. It has **more room** and **fewer zippers than** the others.

⇒ Exercise 15: Describing Problems

Work with a partner. Imagine you are politicians running for election. Use the list of problems below to make a speech about all of the problems caused by the current government. Make up sentences with the comparative form of the nouns in the list to show that there are more problems today than there were four years ago.

Examples: *There is more pollution than there was four years ago.*
There are fewer educational programs than there were four years ago.

Problems

pollution	employment	business opportunities
poverty	strikes	public health problems
hunger	available housing	educational programs
crime	traffic	homeless people

⫸ Exercise 16: Analyzing Data

Rank the vegetables in the following chart for their nutritional value (calories, vitamin A, vitamin C, and so on) using the superlative forms of each category with *the most, the fewest,* and *the least.*

Examples: *Carrots have the most vitamin A.*
Onions have the least vitamin A.

Nutritional Value of Vegetables

	Calories	Carbohydrates (g)	Vitamin A (IU)	Vitamin C (mg)	Calcium (mg)	Sodium (mg)	Iron (mg)
Carrots 1 cup raw	46	11	12,000	9	41	52	.8
Celery 1 cup raw	20	5	320	11	47	150	.4
Cucumber 1 small	25	6	420	19	42	10	1.9
Onions 1 cup raw chopped	65	15	70	17	46	17	.9
Peas 1 cup raw	122	21	930	39	38	3	2.8
Spinach 1 cup raw chopped	14	2	4500	28	51	39	1.7
Sweet Potato 1 medium baked	161	37	9200	25	46	14	1.0

⟱➡ **Exercise 17: Describing Similarities**

Make up six sentences about yourself. Use *the same...as* and the following nouns:
height, weight, hair color, hair length, age, shoe size, shirt size, hobby.

1. My hair is the same length as my mother's.
2. I'm the same height as my sister.
3. _____
4. _____
5. _____
6. _____
7. _____
8. _____

⟱➡ **Exercise 18: Describing Differences**

Make up negative sentences comparing two items that are different using *not the same...as*
and the expressions in parentheses.

1. (size) __A station wagon is not the same size as a sports car.__
2. (shape) _____
3. (length) _____
4. (color) _____
5. (price) _____
6. (distance) _____

⟱➡ **Exercise 19: Describing Similarities and Differences**

Write five sentences about your hometown. Use *the same...as* or *not the same...as* and the
following nouns: *population, size, climate, altitude, problems, industries, weather, crime rate.*

1. My hometown has the same climate as Sydney, Australia.

   My hometown doesn't have the same problems as New York City.

2. _____
3. _____
4. _____
5. _____
6. _____

➡ Exercise 20: Making a Choice

Work with a partner. Imagine you're buying a used car and you're trying to choose between two cars. Read the list of advantages and disadvantages below. Fill in the chart by describing each feature with comparative nouns and adjectives. Put a plus (+) next to an advantage or a minus (−) next to a disadvantage. Then decide which car to buy.

> Example: *I think I should buy the Supergrand because it gets more miles per gallon than the Seagull.*

ADVANTAGES AND DISADVANTAGES

Supergrand	Seagull
4 years old	6 years old
$8,000	$2,500
4-5 passengers	6 passengers
Sedan with small trunk	Station wagon
Has 75,000 miles on it	Has 36,000 miles on it
Gets 28 miles per gallon	Gets 20 miles per gallon
Color is pink	Color is gray
No rust	Small amount of rust
Fabric seats in good condition	Vinyl seats in good condition
Good financing	Poor financing
Air, power windows, cruise control, sunroof	Only air-conditioning

	Supergrand	Seagull
age	+ newer	− older
price	− more expensive	+ cheaper
size		
storage		
total mileage		
gas mileage		
color		
condition of body		
condition of interior		
financing		
extras		

So...That/Such (a)...That: Form

So...That

I was	**so tired that**	I went to bed at 8:30.
I was	**so tired**	I went to bed at 8:30.
He works	**so hard that**	he never takes a break.
He works	**so hard**	he never takes a break.

- Sentences with degree expressions with **so** are followed by a **that** clause.
- **That** can be omitted without a change in meaning.
- **So** comes before an adjective or an adverb.

Such (a)...That

I had	**such a bad cold that**	I missed work.
I had	**such a bad cold**	I missed work.
That was	**such good ice cream that**	I ate more.
That was	**such good ice cream**	I ate more.
They were	**such useful books that**	I bought them.
They were	**such useful books**	I bought them.

- Sentences with degree expressions with **such (a)** are followed by a **that** clause.
- **That** can be omitted without a change in meaning.
- **Such a** comes before an adjective + a singular count noun.
- **Such** comes before an adjective + a noncount noun and before an adjective + a plural count noun.

⇒ **Exercise 21: Working on Form**

Work with a partner. Complete the following conversations with *so*, *such a*, or *such*. For items 4–6, add a *that* clause.

1. **A:** Where're my jeans?

   B: They were _____*so*_____ dirty that I put them in the wash.

2. **A:** What's wrong?

   B: I had _____ bad day that I want to quit my job.

3. **A:** How was your vacation?

 B: Well, we had _____ bad weather that we didn't do much. And yesterday,

 it was _____ foggy that the flight was delayed for three hours.

4. **A:** Why didn't you call me last night?

 B: I was _____ tired that _____

 _____

5. **A:** How did you like the movie?

 B: I thought it was _____ good that _____

 _____

6. **A:** My neighbor moved away.

 B: Do you miss her?

 A: Yes. We were _____ close friends that _____

 _____

So...That/Such (a)...That: Meaning and Use

CAUSE AND RESULT

1. **So** and **such** are used to intensify adjectives, adverbs, and nouns that are modified by adjectives. **So...that** and **such (a)...that** express a cause and a result. They indicate a high degree of the adjective or adverb. This high degree causes or leads to a particular result. The result is expressed in a clause after **that:**

Cause	**Result**
It was **so hot that**	I took off my coat.

2. Since **so** and **such** intensify adjectives, adverbs, and noun phrases, they often express negative feelings, especially complaints:

The sauce is **so spicy that** I can't eat it.

▥➡ **Exercise 22: Complaining**

Work with a partner. Complain about the items in parentheses. For situations 2 and 3, make up sentences with *so...that*. For situations 4–6, make up sentences with *such (a)...that*.

1. You don't like your chemistry course:

   (the lectures) <u>The lectures are so boring that some students fall asleep.</u>

2. You went to a restaurant last night. You didn't like it at all:

   (the food) _____

   (the waitress) _____

   (the music) _____

   (the atmosphere) _____

3. You didn't enjoy your last vacation:

   (the hotel) _____

   (the weather) _____

   (the city) _____

   (the return flight) _____

4. You don't like your chemistry course:

   (difficult exams) <u>We have such difficult exams that most students fail.</u>

5. You don't like your job:

   (noisy printers) _____

   (small office) _____

   (low salary) _____

   (poor benefits) _____

6. You don't like your apartment. You want to move:

   (small kitchen) _____

   (old building) _____

   (busy street) _____

   (nosey neighbors) _____

⫸ **Exercise 23: Describing Results**

Work with a partner. Take turns describing what happened the last time you had the feelings or experiences in parentheses and tell when they happened. Then make up sentences with *so...that* to describe the result.

1. (very angry)

    Example: *I was very angry when a truck carelessly hit my car last week.*
    I was so angry that I lost my temper.

2. (very frightened)

3. (very embarrassed)

4. (very sick)

5. (very cold)

6. (very bored)

7. (very busy)

8. (very late)

9. (very confused)

Summary

Comparative Adjectives and Adverbs: Form

Adjective + *-er:*	The weather is **warmer than** we expected.
More + Adjective:	This suit is **more expensive than** that one.
Less + Adjective:	My sister is **less dependable than** me.
Adverb + *-er:*	Ana runs **faster than** her brother.
More + Adverb:	He calls home **more often than** I do.
Less + Adverb:	She writes **less often than** I do.

Comparative Adjectives and Adverbs: Meaning and Use

The comparative forms of adjectives and adverbs express the differences between two items or situations.

Comparisons:	Which car is **more expensive,** this one or that one?
Preferences:	Fran: Which is **better,** a bath or a shower? Lil: A bath, because it's **more relaxing.**
Opinions:	*Star Trek* is **more interesting than** *Star Wars.*
Compliments:	You look **much healthier** now.
Differences:	This apartment is **larger than** my last one.

Superlative Adjectives and Adverbs: Form

The + Adjective + *-est:*   Dan is **the youngest** child in his class.

The Most + Adjective: That was **the most boring** movie I've ever seen.

The Least + Adjective: This is **the least expensive** car I could find.

The + Adverb + *-est:*   She works **the hardest** of all the students.

The Most + Adverb: Mike writes **the most carefully** of all.

The Least + Adverb: Joe writes **the least carefully** in his class.

Superlative Adjectives and Adverbs: Meaning and Use

The superlative form of adjectives and adverbs is used to compare three or more items. The superlative selects one of these items and ranks the item as first or last in comparison with the other items in the group.

Recommendations: It's **the most popular** bakery in the neighborhood.

Opinions: He's **one of the most talented** musicians I know.

Rankings: George is **the most successful** sales representative in the company. Tom is **the least.**

As...As: Form

As + Adjective + *As:*   I'm **as tall as** my sister.

As + Adverb + *As:*   He doesn't run **as fast as** he used to.

As...As: Meaning and Use

As...as expresses similarities in affirmative sentences and differences in negative sentences.

Approximations: My office is about **as big as** this room.

Promises: I'll be at your house **as soon as** I can.

Similarities: I still work **as hard as** I did ten years ago.

Differences: I don't sleep **as late as** I used to.

Comparative Nouns: Form

More + Count Noun + *Than:*   I have **more bills** now **than** I did before.

More + Noncount Noun + *Than:*   I make **more money than** I used to.

Fewer + Count Noun + *Than:*   There are **fewer students** in this class **than** we expected.

Less + Noncount Noun + *Than:*   I have **less time** to shop **than** I used to.

Superlative Nouns: Form

The Most + Count Noun:	He has **the most problems** in his family.
The Most + Noncount Noun:	This course has **the most homework** of all my courses.
The Fewest + Count Noun:	That's why it has **the fewest students.**
The Least + Noncount Noun:	This town has **the least traffic** of all the college towns I know.

The Same…As: Form

Count Nouns:	This town has **the same restaurants as** that one.
Noncount Nouns:	This town has **the same population as** that one.

Comparative Nouns, Superlative Nouns, *The Same…As:* Meaning and Use

Comparative forms of nouns compare quantities of two nouns. Superlative forms of nouns rank the quantities of three or more nouns by selecting the largest or smallest quantity in the group. **The same…as** expresses the equality of two nouns.

Problems:	We have **more pollution** now **than** we used to.
Data Analysis:	Carrots have **the most vitamin A** in this group of vegetables.
Similarities:	My hair is **the same color as** my father's.
Differences:	I am **not the same size as** my father.
Choices:	I'm buying this car because it costs **less money than** the other one.

So…That/Such (a)…That: Form

So + Adjective + *That:*	I'm **so tired that** I have to leave work early.
So + Adverb + *That:*	I ran **so fast that** I lost my breath.
Such a + Adjective + Count Noun + *That:*	It's **such a popular course that** the enrollment is limited to fifty.
Such + Adjective + Noncount Noun + *That:*	There's **such loud noise** in the hall **that** I can't work.
Such + Adjective + Plural Count Noun + *That:*	They were **such good movies that** I saw them twice.

So…That/Such (a)…That: Meaning and Use

So…that/such (a)…that are degree expressions which indicate that a high degree of an adjective or adverb leads to a particular result. They are frequently used to make complaints.

Results:	I was **so busy that** I forgot to call you back.
Complaints:	The restaurant was **so noisy that** we had to leave.
	We had **such a bad experience** at that restaurant **that** we'll never go there again.

⟹ Summary Exercise: Finding Errors

Most of the sentences have an error in form or appropriate use. Find each error and correct it.

1. My cold was ~~very~~ bad that I went home.   *so*

2. She is taller as I am.

3. We had such a good weather that we stayed for a long time.

4. He's not as tall as me.

5. This one is more prettier than that one.

6. I have as more as he does.

7. Don't go there. It's most expensive restaurant in town.

8. It was so cold that we left early.

9. I don't think that I'm as friendly she is.

10. My hair is the same long as my sister's hair.

11. I work better in the morning that in the afternoon.

12. It was the most interesting one than them all.

Expressing Unreal Situations:
Wish Sentences and Imaginary *If* Sentences

Preview

Two neighbors:

    Mark: **I wish I had** more room for all my books. **Would you mind if I stored** these boxes
        in your basement?
    Kevin: No, go right ahead. We have plenty of room.

Two friends:

    Tina: Are you going to buy the jacket?
    Pat: **I wish I could,** but it's too expensive. **I'd buy** it **if it were** on sale.

Two co-workers:

    Jan: Why didn't you accept the new job? It sounded much better than this one.
    Terry: **If I took** the job, **I'd need** a car. I don't have a car and I can't afford one right now.

Wish sentences describe unreal situations. Sentences with **wish** express a desire to change a real
situation into an unreal one. In the examples above, Mark doesn't have enough room, but he
wishes he did. Pat cannot buy the jacket even though she wants to.

Imaginary **if** sentences express imaginary situations and their imaginary results. In Chapter 5
you studied **if** sentences that talk about real situations. Compare these two kinds of **if** sentences:

    If I **take** the job, **I'll need** a car.
    If I **took** the job, **I'd need** a car.

The first sentence expresses a possible situation and its expected future result. It describes a
situation that still might happen. The second sentence expresses an imaginary situation and its
imaginary result. The real situation in this sentence is *I don't have the job* and therefore, *I don't
need a car.*

In this chapter you will study various uses of **wish** sentences and imaginary **if** sentences that
talk about imaginary situations in the present and the future. Imaginary situations in the past
are discussed in Chapter 15.

Wish Sentences: Form

Wish	Simple Past Clause
I **wish**	**that I had** a different job.
I **wish**	**I had** a different job.
I **wish**	I **were** stronger.
I **wish**	I **could** help you.
I **wish**	you **would** come with me tonight.
I **wish**	you**'d** come with me tonight.

- To form **wish** sentences, use the main verb **wish** in the simple present + a clause with a simple past verb.

- The clause after **wish** must be in the simple past, even when **but** joins it to a simple present sentence:

  I don't have a computer, **but** I **wish** I **did.**
  I **wish** I **had** a computer, **but** I don't.

- **That** is optional after **wish**. It is often omitted.

- **Were** is used for both singular and plural subjects in the unreal simple past clause:

  I wish he **were** stronger.
  I wish they **were** stronger.

- **Could**, the simple past of **can**, is often used in the simple past clause after **wish**.

- **Would**, the simple past of **will**, is often used in the simple past clause. Its contraction is **'d**.

CONVERSATION NOTE

In informal conversation, **was** is often used in the first- and third-person singular instead of **were:**

I wish I **wasn't** so tall.

I wish he **wasn't** so tall.

➡ Exercise 1: Working on Form

Work with a partner. Complete the following conversations using the appropriate form of the verbs in parentheses. Then practice the conversations.

1. **A:** I wish I _____had_____ (have) more money to spend.

   B: I wish you _____did_____ (do) too.

2. **A:** I wish this place _____ (be/not) so crowded.

   B: I know. I wish we _____ (can) leave, but I have to wait until 8:30.

3. **A:** Do you ever wish you _____ (have) a different job?

   B: Yeah. Sometimes I wish I _____ (work) for a smaller company.

4. **A:** Do you like the climate here?

   B: Not particularly. I wish it _____ (rain/not) so often.

5. **A:** Can you help me fix my car?

   B: I wish I _____ (can), but I have an appointment.

6. **A:** I need some help with this. Do you know anything about_____

   _____

   B: No, I wish _____, but I _____

   _____

Wish Sentences: Meaning and Use

UNREAL OR IMPOSSIBLE SITUATIONS

1. Wish expresses a desire for a situation that does not exist right now in the present.
A wish is a desire to change a real situation into an unreal one. This unreal situation is
expressed in the simple past. In a **wish** sentence, the simple past does not indicate past time;
it only indicates that the situation is unreal:

   I **wish** I **lived** in a house, but I don't. I live in an apartment.

2. Wish sentences often express regret about a situation that you would like to change:

   Marie: Can you help me this afternoon?
   Karen: No, I'm sorry. I **wish** I **could,** but I have a doctor's appointment.

3. Would, the simple past of **will,** is used in the simple past clause after **wish** to express
future actions that you want to happen:

   I **wish** the bus **would** come. I'm cold.
   I **wish** you**'d** come with me tonight. I don't want to go alone.

(continued)

4. Sometimes **wish** sentences with **would** express complaints, especially when you want something to change, but you think it probably won't:

I **wish** it **would** stop raining. We can't go anywhere in this weather.
I **wish** you **wouldn't** leave the car windows open.

5. While **wish** expresses a desire for an unreal situation, **hope** expresses a desire for a possible real situation. The difference between unreal and real is expressed by the different tenses that follow **wish** and **hope.** After **wish,** the simple past expresses an unreal situation. After **hope,** the simple present and the future express a possible real situation:

Unreal or Impossible	Possible
I **wish** I **had** a car.	I **hope** I **have** a car soon.
	I **hope** I**'ll have** a car soon.

⇛ Exercise 2: Wishing About the Present

Work in small groups. Take turns making up as many wishes as you can for each situation.

1. Your apartment is too small:

Examples: *I wish I didn't live in such a small apartment.*
I wish I could move.
I wish I had more space.
I wish I could afford a bigger apartment.

2. You're broke. You have no money:

3. You don't like your new class:

4. You're very busy:

5. You live in a big city:

6. You're lonely:

7. You need more exercise:

8. You're lost in the woods:

⇛ Exercise 3: Expressing Regret

Work with a partner. Complete the following conversations with expressions of regret. Use the simple past and then give a reason with *but*, explaining the real situation. Practice the conversations, switching roles.

1. **Roommate A:** Could you please help me with this?

   Roommate B: I'm sorry, I can't. I wish ___I could, but I have to leave right now.___

2. **Customer:** Do you have any more of these?

   Salesclerk: No, I'm sorry. I wish _____, but _____

   _____

3. **Student A:** Can you lend me yesterday's notes?

   Student B: Well, I wish _____, but _____

   _____

4. **Friend A:** Do you have any free time later this afternoon?

   Friend B: No, I wish _____, but _____

   _____

5. **Child:** Are there any more cookies left?

   Parent: No, I wish _____, but _____

   _____

6. **Spouse A:** Is it warm outside this morning?

   Spouse B: No, I wish _____, but _____

   _____

⫸ Exercise 4: Wishing About the Future

Work on your own. Express your wishes for the future by using *wish* sentences with
would clauses.

1. You are going to take a walk and you really want your roommate to come with you:
   I wish you'd take a walk with me.
   _____

2. You want your sister to take better care of herself, but you're afraid that she won't:

   _____

3. You don't like going to concerts alone, but your best friend is always studying. You want her
   to come to the next one:

   _____

4. You think that your father is working too hard. You want to tell him to take a vacation,
   although he probably won't listen:

   _____

5. Your friend dropped by for a few minutes. You want him to stay longer, but he seems to be in a hurry:

_____

6. Your sister has just announced that she wants to quit school and go back home. You want her to stay:

_____

⯈ Exercise 5: Complaining

Work on your own. Imagine you're very unhappy with your roommate this semester. Complain about your roommate's bad habits using *wish* sentences with *would* or *wouldn't*.

1. (makes a lot of noise in the morning)

   I wish he wouldn't make so much noise in the morning. OR

   I wish she would be quieter in the morning.

2. (uses up all the hot water in the shower)

   _____

3. (stays in the bathroom too long)

   _____

4. (doesn't write down phone messages)

   _____

5. (smokes cigarettes)

   _____

6. (leaves dirty clothes in the living room)

   _____

7. (doesn't clean up the kitchen)

   _____

8. (talks on the phone for hours)

   _____

9. (doesn't buy his or her own food)

_____

10. (doesn't turn the lights off)

_____

⟱ Exercise 6: Wishing and Hoping

Work with a partner. You have two friends. Friend A is optimistic and always hopes for something positive. Friend B is usually negative and wishes that the situation were different. Therefore, you get very different answers when you ask them the same question. Make up answers with *wish* and *hope*. Then practice the conversations.

1. Are you coming to the party Saturday night?

   A: _I hope I can. I have to work until 8:30, but I think I can come afterwards._

   B: _I wish I could, but I have to work until 8 :30 and then I'll probably be too tired._

2. Have you decided to go home for vacation?

   A: _____

   _____

   B: _____

   _____

3. Are you going to finish your research paper on time?

   A: _____

   _____

   B: _____

   _____

4. Are you going to the teacher's house for dinner on Friday night?

   A: _____

   _____

   B: _____

   _____

5. Are you going jogging with us tonight as usual?

    A: _____

    _____

    B: _____

    _____

6. Are you going to look for a better job?

    A: _____

    _____

    B: _____

    _____

Imaginary *If* Sentences: Form

Imaginary *If* Clause	Imaginary Result
If I **were** you,	**then** I **would wait**.
If I **were** you,	I **would wait**.
If we **were staying** in Vancouver,	we **could visit** them.

- Imaginary **if** sentences have an **if** clause and a result clause. The **if** clause has a simple past or past continuous verb. The result clause has **would** or **could** + the main verb.
- **Then** in the result clause is optional. It is often omitted.
- **Were** is used for both singular and plural subjects in the unreal simple past or past continuous clause.
- The **if** clause can come before or after the result clause. The meaning is the same.
- When the **if** clause comes first, it is followed by a comma.

Imaginary Result	Imaginary *If* Clause
I **would wait**	**if** I **were** you.
We **could visit** them	**if** we **were staying** in Vancouver.

- When the result clause comes first, there is no comma and **then** is omitted.

CONVERSATION NOTE

In informal conversation, **was** is often used in the first- and third-person singular:

If I **was** taller, there would be no problem.

⫸ Exercise 7: Working on Form

Work with your classmates. Take turns creating imaginary *if* sentences. Use the end of the last person's sentence to begin your own. Continue until everyone has had a turn. Start with: *If I had the day off,….*

> Example: **A:** *If I had the day off, I'd go shopping.*
> **B:** *If I went shopping, I'd spend a lot of money.*
> **C:** *If I spent a lot of money,….*

Imaginary *If* Sentences: Meaning and Use

UNREAL CONDITIONAL SITUATIONS

1. Imaginary **if** sentences express imaginary situations that are not true at the present time. They are also called unreal conditional sentences because the unreal result in the main clause depends on the unreal condition in the **if** clause.

2. In the **if** clause, the simple past or past continuous indicates that the situation is unreal; it does not indicate past time. In the result clause, **would** plus the main verb indicates that the result is unreal:

> If I **had** a problem, **I'd ask** for your help. (I don't have a problem right now, so I don't need help.)
> If it **were snowing, I'd wear** my boots. (It's not snowing right now, so I'm not wearing my boots.)

3. **Could** is possible instead of **would** when it means *would be able to:*

> If you had a computer, you **could work** at home.

4. Imaginary **if** sentences can be used as an indirect way of giving advice. You can make your sentence sound softer and more tentative by using imaginary **if** sentences instead of the modals **should** and **ought to:**

Indirect: **If** I **were** you, **I'd** speak to the instructor.

Direct: You **should** speak to the instructor.

You **ought to** speak to the instructor.

(continued)

5. Imaginary **if** sentences can also be used as an indirect way of asking for permission, especially if you don't want to bother the listener:

You want to open the window but you think your friend might not want you to:

You: **Would you mind if I opened** the window?
Friend: No, go right ahead.

You: **Would it bother you if I opened** the window?
Friend: No, go right ahead.

You: **Would it be OK if I opened** the window?
Friend: Sure, go right ahead.

An affirmative answer to **would you mind** or **would it bother you** is *No* because the speaker is really asking if the request bothers the listener. An affirmative answer means *No, it doesn't bother me. You can do it.*

6. As with giving advice, imaginary **if** sentences used for permission are more indirect than the requests for permission with the modals **may, could,** and **can** that you studied in Chapter 7. Although the meaning of these sentences is very similar, you might choose **would you mind** when you're less sure about the response and you want to be more tentative or indirect:

Indirect: **Would you mind if** I left early?

Direct: **Could** I leave early?

⏵ Exercise 8: Expressing Imaginary Situations

Work on your own. Complete each sentence using the simple past in the imaginary *if* clause and *would* plus a verb in the imaginary result clause.

1. If I missed the bus, I'd have to walk to work. _____

2. If I were much taller, _____

_____

3. If I were late for an appointment, _____

_____

4. If I were sick, _____

_____

5. I'd be embarrassed if _____

_____

6. I'd quit my job if _____

_____

7. I wouldn't get angry if_____

_____

8. I would buy a new computer if _____

_____

⫸ Exercise 9: Expressing Imaginary Situations

Work on your own. Write on a separate sheet of paper five imaginary *if* clauses or result clauses and give them to a classmate to complete.

⫸ Exercise 10: Responding to Imaginary Situations

Work on your own. Complete the following imaginary *if* clauses to form questions that can be as serious or silly as you like. Then, with a partner, take turns asking and answering these questions. Use result clauses with *would* in your answers.

1. **A:** What would you do if _you spilled food all over yourself in a restaurant?_
   B: _I'd try to clean it up very quickly and quietly._

2. **A:** What would you do if _____
   B: _____

3. **A:** What would you say if _____
   B: _____

4. **A:** How would you feel if _____
   B: _____

5. **A:** Where would you go if _____
   B: _____

⫸ **Exercise 11: Giving Advice**

Work with a partner. Take turns giving advice. Complete the conversations with *If I were you, I'd...* or *If I were you, I wouldn't....* Then practice the conversations.

1. **A:** There's a big mistake on my electric bill.
   B: _If I were you, I'd call the business office._

2. **A:** My landlord doesn't repair things when I ask him to.
   B: _____

3. **A:** I'm not doing very well in my math course.
   B: _____

4. **A:** I accepted two invitations to go out Saturday night and now I don't know what to do.
   B: _____

5. **A:** I need to speak to my doctor, but I'm never at home when she calls back.
   B: _____

6. **A:** My boss isn't very nice to me.
   B: _____

7. **A:** I want to buy a computer, but I don't know anything about them.
   B: _____

8. **A:** I'm really having difficulty with my health insurance. I don't understand why the insurance company isn't paying the medical bills that I send.
   B: _____

9. **A:** I'm so embarrassed. I forgot to deposit money into my checking account and my rent check bounced.
   B: _____

10. **A:** I tried to put a quarter into a parking meter, but the quarter got stuck. When I returned to my car, there was a parking ticket on my windshield.
    B: _____

⇒ **Exercise 12: Asking for Permission**

Work with a partner. Read the situations below and take turns asking for permission. Use *Would you mind if…*, *Would it bother you if…*, or *Would it be OK if…*, and respond appropriately.

1. You're supposed to pick your friend up at eight o'clock, but you prefer to pick her up earlier because you're afraid there will be a lot of traffic:

   A: _Would you mind if I picked you up earlier?_

   B: _No, that's OK._

2. You don't have time right now to talk on the phone to your brother. You want to call him back later:

   A: _____

   B: _____

3. You want to listen to the news while your roommate is studying. You don't want to disturb him:

   A: _____

   B: _____

4. You think it's too hot in the classroom and you want to open the window:

   A: _____

   B: _____

5. Your friend has an interesting book that she doesn't seem to be reading right now. You want to borrow it:

   A: _____

   B: _____

6. You're driving your friend home from work. It's late but you want to stop for gas on the way home because you don't want to do it in the morning:

   A: _____

   B: _____

⟹ Exercise 13: Thinking About Meaning

Work with a partner. Read each of the imaginary *if* sentences and decide whether the statements below them are true (T) or false (F).

1. We'd leave if it stopped raining.

    __F__ (a) We left.

    __T__ (b) It's raining.

2. I'd go to the meeting if I weren't so busy.

    _____ (a) I'm not very busy.

    _____ (b) I'm going to the meeting.

3. If it weren't on sale, I couldn't afford it.

    _____ (a) It's on sale.

    _____ (b) I can't afford it.

4. I wouldn't take the exam if I had a choice.

    _____ (a) I have to take the exam.

    _____ (b) I don't have a choice.

5. If you lived in that neighborhood, you'd know Joseph Taylor.

    _____ (a) You know Joseph Taylor.

    _____ (b) You don't live in that neighborhood.

6. If you spoke more slowly, I'd understand you better.

    _____ (a) You speak too fast.

    _____ (b) I understand you very well.

Summary

Wish Sentences: Form

Wish + Simple Past Clause: I **wish that** I **had** a different job.

I **wish** you **were** stronger.

They **wish** they **could get** reservations for next week, but they can't.

I **wish** you **would come** with me tonight.

Wish Sentences: Meaning and Use

Wish sentences express a desire to change a real situation into an unreal or impossible one.

Present Wishes: I **wish** I **had** more free time.

I **wish** I **could stay** longer.

Regrets: Ana: Are you busy tonight?
Sue: Yes, I'm sorry. I **wish** I **weren't,** but I have to study.

Future Wishes: I **wish** you**'d** come with me tonight.

Complaints: I **wish** she **wouldn't make** so much noise in the morning.

Imaginary *If* Sentences: Form

Imaginary *If* Clause + Imaginary Result: **If** we **had** more time**,** we**'d plant** a garden.

If I **were** you, I **would wait.**

Imaginary Result + Imaginary *If* Clause: We'd **plant** a garden **if** we **had** more time.

I **would wait if** I **were** you.

Imaginary *If* Sentences: Meaning and Use

Imaginary **if** sentences express a situation that is not true at the present time and its imaginary result.

Imaginary Situations: Bob: What **would** you **do if** you **were** president?
Mark: I**'d balance** the budget.

Advice: **If** I **were** you, I**'d** look for another job.

Permission: Joe: **Would you mind if** I **came** a little later?
Pat: No, come when you can.

Jan: **Would it bother you if** I **opened** the window?
Alice: No, go right ahead.

Tom: **Would it be OK if** I **left** early?
Kate: Sure, go right ahead.

⟱ **Summary Exercise: Finding Errors**

Some of the following sentences have an error in form or appropriate use. Find each error and correct it.

1. I wish I ~~can~~ go with you, but I have to baby-sit.   *could*

2. What do you do if there were a fire in your kitchen? Would you call the fire department or try to put it out yourself first?

3. I can't play the piano, but I wish I can.

4. I'd call him if I weren't so upset.

5. Would you mind if I left early today?

6. If I know the answer, I wouldn't ask you. But I really don't know the answer.

7. I wish you'll stop smoking so much. I'm worried about you.

8. If I were you, I'll return it to the store.

9. I wish it weren't so cold outside today. I want to go swimming.

10. I really need to talk to you. I hope you'd call me back later.

11. I appreciate her help a great deal. I won't be able to do the job if she weren't helping me.

12. Do you wish you are there right now?

CHAPTER 14

Gerunds and Infinitives

Preview

A summer recreation program guide:

The following classes are available this summer: **swimming, canoeing, fishing, sailing,** tennis, **weight lifting,** and **in-line skating.**

Household advice:

Keeping garlic fresh is easy: **To keep garlic cloves fresh,** store them in the freezer. When you want **to use them,** try **peeling and chopping them** before **thawing.**

Washing your windows: Avoid **washing windows** on sunny days. They will dry too fast and show streaks. **To shine your windows,** it is easier and cheaper **to use newspapers** instead of **using paper towels.**

Gerunds (verb plus **-ing**) and infinitives (**to** plus verb) are verb forms that are used in place of nouns and pronouns. Like nouns, gerunds name things — in this case, activities that are usually expressed by verbs. Gerunds can be the subject of a sentence or the object of prepositions and certain verbs such as **try** and **avoid.** In this chapter you will study common verbs and phrases that are followed by gerunds. You will also study the various uses of the different gerund types.

Infinitives name activities expressed by verbs too, but infinitives are often used differently from gerunds. Infinitives typically follow certain verbs, such as **want, hope,** and **decide.** They can express purpose, as in **[In order] to keep garlic cloves fresh, store them....**

In this chapter you will study common verbs followed by infinitives and other ways in which infinitives are frequently used. You will also study common verbs and expressions that can be followed by either gerunds or infinitives.

Overview of Gerunds: Form and Meaning

Subject	Object	Object of Preposition
Swimming is fun.	Ana likes **swimming**.	She's good at **swimming**.

- To form a gerund, add **-ing** to the simple form of the verb.
- Look at page 485 for spelling rules for adding **-ing** to verbs.
- Gerunds can function as the subject of the sentence, the object of a verb, or the object of a preposition.
- All verbs, including stative verbs, have gerund forms:

  Swimming and **skiing** are my two favorite sports.
  Owning a car is expensive, but I still enjoy **having one.**

- A gerund can be one word or a phrase:

  Did you finish **studying?**
  Did you finish **studying for the test?**

- Gerunds are always singular. They behave like noncount nouns. They take singular verbs and they are replaced by the pronoun **it**:

  Walking is good exercise and **it is** also enjoyable.

Affirmative Gerund	Negative Gerund
Exercising is good for you.	**Not exercising** is bad for you.

- To form a negative gerund, add **not** before the gerund.
- Gerunds name an activity or situation expressed by a verb. As noncount nouns, gerunds express these activities or situations in a general way:

  I don't like **being sick.**
  I don't like **studying.**

⟹ Exercise 1: Identifying Gerunds

Work with a partner. Underline the gerunds or gerund phrases in the conversations below. Then practice the conversations. (Hint: Don't confuse gerunds with continuous verbs.)

1. **A:** I don't like <u>staying home all weekend</u>. I'm really not having any fun.

   B: Well, why don't you make some suggestions instead of <u>complaining?</u>

2. **A:** My doctor said to avoid driving until I finish taking my medicine. So, I've postponed ~~delay~~

   leaving for vacation until tomorrow.

   B: Well, I'm not working this afternoon so I can stop by your apartment. I'd enjoy spending

   more time with you before you leave.

3. **A:** I'm thinking about quitting my job. ~~preposition~~

   B: Really? Don't you like working there anymore?

   A: I don't know. I'm considering going back to school.

4. **A:** Swimming isn't helping my back problem. I'm going to speak to my doctor again.

   B: Have you tried taking hot baths?

5. **A:** Are you nervous about passing the exam?

   B: Yes, I'm not used to studying so hard. I've been reading hundreds of pages every night

   before going to bed.

   A: Then there's no point in worrying.

Subject Gerunds: Form and Use

Subject Gerund	Verb
Swimming	makes me feel good.
Swimming a long distance	makes me tired.
Not swimming for a week	makes me feel lazy.

- Gerunds can replace singular noun or pronoun subjects:

  Exercise makes me tired.
  It
  Swimming

- Subject gerunds are used in general statements such as opinions, and they are also used for listing activities:

  Jogging is good for you.
  My favorite sports are: **jogging, swimming, skiing.**

➠ **Exercise 2: Working on Form**

Complete the following sentences.

1. _____ *Running* _____ is good exercise.
2. _____ ~~Smoking~~ Crossing the road / playing with fire is dangerous.
3. _____ *reading* _____ is easy.
4. _____ *Smoking* _____ is unhealthy.
5. _____ *Drug taking* _____ is against the law.
6. _____ *Going to a concert* _____ is expensive.
7. _____ *Playing video games* _____ takes a lot of time.
8. _____ *Studying* _____ is difficult.
9. _____ *Having a rest / going to sleep* _____ saves energy.
10. _____ *Going to Book Store* _____ is a good idea.
11. Getting up early _____ *is hard when I'm tired.*
12. Raising children _____ *is important when they are young.*
13. Washing dishes _____ *is necessary when we have lunch.*
14. Using a computer _____ *is helpful when we study.*
15. Being able to relax _____ *is good for our ~~physical~~ body.*

➠ **Exercise 3: Listing Problems**

Work with a partner. Choose one of the topics below and make a list of five to ten problems people have in that situation. Use a gerund to express each problem.

    Example: *problems with living in a big city*
          1. parking
          2. making friends

Topics

problems with living in a big city

problems with living in a foreign country

problems with having a pet

problems with owning your own home

➡ Exercise 4: Expressing Opinions

Work with a partner. Take turns asking and answering questions using the words in parentheses with gerunds.

1. (more fun/swim/ski)

   A: *Which is more fun, swimming or skiing?*
   B: *I think skiing is more fun than swimming.*

2. (more relaxing/take a hot bath/sunbathe)

3. (more fun/stay in a hotel/go camping)

4. (more exciting/ride a motorcycle/skydive)

5. (worse/miss a plane/lose your luggage)

6. (more important/enjoy your work/make a lot of money)

7. (more useful/learn to cook/learn to drive)

8. (easier/learn mathematics/learn a second language)

[Handwritten notes:]
which is more relaxing? — Sunbathing.
B: I think taking a hot bath is more relaxing than sunbathing
A: which is more fun? —
B: I think going camping is more fun than staying in a hotel.

Object Gerunds: Form

Subject	Verb	Object Gerund
I	**enjoy**	**working in the garden**.
She	**had fun**	**playing tennis**.

- A gerund can replace a singular noun or pronoun object after a verb:

  I enjoy **my work.**
      it.
      working.

  [Handwritten: 名词 代词]

- Many common verbs and phrases are followed by gerunds:

  Do you **avoid doing homework?**
  Mark **dislikes doing the dishes.**
  I **had trouble running** this morning.

➥ **Exercise 5: Working on Form**

Write five sentences about something that you like or don't like, using these verbs or phrases plus a gerund: *enjoy, dislike, avoid, have trouble, don't enjoy, have fun.* Tell the class about one.

1. I dislike getting up before seven in the morning. That's why I avoid taking eight o'clock classes.

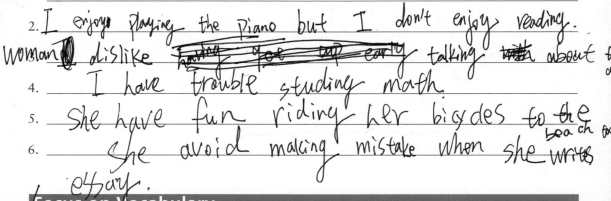

2. I enjoys playing the piano but I don't enjoy reading.

woman dislike ~~having Joe up early~~ talking ~~with~~ about th...

4. I have trouble studying math.

5. She have fun riding her bicycles to the beach...

6. She avoid making mistake when she writes essay.

Focus on Vocabulary

COMMON OBJECT GERUNDS

When you learn the meaning of a verb, it is also important to learn if it is followed by a gerund or an infinitive. These verbs are followed by gerunds; they cannot occur with infinitives. Look at page 495 for a more complete list.

Verb + Gerund

appreciate	I **appreciate living** in a warm climate.
avoid	**Avoid overcooking** the fish.
consider	You should **consider quitting** your job.
delay	Don't **delay calling** the doctor. It's serious.
deny	She **denies taking** the money.
dislike	I **dislike driving** in heavy traffic.
enjoy	Do you **enjoy going** to the theater?
finish	Did you **finish watering** the garden?
go	We **went fishing** yesterday.
imagine	I can't **imagine moving** away.
keep	He **keeps calling** me.
mind	I don't **mind working** late occasionally.

miss	I **miss talking** to you.
postpone	Don't **postpone buying** the tickets.
practice	He never **practices speaking** English at home.
quit	He **quit smoking** last year.
regret	I **regret not calling** you.
suggest	He **suggested taking** a vacation.

Phrase + Gerund

Many common phrases are followed by a gerund, but not by an infinitive:

it's no use	**It's no use worrying.**
be busy	**I'm busy studying** for exams.
it's (not) worth	Forget it. It**'s not worth getting** upset.
can't help	I **can't help telling** the truth.
have a good time	I **had a good time roller-blading** yesterday.
have fun	We **had fun swimming** in the lake.
have trouble	**I'm having trouble concentrating.**
spend time	I **spent a lot of time studying** for the test.
spend an hour	I **spent two hours cleaning** my apartment.
waste time	Don't **waste time worrying.**

➡ Exercise 6: Working on Object Gerunds

Work with a partner. Complete the following conversations with the gerund form of the verbs in parentheses. Then practice the conversations.

1. **A:** I finished _____ *writing* _____ (write) the first few pages of my term paper.

   B: Not me. I keep _____ *postponing* _____ (postpone) it.

2. **A:** Would you mind _____ (help) me with this?

   B: No, in fact, I'd enjoy _____ (do) it.

3. **A:** You should avoid _____ (drink) coffee if it keeps you up at night.

   B: I know, but I can't help _____ (have) a cup of coffee after dinner.

   It's one of my greatest pleasures since I quit _____ (smoke).

4. **A:** I dislike _____ (wait) in line at the grocery store.

   B: Me too. I resent _____ (spend) so much time there after work and on

   Saturdays. I wish they'd hire more help.

   A: It's probably worth _____ (go) there later in the evening. You could

   spend your time _____ (relax) after work and delay _____

   (shop) until after dinner.

5. **A:** Have you considered _____ (visit) your family for the holidays?

   B: It's too late. I had to postpone _____ (go) home until May because there

   weren't any tickets left. I really regret _____ (not/buy) my ticket several

   months ago, but I was busy _____ (look) for a job then.

Object Gerunds: Meaning and Use

LIKES, DISLIKES, FEELINGS, ACTIVITIES

1. Many of the verbs listed on pages 360–361 are used frequently to express likes, dislikes, and feelings:

Likes: We **enjoy sailing.**

Dislikes: I **dislike waiting in line.**

Feelings: He **regrets leaving early.**

2. Go plus gerund is used in many expressions related to recreational activities and shopping:

go boating	go camping	go skating
go canoeing	go hiking	go skiing
go fishing	go hunting	go sledding
go sailing	go jogging	go shopping
go swimming	go mountain climbing	go sightseeing
go waterskiing	go running	go window shopping

   Marie: Do you ever **go swimming** in the lake?
   Karen: Yes, quite often. We also **go boating.** Maybe you can **go fishing** with us sometime.
   Marie: That sounds like a good idea, but first I'll have to **go shopping** for a fishing rod.

3. The verb **mind** plus gerund is frequently used in questions and in negative statements:

Joe: **Do you mind getting up early** for work?
Matt: No, not at all. What about you?
Joe: Well, I **don't mind getting up early** when I'm not tired.

4. The phrase **would you mind** plus gerund is a very common expression for making polite requests. Like the requests for permission with **would you mind** plus **if** clause that you studied in Chapter 13, **would you mind** plus gerund sentences express the idea that the speaker is trying not to bother the listener. The response means *No, it doesn't bother me* or *No, I don't mind:*

Pat: **Would you mind opening the window?**
Ann: No, I'd be glad to.

➡ **Exercise 7: Talking About Likes and Dislikes**

Work with a partner. Take turns asking and answering questions using the words in parentheses. Answer with gerunds or gerund phrases, and then ask *What about you?*

1. (what/enjoy/do/on Sundays)

   A: *What do you enjoy doing on Sundays?*
   B: *I enjoy sleeping late. What about you?*
   A: *I enjoy taking long walks.*

2. (what/avoid/do)

3. (what/dislike/do)

4. (what/enjoy/do/after work)

5. (what/miss/do/in this country)

6. (what/regret/not do/recently)

7. (what/often postpone/do)

8. (what/have trouble/do)

⏩ **Exercise 8: Making Polite Requests**

Work with a partner. Make up polite requests and responses that would be appropriate in each situation. Use *would you mind* and a gerund in your requests.

1. It's pouring outside and you're sitting inside a bus shelter waiting for a bus. The person next to you lights up a cigarette. The smoke is making you sick:

   A: _Would you mind putting out your cigarette?_ The smoke is making me sick.

   B: _No, not at all. I didn't know it was bothering you._

2. You made an appointment with your auto mechanic to check your brakes today. On the way to the garage, you notice that your car horn isn't working:

   A: _____

   It stopped working on the way over here.

   B: _____

3. Your friend is driving you home from work today. You don't feel very well and you are starting to cough. You have no cough medicine at home. You would like your friend to stop at the store on the way home:

   A: _____

   B: _____

4. You are in the computer room at the library. You can't get your computer to work properly. You need some help from the computer assistant:

   A: _____

   B: _____

5. You are having trouble concentrating in class. The professor has just said something important but you missed most of it. You want to know what he said:

   A: _____

   I didn't hear all of it.

   B: _____

6. You were absent from class last week and you would like to borrow from a classmate the notes on the lecture you missed:

   A: _____

   B: _____

Preposition + Object Gerunds: Form and Use

Subject	Verb	Preposition	Object Gerund
We	**talked**	**about**	**taking a trip**.

Subject	Verb Phrase	Preposition	Object Gerund
I	**look forward**	**to**	**swimming**.

- Many common verbs and verb phrases include prepositions. These verbs and phrases can be followed by nouns, pronouns, or gerunds:

  We talked about **a trip.**
                  it.
                  taking a trip.

  I look forward to **my workout.**
                  it.
                  swimming.

Preposition	Object Gerund	(...)
Before	**leaving the room,**	close the window.

- Prepositions also occur with gerunds in separate phrases without verbs. These prepositional phrases often begin or end sentences:

  After calling me, he left.
  He left **after calling me.**

- Prepositional phrases with **by** + gerund explain how to do something:

  Mike: How do you defrost something fast?
  Joe: **By heating it in the microwave.**

- A number of prepositions and prepositional phrase + gerund combinations often present alternatives to a situation:

  Instead of taking math, take a computer course. (Don't take math.)
  Besides taking math, take a computer course. (Take both.)
  In addition to taking math, take a computer course. (Take both.)

⏭ Exercise 9: Offering Solutions

Work with a partner. Answer the following questions with as many solutions as possible using *by* plus gerund.

1. How do you pay for groceries without cash?

   Examples: *By writing a check.*
   By using a credit card (in some stores).
   By using an ATM card (in some stores).

2. How do you get into your locked car if the keys are inside?

3. How do you tie your shoes with one hand only?

4. How do you ask for directions in a foreign country when you don't speak the language?

5. How do you prepare dinner when your stove isn't working?

6. How do you wake up early without an alarm clock?

⏭ Exercise 10: Offering Alternatives

Work with a partner. Offer alternatives to the following situations using *instead of, besides,* or *in addition to* plus gerund.

1. You want to lose weight, but dieting isn't working.

   Examples: *Instead of dieting, start an exercise program.*
   Besides dieting, you need exercise too.
   In addition to dieting, you need exercise too.

2. You keep missing the bus in the morning when you leave at eight o'clock.

3. Your grocery bills are too high.

4. You can't fall asleep until it's very late.

5. You lose your temper very easily these days.

6. People always ask you for favors. You don't know how to say no, even when you want to.

Focus on Vocabulary

COMMON PREPOSITION + OBJECT GERUNDS

These common verbs with prepositions may be followed by a gerund, but not by an infinitive. Look at pages 495–496 for a more complete list.

Verb with Preposition + Gerund

approve of   I don't **approve of smoking.**

disapprove of   I **disapprove of smoking.**

believe in	They don't **believe in eating** red meat.
look forward to	I **look forward to hearing** from you soon.
talk about	We **talked about leaving.**
think about	I often **think about taking** a long trip.
worry about	Do you ever **worry about failing** a course?

Be + Adjective + Preposition + Gerund

Many phrases ending in prepositions are be-plus-adjective expressions. They may be followed by a gerund, but not by an infinitive. Look at page 496 for a more complete list:

be accustomed to	We**'re accustomed to eating** dinner at six o'clock.
be afraid of	I**'m afraid of driving** in snow.
be good at	She**'s** really **good at learning** languages.
be interested in	**Are** you **interested in coming** tonight?
be nervous about	They**'re nervous about taking** the test.
be tired of	I**'m tired of cooking** every night.
be used to	I**'m not used to getting up** so early.
be worried about	He**'s worried about not getting** a raise.

Preposition + Gerund

Prepositions also occur with gerunds in separate phrases without verbs. These prepositional phrases often begin or end a sentence:

after	**After pressing the button,** hang up.
before	Don't eat **before exercising.**
besides	**Besides playing cards,** what else can we do?
by	I got in my car **by forcing the window open.**
in	**In offering the invitation,** she showed her kindness.
in addition to	**In addition to mowing the lawn,** we're going to water the flowers.
instead of	**Instead of complaining,** why don't you do something?
without	He fell asleep **without taking his shoes off.**

⟱ **Exercise 11: Working on Verbs with Prepositions**

Work with a partner. Take turns asking and answering *what* questions using the words in parentheses. Answer with gerunds or gerund phrases and then ask *What about you?*

1. (what/be tired of/do)

   A: *What are you tired of doing?*
   B: *I'm tired of cooking dinner every night. What about you?*
   A: *I'm tired of studying so much.*

2. (be good at/do)

3. (often/think about/do)

4. (be interested in/do)

5. (be afraid of/do)

6. (be used to/do/after dinner)

7. (look forward to/do/next year)

8. (worry about/do)

⟱ **Exercise 12: Working on Prepositions with Gerunds**

Work on your own. Give some helpful advice on some of the topics below. Complete the following sentences by writing a gerund or gerund phrase. Then offer one suggestion to the class.

Topics

take a trip	write a letter
take an exam	buy a car
cook dinner	do the laundry
use a computer	look for an apartment
go shopping	dial a wrong number

1. Before _____taking a trip_____, _____check your car to see if it is_____
   _____working properly._____

2. After _____, _____
   _____

3. Instead of _____, _____
   _____

4. Before _____, _____

_____

5. Besides _____, _____

_____

6. By _____, _____

_____

7. In addition to _____, _____

_____

8. Before _____, _____

_____

Overview of Infinitives: Form and Meaning

Affirmative Infinitive	Negative Infinitive
I expect **to move** soon.	I expect **not to move** before summer.

- To form an infinitive, use **to** + the simple form of the verb.
- All verbs except modal auxiliaries have infinitive forms.
- To form a negative infinitive, use **not** before **to** + verb.
- An infinitive can be a single verb or a verb phrase:

I don't want **to move.**
I don't want **to move out of state.**

Verb + Infinitive	Verb + Gerund
I **like to swim**. He **hates to wash dishes**.	I **like swimming**. He **hates washing dishes**.

- Some verbs are followed by either infinitives or gerunds.

(continued)

It... + Infinitive

It's difficult **to find an apartment**.

- Infinitives also occur in certain sentences beginning with **it**.

In Order + Infinitive

In order to keep garlic cloves fresh, store them in the freezer.
To keep garlic cloves fresh, store them in the freezer.

- Infinitives follow the expression of purpose **in order**.
- Infinitives may begin sentences, but they do not function as subjects.
- Infinitives name an activity or a situation expressed by a verb.

▶ Exercise 13: Working on Form

Work with a partner. Complete the following conversations with infinitives. Then practice the conversations.

1. **A:** When do you expect _____to leave_____ (leave) town?

   B: We promised _____to move out_____ (move out) on the first, so we hope _____ (start) our trip the next day. We'd like _____ (be) in our new apartment on the fifth or sixth.

2. **A:** Let's plan _____ (not arrive) at the party before seven.

   B: But don't we need _____ (help)?

   A: No, I promised _____ (clean up) after the party is over. But I suppose we could offer _____ (arrive) early in order _____ (hang up) the decorations.

3. **A:** How did you manage _____ (complete) all your work?

   B: Well, it wasn't easy _____ (do). I didn't expect _____ (finish) until tonight, but I worked all day and I refused _____ (take) any phone calls.

4. **A:** Is it too late _____ (go) somewhere tonight?

   B: No. We can go to a movie, but we need _____ (leave) in a few minutes.

5. **A:** Did you decide _____ (move) to Florida?

  B: Yes, but I think it makes more sense _____ (not move) until I find a job there.

  A: That sounds sensible. It would be hard _____ (pay) the rent if you quit your job.

Verb + Infinitive: Form

Affirmative Infinitives	Negative Infinitives
I expect **to move** soon.	I expect **not to move** before summer.
She hopes **to stay** for a year.	She hopes **not to leave** this year.

- Affirmative and negative infinitives may follow certain verbs.
- An infinitive can replace a singular noun or pronoun object following a verb:

  I want **a new car.**
        that.
        to buy a new car.

Choice Questions with Infinitives	Answers
Do you want **to sweep or to vacuum**?	**Sweep.**
Do you want **to sweep or vacuum**?	**Sweep.**

- **To** may be omitted before the second infinitive.
- To answer a choice question using only an infinitive, **to** is often omitted.

Yes/No Questions	Short Answers
Will you be ready soon?	Yes, I **expect to**.
Is Fred coming with you?	Yes, he **hopes to**.

- Verb + infinitive can be shortened in response to *yes/no* questions. The short form has a main verb + **to**.
- Verb + infinitive are shortened in the same way after **but** or **and**:

  I don't have to study tonight, **but I want to.**
  I don't have to study tonight, **and I don't want to.**

⮞ Exercise 14: Working on Form

Work with a partner. Make up choice questions with infinitives using the words in parentheses. Omit *to* in your answers where possible.

1. (expect/travel/stay home/next summer)

   A: *Do you expect to travel or stay home next summer?*
   B: *Stay home.*

2. (hope/get high grades/get passing grades)

3. (need/study hard/study a little)

4. (plan/go out/stay home/this weekend)

5. (want/stay in your apartment/find a new apartment)

6. (expect/get a lot of mail/get a little mail/today)

⮞ Exercise 15: Working on Verb + Infinitive Short Answers

Work with a partner. Complete the following conversations using the verbs in parentheses to form shortened verb plus infinitive answers.

1. **A:** Are you going to graduate in June?

   B: I _____ hope to. _____ (hope)

2. **A:** Are you taking a vacation this summer?

   B: Yes, I _____ (expect)

3. **A:** Do you think you'll come to the party?

   B: We _____ (hope)

4. **A:** Are you interested in going with us?

   B: No thanks. I _____ (not/want)

5. **A:** Are you still going to get married?

   B: Yes, we _____ (plan) soon.

6. **A:** Please don't leave so early.

   B: I'm sorry, but I really _____ (need)

Focus on Vocabulary

COMMON VERBS + INFINITIVES

When you learn the meaning of a verb, it is also important to learn if it is followed by an infinitive or a gerund. These verbs are followed by infinitives; they cannot occur with gerunds. Look at page 497 for a more complete list:

decide	We **decided to stay.**
expect	I **expect to have** a good time.
hope	I **hope not to be** late.
learn	We **learned to use** the new software in an hour.
manage	Did you **manage to find** your glove?
need	I **need to mail** these letters.
offer	He **offered to help** me.
plan	Do you **plan to stay** in this country?
promise	He **promised to water** my plants while I'm out of town.
refuse	Did you **refuse to pay** the bill?
seem	She **seems to be** shy.
wait	I'll **wait to make** an appointment.
want	I **want to find** a new apartment.
would like	**Would** you **like to borrow** my notes?

➠ Exercise 16: Working on Verbs + Infinitives

Imagine you are a public figure and you have an interview with the press. Choose either Situation A or B and complete the sentences that you might say during your interview.

Situation A: You are going to run for president.

Situation B: You are going to resign from your position because of a scandal.

1. I have decided _to run for president._

2. I expect _____

3. I hope _____

4. I refuse_____

5. I can't promise _____

6. I plan _____

7. I have managed _____

8. I need _____

9. I would like _____

10. I've learned _____

11. I want _____

12. My opponents seem _____

Verb + Infinitive: Meaning and Use

ATTITUDES, OPINIONS, FEELINGS

1. Infinitives often express attitudes, opinions, and feelings following verbs such as **want, would like, hope, expect,** and **seem:**

I **would like** to travel, but I don't have enough money.

2. The verb **would like** does not have the same meaning as **like.** Compare these sentences:

I **would like** to travel, but I don't have enough money.
I **like** to travel. I take a long trip every summer.
I **like** traveling.

In the first sentence, **would like** expresses a wish or a desire for something that hasn't happened yet. It only occurs with an infinitive. In the other sentences, **like** tells what you enjoy. It can be used with either an infinitive or a gerund.

3. Infinitives are not used with verbs and phrases that end with prepositions. These verbs and phrases take only gerunds:

I **look forward to** swimming.
*I look forward to swim. (INCORRECT)

I'm not accustomed to staying up late.
*I'm not accustomed to stay up late. (INCORRECT)

➡ Exercise 17: Distinguishing Verb + Infinitive from Verb + Gerund

Work on your own. Imagine some people are discussing a new movie that is very controversial. Complete each sentence with the gerund phrase *seeing it* or the infinitive phrase *to see it.*

1. I'm planning _to see it._ _____

2. I've thought about _seeing it._ _____

3. You should consider _____

4. I've decided _____

5. I suggest _____

6. Do you want_____

7. Don't expect _____

8. He refuses _____

9. I hope _____

10. There's no point in_____

11. We managed _____

12. Do you regret _____

13. I would like_____

14. You should avoid _____

15. I look forward to _____

16. Do you really need_____

Verb + Infinitive or Gerund: Form

Verbs	Infinitives	Gerunds
begin	It **began to snow**.	It **began snowing**.
start	He **started to laugh**.	He **started laughing**.
continue	We **continued to read**.	We **continued reading**.
like	I **like to swim**.	I **like swimming**.
love	I **love to ski**.	I **love skiing**.
hate	They **hate to move**.	They **hate moving**.
prefer	We **prefer to watch**.	We **prefer watching**.
remember	I **remembered to vote**.	I **remembered voting**.
forget	I never **forget to call**.	I never **forget calling**.
stop	I **stopped to smoke**.	I **stopped smoking**.
regret	I **regret to say** this.	I **regret saying** that.
try	I **tried to call**.	I **tried calling**.

- Some verbs may be followed by either an infinitive or a gerund. The meanings of the infinitives and gerunds can be the same or very different. (This is discussed in the Meaning and Use section on pages 376–377.)
- Look at page 497 for a more complete list of verbs that can be followed by infinitives or gerunds.
- If the main verb is in the continuous, the infinitive form is used instead of the gerund:

  It was beginning **to snow.**

➡ **Exercise 18: Working on Form**

Work with a partner. Change each verb plus gerund to a verb plus infinitive, and each verb plus infinitive to a verb plus gerund. Then practice the conversations. Notice that the meaning is the same or very similar.

1. **A:** I love skiing. What about you?

   B: I like skiing, but I prefer staying indoors in the winter.

   A: *I love to ski. What about you?*

   B: *I like to ski, but I prefer to stay indoors in the winter.*

2. **A:** I hate to drive in traffic.

   B: Then you should continue to take the bus home.

3. **A:** Karen began smoking as a teenager.

   B: Well, she'll probably continue coughing until she gives up the habit.

4. **A:** It started to rain a few minutes ago.

   B: Let's wait for a while. I don't like to walk in the rain.

5. **A:** I hate waiting in line.

   B: So do I. That's why I prefer to shop at night when there are fewer people.

Verb + Infinitive or Gerund: Meaning

SAME OR DIFFERENT?

Because infinitives are more like verbs and gerunds are more like nouns, there may sometimes be differences in meaning between the infinitive and the gerund that can follow the same verb. The verbs in this section are in groups according to whether or not there are differences in meaning.

1. After **begin, start,** and **continue,** the infinitive and the gerund have the same meaning:

Infinitive: It **began to snow** after dinner.

Gerund: It **began snowing** after dinner.

2. After **like, love, hate,** and **prefer,** the infinitive and the gerund are very similar in meaning, but not exactly the same. Sometimes it is more common to use an infinitive to talk about one specific occasion, especially in the future. It is more common to use a gerund to talk about an activity in general, without referring to a specific time:

Specific Occasion: Do you prefer **to play tennis** or **to swim** this afternoon?

In General: Do you prefer **playing tennis** or **swimming?**

3. After **remember, forget, stop,** and **regret,** the difference between the infinitive and the gerund concerns time and order of events. The infinitive refers to an action that happens later than the main verb (after the remembering, forgetting, stopping, etc.). The gerund refers to an action that happens earlier (before the remembering, forgetting, stopping, etc.):

Infinitive: I remembered **to mail the letter.** (First I remembered. Then I mailed the letter.)

Gerund: I remembered **mailing the letter.** (First I mailed the letter. Then I remembered it.)

Infinitive: I forgot **to go there.** (First I forgot. So I didn't go.)

Gerund: I'll never forget **going there.** (First I went there. Now I'll never forget it.)

Infinitive: I stopped **to smoke.** (First I stopped what I was doing. Then I smoked.)

Gerund: I stopped **smoking.** (First I was a smoker. Then I stopped.)

Infinitive: I regret **to tell** you that… (First I regretted it. Then I told you that…)

Gerund: I regret **telling** you that… (First I told you something. Then I regretted it.)

Forget and **regret** have some special restrictions: **Forget** is more commonly used with an infinitive. With a gerund, it occurs mostly in sentences with **will never:**

Infinitive: I **forgot to pay** my telephone bill.

Gerund: I **will never forget living** in Ecuador.

Regret takes either an infinitive or gerund with such verbs as **inform, tell, say,** and **announce.** With all other verbs, **regret** takes a gerund:

Infinitive: I **regret to announce** my resignation.

Gerund: I **regret announcing** my resignation.

Gerund: I **regret leaving.**

Gerund: I **regret quitting** my job.

4. After **try,** the infinitive and the gerund sometimes have different meanings:

Unsuccessful Attempt: I **tried to take some aspirin** for the pain, but I couldn't open the bottle.

Experiment: I **tried taking some aspirin** for the pain, but it didn't help.

Sometimes, however, infinitives and gerunds after **try** may have the same meaning. In both sentences below, Mark made the phone call:

Mark is talking to his friend:

  I tried **to call you** but you weren't home.
  I tried **calling you** but you weren't home.

⟫ Exercise 19: Expressing Feelings and Preferences

Work with a partner. Two cousins, who are very different, are spending the weekend together. Cousin A is very positive about everything. Cousin B is very negative. Complete the conversation using gerunds or infinitives. In some cases, you may use either one.

1. The alarm clock rings:

    A: Another beautiful day! I love _____ *getting up* OR *to get up* _____ (get up) in the

    morning. Before _____ (get out) of bed, I think about

    _____ (do) all sorts of wonderful things.

    B: You're kidding! I really dislike _____ (get up) in the

    morning. I immediately start _____ (worry) about all of

    the things I need _____ (do).

2. They plan their day:

    A: Let's go _____ (shop). I like

    _____ (watch) the crowds, and I would like

    _____ (buy) some gifts.

    B: Do we have to? I hate _____ (fight) my way through the

    crowds.

    A: Then let's go to the zoo. I enjoy _____ (look at) all the

    animals.

    B: Are you sure you want _____ (go) to the zoo? I don't like

    _____ (go) to the zoo. The animals smell, and there are so

    many flies.

    A: Well, would you like _____ (go) to the top of the Sears

    Tower? I enjoy _____ (be) high up. The view is great. I think

    you can see the lake from there.

    B: I remember _____ (go) up there once. It was terrible. I prefer

    _____ (have) both of my feet on the ground.

3. They return after _____ (sightsee) all day.

   Cousin A stops _____ (check) the mailbox before

   _____ (go) upstairs:

   A: I like _____ (get) mail, especially from my family.

   B: Not me. I hate _____ (get) mail. It's always bills and

   junk mail.

4. They enter the apartment:

   A: I'm beginning _____ (feel) hungry. Let's change clothes and

   go out for dinner. I don't want _____ (stay home) on such a

   nice evening. Let's try _____ (find) a good restaurant.

   B: I hate _____ (eat out). I try _____

   (avoid) the restaurants around here. You wouldn't mind _____

   (cook) something here, would you?

➤ Exercise 20: Giving Advice

Work in small groups and choose one of the suggested topics. Give advice by completing each
sentence with a gerund or infinitive. Be prepared to read your advice to the class without
mentioning your topic. Ask the class to guess what the advice is for.

Topics

Tips for cleaning your apartment

Tips for washing your car

Tips for studying for a test

Tips for finding a job

   Example: *Tips for cleaning your apartment*

1. Try _to make a plan before you begin._____

2. Consider _getting some help._____

3. Think about _____

4. Plan _____

5. Remember_____

6. Spend some time _____

7. Avoid _____

8. Don't postpone_____

9. Don't stop_____

10. Finally, don't forget_____

⟼ **Exercise 21: Discussing Attitudes**

Work in small groups. Share information about how people feel about restaurants, newspapers, or clothing in your country. Use as many of the suggested expressions as possible with gerunds or infinitives.

Expressions

people love	people hate
people like	people usually don't like
they're accustomed to	they're not accustomed to
they think it's worth	they think it's not worth
people approve of	they generally disapprove of
they usually prefer	people avoid
many people want	
some people need	
most people would like	

Example: *People usually don't like wearing bright clothing in my country.*

It... + Infinitive: Form

It Subject	*Be* + Adjective	Infinitive
It	is difficult	**to drive home in bad weather**.

- In **it...** + infinitive sentences, an **it** subject begins the sentence. It is often followed by **be** + an adjective and an infinitive or infinitive phrase.
- **It** substitutes for the infinitive. (**It** = **to drive home in bad weather.**)

It Subject	Verb	Infinitive
It	takes an hour	**to drive home in bad weather**.

- **It** can also be followed by a verb such as **take** or **cost**.

⫸ Exercise 22: Working on Form

Work with a partner. Take turns making up *yes/no* questions using the words in parentheses and *it...* plus an infinitive. Answer each question with a short answer.

1. (be unhealthy/worry a lot)

   A: *Is it unhealthy to worry a lot?*
   B: *Yes, it is.*

2. (cost a lot/go to college)

   A: *Does it cost a lot to go to college?*
   B: *Yes, it does.*

3. (be polite/phone people late at night)

4. (be necessary/sleep eight hours every night)

5. (cost much/travel to your relatives)

6. (be important/graduate from high school)

7. (take a long time/get a driver's license)

8. (be a good idea/get married)

9. (be unhealthy/eat a lot of eggs)

It... + Infinitive: Meaning and Use

REPLACING SUBJECT INFINITIVES WITH *IT*

1. Since the typical position of an infinitive is toward the end of a sentence, the pronoun **it** often replaces an infinitive as the subject of the sentence. **It** has the same meaning as the infinitive that it replaces:

   It is difficult **to learn Chinese. (It = to learn Chinese.)**

2. It... plus infinitive sentences have the same meaning as similar sentences with subject gerunds:

   It takes an hour **to drive home.**
   Driving home takes an hour.

3. A limited group of verbs and phrases can follow **it** in **it...**plus infinitive sentences. These include **be** and similar stative verbs (such as **seem, appear, look**) followed by an adjective, and a few other verbs including **cost** and **take**:

   It is too heavy to lift.
   It looks too heavy to lift.
   It costs a lot to fly to Asia.
   It takes twelve hours to get there.

➠ **Exercise 23: Expressing Opinions with *It* Sentences**

Rewrite each of the following sentences. Change the gerund to *it* and add the infinitive later in the sentence.

1. Raising children is not easy.

   It's not easy to raise children.
   _____

2. Studying all night is a bad idea.

   _____

3. Walking to work takes too much time.

   _____

4. Getting exercise is important.

   _____

5. Smoking cigarettes is dangerous.

   _____

6. Knowing a foreign language is useful.

   _____

➠ **Exercise 24: Expressing Opinions with Gerunds**

Complete each sentence with an infinitive. Then rewrite the sentence using a gerund as the subject.

1. It's not easy _to live in a big city._

   Living in a big city is not easy.
   _____

2. It's not necessary _____

   _____

3. It's difficult _____

   _____

4. It costs too much _____

_____

5. It's worthwhile for me _____

_____

6. It makes me happy _____

_____

7. It's easy _____

_____

8. It's important _____

_____

In Order + Infinitive: Form

Affirmative

In order to open, twist gently.
To open, twist gently.
Twist gently **to open**.

- Sentences with **in order** + an infinitive express purpose.
- Purpose infinitives often begin with **in order,** but **in order** is not necessary with affirmative infinitives.
- Purpose infinitives can occur at the beginning of a sentence or at the end of a sentence; the meaning is the same. There is no comma when the purpose infinitive is at the end of the sentence.

Negative

In order not to miss the bus, she left early.
She left early **in order not to miss the bus**.

- With negative purpose infinitives, **in order** is necessary.

⇒ **Exercise 25: Working on Form**

Complete the following sentences with purpose infinitives.

I spent a lot of time doing errands this morning. First I went to the bank
_____to get some money_____ and I went to the post office _____.
Then I stopped at the dry cleaners _____, and I went to the drugstore
nearby _____. After that, I stopped at the library
_____, and then I went to the supermarket
_____. On the way back home, I stopped at the gas station
_____. Finally, I went home _____.

In Order + Infinitive: Meaning and Use

PURPOSE OR REASON

1. Purpose infinitives express the reason for doing something:

I pressed the button (**in order**) **to start the machine.**

2. In order is often left out of purpose infinitives, especially in instructions on signs and packages and in conversation:

Instructions at a laundromat:

To operate this machine, press the red button first.

A conversation:

Pat: What is Tina doing these days?
Ana: She went back to school **to study biology.**

⇒ **Exercise 26: Expressing Purpose**

Work with a partner. Take turns asking and answering the following questions. Use as many purpose infinitives as possible in your responses.

1. Why do people exercise?

Example: *To stay healthy, to feel good, to lose weight.*

2. Why do people watch TV?

3. Why do people drink coffee?

4. Why do people go to the dentist?

5. Why do people use microwave ovens?

6. Why do people go to college?

7. Why do people put money in the bank?

8. Why do people go to the library?

9. Why do people read the newspaper?

10. Why do people study English?

11. Why do people travel?

12. ～～～～

➠ **Exercise 27: Giving Instructions**

1. Work with a partner. Choose two of the suggested topics below and write on a separate sheet of paper simple instructions starting with a purpose infinitive.

Topics

How to open a container of milk.

How to open a jar of jelly, a can of beans, a box of crackers, or a bottle of wine.

How to operate your TV, radio, VCR, or computer.

How to start your car.

To open a container of milk, push up the flap.

2. On your own, bring to class two examples of instructions, on signs or packages, with purpose infinitives.

➠ **Exercise 28: Thinking About Meaning**

Work with a partner. Read the explanation following each sentence. Decide whether it is true (T) or false (F).

1. I forgot to mail the letter.

   ___F___ I mailed the letter.

2. I didn't remember to take out the dog.

   _____ I took out the dog.

3. I regret quitting my job.

   _____ I quit my job.

4. I'll never forget winning the prize.

_____ I won the prize.

5. I always avoid eating sweets.

_____ I eat sweets.

6. I remember locking the door.

_____ I locked the door.

7. She stopped to eat lunch.

_____ She doesn't eat lunch.

8. I tried soaking my ankle, but it still hurts.

_____ I soaked my ankle.

9. I tried to catch the bus, but I missed it.

_____ I caught the bus.

10. She stopped drinking coffee.

_____ She drinks coffee.

Summary

Gerunds: Form

Subject Gerunds:	**Swimming** is good exercise.
	Not exercising is bad for your health.
Object Gerunds:	I **enjoy reading books.**
	I **regret not calling you.**
Preposition + Object Gerund:	I **thought about staying home.**
	People should be more careful **about not polluting** the environment.
Preposition + Gerund:	Wipe your feet **before entering.**

Gerunds: Meaning and Use

Gerunds name an activity or situation expressed by a verb.

Likes and Dislikes:	I enjoy **swimming in a pool** but I dislike **swimming in the ocean.**
Polite Requests:	Would you mind **helping me?**
Feelings:	I dislike **waiting in line.**

Solutions:	Tom: How would you get into your house without a key? Matt: **By climbing through a window.**
Advice:	Before **taking an exam,** relax.
Opinions:	Jim: Which is worse? **Driving in fog** or **driving in snow?** Joe: **Driving in snow.**
Lists:	These are her two most serious problems: **using the language lab** and **understanding the lectures.**
Alternatives:	**Instead of leaving late,** leave ten minutes earlier.

Infinitives: Form

Verb + Infinitive:	I **want to eat dinner.**
Verb + Negative Infinitive:	I **hope not to be late.**
Verb + Infinitive or Gerund:	I like **to draw pictures.**
	I like **drawing pictures.**
	I tried **not to take aspirin.**
	I tried **not taking aspirin.**
It… + Infinitive:	**It**'s difficult **to learn a new language.**
	It's better **not to arrive late.**
In Order + Infinitive:	**To open,** twist gently.
	Use a potholder **in order not to burn yourself.**

Infinitives: Meaning and Use

All infinitives name an activity or a situation expressed by a verb. Purpose infinitives express the reason or purpose for doing something.

Feelings:	I love **to get up** early in the morning.
Opinions:	I think that **it**'s important **to get a college degree.**
Preference:	Do you prefer **to come with me** tonight?
Attitudes:	I don't like **to study** on Saturday night.
Advice:	Try **not to worry** so much. It's not good for you.
Purpose:	Many people exercise **in order to lose weight.**
Instructions:	**To operate this machine,** read the instruction manual carefully.

⟫ **Summary Exercise: Finding Errors**

Most of the sentences have an error in form or use. Find each error and correct it.

1. ~~Play~~ tennis is good exercise. *Playing*

2. Please remember taking out the trash tomorrow morning.

3. I'm not used to getting up so early.

4. We don't want to leave, but we need to do.

5. I arrived early not to miss her speech.

6. Did you decide stay here?

7. We're looking forward to see them this weekend.

8. It's easy take the bus downtown.

9. Instead of driving, why don't you take the train?

10. It's beginning raining again.

11. When do you expect getting your degree?

12. I went to the supermarket for buying some milk.

13. Before leave for work, close the windows.

14. Would you mind to help me with this, please?

15. I used to writing a lot of letters when I lived far away from my family.

The Past Perfect and the Past Perfect Continuous, Past *Wish* Sentences, and Past Imaginary *If* Sentences

Preview

News report:

> By the time the stolen credit cards were reported to the police, the suspect **had left** town. He **had been staying** at the most expensive hotel in town until he checked out early Monday morning...

Two friends are talking:

> Tina: A waiter charged me three dollars too much today, but I didn't say anything because I was embarrassed. What **would** you **have done?**
>
> Eva: **If** that **had happened** to me, I **would have shown** him the mistake. I certainly **wouldn't have paid** the extra three dollars.
>
> Tina: I **wish** you **had been** there.

In Chapters 3 and 5 you learned several ways of talking about the past. Another way of talking about the past is with the past perfect and the past perfect continuous in various types of sentences including past wishes and past imaginary **if** sentences.

In the news report above, the past perfect (**had left**) expresses a relationship between two past times (*reporting stolen credit cards* and *leaving town*). The past perfect indicates the earlier, completed activity or situation (*the suspect had left*). The simple past indicates the later activity (*The stolen credit cards were reported to the police*). The past perfect continuous is similar to the past perfect, but it emphasizes the continuation of the earlier activity (**had been staying**) up to a specific time in the past.

The conversation between friends above describes an unreal situation with the past perfect in **wish** sentences and past imaginary **if** sentences. The past perfect (**had happened, had been**) indicates that the situation never happened to Eva; she was not in the restaurant.

In this chapter you will study the past perfect and the past perfect continuous along with past wishes and past imaginary **if** sentences.

The Past Perfect: Form

Statements	Contraction
I **had finished** by then.	I**'d**
You	You**'d**
She	She**'d**
He	He**'d**
It	It**'d**
We	We**'d**
They	They**'d**

- To form the past perfect, use **had** + the past participle of the main verb.
- The past participle of regular verbs is the same form as the simple past form (verb + **-ed**).
- Look at pages 486–487 for spelling and pronunciation rules for regular past participles.
- Look at pages 488–491 for a list of irregular verbs and their past participles.

Negative Statements	Contraction
I **had not started** by then.	I **hadn't**

- To form negative statements, use **had** + **not** or its contraction and the past participle of the main verb.

Yes/No Questions	Short Answers	Contraction
Had he **arrived** yet?	Yes, he **had**.	
	No, he **had not**.	No, he **hadn't**.

- To form *yes/no* questions, use **had** before the subject. The past participle of the main verb follows the subject.
- Short answers to *yes/no* questions have a subject pronoun + **had**.
- Affirmative short answers do not have contracted forms.

Information Questions	Answers
Why had you **left**?	To pick up my brother.

- The *wh-* word is followed by **had**, the subject, and the past participle of the main verb.

Information Questions (Subject)	Answers
Who had finished?	Mike **had**.
What had happened?	Nothing much.

- If **who** or **what** is the subject of the question, the word order is the same as for affirmative statements.

CONVERSATION NOTE

Had is contracted with subject pronouns in speaking and informal writing. With names and other nouns, **had** is not contracted in writing, although it may sound contracted in conversation. In fast speech, the *h* sound is dropped:

Written Form	**Spoken Form**
He**'d** already gone.	"He**'d** already gone."
They**'d** stopped.	"They**'d** stopped."
Dan **had** already gone.	"Dan**'d** already gone." (SPOKEN ONLY)
The cars **had** stopped.	"The cars**'d** stopped." (SPOKEN ONLY)

⏩ Exercise 1: Working on Form

Work with a partner. Complete the following conversations with the past perfect, using contractions wherever possible. Then practice the conversations.

1. **A:** We arrived at the theater late. The show _____had already begun_____ (already/begin).

   B: You didn't miss anything. Nothing really important _____ (happen) yet.

   A: But the first dance _____ (already/end) by the time we arrived, and I _____ (want) to see it so much.

2. **A:** No one wanted to go to the movies with Kate last night.

   B: I know. I _____ (already/see) the film that was playing, Rita _____ (read) the book, and Lisa _____ (go) to visit her aunt.

3. **A:** _____ (you/make) any arrangements before you arrived here?

   B: Yes, before I came, I _____ (already/arrange) for a place to live, but I _____ (not/register) for this course yet.

4. **A:** The building was empty when I got to work. No one _____
(come in) yet.

   B: That's because the train that we all take _____ (break down).
   By the time it came to the station, we _____ (be) there for over
   an hour.

5. **A:** When I saw my old friends, I couldn't believe it. Everyone _____
(change) so much. A lot of them _____ (gain) weight, and their hair
_____ (turn) gray. Some of the men _____
(lose) their hair.

   B: Well, what did you expect? The last time you saw them, you
   _____ (just/graduate) from high school.

⇒ Exercise 2: Asking and Answering Questions

Work with a partner and take turns asking and answering questions in the past perfect.
Start with *Before you started this course…* and use the phrases in parentheses with *ever*.
Respond with short answers and an explanation.

1. (take any other English courses)

   A: *Before you started this course, had you ever taken any other English courses?*
   B: *Yes, I had. I'd studied English for a year in high school.*

2. (study English grammar)

3. (read any English-language newspapers)

4. (speak on the phone in English)

5. (write any letters in English)

6. (see any movies in English)

7. (read any English-language books)

8. (make any English-speaking friends)

9. (order from a menu in English)

10. (watch any TV programs in English)

The Past Perfect: Meaning and Use

ORDER OF TWO PAST EVENTS

1. The past perfect expresses a relationship in time between two past events or situations. It indicates the first event or situation:

1st Event   **2nd Event**

I **had completed** the exam   when the bell rang.

2. The two past times can be recent or distant. The past perfect is not used only to talk about things that happened a long time ago:

Recent Time: When you called this morning, I **had gone** to a meeting. 最近的时间

Distant Time: He **had** never **left** home until he sailed to America in 1801. 遥远的时刻)

3. When you use the past perfect, make sure that two past times are involved. The later activity or time doesn't have to be stated in every sentence, but it must be stated in an earlier sentence or understood in the situation:

I **noticed** something strange by the back door. There **were** tools everywhere. Someone **had tried** to break the lock.

4. Past perfect sentences often combine with simple past time clauses beginning with **when, by the time, before,** and **until.** The past perfect is usually used in the main clause to indicate the first event or situation:

2nd Event   **1st Event**

When she **called** the police,   the thief **had escaped.**

By the time she **called** the police,   the thief **had escaped.**

Before she **called** the police,   the thief **had escaped.**

1st Event   **2nd Event**

He **had been** unhappy   **until** he **changed** jobs.

5. The meaning of **when** depends on the tense that is used in the main clause. Compare these sentences:

I had eaten **when** he left. (I ate before he left.)
I ate **when** he left. (I ate right after he left.)
I was eating **when** he left. (During the time that I was eating, he left.)

(continued)

6. The past perfect is often used in time clauses with **after** to indicate the earlier event. The later event in the main clause is expressed in the simple past:

1st Event	**2nd Event**
After I **had called** her,	I realized my mistake.

7. Since the sequence of events is already clear in sentences with **before** and **after**, the past perfect is sometimes replaced by the simple past. This means that the simple past can be used in both clauses:

> I **entered** the room **before** I took off my coat.
> I **had entered** the room **before** I took off my coat.

> **After** I **entered** the room, I took off my coat.
> **After** I **had entered** the room, I took off my coat.

8. One important difference between the present perfect and the past perfect is that the past perfect can be used with a phrase that indicates a definite point in time. The present perfect cannot:

> I found out that the plane **had arrived at three o'clock.**
> I found out that the plane has already arrived.

9. The past perfect is used with the same adverbs that are used with the present perfect with the same meanings: **ever, never, already, still, yet, just, for, since.** Therefore, past perfect sentences with these adverbs are often used to describe changes and accomplishments:

Changes:	When she came to the United States, she **had never eaten** a hot dog before.
Accomplishments:	By lunchtime, we **had discussed** the new budget, we **had written** a hiring policy, but we **hadn't approved** the new health care plan **yet.**

⟱ Exercise 3: Expressing Sequences

Work on your own. Read the following pairs of sentences and decide which event happened first by numbering the sentences *1* and *2*. Then combine the two sentences with the adverb in parentheses. Use the past perfect for the first event and the simple past for the second event.

1. __2__ He took some aspirin.

   __1__ He had a headache.

   (until)_He had had a headache until he took some aspirin._

2. _____ The sink overflowed.

_____ I left the water running.

(after)_____

3. _____ I didn't study.

_____ I failed the exam.

(because) _____

4. _____ They were married for five years.

_____ They got divorced.

(by the time) _____

5. _____ He was robbed.

_____ He called the police.

(after)_____

6. _____ The doctor said she was very healthy.

_____ She was worried.

(until)_____

7. _____ She slept for ten hours.

_____ She felt rested.

(when) _____

8. _____ His wife gave birth.

_____ He never held a newborn baby.

(until)_____

⬛➡ **Exercise 4: Describing Changes**

Work on your own. Describe some changes that took place as a result of each new experience. Use the past perfect with *never* and the phrases in parentheses.

1. Brian and JoAnn have just had their first child:

    (a) (hold a newborn baby) _Brian had never held a newborn baby before._

    (b) (diaper a baby) _____

    (c) (bathe a baby)_____

2. Eva started college last week:

    (a) (be on her own) _____

    (b) (live in a dormitory) _____

    (c) (do her own laundry)_____

3. Ryan just got his first summer job at a supermarket:

    (a) (use an electronic cash register) _____

    (b) (pack groceries) _____

    (c) (get a paycheck) _____

4. Nora took her first driving lesson:

    (a) (start a car) _____

    (b) (drive a car) _____

    (c) (be so scared) _____

⬛➡ **Exercise 5: Describing Personal Changes**

Think of something that you did for the first time. Describe some of the changes that took place as a result of this experience. Write three to five sentences with the past perfect and *never*.

New Experience: _I decided to have a surprise party for my friend._

I had never cooked for thirty people before.

New Experience: _____

1. _____

2. _____

3. _____

4. _____

5. _____

⫸ Exercise 6: Discussing Accomplishments

Work with a partner. Tell what was already done and what was not yet done. Use the past perfect with *already* and *not...yet* and the expressions in parentheses.

1. Sonia was hoping to move into her new apartment a few days early. Yesterday she went to see if it was ready yet:

   (the painters/paint/apartment)

   Example: *The painters had already painted the apartment.*

   (they/clean/carpet)

   Example: *They hadn't cleaned the carpet yet.*

   (they/fix/refrigerator)

   (plumbers/repair/pipes)

2. Martin checked the requirements for graduation last week:

   (complete/the English requirement)

   (take/a math course)

   (pass/the writing test)

3. Emma arrived at school late:

   (the class/check/the homework)

   (the teacher/give/a new assignment)

   (the class/begin/a new chapter)

4. When you spoke to your cousin, he had been looking for a job for three weeks and he still hadn't found anything yet:

   (answer/the classified ads)

   (go to an employment agency)

   (send/letters of inquiry)

The Past Perfect Continuous: Form

Statements				Contraction
I	**had**	**been**	**waiting**.	I**'d**
We	**had**	**been**	**waiting**.	We**'d**

- To form the past perfect continuous (also called the past perfect progressive), use the past perfect form of **be (had been)** + the main verb + **-ing**.
- Look at page 485 for the spelling rules for verbs ending in **-ing**.

Negative Statements					Contraction
We	**had**	**not**	**been**	**waiting**.	We **hadn't**

- To form negative statements, use **had** + **not** + **been** + verb + **-ing**.

Yes/No Questions				Short Answers	Contraction
Had	you	**been**	**working**?	Yes, I **had**.	
				No, I **had not**.	No, I **hadn't**.

- To form *yes/no* questions, use **had** before the subject, and use **been** + verb + **-ing**.
- Short answers have a subject pronoun + **had**.

Information Questions					Answers
What	**had**	she	**been**	**doing**?	Working.
Where	**had**	she	**been**	**working**?	Downtown.

- The *wh-* word is followed by **had**, the subject, **been**, and the main verb + **-ing**.

Information Questions (Subject)				Answers
Who	**had**	**been**	**working**?	Maria **had**.
What	**had**	**been**	**happening**?	Nothing much.

- If **who** or **what** is the subject, then the word order is the same as for affirmative statements.

➠ Exercise 7: Working on Form

Work with a partner. Complete each conversation with the words in parentheses, using the past perfect continuous form of the verb. Then practice the conversations.

1. **A:** You really looked tired when I met you. What _____*had you been doing*_____ (you/do)?

    B: I _____ (jog) for an hour, and before that I _____ (play) tennis.

2. **A:** He was arrested because he _____ (steal) money from the company.

    B: How long _____ (this/go on)?

    A: I'm not sure, but it appears that the police _____ (watch) him for several weeks.

3. **A:** I _____ (wait) for an hour when I finally complained to the receptionist.

    B: What was wrong?

    A: She _____ (look) at the wrong list of patients, and my name wasn't on it.

4. **A:** Why did the software company on Fourth Street go out of business?

    B: It seems that they _____ (lose) money for a long time.

    A: That's too bad. I _____ (hope) to speak to them about a summer job.

5. **A:** What made you quit your job?

    B: Well, it _____ (bother) me for a long time.
    I _____ (work) too hard.

The Past Perfect Continuous: Meaning and Use

FOCUS ON PAST CONTINUING ACTIONS

1. The past perfect continuous is used instead of the past perfect to emphasize that an activity was in progress during a certain period of time before another past time:

> Julie was exhausted at breakfast. She**'d been studying** all night.

2. The past perfect continuous focuses on longer activities or situations that continued up to or just before a particular moment:

> Joe **had been watering** the garden before I arrived. (Joe watered the garden a few minutes before I arrived. The garden was still wet.)

A past perfect action, however, could be recent or distant:

> Joe **had watered** the garden before I arrived. (Joe could have watered it five minutes before I arrived, or many hours before I arrived.)

3. Since duration is important with the past perfect continuous, it is often used with **for** and **since**:

Marie left her office at 6:00 P.M.:

> She**'d been working since** 8:30 A.M.
> She**'d been working for** nine and a half hours.

4. Like other continuous forms, the past perfect continuous is not used with stative verbs. The past perfect is used instead:

> I **had known** him for many years when he was hired.
> *I had been knowing him for many years when he was hired. (INCORRECT)

5. The past perfect continuous is used to give reasons with **because**, to draw conclusions, and to tell stories:

Reasons: She looked very tired **because** she **had been studying** all night.

Conclusions: He was embarrassed when I greeted him at the party. I realized that he **had** just **been criticizing** my work.

Stories: Before I graduated, I **had been planning** to work for a large company. For several weeks, I **had been writing** to various organizations and…

⫸ **Exercise 8: Combining Sentences**

Write two sentences for each situation. Each sentence should have a past perfect continuous clause and a simple past clause with *when*. Use *for* or *since* in each sentence.

1. Julia worked from 1992 to 1994. Then she went back to school:

   When Julia went back to school, she had been working for two years.

   When Julia went back to school, she had been working since 1992.

2. Steve went to the dentist at 2:00 P.M. He waited until 2:30 and then the receptionist called his name:

3. Brigette studied English from 1993 to 1994. Then she came to the United States:

4. Michael lived in Indonesia from April until September. Then he was offered a job in Thailand:

5. The chicken started baking at 5:30. The electricity went off at 5:45:

⫸ **Exercise 9: Giving Reasons**

Complete each sentence with a reason in the past perfect continuous.

1. He looked very tired because ___he had been sleeping poorly.___

2. He didn't hear the doorbell because _____

3. I turned off the computer because _____

4. The student was expelled from school because _____

_____

5. We were perspiring because _____

_____

6. Her parents were unhappy because_____

_____

7. She stopped staying out so late because _____

_____

8. I bought a new toaster because _____

_____

⬛▶ **Exercise 10: Drawing Conclusions**

Work in small groups. Give one or more conclusions for each situation based on the evidence.
Use the past perfect continuous.

1. When you saw your friend, her eyes were red and swollen. You were sure that...

   ...she had been crying. OR
   ...she had been suffering from allergies. OR
   ...she had been chopping onions.

2. Two months ago, Tom's doctor said Tom was overweight. When you saw him last night, he
   looked much thinner. You assumed that...

3. When you called Martin, it took a long time for him to answer the phone and he sounded
   tired. Although he didn't say anything, you thought that...

4. When the police stopped the car, they smelled alcohol on the driver's breath. It seemed that...

5. When you got on the bus, you smelled cigarettes. Despite the NO SMOKING sign, it appeared
   that...

6. Your friend said he was going to the laundromat the day before your birthday. He came
   back with a gift-wrapped package instead of clean laundry. You were sure that...

7. You saw several of your friends talking together. When you went over to them, they became
   very quiet. You wondered if...

8. The suspect said he had been out of town on the night of the murder. But then the police
   found the murder weapon in his car. Everyone began to think that...

⟾ **Exercise 11: Telling a Story**

Work on your own. Pick a past time in your life, for example, when you were five, ten, or fifteen years old. Write four or five sentences about things that happened before that time. Use the past perfect and the past perfect continuous. Start with a simple past sentence beginning with *I remember when I was....*

I remember when I was five years old. My family had just moved from a small

apartment in the city to a much bigger house in the country. I had been living in

that small apartment my whole life and I hadn't wanted to move...

Past *Wish* Sentences: Form

Wish	Past Perfect Clause
I **wish**	**that** I **had taken** a vacation last year.
I **wish**	I **had taken** a vacation last year.
I **wish**	I **could have gone** to the show.

- To form past **wish** sentences, use the main verb **wish** in the simple present + a clause in the past perfect.
- **That** is optional after **wish**. It is often omitted.
- The short form of the clause after **wish** has a subject + **had**:

  I didn't take a vacation last year, but I wish **I had.**

- The clause after **wish** must be in the past perfect, even when **but** combines it with a simple past clause:

  I **didn't take** a vacation last year, **but** I wish I **had.**

- **Could have**, the past form of **could**, is often used in the clause after **wish** instead of **had been able to**.

⟫ **Exercise 12: Working on Form**

Work with a partner. Complete the conversations with the appropriate forms of the verbs in parentheses to form past wishes. Then practice the conversations.

1. **A:** ___Does he ever wish___ (he/ever/wish) that he ___had chosen___ (choose) a different career when he graduated?

   B: Yes. Sometimes he _____ (wish) he _____ (go) to graduate school right after college.

2. **A:** I _____ (wish) we _____ (come) at nine o'clock instead of at eight.

   B: I know. I _____ (wish) they _____ (tell) us when we called for information.

3. **A:** My sister _____ (wish) she _____ (see) this apartment when she was looking for one.

   B: I didn't know she was interested in a two-bedroom apartment. I _____ (wish) I _____ (show) it to her. Then we could have been neighbors.

4. **A :** _____ (you/ever/wish) you _____ (learn to ski) when you were younger?

   B: Not really. But sometimes I _____ (wish) I _____ (be in the Olympics).

Past *Wish* Sentences: Meaning and Use

UNREAL SITUATIONS IN THE PAST

1. Past **wish** sentences refer to past actions that did not happen. They express a desire for something that wasn't true in the past. When you use a past **wish** sentence, you express regret about a past situation. Compare these sentences to see if you understand the difference between the present **wish** sentences in Chapter 13 and these past **wish** sentences:

Present: I **wish** the weather **were** nice. (It's raining now.)

Past: I **wish** the weather **had been** nice yesterday. (It rained yesterday.)

2. Sometimes the speaker expresses dissatisfaction about a past situation:

I **wish** you **had gone** to the bank before paying the rent. I'm upset that our rent check bounced.

⟹ Exercise 13: Expressing Regret

Work with a partner. Take turns making up past *wish* sentences that express regret. Think of as many sentences as you can for each situation.

1. You refused to lend your brother money. Now you regret it:

   Examples: *I wish I'd lent him the money.*
                I wish I'd helped him.

2. You lost your temper today when you were baby-sitting your nephew. Now you're sorry:

3. You didn't tell your boss how you felt when you spoke to her today. Now you regret it:

4. You didn't call the doctor last week when you got sick. You're still sick:

5. You forgot to pack a number of important items before you left for vacation. Now you need them:

6. You didn't make any plans for the weekend. Now you're bored and lonely:

7. You forgot your best friend's birthday. You feel terrible:

8. You accepted a job offer on Monday. On Tuesday you got a better offer from another company:

⟹ Exercise 14: Expressing Complaints and Regrets

Work with a partner. Take turns reacting to the statements by using a present or past *wish* sentence with short forms.

1. **A:** The library is closed today.
   B: _I wish it weren't._____

2. **A:** Our team didn't win first prize.
   B: _I wish we had._____

3. **A:** The president raised taxes again.
   B: _____

4. **A:** My TV is broken.
   B: _____

5. **A:** The train came late.
   B: _____

6. **A:** I didn't invite Peter.

   B: _____

7. **A:** It's snowing.

   B: _____

8. **A:** He loves to stay up late.

   B: _____

9. **A:** They didn't call back.

   B: _____

10. **A:** I didn't see that movie.

   B: _____

Past Imaginary *If* Sentences: Form

Past Imaginary *If* Clause	Past Imaginary Result
If I **had known** the answer,	**then** I **would have passed** the test.
If I **had known** the answer,	I **would have passed** the test.
If I **had known** the answer,	I **could have passed** the test.

- Like the present imaginary **if** sentences in Chapter 13, past imaginary **if** sentences have an **if** clause and a result clause.
- The **if** clause is in the past perfect, and the result clause has **would have** or **could have** + the past participle of the main verb.
- **Then** in the result clause is optional. It is often omitted.
- The **if** clause can come before or after the result clause with the same meaning.
- When the **if** clause comes first, it is followed by a comma.

Past Imaginary Result Clause	Past Imaginary *If* Clause
I **would have passed** the test	if I **had known** the answer.

- When the result clause comes first, there is no comma and **then** is omitted.

CONVERSATION NOTE

The contractions of **would have** are **would've** and **'d have. Could have** has only one contraction: **could've:**

If we'd driven, we **would have** arrived earlier.

"If we'd driven, we **would've** arrived earlier." (SPOKEN ONLY)

If we'd driven, we **'d have** arr~~ived e~~arlier.

If we'd dr~~iven~~ d earlier.

"If w~~e~~ ~~e~~arlier." (SPOKEN ONLY)

➡ **Ex** **rm**

Work in ~~groups practicing~~ past imaginary *if* sentences. Person A begins with *If I hadn't*~~...~~ a result. Person B uses the end of Person A's sentence to ~~...~~ adds a new result. Continue until everyone has had a turn.

Person A: ~~...~~ *ave been exhausted this morning.*
Person B: ~~...ing,~~ *I would have stayed home from work.*
Person C: *I*~~...~~

[handwritten appointment card overlay: Please give 24 hour notice if you need to change appointment — NAME: Sia 4-11-16 — NEXT APPOINTMENT: 7:00 am — TIME — WITH: Dr. Leopold — www.AHmedicalgroup.org]

Past Imagi~~nary If Sentences: M~~eaning and Use

PAST UNREAL ~~PAST UNREA~~L SITUATIONS

1. Past imaginary *if* sentences express imaginary situations that were not true in the past. They are also called past unreal conditional sentences because the past unreal result in the main clause depends on the past unreal condition in the **if** clause.

2. In the **if** clause, the past perfect indicates that the situation was unreal in the past. In the result clause, **would have** or **could have** plus the main verb indicates that the result was unreal in the past:

If I **had been** the boss, I **would have fired** her. (But I wasn't the boss, so I didn't fire her.)

3. Could have is possible instead of **would have** when it means *would have been able to:*

If you'**d had** a computer, you **could have worked** at home.

(continued)

4. Past imaginary **if** sentences sometimes express advice about the past in a softer, more indirect way than advice with **should have.** The **if** clause is often omitted:

Pat is complaining to Jan about the party last night. Jan is offering this advice:

Indirect: (If I had been you,) I **would have left** early.

Direct: You **should have** left early.

5. Past imaginary **if** sentences (like all imaginary **if** sentences) are often used to further explain an unreal situation expressed in a wish:

I **wish** I **had made** a dinner reservation. If I **had made** a reservation, I **wouldn't have had** to wait in line so long.

⇒ Exercise 16: Expressing Past Imaginary Situations

Work on your own. Complete the sentences by using the past perfect in the *if* clause and *would have* or *could have* in the result clause. Then write two imaginary *if* clauses or result clauses and ask your partner to complete each sentence.

1. If I had been born a boy, _my parents would have named me Joseph._

2. If I had known then what I know now, _____

   _____

3. I would have been sorry if _____

   _____

4. I wouldn't have taken this course if _____

   _____

5. If I had listened to my parents, _____

   _____

6. If I hadn't ever learned to read, _____

   _____

7. I would have been frightened if _____

   _____

8. I wouldn't have been surprised if _____

_____

9. _____

_____

10. _____

_____

⟱ Exercise 17: Giving Indirect Advice

Work with a partner. Take turns giving indirect advice to your partner by telling what you
would have done. You can omit the *if* clauses if you want.

1. **A:** I didn't understand last week's homework assignments, but I didn't do anything about it.
   B: ___(If I were/had been you,) I would have gone to see the instructor.___

2. **A:** My best friend asked to borrow a lot of money. I gave it to him without asking any
   questions.
   B: _____

3. **A:** A salesperson was rude to me yesterday in the department store.
   B: _____

4. **A:** My doctor didn't answer all my questions.
   B: _____

5. **A:** My boss didn't offer me the raise that I wanted. I was disappointed.
   B: _____

6. **A:** The airlines refused to change my ticket even though it was an emergency.
   B: _____

⟹ **Exercise 18: Explaining Wishes**

Work on your own. Think of two past events in your life that you wish you could have changed. Then write two sentences about each of these situations. First, write a past *wish* sentence. Then, explain your wish using a past *if* sentence.

1. I wish my family hadn't moved when I was young. If they hadn't moved,
    I wouldn't have been so lonely.

2. _____
    _____

3. _____
    _____

⟹ **Exercise 19: Thinking About Meaning**

Work with a partner. Read each sentence and decide whether the statements below them are true (T) or false (F). Discuss your answers with the class.

1. After he had eaten a sandwich, he ate a salad.

    ___F___ (a) He ate the salad first. Then he ate the sandwich.

    _____ (b) He ate the salad and sandwich together.

2. He had left before the play ended.

    _____ (a) The play ended. Then he left.

    _____ (b) He was gone at the end of the play.

3. I would have reached you if the phone had been working.

    _____ (a) The phone was working.

    _____ (b) I didn't reach you.

4. I wish I had taken a vacation.

    _____ (a) I should have taken a vacation.

    _____ (b) I took a vacation.

5. She wouldn't have taken the medication if she had known about the risks.

    _____ (a) She knew about the risks.

    _____ (b) She took the medication.

Summary

The Past Perfect: Form

Statements:	At that moment, I **had** just **walked** in.
Negative Statements:	Until then, we**'d** never **taken** the train.
Yes/No Questions:	**Had** you ever **been** late before?
Short Answers:	Yes, we **had.** OR No, we **hadn't.**
Information Questions:	Why **hadn't** she **arrived** yet?
Information Questions (Subject):	Who **had** already **finished?**

The Past Perfect: Meaning and Use

The past perfect expresses a relationship between two past times. It indicates the earlier event or situation.

Sequences:	When I arrived, he **had cleaned up** the mess.
	The building collapsed after he **had left.**
	I **hadn't heard** about it until I met her.
Changes:	I **had** never **lived** alone until I started college.
Accomplishments:	By last night, the apartment **had been painted,** but the windows **hadn't been repaired** yet.

The Past Perfect Continuous: Form

Statements:	I **had been waiting** for an hour.
Negative Statements:	She **hadn't been sleeping** very well.
Yes/No Questions:	**Had** you **been waiting** long?
Short Answers:	Yes, I **had.** OR No, I **hadn't.**
Information Questions:	How long **had** you **been waiting?**
Information Questions (Subject):	Who **had been using** the computer?

The Past Perfect Continuous: Meaning and Use

The past perfect continuous is similar to the past perfect, but it emphasizes the duration of the earlier event or situation.

Reasons: They looked tired because they**'d been playing** tennis.

Conclusions: It appeared that he**'d been smoking.**

Stories: I **had been living** in that small apartment my whole life and I hadn't wanted to move.

Past *Wish* Sentences: Form

Wish + Past Perfect Clause: I **wish (that)** I **had known** the answer.

Wish + *Could Have* Clause: I **wish** I **could have gone** with you.

Past *Wish* Sentences: Meaning and Use

Past **wish** sentences express a desire for something that wasn't true in the past. They express complaints or regrets about a past situation.

Regrets: I **wish** I **had gone** to the party.

Complaints: The president raised taxes again. I **wish** he **hadn't raised** them.

Past Imaginary *If* Sentences: Form

Past Imaginary *If* Clause + Past Imaginary Result Clause: If I **had left** earlier, I **would have arrived** on time.

Past Imaginary Result Clause + Past Imaginary *If* Clause: I **would have arrived** on time if I **had left** earlier.

Past Imaginary *If* Sentences: Meaning and Use

Past imaginary **if** sentences express an unreal condition about the past and its imaginary past result.

Imaginary Situations: If I **had lived** in the nineteenth century, I**'d have owned** a horse and carriage.

Advice: If I**'d been** you, I**'d have complained** to the manager.

Explanations: I **wish** my family **hadn't moved.** If my family **hadn't moved,** I **wouldn't have been** so lonely.

⇒ **Summary Exercise: Finding Errors**

Most of the sentences have an error in form or appropriate use. Find each error and correct it.

1. Why ~~she hadn't~~ called you before she left?   *hadn't she*
2. I'd never driven a car until I took my first lesson.
3. If we'd arrived earlier, we wouldn't miss the bus.
4. When I had entered the building, the window had already been broken.
5. Excuse me. I'd been waiting for an hour. Is Ms. Cole in yet?
6. If I'd been there, I'd have helped you.
7. I wish you've gone to the doctor.
8. She'd already answer the door when I got there.
9. What would you do if they had lied?
10. She wishes she could have read the whole book.
11. I wish I saw her yesterday.
12. If I had taken the exam, I would pass it.

Passive Sentences

Preview

Hotel information:

Dinner **is served** from 5:00 to 9:00 P.M.

News report:

Five people **were injured by a tornado** last night in Plainfield.

Sign:

NO TRESPASSING. VIOLATORS **WILL BE PROSECUTED.**

Sentences are active when the subject performs an action, and an optional object receives or is the result of an action:

Scott **mailed** the letter yesterday. (The active subject **Scott** did something to the object **letter.**)

Sentences are passive when the subject does not perform an action. The subject of a passive sentence receives an action or is the result of an action. The person or thing that performed the action may be unimportant or unknown in a passive sentence:

The letter **was mailed** yesterday. (The passive subject **the letter** did not perform the action. Instead, something happened to **the letter.** This sentence doesn't tell who mailed the letter.)

Compare the sentence above with the following sentence:

The letter **was mailed by Scott.** (This sentence says that **Scott** mailed the letter. **By** plus a noun tells who performed the action in a passive sentence.)

The passive voice is important in spoken and written English, especially in technical writing. Passive sentences affect the way we think about the information in a sentence, by changing the usual order of the subject and object of an active sentence. You can choose an active sentence to emphasize who or what did the action, or a passive sentence to focus on the receiver of the action. The kind of sentence you choose depends on the sentences that have come before, and on whether you need to begin your sentence with the noun that performed the action or the noun that received the action.

Overview of Passive Sentences: Form

Tense or Modal	Passive Sentence
Simple Present:	The exam **is given** every year.
Simple Past:	The exam **was given** every year.
Simple Future:	The exam **will be given** every year.
Present Continuous:	The exam **is being given** every year.
Past Continuous:	The exam **was being given** every year.
Present Perfect:	The exam **has been given** every year.
Past Perfect:	The exam **had been given** every year.
Simple Modal:	The exam **should be given** every year.
Past Modal:	The exam **should have been given** every year.

- To form the passive, use the appropriate tense or modal with the auxiliary verb **be** + the past participle of a transitive verb.

- A transitive verb is a verb that can be followed by an object.

- Verbs that cannot be followed by objects are called intransitive verbs. Intransitive verbs have no passive forms. The most common intransitive verbs include: **appear, arrive, come, cry, die, go, happen, occur, rain, sleep, stay,** and **walk.**

- A few transitive verbs do not have passive forms. These verbs include the stative verbs **have, become**, **weigh** (stative use), **resemble, fit,** and **cost.** Therefore, these sentences have no related passive forms:

  Joe **has** a CD player.
  She **became** an engineer.
  He **weighs** 150 pounds.
  Jenny **resembles** Bob.
  The dress **fits** Valerie.
  The dress **costs** fifty dollars.

- **By** + a noun is optional at the end of passive sentences:

  The exam **is given** every year (**by the police department**).

⇒ Exercise 1: Identifying Passive Sentences

Work with a partner. Read the following sentences and mark them either active (A) or passive (P). Underline the passive verbs.

1. __A__ I've been going to school.
2. __P__ It's being cooked. ~~Present~~ ~~for~~ Continue,
3. __P__ He's been weighed.

4. ___ You've failed.   tense : Present Perfect
5. ___ We'll be studying by that time.   Simple Future.
6. ___ She was dead.
7. ___ They were fired.   Simple Past
8. ___ I arrived by car.
9. ___ We're forbidden to take it.
10. ___ They've stopped by the lake.
11. ___ You'll be called again about it.
12. ___ It could be refilled.
13. ___ He's sending it by airmail.
14. ___ She's been injured.

Overview of Passive Sentences: Meaning and Use

FOCUS ON THE RECEIVER OF THE ACTION

The passive usually doesn't affect the meaning of a sentence. However, it does affect the way you think about the information in a sentence because it changes the usual order of the subject and object of an active sentence. Passive sentences focus on the noun that is the receiver or result of an action rather than the noun that is performing the action (the agent). In fact, passive sentences very often do not mention the agent at all.

Here are the basic reasons for choosing a passive sentence instead of an active sentence:

1. The passive is used when the agent is unimportant or unknown, and the sentence emphasizes the action, process, or result instead. The agent is frequently omitted from passive sentences, especially in factual writing found in scientific articles and in journalism:

Scientific article:

Supercomputers **were developed** in order to solve complex problems.
(The agent is unimportant. The sentence emphasizes the result.)

News report:

Five people **were killed** by a tornado last night.
(The result is emphasized more than the agent.)

Headline:

Two Houses **Robbed** (The agent is unknown. The result is important.)

(continued)

2. The passive is preferred when it's not necessary to mention the agent because the agent is obvious from the meaning of the sentence:

My mail **is delivered** at noon. (It's obvious that a mail carrier delivers it.)

Definition:

Paella is a Spanish dish that **is made** with seafood. (It's obvious that people make paella.)

3. The passive is used to make a sentence sound more impersonal. It is common in formal announcements, rules, and signs, and especially when you don't want to mention the agent:

Airplane announcement:

Passengers **are requested** to remain seated. (The passive is more impersonal than *We request you to…*)

Registration information:

All fees **must be paid** at registration. (The passive is more impersonal than *You must pay all fees at registration.*)

A boss is speaking to her employees:

A serious error **was made** in this week's payroll. (The boss intentionally doesn't say who made the mistake.)

4. A passive sentence without an agent is often used instead of an active sentence that has a very general subject such as **people, someone, somebody,** or impersonal **you** and **they:**

A sign:

SPANISH **IS SPOKEN** HERE.
(Active sentence: **People speak Spanish** here.)

An opinion:

I think the health department **should be called** immediately.
(Active sentence: I think **somebody should call** the health department immediately.)

5. The passive is often used to keep the focus on a noun that was mentioned in a previous sentence. This noun is old information, and old information is usually found in subject position in a sentence:

Lynda had three job interviews. Eventually, **she was hired** by a new computer company in Dallas. In her last letter, she said she was very happy there.
(This discussion is about Lynda. The passive is used so that Lynda can be the subject of the second sentence.)

Yesterday, the old man lost **his wallet. It was found** by a policeman a few hours later.
(This discussion is about a wallet. The passive is used so that the wallet can be the subject of the second sentence.)

⟱ **Exercise 2: Working on Meaning**

Read each situation and the two statements below it. Put a checkmark next to all the sentences that have the same meaning as the passive sentence. Then explain your answers in small groups.

1. Visitors are asked not to smoke in this building.

_____✓ (a) You shouldn't smoke in this building.

_____✓ (b) We ask visitors not to smoke in this building.

2. French is spoken in Quebec.

_____ (a) They speak French in Quebec.

_____ (b) Nobody speaks French in Quebec.

3. All fees must be paid by July 30.

_____ (a) You need to pay all fees by July 30.

_____ (b) All fees have to be paid by July 30.

4. We called Julie at the hospital yesterday. She was permitted to speak to us briefly.

_____ (a) We permitted Julie to speak.

_____ (b) They permitted Julie to speak.

5. Several people were injured by a falling tree.

_____ (a) A falling tree injured several people.

_____ (b) Several people injured a tree.

6. He was arrested for burglary.

_____ (a) The police arrested him for burglary.

_____ (b) The authorities arrested him for burglary.

7. The mail is delivered six days a week.

_____ (a) We don't know who delivers the mail six days a week.

_____ (b) The mail carrier delivers the mail six days a week.

8. The book was written in 1966.

_____ (a) The author wrote the book in 1966.

_____ (b) Someone wrote the book in 1966.

9. My dog Rover disappeared at about 6:00 P.M. He was last seen at the park entrance. Later in the evening, he was picked up by the park ranger near the lake.

_____ (a) The park ranger saw Rover at the park entrance.

_____ (b) Someone found Rover near the park ranger.

10. Your assistance will be appreciated.

_____ (a) You will appreciate our assistance.

_____ (b) We will appreciate your assistance.

Simple Present and Simple Past Passives: Form

Statements				Contractions
I	**am**	**invited**	(**by** Joe).	I**'m**
She	**is**	**invited**.		She**'s**
He				He**'s**
It				It**'s**
We	**are**	**invited**.		We**'re**
You				You**'re**
They				They**'re**
I	**was**	**invited**.		
She				
He				
It				
We	**were**	**invited**.		
You				
They				

- To form the simple present passive, use **am, is,** or **are** + the past participle of a transitive verb.
- To form the simple past passive, use **was** or **were** + the past participle of a transitive verb.
- **By** + a noun is optional at the end of a passive sentence.
- The auxiliary **be** in passives follows the same contraction rules that you learned in previous chapters.
- Look at pages 486–487 for spelling and pronunciation rules for regular past participles.
- Look at pages 488–491 for a list of irregular verbs and their past participles.

Negative Statements				Contractions
I	**am**	**not**	**elected**.	I**'m not**
She	**is**	**not**	**elected**.	She**'s not**/She **isn't**
You	**are**	**not**	**elected**.	You**'re not**/You **aren't**
I	**was**	**not**	**elected**.	I **wasn't**
You	**were**	**not**	**elected**.	You **weren't**

- In negative statements, **not** or the contraction **-n't** follows the auxiliary **be**.

Yes/No Questions			Short Answers	Contractions
Am	I	**invited**?	Yes, you **are**.	
			No, you **are not**.	No, you**'re not**./No, you **aren't**.
Was	it	**required**?	Yes, it **was**.	
			No, it **was not**.	No, it **wasn't**.

- To form a *yes/no* question, use a form of the auxiliary **be** before the subject.
- Short answers to passive *yes/no* questions have a subject pronoun + the auxiliary **be**. Affirmative short answers don't have contracted forms.

Information Questions				Answers
Why	**is**	it	**required**?	For your safety.
When	**were**	they	**elected**?	In November.

- The *wh-* word comes before the auxiliary **be** and the subject.

Information Questions (Subject)			Answers	Contraction
Who	**is**	**invited**?	Everyone.	**Who's**
What	**was**	**required**?	A driving test.	

- If **who** or **what** is the subject of the question, the word order is the same as for affirmative statements.

⟫ Exercise 3: Working on Simple Present Passives

Work with a partner. Complete the following paragraph with the underlined simple present form of the passive. (Note: To join two or more passive verb phrases with *and,* use a form of *be* in the first verb phrase only, but omit *be* in the remaining verb phrases.)

When glass _____ *is made* _____ (make), certain materials ~~are~~ *is* **melted** ✓ (melt) together and then _____ ~~are~~ *is* **cooled** ✓ (cool). The materials _____ *are heated* _____ (heat) in large furnaces that *usually are* ~~built~~ *built* (usually/build) of ceramic blocks. When the bubbles _____ *are removed* _____ (remove) from the hot mixture, the hot liquid _____ *is poured* _____ (pour) into molds and _____ *is formed* _____ (form) into different shapes. ✓

⟫ Exercise 4: Asking and Answering Questions with Simple Present Passives

Work with a partner. Complete the following conversation with the appropriate simple present form of the passive, using contractions whenever possible. Then practice the conversation.

A: When *'s the trash collected* _____ (collect/trash) in your neighborhood?

B: It _____ *is picked up* _____ (pick up) on Mondays, but we don't have much trash anymore. Almost everything we use _____ *recycle* _____ (recycle).

A: And *what the recycled items are collected* _____ (collect/the recycled items) too?

B: Some of them _____ *are collected* _____ (collect). Newspapers, glass, and cans _____ *are taken away* _____ (take away) by a private recycling company that _____ *is paid* _____ (pay) by the city.

A: And then what _____ *can be done* _____ (do) with all of that stuff?

B: It _____ *is separated* _____ (separate) once more and _____ *is sold* _____ (sell) to other companies for recycling.

⟹ **Exercise 5: Working on Simple Past Passives**

Work on your own. Create meaningful active or passive sentences in the past with the words in parentheses. Make the first word in parentheses the subject of your sentence.

1. (the medicine/take/the patient)

   Example: *The medicine was taken by the patient.*

2. (the patient/take/the medicine)

   Example: *The patient took the medicine.*

3. (the glass/drop/the child)

4. (the concert/attend/thousands of people)

5. (the cake/cost/quite a bit)

6. (soccer/play/on Sundays at 2:00 P.M.)

7. (we/cancel/the appointment)

8. (the waiter/take/the order)

9. (the car/repair/two mechanics)

10. (the baby/cry/for an hour)

11. (the package/mail/the woman/early in the morning)

12. (the shoes/buy/at the mall)

Simple Present and Simple Past Passives: Meaning and Use

FOCUS ON THE RECEIVER OF THE ACTION

1. Like all passives, simple present and simple past passives affect the way we think about the information in a sentence by changing the usual order of the subject and object of an active sentence. (Look at Overview of Passive Sentences: Meaning and Use, pages 417–418.)

2. Simple present and simple past passives are used in signs (with forms of **be** omitted), to define words, to express facts, to describe results, and to arrange old and new information in a sentence:

Sign:	NO PETS **ALLOWED**
Definitions:	Parsley is an herb that **is used** as a seasoning and a garnish.
Facts:	The weight of the Earth **is estimated** at 6,600 billion billion tons.
Results:	Many homes **were damaged** by the flood.
Old Information:	Sushi is a rice delicacy in Japan. It **is shaped** into many forms and **stuffed** with raw fish.

➠ **Exercise 6: Understanding Signs**

Work with a partner. Read each sign and write a full sentence that explains its meaning.
Use the simple present passive. Then decide where you might see each sign.

1. RESERVATIONS REQUIRED

   Reservations are required.

   Location: In a restaurant

2. CREDIT CARDS ACCEPTED

   Location:

3. VOLUNTEERS NEEDED

   Location:

4. ID REQUIRED

   Location:

5. LOTTERY TICKETS SOLD HERE

   Location:

6. CHINESE SPOKEN HERE

   Location:

7. SATISFACTION GUARANTEED

   Location:

8. PARKING PROHIBITED

   Location:

9. NO CAMERAS ALLOWED

_____

Location: _____

10. PRICES REDUCED

_____

Location: _____

11. CHECKS CASHED HERE

_____

Location: _____

12. CHILDREN UNDER 12 ADMITTED FREE

_____

Location: _____

⯈ Exercise 7: Defining Words

Work with a partner. Use the simple present passive form of the verbs in parentheses to complete each definition. For numbers 6–10, use the verb in parentheses and your own words.

1. Wine is an alcoholic beverage that _____is made_____ (make) from grapes.

2. A guide dog is a canine that _____is trained_____ (train) to lead a blind person.

3. Grizzly bears are large, powerful animals that _____are found_____ (find) in North America.

4. Thanksgiving is an American holiday that _____is celebrated_____ (celebrate) on the fourth Thursday in November.

5. Silk is a smooth, soft cloth that _____is made_____ (make) from fine thread. The thread _____are produced_____ (produce) by a silkworm.

6. Caffeine is a stimulant that _____is found in coffee._____ (find)

7. Labor Day is an American holiday that _____is celebrated by all of people in USA._____ (celebrate)

8. Garlic is a plant that _____ *is used to make delicious* _____ *foods* _____ (use)

9. A tuxedo is a garment that _____ *is worn by gentleman.* _____ (wear)

10 A mango is a fruit that _____ *is used to make salad* _____ (use)

⫸ Exercise 8: Expressing Facts

Work with a partner. Take turns reading the following statements aloud to each other. Tell whether the statement is true or false. If the statement is false, make it negative. Then add another sentence in the present or past passive which states the correct fact.

1. Oxygen is carried by white blood cells.

   Example: *False. Oxygen isn't carried by white blood cells.*
   It's carried by red blood cells.

2. Penicillin was discovered by Sir Arthur Fleming.

   Example: *True.*

3. Nitrogen is required for a fire to burn. *Nitrogen isn't required for a fire to b*

4. Microwaves are used in refrigerators.

5. Bread is usually made from wheat.

6. Earthquakes are measured by a device called a polygraph. *Seismogaph*

7. The telephone was invented in ancient times.

8. Antibiotics were developed to kill viruses.

9. Rice is grown in cold, dry climates.

10. Nuclear energy is used to generate electricity in many countries.

11. Cholesterol is needed for strong bones.

12. Computer data are stored on disks.

➠ **Exercise 9: Describing Results**

Work with a partner. Describe the results of the following situations using simple past passive sentences with the words in parentheses.

1. An earthquake rocked southern California last night:

   (several homes/damage)

   Example: *Several homes were damaged.*

   (one major road/close for an hour) *one major road was closed for an hour*

   (twelve people/injure) *twelve people were injured.*

   (one person/kill) *one person was killed*

   (many windows/shatter) *many windows were shattered.*

   (one building/destroy) *one building was destroied.*

   (one person/hospitalize) *one person was hospitalized*

   (no major power lines/affect) *no major power lines were affected*

2. A serious flu epidemic spread through your area last month:

   (some schools/close) *some schools were closed*

   (several businesses/shut down) *several businesses were shut down*

   (many public events/cancel) *many public events were canceled*

   (more doctors/need) *more doctors were needed*

   (several new treatments/try) *several new treatments were tried*

   (many flu shots/give) *many flu shots were given*

   (hundreds of people/treat) *hundreds of people were treated*

Exercise 10: Arranging Old and New Information

Work on your own. Underline the active or passive sentence that best completes each passage. Remember that old information is usually found in subject position.

1. Charlotte opened the door

   (a) <u>and (she) was greeted by a strange dog.</u>

   (b) and a strange dog greeted her.

2. When we lived in that house,

   (a) a garden was never planted by us.

   (b) we never planted a garden.

3. Golf is one of the most popular sports in the United States.

   (a) It is played by people of all ages.

   (b) People of all ages play it.

4. Gold is a valuable yellow metal.

   (a) It is found in many places in nature.

   (b) People find it in many places in nature.

5. In 1994, she wrote a best-selling novel.

   (a) After that, many offers were received to write more fiction.

   (b) After that, she received many offers to write more fiction.

6. Asia has more mountains than any other continent.

   (a) Transportation is made difficult by the mountains in many areas.

   (b) The mountains make transportation difficult in many areas.

7. The Great Lakes are the largest group of freshwater lakes in the world.

   (a) These lakes were formed by glaciers about 250,000 years ago.

   (b) Glaciers formed these lakes about 250,000 years ago.

8. As soon as the bank robber tried to leave the bank,

   (a) he was arrested by a detective waiting outside.

   (b) a detective waiting outside arrested him.

Simple Future Passives: Form

Statements	Contraction
I **will** **be** **helped** (**by**) the medicine.	I**'ll**
You	You**'ll**
She	She**'ll**
He	He**'ll**
It	It**'ll**
We	We**'ll**
They	They**'ll**

- To form the future passive, use **will be** + the past participle of a transitive verb.
- **By** + a noun is optional.
- Contractions are used with the first auxiliary, **will**, only.
- **Be going to** is also used in future passive forms:

  Food production **is going to be affected** by the drought.

Negative Statements	Contraction
I **will** **not** **be** **elected**.	I **won't**

- **Not** or its contraction follows the first auxiliary.

Yes/No Questions	Short Answers	Contraction
Will he **be** **elected**?	Yes, he **will**.	
	No, he **will not**.	No, he **won't**.

- The first auxiliary comes before the subject.
- Short answers have a subject pronoun + the first auxiliary.
- Affirmative short answers are not contracted.

Information Questions	Answers
When will he **be called**?	Soon.

- The *wh-* word comes before the first auxiliary and the subject.

Information Questions (Subject)	Answers
Who will be elected?	Martinez **will**.

- If **who** or **what** is the subject, the word order is the same as for affirmative statements.

⟫ Exercise 11: Working on Future Passives

Complete the following sentences with the future passive.

1. Community Center policies:

    (a) New courses _____will be offered_____ (offer) every six weeks.

    (b) Instructor schedules _____ (post) at the front desk.

    (c) Schedule changes _____ (announce) approximately one week in advance.

    (d) Classes with fewer than five participants _____ (cancel).

2. Mail-ordering information:

    (a) Your order _____ (ship) within forty-eight hours.

    (b) Postage and handling _____ (add) to all orders.

    (c) Orders _____ (send) by U.S. mail.

    (d) Refunds for credit card purchases _____ (credit) to your account.

    (e) Cash or check purchases _____ (refund) within ten days of receipt of merchandise.

3. Recorded announcement:

    Please continue to hold. Your call _____ (answer) by the next available customer service agent. This announcement _____ (not/repeat).

Continuous and Perfect Passives: Form

Statements				Contractions
I	**am**	**being**	**helped**.	**I'm**
He	**is**	**being**	**helped**.	**He's**
We	**are**	**being**	**helped**.	**We're**
I	**was**	**being**	**helped**.	
They	**were**	**being**	**helped**.	
I	**have**	**been**	**helped**.	**I've**
He	**has**	**been**	**helped**.	**He's**
I	**had**	**been**	**helped**.	**I'd**

- Continuous and perfect forms of the passive all have two auxiliaries before the past participle of a transitive verb.
- To form the present continuous passive, use **am, is,** or **are** + **being** + the past participle.
- To form the past continuous passive, use **was** or **were** + **being** + the past participle.
- To form the present perfect passive, use **have** or **has** + **been** + the past participle.
- To form the past perfect passive, use **had** + **been** + the past participle.
- Look at pages 486–487 for spelling and pronunciation rules for regular past participles.

Negative Statements					Contractions
I	**am**	**not**	**being**	**invited**.	**I'm not**
She	**is**	**not**	**being**	**invited**.	She**'s not**/She **isn't**
We	**are**	**not**	**being**	**invited**.	We**'re not**/We **aren't**
I	**was**	**not**	**being**	**helped**.	I **wasn't**
You	**were**	**not**	**being**	**helped**.	You **weren't**
I	**have**	**not**	**been**	**elected**.	I **haven't**
He	**has**	**not**	**been**	**elected**.	He **hasn't**
I	**had**	**not**	**been**	**helped**.	I **hadn't**

- **Not** or its contraction follows the first auxiliary.

(continued)

Yes/No Questions				Short Answers	Contractions
Is	it	**being**	**painted**?	Yes, it **is**. No, it **is not**.	No, it **isn't**.
Was	it	**being**	**washed**?	Yes, it **was**. No, it **was not**.	No, it **wasn't**.
Has	he	**been**	**called**?	Yes, he **has**. No, he **has not**.	No, he **hasn't**.
Had	he	**been**	**told**?	Yes, he **had**. No, he **had not**.	No, he **hadn't**.

- The first auxiliary comes before the subject.
- Short answers have a subject pronoun + the first auxiliary.

Information Questions					Answers	Contractions
Why	**is**	she	**being**	**fired**?	For being late.	**Why's**
When	**was**	she	**being**	**helped**?	This morning.	
How	**have**	they	**been**	**ordered**?	By mail.	
Why	**had**	they	**been**	**called**?	For jury duty.	

- The *wh-* word comes before the first auxiliary and the subject.

Information Questions (Subject)				Answers	Contractions
What	**is**	**being**	**done**?	Not much.	**What's**
What	**was**	**being**	**collected**?	Donations.	
Who	**has**	**been**	**fired**?	Pat has.	**Who's**
Who	**had**	**been**	**elected**?	The president.	

- If **who** or **what** is the subject, the word order is the same as in affirmative statements.

⟹ **Exercise 12: Working on Present Continuous Passives**

Work on your own. Complete the following paragraph using the present continuous passive.

The building where I work _____ is being renovated _____ (renovate) right now, and a

number of changes _____ (make). For example, all of the offices

_____ (paint) and the carpeting _____

(replace). New shelves _____ (build) and a new computer system

_____ (install). And finally, a new kitchen

_____ (add) for the staff. A refrigerator, microwave, and sink

_____ (put in) near the lounge.

➠ **Exercise 13: Working on Past Continuous Passives**

Change the paragraph in Exercise 12 to the past continuous passive. Start your paragraph with the following sentence:

Last month, while I was trying to complete an important project at work,

the building was being renovated....

➠ **Exercise 14: Working on Perfect Passives**

Use the words in parentheses to create meaningful active or passive sentences in the present perfect. The first word in parentheses should be the subject of your sentence.

1. (the exam/cancel/the teacher) *The exam has been canceled by the teacher.*
2. (the company/manufacture/the product) *The company has manufactured the product.*
3. (this book/translate/into many languages)
4. (the senator/call/dishonest)
5. (the man/eat/the steak)
6. (a new prescription/recommend/the doctor)
7. (the computer/use/the whole class)
8. (the school newspaper/receive/an award)

➠ **Exercise 15: Asking and Answering Questions with Future, Continuous, and Perfect Passives**

Work with a partner. Make questions with the words in parentheses. Use every word. Then take turns asking and answering the questions.

1. (been/you/invited/have/parties/any/lately/to)
   A: *Have you been invited to any parties lately?*
   B: *Yes, I have.*
2. (will/apartment/painted/this/your/be/year)
3. (been/your/recently/class/has/canceled)
4. (telephone/used/your/being/is/right now)
5. (ever/you/robbed/been/had/before)
6. (rent/soon/be/your/raised/will)
7. (this/being/course/by/is/a/man/taught)
8. (being/course/English/this/given/was/semester/last)

Future, Continuous, and Perfect Passives: Meaning and Use

FOCUS ON THE RECEIVER OF THE ACTION

1. Like all passives, the future, continuous, and perfect passives affect the way we think about the information in a sentence by changing the usual order of the subject and object of an active sentence. (Look at Overview of Passive Sentences: Meaning and Use, pages 417–418.)

2. Future passives can be used to describe future processes:

His arm **will be x-rayed.**

3. Past continuous passives are used to focus on past actions and processes:

When I arrived at the party, dinner **was being served.**

4. Present perfect passives are not stated, but are often understood in headlines:

SMITH **FOUND** GUILTY IN MURDER TRIAL

5. In all passive sentences, the agent is often omitted because it is unimportant or unknown:

The windows **were being replaced.**

⟶ **Exercise 16: Describing Processes**

Work on your own. Rewrite the following descriptions of processes using the present or future passive. Then work in small groups and discuss whether you need to use the agent in any of your sentences. What is the difference between the active and passive descriptions?

1. When John arrives at the emergency room, they will examine his arm, and then they will send him for an X ray. After they x-ray his arm, they will tell him whether it is broken. If his arm is broken, they will send him back to the emergency room, where they will put a cast on his arm. First, they will put his arm in the proper position. Then, they will put a cotton sleeve over his arm and they will wrap it with wet bandages.

> *When John arrives at the emergency room, his arm will be examined and he will be sent for an X ray...*

2. The research assistant will give each subject two lists of words. He will ask the subjects to read each list once. Then he will show them some pictures and he will ask them to press a bell...

     Each subject will be given two lists of words... _____

_____

_____

_____

_____

_____

⟹ **Exercise 17: Focusing on Past Actions and Processes**

Work with a partner. Use the words in parentheses and the past continuous passive to tell what was happening.

1. Your friend's wedding reception started at 2:00 P.M. When you arrived at 2:15:

    (a) (the guests/greet) _*The guests were being greeted.*_____

    (b) (the bride and groom/photograph) _____

    _____

    (c) (drinks/serve) _____

2. You couldn't decide whether to rent the apartment that you looked at today because when you got there:

    (a) (the rooms/paint) _____

    (b) (the carpets/clean) _____

    (c) (the appliances/repair) _____

3. You and your roommate cooked an elaborate meal for your friends. When they arrived, you weren't finished yet:

    (a) (the wine/chill) _____

    (b) (the salad/prepare) _____

    (c) (the table/set) _____

4. When you arrived at the scene of the accident:

    (a) (one person/lift into an ambulance)_____

_____

    (b) (a man/give oxygen) _____

    (c) (two witnesses/question by the police) _____

_____

⮞ Exercise 18: Understanding Headlines

Work on your own. Change each newspaper headline into a full sentence using the present perfect passive or the simple past passive. If necessary, add articles and other deleted words.

1. TWO CHILDREN INJURED IN TRAIN ACCIDENT

    Two children have been injured in a train accident. OR

    Two children were injured in a train accident.

2. NEW CANCER TREATMENT DISCOVERED

_____

3. PRESIDENT'S TRIP POSTPONED; NEW PLANS ANNOUNCED

_____

4. BUILDING DAMAGED BY EXPLOSION

_____

5. SITE SELECTED FOR RECYCLING PLANT

_____

6. RESTAURANT CLOSED BY HEALTH DEPARTMENT

_____

7. LOCAL BANK ROBBED; 2 KILLED

_____

8. HIGHER WAGES DEMANDED BY STRIKERS

_____

9. GOLFER STRUCK BY LIGHTNING

_____

10. THREE JOURNALISTS RELEASED FROM JAIL

_____

11. TEEN CHARGED WITH BURGLARY

_____

12. MAN HOSPITALIZED AFTER MOTORCYCLE CRASH

_____

➠ Exercise 19: Reading the Headlines

Work on your own. Find three examples of the passive in newspaper headlines and bring them to class. Ask the class to make full passive sentences out of the headlines.

➠ Exercise 20: Using or Omitting Agents

Work with a partner. Change each sentence to the present continuous, past continuous, or future form of the passive. Omit the agent whenever it isn't necessary. Discuss your reasons.

1. Some painters were painting the office yesterday.

   Example: *The office was being painted yesterday.*
   (The agent is obvious from the meaning of the sentence.)

2. A painter from Dryden will paint the house.

   Example: *The house will be painted by a painter from Dryden.*
   (The sentence tells us something about the agent.)

3. The vendors are always reducing the prices at the farmer's market.

4. At the meeting, the president will announce the new regulations.

5. They're accepting applications for summer employment at the supermarket.

6. When a pipe burst in our house, the water ruined our new carpet.

7. The police will arrest the strikers if they don't leave.

8. At that moment, somebody was unlocking the door.

9. A mechanic was repairing my aunt's car at the service station.

10. People who drink alcohol are causing many accidents.

11. Authors are writing many books about health and nutrition.

12. Next semester, the university will require undergraduates to take five courses each semester.

Modal Passives: Form

Statements

| I | **should** | **be** | | **hired** | (**by** the company). |
| I | **might** | **have** | **been** | **called**. | |

- To form a simple modal passive, use the modal + **be** + the past participle of a transitive verb.
- To form a past modal passive, use the modal + **have been** + the past participle of a transitive verb.

Negative Statements   Contractions

| You | **could** | **not** | **be** | **reached**. | | You **couldn't** |
| You | **must** | **not** | **have** | **been** | **selected**. | |

- **Not** or the contraction **-n't** follows the first auxiliary.

Yes/No Questions   Short Answers   Contractions

| **Can** | it | **be** | **painted**? | | Yes, it **can**. |
| | | | | No, it **cannot**. | No, it **can't**. |

| **Should** he **have** **been** **paid**? | Yes, he **should have**. | |
| | No, he **should not have**. | No, he **shouldn't have**. |

- The first auxiliary comes before the subject.
- Short answers to simple modal passives have a subject pronoun + the first auxiliary.
- Short answers to past modal passives have a subject + the first and the second auxiliary.

Information Questions   Answers

| **When** | **should** | it | **be** | **used**? | Within a week. |
| **How** | **could** | she | **have** | **been** | **fired**? | Who knows? |

- The *wh-* word comes before the first auxiliary and the subject.

Information Questions (Subject)   Answers

What should be fixed?   The air conditioner.
Who should have been invited?   The whole family.

- If **who** or **what** is the subject of the question, the word order is the same as in affirmative statements.

➠ Exercise 21: Working on Simple Modal Passives

Complete each sentence with a simple modal passive.

1. Product instructions:
   (a) This product _____should be refrigerated_____ (should/refrigerate) after opening.
   (b) This prescription _____ (can/not/refill).
   (c) This product _____ (should/keep) out of the reach of children.
   (d) This container _____ (must/discard) after use. Do not reuse.
   (e) After opening, this product _____ (may/store) for up to three months in a cool, dry place.
   (f) This product _____ (should/not/freeze).

2. Mail-ordering information:
   (a) Your order _____should be examined_____ (should/examine) carefully when you receive it.
   (b) Any damage _____ (must/report) within two weeks.
   (c) Each return _____ (must/accompany) by an explanation and a receipt.
   (d) Mail orders _____ (should/send) to the Mail Order Department at the address below.
   (e) All orders _____ (must/pay) in advance.
   (f) Telephone orders _____ (can/place) twenty-four hours a day.

➠ Exercise 22: Working on Past Modal Passives

Work with a partner. Complete each conversation with the appropriate past modal passive form of the words in parentheses. Then practice the conversations.

1. **A.** Look at that house. I can barely recognize it.
   B: It _____must have been damaged_____ (must/damage) in the fire last week.

2. **A:** My new driver's license never arrived. My old one has expired.
   B: It _____ (could/send) to your old address. Did you notify them when you moved?

3. **A:** That tree isn't growing very well.

   B: I know. It _____ (should/not/plant) in the shade. That was a mistake.

4. **A:** Her flight _____ (must/delay) by the bad weather.

   B: What time was she supposed to arrive?

5. **A:** I heard that you were accepted into the graduate program.

   B: That's impossible. I _____ (could/not/accept). I didn't even send in all the application forms.

6. **A:** I'm trying to reach Extension 4371, but no one answers.

   B: Your call _____ (must/transfer) incorrectly. Why don't you call the operator again?

7. **A:** No one told me about the meeting.

   B: You _____ (should/notify) last week.

8. **A:** They should have called 911 for help. John _____ (could/save).

   B: I don't think so. He _____ (could/not/help). His heart had already stopped.

Modal Passives: Meaning and Use

FOCUS ON THE RECEIVER OF THE ACTION

1. Like all passive sentences, simple modal passives and past modal passives affect the way we think about the information in a sentence by changing the usual order of the subject and object of an active sentence.

2. Modal passives also express the same meanings of the modals presented in Chapters 7 and 8. For example, modal passives often express opinions with **should,** rules and requirements with **must,** and possibilities with **could, might,** and **may:**

Opinion:	I don't think smoking **should be permitted** in public places.
Requirement:	Applications **must be submitted by** June 1.
Possibility:	The sales meeting **might have been canceled.**

➠ **Exercise 23: Writing Rules**

Work on your own. Change the following rules to a more formal, impersonal style by using passive instead of active sentences. Write your rules on the sign.

1. Members must show their membership passes at the gate.
2. Members can buy guest passes at the main office.
3. We may limit the number of guests on weekends.
4. We do not admit children under 12 unless an adult accompanies them.
5. You must supervise small children at all times.
6. You must take a shower before entering the pool.
7. You must obey the lifeguard at all times.
8. We permit diving in designated areas only.
9. We prohibit smoking, gum-chewing, and glass bottles.
10. You may eat food in the picnic area only.

Community Swimming Pool Rules

1. Membership passes must be shown at the gate. _____
2. _____
3. _____
4. _____
5. _____
6. _____
7. _____
8. _____
9. _____
10. _____

⫸ **Exercise 24: Expressing Opinions**

Work in small groups. Take turns asking and answering questions using the passive forms of the words in parentheses with the modal *should*.

1. (permit/smoking in public places)

   A: *Should smoking be permitted in public places?*
   B: *Yes, it should.* OR
       No, it shouldn't.

2. (allow/bicyclists/on busy streets)

3. (ban/violence/from television)

4. (guns/sell/in stores)

5. (pilots/test/for drugs and alcohol)

6. (women/pay/the same wages as men)

7. (men/give/parental leave)

8. (animals/use/medical research)

9. (children/give/allowance)

10. (⌇⌇⌇⌇)

⫸ **Exercise 25: Expressing Possibilities**

Work in small groups. Make guesses about the following situations using *could have, may have,* and *might have* with the passive. Offer as many possibilities as you can.

1. I didn't receive the letter that was supposed to come:

   Examples: *It could have been delivered incorrectly.*
             It may have been sent to the wrong address.
             It might have been lost.

2. The president's speech was supposed to be on TV at 9:00 P.M. It's 9:30 and the speech is still not on:

3. Jane just walked out of the manager's office. She was angry:

4. A failing student wrote a brilliant term paper. The teacher is very suspicious:

5. Joe entered his house, looked around, and called the police:

6. A million-dollar shipment of sardines disappeared off the coast of California near Monterey:

⬤ Exercise 26: Thinking About Meaning

Read each passive sentence and the two statements below it. Circle the statement that best explains the meaning of the sentence. Then explain your answers in small groups.

1. Students are required to take the final exam.

    (a) The students require the final exam.

    (b) The professor requires the final exam.

2. Your order should be accompanied by a check.

    (a) A check should accompany your order.

    (b) You should accompany your order.

3. He has been called a liar by the mayor.

    (a) The mayor has called him a liar.

    (b) He has called the mayor a liar.

4. Laser beams are used in surgery.

    (a) Laser beams use surgery.

    (b) Surgeons use laser beams in surgery.

5. He was asked to resign by the board of directors.

    (a) He asked the board of directors to resign.

    (b) The board of directors asked him to resign.

6. The accident could have been prevented.

    (a) The accident was prevented.

    (b) No one prevented the accident.

7. The letter was sent to all patients by the doctor.

    (a) The patients sent the letter.

    (b) The doctor sent the letter.

8. He is not being hired for the job.

    (a) He is not hiring us for the job.

    (b) He is not going to get the job.

Summary

Passive Sentences: Form

Simple Present:	Dinner **is served** from 5:00 to 9:00 P.M.
Simple Past:	The letter **was sent** on Monday.
Simple Future:	The Smith trial **will be heard** in Courtroom 2000.
Present Continuous:	Prices **are being lowered** for our special sale.
Past Continuous:	The children **were being driven** to school.
Present Perfect:	The weather **has been affected by** recent volcanic eruptions.
Past Perfect:	He **had been arrested** once before.
Simple Modal:	This product **should be kept** out of the reach of children.
Past Modal:	Her flight **must have been delayed.**

Passive Sentences: Meaning and Use

The passive in all tenses affects the way we think about the information in a sentence by changing the usual order of the subject and object of an active sentence. Passive sentences focus more on processes and results than on the person or thing that causes the action in the sentence.

Announcements:	Passengers **are requested** to remain seated.
Signs:	RESERVATIONS **REQUIRED**
Facts:	Oxygen **is carried** by red blood cells.
Processes:	The mixture **was boiled** and then **cooled** before it **was poured** into two bowls.
Results:	The car **was damaged by** the explosion.
Definitions:	Wine is an alcoholic beverage that **is made** from grapes.
Old Information:	Antibiotics are drugs. They **are used** to treat certain types of bacteria.
Headlines:	TWO **ARRESTED** IN SUPERMARKET BURGLARY
Opinions:	**Should** smoking **be permitted** in public places?
Possibilities:	The president's speech **might have been canceled.**
Rules:	Membership passes **must be shown** at the gate.

⟱➡ **Summary Exercise: Finding Errors**

Most of the sentences below have an error in form or appropriate use. Find each error and correct it.

1. These pills should be ~~take~~ every four hours.   *taken*

2. They were questioning by the police.

3. The letter should have be delivered in the afternoon.

4. The bell was rang several times.

5. The package was lost by the mail carrier.

6. A young man has put in prison.

7. This carpet being cleaned by a professional carpet cleaner.

8. The show must had been canceled.

9. The mail has sent to the wrong address.

10. The baby was weighed at the doctor's office.

11. He was died at the age of twenty.

12. Will the new road built soon?

13. The phone is being used when I needed it.

14. It will be not needed any longer.

15. It may not have been discovered early enough.

Noun Clauses and Reported Speech

Preview

In the supermarket:

Customer: Excuse me. Can you tell me **where the manager is?**
Cashier: I'm sorry. I'm not sure **if she's available right now,** but the assistant manager is over there....

Survey questions:

Do you believe **that we need a national space program?**
Do you think **that people should be allowed to carry hand guns?**

News report:

The president said in his speech last night **that he would not raise taxes this year.**

Three different types of noun clauses are: **wh-** clauses, **if/whether** clauses, and **that** clauses. Noun clauses are dependent clauses that can occur in the same place as a noun or noun phrase in a sentence. In the following sentence, the three kinds of noun clauses can take the place of the noun phrase *the answer:*

I didn't know **the answer.**
            where his key was.
            if he had his key.
            whether he had his key.
            that he had his key.

In this chapter you will study the different uses of noun clauses following mental activity verbs (for example, **know, think,** and **believe**). You will also study the uses of these noun clauses following verbs of communication (for example, **say, ask,** and **tell**) for reporting the general meaning of something that has been said or written.

Wh- Clauses: Form

Main Clause		*Wh-* Clause		
He	wondered	**who**	**I**	**was**.
		what	**she**	**was wearing**.
		why	**I**	**called**.
I	know	**where**	**he**	**is**.
		when	**the train**	**arrives**.
		how	**they**	**do it**.

- **Wh-** clauses begin with **wh-** words. They are sometimes called indirect questions or embedded questions.
- Like other clauses, **wh-** clauses have a subject and a verb.
- **Wh-** clauses are connected to the main clause by a **wh-** word (**who, what, why, where, when, how**). There's no comma between the main clause and the **wh-** clause.
- Although **wh-** clauses begin with **wh-** words, they do not use question word order. They use statement word order with the subject of the **wh-** clause always before the verb.
- When **who** or **what** is the subject of a question, the question is already in statement word order. Therefore, the word order stays the same when these questions become part of indirect questions:

  Joe: What happened?
  Matt: I don't know **what happened.** I wasn't home.

- A question mark is at the end of the sentence if the main clause is a question:

  Can you tell me what time it is**?**

- A period is at the end of the sentence if the main clause is a statement:

  I was wondering where you bought that shirt**.**

⫸ **Exercise 1: Working on Form**

Work with a partner. Complete the noun clauses with the subjects and verbs in parentheses.
Be sure to use appropriate tenses. Then practice the conversations.

1. Person A is looking for Eric:

   A: Do you know where _____ *Eric went* _____ (Eric/go)?

   B: No, and I don't know what time _____ *he came back* _____ (he/come back)

   either. OR

   No, and I don't know what time _____ *he's coming back* _____ (he/come back) either.

2. Person A is waiting for the mail:

   A: I wonder why _____ (the mail/not/come) today.

   B: Maybe I'll call the post office and ask what _____ (happen).

   Do you know what time _____ (the post office/close)?

3. Person A wants to take Person B out for her birthday:

   A: Please tell me where _____ (you/want/go) for your birthday.

   I don't care how much _____ (it/cost).

   B: I don't know. You can decide where _____ (we/should/go).

   Just tell me what time _____ (I/should/be ready).

4. Person A needs information about the chemistry exam:

   A: Do you know when _____ (the chemistry exam/be)?

   B: Yes, it's on Thursday, but I'm not sure where _____ (it/be) or

   how long _____ (it/be).

5. Person A can't find his keys:

   A: I can't find my keys. I have no idea where _____ (they/be).

   B: You had them last night. Do you remember what _____

   (you/do) when you came into the house?

6. Person A is in a department store:

   A: I'd like to find out how much _____ (this/cost).

   B: I'm not sure, but I'll ask the manager as soon as I find out where

   _____ (he/be).

Wh- Clauses: Meaning and Use

STATEMENTS OF UNCERTAINTY AND CURIOSITY; POLITE QUESTIONS

1. Wh- clauses often occur in statements following mental activity verbs such as **know, understand, remember,** and **wonder.** These statements frequently express uncertainty and curiosity, especially in response to questions and statements:

> Pat: Olga left yesterday.
> Tim: I don't know **why she left.** I don't understand **what happened.**
> Pat: When did her train leave?
> Tim: I can't remember **when it left.**
> Pat: You know, her parents have eight children.
> Tim: I wonder **how they manage.**

2. Wh- clauses often replace direct questions because they make a question more indirect and therefore more polite:

Direct Question: When does the train arrive?

Polite Question: Can you (please) tell me **when the train arrives?**

Could you (please) tell me **when the train arrives?**

Do you know **when the train arrives?**

I was wondering if you could tell me **when the train arrives.**

I'd like to find out **when the train arrives.**

⇒ Exercise 2: Expressing Uncertainty

Work with a partner. Imagine you are at the scene of a hit-and-run accident. A speeding truck crashed into a car and a bicyclist, and then the truck drove off. The police are interviewing possible witnesses without much success. Take turns asking and answering the questions below, using a statement of uncertainty (*I can't remember, I'm not sure, I don't know, I'm not certain, I have no idea*) and a *wh-* clause.

1. **Police:** Who was driving the truck?

   Witness 1: *I'm not sure who was driving it.*

2. **Police:** What time did the accident occur?

   Witness 1:

3. **Police:** What was the license plate number on the truck?

   Witness 2:

4. **Police:** Where was the bicyclist?

   Witness 2:

5. **Police:** What did the truck look like?

   Witness 3:

6. **Police:** How many people were in the truck?

   Witness 3:

7. **Police:** What were you doing at the time of the accident?

   Witness 4:

8. **Police:** How fast was the truck going?

   Witness 4:

9. **Police:** What color was the truck?

   Witness 5:

10. **Police:** What did the driver look like?

    Witness 5:

⮕ Exercise 3: Expressing Curiosity

Work on your own. Write five sentences about different things that you are uncertain or curious about. Begin your sentences with some of these expressions: *I've always wondered, I'm not sure, I don't know, I can't understand, I can't remember, I'm not certain.* Then tell the class one of your sentences.

1. I've always wondered what it's like in Alaska.

2. _____

3. _____

4. _____

5. _____

6. _____

⟱ **Exercise 4: Asking Polite Questions**

Work with a partner. Make up polite questions for each situation. Then practice asking and answering each question.

1. At the airport — you're looking for a restroom:

   A: *Excuse me. Can you please tell me where the restroom is?* OR
       Excuse me. Could you please tell me where the restroom is?
   B: *It's downstairs on the left.*

   Now you're looking for the baggage claim:

   A: *Excuse me. Could you please tell me where the baggage claim is?*
   B: *It's straight ahead on your right.*

2. At the bus stop — you're asking someone for the time:

   Now you're looking for the bus schedule:

3. In a department store — you're asking a salesperson the price of a shirt:

   Now you're asking a salesperson the size of a pair of socks:

4. In the supermarket — you're looking for the manager:

   Now you're asking the clerk for the price of broccoli:

5. On campus — you're applying for a new ID card:

   Now you're paying your tuition bill:

If/Whether Clauses: Form

Main Clause	*If/Whether* Clause
I don't know	**if he left (or not).**
Can you tell me	**whether it arrived (or not)?**

- **If** clauses and **whether** clauses are noun clauses that begin with **if** or **whether.** They are also called embedded or indirect *yes/no* questions.
- Like other clauses, **if/whether** clauses have a subject and a verb.
- **If/whether** clauses are like *yes/no* questions, but they use statement word order:

   Do you know **if you are coming with us?**
   *Do you know if are you coming with us? (INCORRECT)

- The phrase **or not** can be added to the end of **if/whether** clauses if the clauses are not very long:

  I wonder **if** she left **or not.**
  I wonder **whether** she left **or not.**

- **Or not** can also immediately follow **whether,** but it can't follow **if**:

  I wonder **whether or not** she left.

- There is no comma between the main clause and the **if/whether** clause.
- A period is at the end of the sentence if the main clause is a statement.
- A question mark is at the end of the sentence if the main clause is a question.

⇒ Exercise 5: Working on Form

Work with a partner. Use your own words to complete the following conversations with *if/whether* clauses. Then practice the conversations.

1. Two friends are on the way home from work:

   A: Do you know if the bank _____ *is open today?* _____

   B: I'm not sure if _____ *it is or not.* _____ They've recently changed their hours.

2. Person A is getting ready to leave for work:

   A: I wonder whether or not _____

   B: Take your umbrella if you're not sure.

3. Two co-workers are talking about their manager:

   A: Do you remember if _____

   B: I really don't know whether _____ or not. Let's ask someone.

4. Person A is buying groceries:

   A: Can you tell me if _____

   B: I'm not sure if _____ or not. I'll ask the manager.

5. Person A is buying tickets for a concert:

A: I was wondering if you could tell me whether _____

_____

B: There aren't any seats left on that date, and I don't know if

_____. I'll have to check.

If/Whether Clauses: Meaning and Use

STATEMENTS OF UNCERTAINTY AND POLITE QUESTIONS

1. **If** and **whether** have the same meanings when they begin noun clauses. They are used both in speaking and in writing, although **if** is more common in informal situations and **whether** is more common in more formal situations.

2. **Whether** is often used instead of **if** to emphasize that there are alternatives:

I don't know **whether she's at home or at work.**

3. Like embedded **wh-** clauses, **if/whether** clauses are often used in statements following mental activity verbs:

I can't remember **if I locked the door** or not.
I wonder **whether the mail has arrived yet.**

4. **If/whether** clauses are also used to make polite questions:

Do you know **if the train has come yet?**
Can you please tell me **whether there's any space on the 4:05 flight to Dallas?**

⇒ Exercise 6: Expressing Uncertainty

Work with a partner. Complete each sentence with an *if/whether* clause in an appropriate tense. You can add *or not* to some of your noun clauses.

1. Peter overslept this morning. He had to get dressed very quickly because he had an important appointment. On the way to work, he realized that he left his apartment so quickly that he couldn't remember if he had done everything that he was supposed to do:

(a) He couldn't remember _if he'd locked the door (or not)._____

(b) He wasn't sure whether_____

(c) He didn't know if_____

(d) He wondered if _____

2. This is the first day of your new job. You're nervous on your way to work:

    (a) You wonder whether _____

    (b) You're not sure if _____

    (c) You have no idea whether_____

    (d) You don't know if _____

3. You've met the man or woman of your dreams. You're going to meet his or her parents tonight. You've been worrying about it all day:

    (a) You wonder if_____

    (b) You don't know whether _____

    (c) You're not sure whether _____

    (d) You can't remember if_____

⇒ Exercise 7: Expressing Uncertainty

Work on your own. Think of a situation where you did something for the first time and you were uncertain about it. Write four sentences using statements of uncertainty followed by *if/whether* clauses.

1. When I decided to move to another city, I wasn't sure if I should sell my furniture or not.

2. _____

3. _____

4. _____

5. _____

⮞ Exercise 8: Asking Polite Questions

Work with a partner. Here are some direct questions that you might ask another student. Make each question more polite by using *I was wondering…, Can/Could you (please) tell me…, Do you know…, Do you have any idea…*.

1. Is the assignment due tomorrow?

   Example: *Do you know if the assignment is due tomorrow?*

2. Is the library closed during vacation?

3. Is the teacher going to show a film today?

4. Could you repeat that, please?

5. Did you have any trouble with the last assignment?

6. Is the new language lab open yet?

7. Did I miss anything important yesterday?

8. Can you give me a ride home this afternoon?

⮞ Exercise 9: Asking Polite Questions

Think of another situation where you might need to get some information (for example, at the airport, the bank, the supermarket, the library). Make up three direct *yes/no* questions on your own. Then have your partner change them into polite questions.

1. Situation: In a store

   Direct Question: Is this on sale?

   Polite Question: Could you please tell me if this is on sale?

2. _____

   _____

   _____

3. _____

   _____

   _____

4. _____

   _____

   _____

That Clauses: Form

Main Clause	*That* Clause
I think	**(that) he called**.
They didn't think	**(that) it would break**.

- **That** clauses are noun clauses which begin with **that.**
- Like other clauses, **that** clauses have a subject and a verb.
- There is no comma between the main clause and the **that** clause.
- **That** can usually be omitted.

⇒ **Exercise 10: Working on Form**

Work with a partner. Unscramble the words to make a statement or a question with a *that* clause. Use every word.

1. (was/that/you/he/angry/notice/did)

   Did you notice that he was angry?

2. (is/doubt/she/we/coming)

3. (predict/it/soon/happen/they/will)

4. (help/I/some/need/I/that/guess)

5. (that/due/remembered/my/was/rent/I/tomorrow)

6. (proved/could/he/do/it/he)

7. (tomorrow/register/I/can/you/assume)

8. (he/that/is/you/guilty/believe/do)

That Clauses: Meaning and Use

OPINIONS, THOUGHTS, FEELINGS

1. **That** clauses follow mental activity verbs to express opinions, thoughts, and feelings:

agree	dream	find out	notice	recognize
assume	estimate	forget	predict	regret
believe	expect	guess	presume	remember
bet	fear	hope	pretend	suppose
decide	feel	imagine	prove	suspect
discover	figure out	know	realize	think
doubt	find	learn	recall	understand

2. **That** is often omitted, especially in conversation. The meaning of the sentence does not change:

Joe: I think **I might go with you tonight.**
Kate: I hope **you do.** It'll be fun.

3. When the mental activity verb is in the present tense, the verb in the noun clause can be in the present, past, or future. The tense depends on the meaning of the sentence:

I think **it's OK.**
I believe **she sent the letter this morning.**
I assume **they'll come later.**

4. When the mental activity verb is in the past, the verb in the noun clause usually shares the same past point of view:

I thought **that I was working too hard.**

5. The past perfect is used in the noun clause to refer to an earlier past time:

I knew **that she had left.**

6. **Was** or **were going to** or **would** are used in the noun clause to refer to a later time:

I thought **she was going to come later.**
I thought **he would come later.**

7. In some cases, however, the verb in the noun clause doesn't use the past tense verb after a past mental activity verb. If the noun clause is a generalization that's true at the present, the present tense can be used in the noun clause:

Columbus believed **that the world is round.**

If the verb is a mental activity that takes place very quickly (for example, **decide, realize**), the present or future tense can be used in the noun clause:

Last night I realized **that my report is too long.**
He decided **he'll be here by lunchtime.**

Mental activity verbs that take place very quickly include: **decided, discovered, figured out, forgot, found out, learned, noticed, proved, realized, recalled,** and **remembered.**

8. In conversation, **so** often replaces a **that** clause after verbs like **think, believe,** and **hope** in affirmative responses to *yes/no* questions:

Janet: Did it stop raining?
Susan: Yes, I **think so.** (so = **that it stopped raining**)

9. Other verbs and expressions that can be followed by **so** in affirmative answers include: **assume, be afraid, guess, imagine, suppose, it seems,** and **it appears.**

10. There are two ways to make shortened negative answers with the verbs that can be followed by **so:**

Negative verb + **so**
Pat: Is he leaving?
Dan: I **don't think so.**

Verb + **not**
Pat: Is he leaving?
Dan: I **think not.**

11. Hope, be afraid, and **guess** have only one shortened negative form. They can only be followed by **not:**

Pat: Is he leaving?
Dan: I **hope not.** OR
I'm **afraid not.** OR
I **guess not.**

⫸ **Exercise 11: Expressing Opinions**

Work in small groups. Take turns expressing your own opinions about each statement. Use as many mental activity verbs as you can.

1. Smokers are often treated unfairly.

   Example: *I agree that smokers are often treated unfairly. I think…*

2. Middle age starts at forty.

3. The media discusses nutrition too much.

4. Marriage contracts are a good idea.

5. You can't really change someone.

6. Some people can't learn a second language.

⫸ **Exercise 12: Expressing Thoughts and Feelings**

Work with a partner. Take turns asking and answering each question. Choose a different mental activity verb using *so, not,* or *don't/doesn't…so* in each answer. Then add another sentence to explain your answer.

1. Are you making progress in English?

   Examples: *Yes, I hope so. It's getting easier.* OR
             No, I don't think so. I'm still having a lot of trouble.

2. Would you like to be in politics?

3. Do you ever want to be someone else?

4. Are you generally a happy person?

5. Are computers making your life easier?

6. Is money necessary for your happiness?

7. Are your friends available to you when you need them?

8. 〜〜〜〜〜

⫸ **Exercise 13: Combining *That* Clauses**

Work with a partner. Make up as many sentences as you can using the mental activity verbs in Column A and the *that* clauses in Column B. Be prepared to discuss why some combinations don't work.

   Example: *I thought that something happened.*
            I thought that he had won.
            I thought that…

Column A	Column B
1. I thought	a. that he'll change.
2. She doubts	b. that it's raining.
3. I hoped	c. that something happened.
4. They realized	d. that he had won.
	e. that we were going to complain.
	f. that Joe could win.
	g. that water freezes at 32° Fahrenheit.

Overview of Reported Speech: Form

Reported Statements

She **says (that) she wants to leave**.

Reported *Yes/No* Questions

They **asked if I needed a ride**.

Reported Information Questions

I **asked what time it was**.

Reported Imperatives

I **told him to stay home**.
I **told him not to stay home**.

- Reported speech (also called indirect speech) has a reporting verb in the main clause (for example, **say, ask, tell**) followed by a noun clause or an infinitive.
- In reported statements, the quoted statement changes to a **that** clause.
- In reported *yes/no* questions, the quoted *yes/no* question changes to an **if/whether** clause. Like other **if/whether** clauses, reported *yes/no* questions have statement word order.
- In reported information questions, the quoted information question changes to a **wh-** clause. Like other **wh-** clauses, reported information questions have statement word order.
- In reported imperatives, the quoted command is changed to an infinitive. In negative imperatives, **not** comes before the infinitive.
- Look at page 498 for a list of reporting verbs (verbs of communication).

⟶ **Exercise 14: Identifying Reported Speech**

Underline all examples of reported speech in the following conversations.

1. **A:** I don't think that the new manager is doing a good job.

   B: Me neither. <u>He told me to come in early yesterday for a meeting,</u> and he forgot to show up.

   A: You're kidding. Julia said the same thing happened to her on Tuesday. I wonder whether we should complain to Allison. She hired him.

   B: I'm not sure if we should say anything yet. I asked Tom what he thought. He suggested that we wait one more week.

2. **A:** Did you hear the news? Channel 7 reported that the superintendent resigned.

   B: I know. I wonder if something happened. Everyone says she was pleased with the way things were going.

   A: Yesterday's news mentioned that she hadn't been feeling well lately. Maybe it's something serious and she was advised to step down.

3. **A:** Did you speak to the travel agent?

   B: I asked whether I needed to change the flight. He said he'd take care of it, and he admitted that he'd made a mistake. He assured me that everything would work out.

   A: Let's hope so. I told you to be careful during the holiday season. They're so busy that they often make mistakes.

Quoted Speech versus Reported Speech: Form

Quoted Speech		Reported Speech
"The report is on my desk."	→	She **says that the report is on her desk**.
"Are you staying here?"	→	He **asked if I was staying there**.
"Where did you go?"	→	I **asked where she had gone**.
"Press the green button."	→	He **told me to press the green button**.
"Don't press the red button."	→	He **told me not to press the red button**.

- Reported speech has no quotation marks or question marks.
- Reported speech often has pronouns and adverbs different from the quoted speech (look at page 466):

"Did **you** see **this?**" → He asked if **I** had seen **that.**

Quoted Speech	Reported Speech (Present Tense Report)
"It**'s raining**."	→ Joe **says** it**'s raining**.
"It**'s going to rain**."	→ Joe **says** it**'s going to rain**.
"It **rained**."	→ Joe **says** it **rained**.

- If the reporting verb (**say**) is in the present tense, the tense in the **that** clause doesn't change.

Quoted Speech	Reported Speech (Past Tense Report)
"I **need** a vacation."	→ I **said** that I **needed** a vacation.
"I**'m working**."	→ I **said** that I **was working**.
"I **left** early."	→ I **said** that I**'d left** early.
"I**'ve finished**."	→ I **said** that I**'d finished**.
"I**'ll see** you soon."	→ I **said** I **would see** you soon.
"I**'m going to win**."	→ I **said** I **was going to win**.
"I **can win**."	→ I **said** I **could win**.
"I **may leave**."	→ I **said** I **might leave**.
"I **have to try**."	→ I **said** I **had to try**.
"I **must take** a vacation."	→ I **said** I **had to take** a vacation.
"I **should stay**."	→ I **said** I **should stay**.
"I **ought to stay**."	→ I **said** I **ought to stay**.

- If the reporting verb (**said**) is in the past tense, the tense in the **that** clause often changes.
- The modals **should** and **ought to** do not change to a past form.

⤷ **Exercise 15: Working on Form**

Work with a partner. Complete the following conversations by changing the quoted speech in parentheses to reported speech. If the reporting verb is in the past tense, you can change the verb in the noun clause to the past tense. Pronouns may also change. Then practice the conversations.

1. **Martha:** Your mother called.

   John: What did she say?

   Martha: She wanted to know _____ how you were feeling. _____ ("How is John feeling?") She also asked _____ if we could come over for dinner Sunday. _____ ("Could you and John come over for dinner on Sunday?")

   John: That's strange. I told her yesterday that

   _____ ("We are busy on Sunday.")

   Martha: You'd better call her back because I said _____

   _____ ("I think we can, but I'll have to check with John first.")

2. **A:** The recipe says _____ ("Use fresh herbs.")

   B: I know. It also says _____ ("Make the sauce a day ahead.")

3. **A:** Nina wants to know _____ ("What does Jim's letter say?")

   B: It says _____ ("I'm having a great time.")

   It also says that _____

   _____ ("I'm going to come home on the twenty-ninth at 6:30 P.M.") and _____

   _____ ("I hope Nina can pick me up at the airport.")

   A: I'll tell Nina _____

   _____ ("Pick Jim up at the airport at 6:30 P.M. on the twenty-ninth.")

4. **A:** What did the doctor say?

 B: Not much. He said _____ ("Get some rest
 for a few days.")

 A: Did you ask him _____ ("Do I need an
 X ray?")?

 B: Yes. He said _____

 _____ ("Wait until Monday and then call my office.")

Reported Speech: Meaning and Use

THE REPORTER'S POINT OF VIEW

Reported speech is used in speaking and writing to tell what someone has said or written.
It expresses the same meaning as quoted speech, but it expresses the quoted speech from the
reporter's point of view. This explains why sometimes there are changes in tense, pronouns,
and adverbs between reported speech and related quoted speech.

Tense Changes

Tense changes depend on the tense of the reporting verb and on the reporter. If the reporting
verb is in the past tense, then the tense in the **that** clause may change to the past. This tense
change usually depends on how the reporter views the relationship between the quoted
sentence and the present time. There are many reasons why the reporter may not change the
reported speech to the past:

1. If the quoted speech just happened, the reporter often uses the same tense in the
that clause because the time has not really changed very much:

 Cindy: **I'm going out** for a while.
 Maria: What did she say?
 Rosa: She said she**'s going out** for a while.

Announcement: "Flight 403 **has arrived** at Gate 9."
 Mark: What did the announcement say? I couldn't hear it.
 Pat: It said that flight 403 **has arrived** at Gate 9.

2. If the reporter wants to show that the quoted speech is a generalization that is still true,
the present tense is used:

 The manager told me that the supermarket **doesn't accept** checks.

3. If the event in the quoted speech hasn't happened yet, the future is often used:

 The president announced that he **is going to appoint** a new judge next week.

(continued)

Pronoun Changes

1. Personal pronouns often must be changed to represent the reporter's point of view, instead of the original speaker's point of view:

"Please take **your** book." → She told me to take **my** book.

"I like **your** hat." → I said I like **his** hat.

2. Sometimes the pronouns stay the same when the reporter is repeating his or her own words:

"I can't find **my** key." → I said I can't find **my** key.

3. **This, that, these,** and **those** are used from the reporter's point of view, not the speaker's. Therefore, sometimes they change to **a** or **the,** and sometimes **this/these** change to **that/those:**

"I like **this** book." → He said he likes **this** book (right here).

→ He said he likes **that** book (over there).

→ He said he likes **a** book. (It doesn't matter which one.)

→ He said he likes **the** book (you bought him).

Adverb Changes

Adverbs of time (**today, yesterday**) and place (**here, there**) may change depending on the time of the reported speech and the location of the reporter. Once again, they need to express the reporter's point of view of the quoted speech, not the speaker's. For example, there are numerous ways to report the following phone messages:

"I'll call you **tomorrow**." → He said he would call me **the next day.**

He said he'd call me **on Monday.**

He said he'll call me **tomorrow.**

"I'll be **here** until 6:00 P.M." → He said he'd be **there** until 6:00 P.M.

He said he'll be **here** until 6:00 P.M.

Reporting Verbs

Reporting verbs are all communication verbs followed by noun clauses. **Say, tell,** and **ask** are the most common reporting verbs, but many other reporting verbs such as **admit** and **complain** are used instead to express more clearly the reporter's interpretation of the quoted words. There are some differences between the various reporting verbs:

1. Tell is followed by a noun or pronoun before the **that** clause. The noun or pronoun refers to the listener:

> He **told me** that it was too late.
> I **told Julia** I'd be there soon.

2. With **say,** you don't need to mention the listener:

> He **said** that it was too late.
> I **said** I'd be there soon.

If the listener is mentioned, **to** is needed. However, **tell** is much more common than **say to:**

> He **said to me** that it was too late.
> He **told me** that it was too late.

3. Ask or **want to know** are used instead of **say** and **tell** to report questions:

> She **asked** what time it was.
> She **wanted to know** what time it was.

4. The following reporting verbs are similar to **say** because the listener doesn't have to be identified. If the listener is mentioned, **to** is needed:

> He **admitted (to me)** that he was sorry.
> I **explained (to John)** that it was OK.

admit	confess	point out	shout
announce	explain	remark	state
comment	indicate	reply	swear
complain	mention	report	whisper

5. The following reporting verbs are similar to **tell** because the verb must be followed by the listener: **assure, convince, inform, notify, persuade,** and **remind:**

> He **reminded me** that I had an appointment at three o'clock.

News report:

> The president **informed the Congress** that he was going to form a special committee.

6. The listener is optional with **answer** and **promise:**

> She **answered (me)** that he was coming soon.
> She **promised (me)** that he was coming soon.

(continued)

7. When a **that** clause follows the verbs **ask, require, insist, demand, suggest, recommend, advise,** and **propose,** the verb in the **that** clause is always in the simple form even if these verbs are in the past tense:

I **recommend**	that he stay.
I **recommended**	that he stay.
They **suggest**	that she take a vacation.
They **suggested**	that she take a vacation.

8. Should is often used instead of an infinitive to report imperatives:

Advice:

Doctor: Don't eat any spicy foods for a few days.
Patient: The doctor said I **shouldn't eat** any spicy foods for a few days. OR
The doctor said **not to eat** spicy foods for a few days.

⏩ Exercise 16: Completing Sentences with Reported Speech

Work with a partner. Make as many sentences as you can using the reporting verbs in Column A and the phrases in Column B. Be prepared to discuss why some combinations don't work.

Example: *She told me that he was leaving.*
She told him to stay.
She told…

Column A	Column B
1. She told	a. to the woman that it was impossible.
2. He explained	b. me that he was leaving.
3. They require	c. him to stay.
4. I admitted	d. I was tired.
5. We asked	e. that the bridge was open.
6. He suggested	f. that it was too late.
7. You said	g. that the student take an exam.
8. I answered	h. if he was leaving.
	l. them that they were next.
	j. to me that I should try.

⇒ Exercise 17: Repeating Yourself

Work with a partner. Person A makes a statement or asks a question, and Person B uses the polite expressions below to ask Person A to repeat himself or herself. Person A uses reported speech to repeat what he or she has just said. Be prepared to discuss why you did or didn't change the tenses in the reported speech.

Polite Expressions

Excuse me. I didn't hear you.

Could you repeat that, please?

I'm sorry. What did you say?

Could you please say that again?

1. Two students:

   Person A: Class is canceled today.
   Person B: *Excuse me. I didn't hear you.*
   Person A: *I said that class is canceled today.*

2. Two roommates:

   A: Where are the stamps?

3. Two friends:

   A: Are you going with us tonight?

4. A customer and a cashier at a supermarket:

   A: Can I give you a check?

5. A teller and a customer at a bank:

   A: Take this to the front desk.

6. Two roommates:

   A: Your mother called this afternoon.

7. A parent and child at home:

   A: Did you finish your homework?

8. A supervisor and a secretary at an office:

   A: Don't worry about the report. You can finish it tomorrow.

▶ Exercise 18: Reporting Advice

Work on your own. Maria is a thirty-year-old elementary school teacher who has taught for eight years. She's thinking about quitting her job and finding a new career. Her family and friends give her a lot of different advice. Complete each sentence by reporting each person's advice with an infinitive, a clause with *should*, or a clause with the simple form of the verb.

Advice from Family and Friends

Friend: Don't quit your job until you know what you want to do.

Husband: Think about getting another degree.

Mother: If I were you, I'd find out about different types of graduate programs.

Father: Don't quit. Just take a leave of absence for a year.

Aunt: Quit your job and have a baby.

Uncle: Do whatever makes you happy!

Sister: Ask for a raise.

Brother-in-law: Go to an employment agency.

Colleague: Ask to teach a different grade next year.

Neighbor: Try to get a job in my company.

1. Her friend told her *not to quit her job until she knows what she wants to do.*

2. Her husband says_____

3. Her mother suggested _____

4. Her father told her_____

5. Her aunt advises _____

6. Her uncle says _____

7. Her sister recommended _____

8. Her brother-in-law_____

9. Her colleague _____

10. Her neighbor _____

⏩ **Exercise 19: Reporting Messages**

Work on your own. Imagine your friend is in the hospital. He asks you to listen to the phone messages on his answering machine and report the messages to him. Today is Thursday, March 23. You're reporting the messages from March 20 to 23. Change each message to reported speech using appropriate verb tenses, pronouns, and adverbs.

1. Monday, March 20:

   (a) "This is Nora Green. Please call me back."

   Nora Green called on Monday. She said to call her back.

   (b) "This is Joe's Repair Shop. Your TV will be ready at noon today."

   _____

2. Tuesday, March 21:

   (a) "This is Bob. I'll call back later."

   _____

   (b) "My name is Richard Smith. I'd like to speak to you about an insurance policy. My number is 324-1221."

   _____

3. Wednesday, March 22:

   (a) "This is Jill. I'm just calling to say hello. I'll be home all evening."

   _____

   (b) "This is Stuart Lee. I've been calling for several days. Is anything wrong? Please call me back soon."

   _____

4. Thursday, March 23:

   (a) "This is Eric Martin. I'm calling to remind you about the board meeting on the twenty-ninth. Call me back if you have any questions."

   _____

   (b) "This is Gibson's. We'll be able to deliver the desk you ordered on Monday, March 27. Please call if this is inconvenient."

   _____

➠ **Exercise 20: Reporting the Weather**

Work on your own. Rephrase the following weather forecast using reported speech and the reporting verbs *predict* and *say*.

"Tonight a cold front will move in from the west and temperatures will drop into the fifties. Tomorrow the skies will turn cloudy with a 30 percent chance of afternoon showers. Temperatures will remain in the fifties all day. On Sunday, you can expect sunny skies. It will be warmer than Saturday, with highs in the upper sixties."

The weather report said that a cold front will move in from the west tonight.

It predicted that...

_____

_____

_____

_____

_____

_____

_____

_____

➠ **Exercise 21: Reporting the Weather**

Listen to a radio or TV weather report and write three or four sentences about it using reported speech.

The announcer predicted that the weather is going to get much colder

by Sunday...

_____

_____

_____

_____

_____

⫸ Exercise 22: Reporting the News

Listen to the news on the radio or TV and write three or four sentences about a topic in the news that interests you. Use reported speech to restate what you heard.

The local news station announced that the new recycling program begins next week.

They said that...

_____

_____

_____

_____

_____

⫸ Exercise 23: Restating Statements

Work in small groups. First discuss comments and advice from your parents and other family members when you were growing up. Use statements with reported speech. Then write four examples of comments or advice.

1. My father often told me not to be a teacher.

2. _____

3. _____

4. _____

5. _____

⫸ Exercise 24: Restating Questions

Work in small groups. First discuss what kinds of questions people ask you when they first meet you. Then write down four examples of these questions.

1. People often ask me how long I've been living here.

2. _____

3. _____

4. _____

5. _____

Summary

Wh- Clauses: Form

Main Clause + *Wh-* Clause: He forgot **who I was.**

Can you tell me **where he is?**

If/Whether Clauses: Form

Main Clause + *If/Whether* Clause: I don't know **if it arrived yet (or not).**

I wonder **whether (or not) she left.**

Wh- Clauses and *If/Whether* Clauses: Meaning and Use

Wh- clauses and **if/whether** clauses express thoughts and polite questions when they follow mental activity verbs.

Uncertainty: I don't know **where it is.**

I'm not sure **whether she's here or not.**

Curiosity: I wonder **if she left yet.**

Polite Questions: Could you please tell me **what time it is?**

That Clauses: Form

Main Clause + *That* Clause: I think **(that) he called.**

That Clauses: Meaning and Use

That clauses express opinions, thoughts, and feelings when they follow mental activity verbs.

Opinions: I don't think **that they should raise the sales tax.**

Thoughts: I dreamed **that she called me.**

Feelings: I hope **he'll come soon.**

I felt **that he was innocent.**

Reported Speech: Form

Reported Statements: He said **that he was having a great time.**

Reported *Yes/No* Questions: I asked **if my order was ready.**

I asked **whether my order was ready.**

Reported Information Questions: She wants to know **when the bank opens.**

Reported Imperatives: They told me **to wait here.**

They said **not to stay.**

Reported Speech: Meaning and Use

Reported speech expresses the meaning of quoted speech or writing from the point of view of the reporter. **Wh-** clauses, **if/whether** clauses, and **that** clauses express reported speech when they follow communication verbs.

Repeating:	Waiter: Excuse me. Could you repeat that, please? Customer: I said **I'd like to pay the bill now.**
Reported Advice:	The doctor told him **to get some rest.**
	She suggested **that he take a vacation.**
Reported Messages:	Ana called. She said **she'd call back later.**
Reported News:	The mayor announced **that he was going to resign at the end of the year.**
Reported Weather:	The weather report predicts **that it'll be sunny tomorrow.**
Restatements:	My grandmother always said **I was too thin.**

⥤ Summary Exercise: Finding Errors

Most of the sentences have an error in form or appropriate use. Find each error and correct it.

1. I wonder where ~~is he.~~ *he is*

2. I asked if I could borrow her pen.

3. She spoke to me that it was too late.

4. **A:** Is Nina coming?
   B: Yes, I think.

5. **A:** Are you going home this weekend?
   B: Yes, I suppose so.

6. I think she said me the truth.

7. I didn't realize, that she was absent.

8. She thought he will come later.

9. They told me that why she left.

10. I can't remember who called.

11. They told that the store was closed.

12. Do you know if or not he's staying?

13. Please tell if you want to come or not.

14. They recommended that she left early.

15. She said if I wanted a ride home.

Appendix

Two- and Three-Word Verbs

Many common verbs have two or even three words. These two- and three-word verbs are also known as phrasal verbs. The meaning of the whole phrase is usually different from the individual meanings of the two or three words that make up the phrasal verb.

Several of the two- and three-word verbs in this section are used in the explanations, examples, and exercises throughout the book.

1. Many two-word verbs are separable. This means that a noun object can separate the two words of the phrasal verb, or the noun object can follow the phrasal verb. But if the object is a pronoun (**me, you, him, her, it, us, them**), the pronoun must separate the two words. Pronouns cannot follow a separable two-word verb:

Noun Object	Pronoun Object
She **turned** the offer **down.**	She **turned** it **down.**
She **turned down** the offer.	*She turned down it. (INCORRECT)

2. If the object noun phrase is long, the two-word verb is not separated:

She **turned down** the offer that she received in the mail yesterday.
*She turned the offer that she received in the mail yesterday down. (INCORRECT)

3. Some two-word verbs are nonseparable. This means that a noun or pronoun object cannot separate the two parts of the phrasal verb. They must follow a nonseparable two-word verb:

Noun Object	Pronoun Object
The teacher **went over** the lesson.	The teacher **went over** it.
*The teacher went the lesson over. (INCORRECT)	*The teacher went it over. (INCORRECT)

4. Three-word verbs are almost always nonseparable. Noun and pronoun objects follow the entire three-word verb phrase:

Noun Object

Don't **put up with** the noise.

*Don't put up the noise with. (INCORRECT)

Pronoun Object

Don't **put up with** it.

*Don't put up it with. (INCORRECT)

5. These three-word verbs are separable:

make (something) **up to** (someone)

put (something) **over on** (someone)

6. The following list includes some common separable and nonseparable two-word verbs, and some common three-word verbs, and their meanings. Many of these verbs have more than one meaning. If a phrasal verb is separable, its parts are separated in the list by (someone) or (something):

ask (someone) out	invite someone to go out
ask (someone) over	invite someone to come to your house
beat (someone) up	give someone a severe beating
blow up	explode
blow (something) up	inflate; cause something to explode
boot (something) up	start or get a computer ready for use
break down	stop functioning properly
break up with (someone)	end a relationship with
bring (someone) up	raise a child
bring (something) up	introduce or call attention to a topic
burn down	be destroyed by fire
burn (something) down	destroy by fire
call (someone) back	return a phone call to someone
call (something) off	cancel something
call on (someone)	ask someone to answer or speak in class; visit someone
call (someone) up	telephone
call (something) up	retrieve from the memory of a computer
catch up with (someone or something)	travel fast enough to overtake someone who is ahead
check (something) out	borrow a book, video, tape from the library; verify

check out of (a hotel)	leave a hotel after paying the bill
clean (something) out	clean the inside of something thoroughly
clean (something) up	clean thoroughly and remove anything unwanted
clear up	become fair weather
clear (something) up	explain a problem
come back	return
come over	visit
come up with (something)	think of a plan or reply
cross (something) out	draw a line through
cut down on (something)	reduce
cut (something) up	cut into little pieces
do (something) over	do something again
eat out	have a meal in a restaurant
face up to (something)	be brave enough to accept or deal with
fall down	leave a standing position; perform in a disappointing way
figure (something) out	solve a problem
fill (something) in	write in a blank or a space
fill (something) out	write information on a form
fill (something) up	fill completely with something
find (something) out	discover information
get away with (doing something)	not be punished for doing something wrong
get down to (something)	begin to give serious attention to
get off (something)	leave a plane, bus, train
get on (something)	enter a plane, bus, train
get over (something)	recover from an illness or a serious life event
get up	arise from a bed or chair
give (something) back	return something
give up	stop trying, lose hope
give (something) up	quit something; get rid of something
go back	return
go down	(of computers) stop functioning; (of prices or temperature) become lower; (of ships) sink; (of the sun or moon) set

go off	stop functioning; (of alarms) start functioning; explode or make a loud noise
go on	take place; happen (especially in the continuous tenses)
go out	leave one's house to go to a social event
go out with (someone)	spend time regularly with someone
go over (something)	review
grow up	become an adult
hand (something) in	submit homework, a test, an application
hand (something) out	distribute something
hang (something) up	put on a hook or on a clothes hanger; end a telephone call
hold on	wait on the telephone
keep on (doing something)	continue doing something
keep (someone) up	prevent someone from going to sleep
keep up with	stay at the same level or position
kick (someone) out	force someone to leave
leave (something) out	omit
light (something) up	make light or bright with color; begin to smoke a cigar, cigarette, or pipe
look out for (something/someone)	be careful of
look (something) over	examine carefully
look (something) up	look for information in a book
make (something) up	create or invent something; do work that was missed
make (something) up to (someone)	return a favor
move out	stop occupying a residence, especially by removing one's possessions
pack up	prepare all of one's belongings for moving
pay (someone) back	return money owed to someone
pick (something) out	choose
pick (something/someone) up	lift something or someone; stop to get something or someone
point (something) out	mention; draw attention to something
put (something) away	put something in its usual place

put (something) back	return something to its original place
put (something) down	stop holding something
put (something) in	install
put (something) off	postpone
put (something) on	get dressed
put (something) out	extinguish a fire, cigarette, or cigar
put (something) over on (someone)	deceive someone
put up with (something/someone)	tolerate
run out	come to an end; be completely used up
run out of (something)	have no more of something
set (something) up	make something ready for use
show up	appear, be seen, arrive at a place
shut (something) off	turn off a machine
sit down	get into a sitting position
start (something) over	start again
stay out	remain out of the house, especially at night
stay up	remain awake, not go to bed
take (something) away	remove
take off	leave (usually by plane)
take (a time period) off	have a break from work or school
take (something) off	remove
take (someone) out	accompany someone to the theater, a restaurant, a movie
take (a dog) out	walk a dog
take (something) out	remove something from something else
tear (something) down	destroy completely
tear (something) off	detach something
tear (something) up	tear into pieces
think (something) over	reflect upon something before making a decision
think (something) up	invent
throw (something) away	put something in the trash
throw (something) out	put something in the trash

tie (someone) up	bind with rope to keep from escaping
try (something) on	put on clothing to see how it looks
turn (something) down	lower the volume; refuse an offer or invitation from someone
turn (something) in	return; submit homework, a test, an application
turn (something) off	stop a machine or light
turn (something) on	start a machine or light
turn up	appear
turn (something) up	increase the volume
use (something) up	use something until no more is left
wake up	stop sleeping
wake (someone) up	cause someone to stop sleeping
wear (something) out	cause something to become useless or threadbare through repeated use
wear (someone) out	cause someone to become exhausted
write (something) down	write something on a piece of paper
work out	exercise vigorously
work (something) out	solve something

There are many more phrasal verbs in English. New ones are being created all the time. You may wish to add more two-word verbs to this list as you learn them.

Spelling of Verbs and Nouns Ending in -s and -es

These spelling rules apply to verbs and nouns ending in -s and -es:

- third-person singular verbs in the simple present (Chapter 1)
- regular plural count nouns (Chapter 10)

1. For most third-person singular verbs and plural nouns, add -s to the simple form:

Verbs	Nouns
swim — swims	lake — lakes

2. If the simple form ends with the letters **s, z, sh, ch,** or **x,** add -es:

Verbs	Nouns
miss — misses	box — boxes

3. If the simple form ends with a consonant + **y**, change **y** to **i** and add -es:

Verbs	Nouns
try — tries	baby — babies

(Compare vowel + **y:** obey — obeys, toy — toys.)

4. If the simple form ends with a consonant + **o**, add -s or -es. Some words take:

-s	-es	Both -s and -es
auto — autos	do — does	tornado — tornados/tornadoes
photo — photos	echo — echoes	volcano — volcanos/volcanoes
piano — pianos	go — goes	zero — zeros/zeroes
solo — solos	hero — heroes	
	potato — potatoes	
	tomato — tomatoes	

(Compare vowel + **o:** radio — radios, zoo — zoos.)

5. If the simple form ends in a single **f** or in **fe,** change the **f** or **fe** to **v** and add -es:

calf — calves	knife — knives
shelf — shelves	

Exceptions

belief — beliefs	hoof — hoofs/hooves
chief — chiefs	scarf — scarfs/scarves
roof — roofs	

Pronunciation of Verbs and Nouns Ending in *-s* and *-es*

These pronunciation rules apply to verbs and nouns ending in -s and -es:

• third-person singular verbs in the simple present (Chapter 1)
• regular plural count nouns (Chapter 10)

Slashes are used to talk about sounds. The symbols that are used below are not standard IPA (International Phonetic Alphabet) symbols.

The endings -s and -es are pronounced as **/s/, /z/,** or as an extra syllable **/iz/** at the end of third-person singular verbs and plural nouns. The pronunciation depends on the final sound of the simple form of the verb or noun:

1. If the simple form ends with the sounds **/s/, /z/, /sh/, /zh/, /ch/, /j/, /ks/,** then pronounce -s and -es as an extra syllable **/iz/**:

Verbs	Nouns
slice — slices (c = /s/)	price — prices (c = /s/)
lose — loses (s = /z/)	size — sizes
wash — washes	dish — dishes
	garage — garages (ge = /zh/
watch — watches	inch — inches
judge — judges	language — languages
relax — relaxes (x = /ks/	tax — taxes (x = /ks/

2. If the simple form ends with the voiceless sounds **/p/, /t/, /k/, /f/,** or **/th/,** then pronounce -s and -es as **/s/**:

Verbs	Nouns
sleep — sleeps	grape — grapes
hit — hits	cat — cats
work — works	book — books
laugh — laughs (gh = /f/)	cuff — cuffs
	fifth — fifths

3. If the simple form ends with any other consonant or with a vowel sound, then pronounce -s and -es as **/z/**:

Verbs	Nouns
learn — learns	name — names
go — goes	boy — boys

Spelling of Verbs Ending in *-ing*

These spelling rules are for adding **-ing** to verbs:

- in the present continuous (Chapter 1)
- in the past continuous (Chapter 3)
- in the present perfect continuous (Chapter 6)
- to form gerunds (Chapter 14)
- in the past perfect continuous (Chapter 15)

1. For most verbs, add **-ing** to the simple form of the verb:

sleep — sleeping

talk — talking

2. If the simple form ends in a single **e**, drop the **e** and add **-ing**:

live — living

write — writing

3. If the simple form ends in **ie**, change **ie** to **y** and add **-ing**:

die — dying

lie — lying

4. If the simple form of a one-syllable verb ends with a single vowel + consonant, double the final consonant and add **-ing**:

hit — hitting

stop — stopping

(Compare two vowels + consonant: eat — eating.)

5. If the simple form of a verb with two or more syllables ends in a single vowel + consonant, double the final consonant only if the stress is on the final syllable. Do not double the final consonant if the stress is not on the final syllable:

admít — admitting   devélop — developing

begín — beginning   lísten — listening

The final **l** is always doubled in British English, but not in American English:

travel — travelling (British)   travel — traveling (American)

6. Do not double the final consonants **x, w,** and **y**:

fix — fixing

plow — plowing

obey — obeying

Spelling of Verbs Ending in *-ed*

These spelling rules are for adding **-ed** to verbs:

- in the simple past (Chapter 3)
- in the present perfect (Chapter 6)
- in the past perfect (Chapter 15)
- in the passive (Chapter 16)

1. To form the simple past and past participle of most regular verbs, add **-ed** to the simple form:

brush — brushed

play — played

2. If the simple form ends with **-e**, just add **d**:

race — raced

trade — traded

3. If the simple form ends with a consonant + **y**, change the **y** to **i** and add **-ed**:

bury — buried

dry — dried

(Compare vowel + **y**: play — played, enjoy — enjoyed.)

4. If the simple form of a one-syllable verb ends with a single vowel + consonant, double the final consonant and add **-ed**:

plan — planned

shop — shopped

5. If the simple form of a verb with two or more syllables ends in a single vowel + consonant, double the final consonant and add **-ed** only when the stress is on the final syllable. Do not double the final consonant if the stress is not on the final syllable:

prefér — preferred   énter — entered

The final **l** is always doubled in British English, but not in American English:

travel — travelled (British)   travel — traveled (American)

6. Do not double the final consonants **x, w,** and **y:**

coax — coaxed

snow — snowed

stay — stayed

Pronunciation of Verbs Ending in *-ed*

These pronunciation rules are for verbs ending in **-ed**:

- in the simple past (Chapter 3)
- in the present perfect (Chapter 6)
- in the past perfect (Chapter 15)
- in the passive (Chapter 16)

The ending **-ed** is pronounced as an extra syllable **/id/**, or as **/t/** or **/d/** at the end of the simple past and past participle forms of verbs. The pronunciation depends on the final sound of the simple form of the verb:

1. If the simple form of the verb ends with the sounds **/t/** or **/d/**, then pronounce **-ed** as an extra syllable **/id/**:

/t/	**/d/**
start — started	need — needed
wait — waited	decide — decided

2. If the simple form ends with the voiceless sounds **/f/, /k/, /p/, /s/, /sh/, /ch/, /ks/,** then pronounce **-ed** as **/t/**:

laugh — laughed (gh = /f/)	wish — wished
look — looked	watch — watched
jump — jumped	fax — faxed (x = /ks/)
slice — sliced (c = /s/)	

3. If the simple form ends with the voiced sounds **/b/, /g/, /j/, /m/, /n/, /ng/, /l/, /r/, /th/, /v/, /z/,** or with a vowel, then pronounce **-ed** as **/d/**:

rob — robbed	call — called
brag — bragged	order — ordered
judge — judged	bathe — bathed
hum — hummed	wave — waved
rain — rained	close — closed (s = /z/)
bang — banged	play — played

Irregular Verbs

These irregular verb forms are used for:

- the simple past (Chapter 3)
- the present perfect (Chapter 6)
- the past perfect (Chapter 15)
- the passive (Chapter 16)

Simple Form	Simple Past	Past Participle
arise	arose	arisen
be	was/were	been
beat	beat	beaten
become	became	become
begin	began	begun
bend	bent	bent
bet	bet	bet
bind	bound	bound
bite	bit	bitten
bleed	bled	bled
blow	blew	blown
break	broke	broken
bring	brought	brought
build	built	built
buy	bought	bought
catch	caught	caught
choose	chose	chosen
come	came	come
cost	cost	cost
creep	crept	crept
cut	cut	cut
dig	dug	dug
dive	dove (or dived)	dived
do	did	done
draw	drew	drawn
drink	drank	drunk
drive	drove	driven

Simple Form	Simple Past	Past Participle
eat	ate	eaten
fall	fell	fallen
feed	fed	fed
feel	felt	felt
fight	fought	fought
find	found	found
fit	fit	fit
fly	flew	flown
forbid	forbade	forbidden
forget	forgot	forgotten
freeze	froze	frozen
get	got	gotten
give	gave	given
go	went	gone
grow	grew	grown
hang	hung	hung
have	had	had
hear	heard	heard
hide	hid	hidden
hit	hit	hit
hold	held	held
hurt	hurt	hurt
keep	kept	kept
know	knew	known
lay (put, place)	laid	laid
lead	led	led
leave	left	left
lend	lent	lent
let	let	let
lie (recline)	lay	lain
light	lit	lit
lose	lost	lost
make	made	made

Simple Form	Simple Past	Past Participle
mean	meant	meant
meet	met	met
pay	paid	paid
prove	proved	proven (or proved)
put	put	put
quit	quit	quit
read	read (rhymes with *bed*)	read (rhymes with *bed*)
ride	rode	ridden
ring	rang	rung
rise	rose	risen
run	ran	run
say	said (rhymes with *bed*)	said (rhymes with *bed*)
see	saw	seen
sell	sold	sold
send	sent	sent
set	set	set
sew	sewed	sewn
shake	shook	shaken
shine	shone	shone
shoot	shot	shot
show	showed	shown
shrink	shrank	shrunk
shut	shut	shut
sing	sang	sung
sink	sank	sunk
sit	sat	sat
sleep	slept	slept
slide	slid	slid
speak	spoke	spoken
speed	sped	sped
spend	spent	spent
spin	spun	spun
split	split	split

Simple Form	Simple Past	Past Participle
spread	spread	spread
spring	sprang	sprung
stand	stood	stood
steal	stole	stolen
stick	stuck	stuck
sting	stung	stung
stink	stank	stunk
strike	struck	struck
string	strung	strung
swear	swore	sworn
sweep	swept	swept
swell	swelled	swollen
swim	swam	swum
swing	swung	swung
take	took	taken
teach	taught	taught
tear	tore	torn
tell	told	told
think	thought	thought
throw	threw	thrown
understand	understood	understood
undertake	undertook	undertaken
upset	upset	upset
wake	woke	woken
wear	wore	worn
weave	wove	woven
weep	wept	wept
wet	wet	wet
win	won	won
wind	wound	wound
wring	wrung	wrung
write	wrote	written

The Definite Article with Proper Nouns

In general, **the** is not used with proper nouns (Chapter 10). The following are exceptions to this rule:

1. The is used with plural proper nouns:

the Alps	the Netherlands
the Andes	the Philippines
the Bahamas	the United States
the Great Lakes	the West Indies

2. The is frequently used with singular proper nouns referring to oceans, seas, rivers, canals, and deserts:

the Atlantic (Ocean)	the Mississippi (River)
the Pacific (Ocean)	the Nile (River)
the Mediterranean (Sea)	the Panama Canal
the Caribbean (Sea)	the Sahara (Desert)

3. The is also used with certain singular proper nouns. For example:

the Dominican Republic	the Middle East	the South Pole
the Eiffel Tower	the Orient	the Taj Mahal
the Hague	the Riviera	the United Kingdom

4. The is generally used with nouns that are followed by **of** phrases:

the emperor of Japan

the president of the United States

the queen of England

the Prince of Wales

Comparative and Superlative Adjectives and Adverbs

The same spelling rules for adjectives and adverbs ending in **-er** and **-est** are used to form comparatives and superlatives (Chapter 12). When to use **-er** or **-est** versus **more** or **most** is explained below. Irregular forms are also listed.

1. Add **-er** or **-est** to one-syllable adjectives and adverbs:

cheap — cheaper, the cheapest

fast — faster, the fastest

2. If a one-syllable adjective or adverb ends in **-e** or a two-syllable adjective ends in **-le**, just add **-r** or **-st**:

late — later, the latest

simple — simpler, the simplest

3. If a one-syllable adjective or adverb ends with a single vowel + consonant, double the final consonant and add **-er** or **-est**:

big — bigger, the biggest

fat — fatter, the fattest

(Compare two vowels + consonant: cheap — cheaper, the cheapest.)
(Compare two final consonants: hard — harder, the hardest.)

Do not double the final consonants **x, w,** and **y**:

low — lower, the lowest

4. If a two-syllable adjective ends in a consonant + **y**, change **y** to **i** and add **-er** or **-est**:

happy — happier, the happiest

easy — easier, the easiest

5. For two-syllable adjectives ending in **-ous, -ish, -ful, -ed, -nt, -st, -ing**, use **more** or **the most**:

famous — more famous, the most famous

ticklish — more ticklish, the most ticklish

painful — more painful, the most painful

frightened — more frightened, the most frightened

patient — more patient, the most patient

honest — more honest, the most honest

boring — more boring, the most boring

6. For most adverbs of two or more syllables ending in **-ly,** use **more** and **most** instead of **-er** and **-est:**

quickly — more quickly, the most quickly

clearly — more clearly, the most clearly

Exception: early — earlier, the earliest

7. Add **more** or **the most** to adjectives of three or more syllables:

beautiful — more beautiful, the most beautiful

expensive — more expensive, the most expensive

8. Use either **-er** or **more** for adjectives ending in **-ly, -ow, -er, -some, -ite:**

lonely — lonelier/more lonely, the loneliest/the most lonely

shallow — shallower/more shallow, the shallowest/the most shallow

clever — cleverer/more clever, the cleverest, the most clever

handsome — handsomer/more handsome, the handsomest, the most handsome

polite — politer/more polite, the politest, the most polite

9. If you are not sure whether to use **-er** or **more** with words of two or more syllables, it is usually correct to use **more.**

10. Some irregular comparative and superlative forms include:

Adjective	Adverb	Comparative	Superlative
good	well	better	the best
bad	badly	worse	the worst
far	far	farther (distance)	the farthest
		further	the furthest
(a) little	(a) little	less	the least
much	much	more	the most
many	more	more	the most
a lot	a lot	more	the most

Gerunds and Infinitives

Verb + Gerund

These verbs may be followed by gerunds, but not by infinitives (See Chapter 14). Note: In some dialects of English, some of these verbs are not followed by gerunds.

acknowledge	escape	prevent
admit	excuse	quit
anticipate	finish	recall
appreciate	go	recollect
avoid	imagine	recommend
consider	involve	regret
defend	keep	resent
defer	loathe	resist
delay	mean (mean = involve)	resume
deny	mention	risk
detest	mind (mind = object)	(can't) stand
discuss	miss	suggest
dislike	omit	tolerate
endure	postpone	understand
enjoy	practice	

Verb with Preposition + Gerund

These verbs or phrases with prepositions may be followed by a gerund, but not by an infinitive (Chapter 14):

adapt to	complain (to someone) about
adjust to	concentrate on
agree (with someone) on	consist of
apologize (to someone) for	decide on
approve of	depend on
argue (with someone) about	disapprove of
ask about	discourage (someone) from
believe in	engage in
blame for	forgive (someone) for
care about	help (someone) with

inquire about	quarrel (with someone) about
insist on	result from
interfere with	result in
keep on	succeed in
look forward to	suffer from
object to	talk about
participate in	there's no point in
persist in	think about
prepare (someone/something) for	warn (someone) about
profit from	work on
prohibit (someone) from	worry about

Be + Adjective + Preposition + Gerund

Adjectives with prepositions typically occur in **be + adjective** phrases (**be happy about, be concerned with**). These phrases may be followed by gerunds, but not infinitives (Chapter 14):

be accustomed to	be interested in
be afraid of	be jealous of
be angry (at someone) about	be known for
be ashamed of	be nervous about
be capable of	be perfect for
be certain of/about	be proud of
be concerned with	be responsible for
be critical of	be sad about
be discouraged from	be successful in
be enthusiastic about	be suitable for
be familiar with	be tired of
be famous for	be tolerant of
be fond of	be upset about
be glad about	be used to
be good at	be useful for
be happy about	be worried about
be incapable of	

Verb + Infinitive

The following verbs may be followed by infinitives, but not by gerunds (Chapter 14). Note: In some dialects of English, some of these verbs are not followed by infinitives.

agree	demand	pretend
aim	desire	promise
appear	expect	refuse
arrange	fail	resolve
ask	guarantee	seem
beg	know	tend
(can't) bear	hope	struggle
can't stand	intend	swear
care (negative)	learn	volunteer
choose	manage	wait
claim	need	want
consent	offer	wish
dare	plan	would like
decide	pledge	
decline	prepare	

Verb + Infinitive or Gerund

The following verbs may be followed by infinitives or gerunds (Chapter 14). Note: In some dialects of English, some of these verbs are not followed by both gerunds and infinitives.

attempt	love
begin	neglect
can/could bear (often used in the negative)	prefer
can/could stand	propose
cease	regret
continue	remember
forget	start
hate	stop
like	try

Reporting Verbs

1. These reporting or communication verbs are followed by noun clauses to report what someone has said or written (Chapter 17):

acknowledge	deny	protest
add	emphasize	remark
admit	estimate	remind (someone)
affirm	exclaim	repeat
agree	explain	reply
announce	growl	report
answer	grumble	respond
argue	guess	roar
ask	imply	say
assert	indicate	scream
assure (someone)	inform (someone)	shout
boast	insist	shriek
brag	instruct (someone)	sneer
caution	maintain	stammer
claim	murmur	state
complain	mutter	suggest
conclude	note	tell (someone)
confess	notify (someone)	threaten
confirm	observe	warn
convince (someone)	persuade (someone)	whisper
cry	point out	write
declare	promise	yell

2. These reporting verbs are used with infinitives to report advice, requests, commands, and obligations:

advise (someone) to	forbid (someone) to	tell (someone) to
ask (someone) to	instruct (someone) to	urge (someone) to
beg (someone) to	oblige (someone) to	want (someone) to
command (someone) to	order (someone) to	
direct (someone) to	request (someone) to	

Glossary of Grammar Terms

ability modal *See* modal of ability.

active voice The active voice emphasizes the person or thing that performs or causes an action. A sentence is in the active voice when the subject of the sentence performs an action and when the object receives or is the result of the action. In the following sentence, the subject **Ivan** performed the action, and the object **letter** received the action.

> **Ivan** mailed the **letter.**

adjective A word that describes or modifies the meaning of a noun.

> the **orange** car
> a **strange** noise

adjective phrase A phrase that functions as an adjective.

> These shoes are **too tight.**

adverb A word that describes or modifies the meaning of a verb, another adverb, an adjective, or a sentence. Adverbs answer such questions as *How? When? Where?* or *How often?* They often end in **-ly.**

> She ran **quickly.**
> She ran **very** quickly.
> a **truly** wonderful performance
> **Maybe** she'll leave.

adverb of frequency An adverb that tells how often an action occurs. Adverbs of frequency range in meaning from *all of the time* to *none of the time.*

> She **always** eats breakfast.
> He **never** eats meat.

adverbial phrase A phrase that functions as an adverb.

> Sheila spoke **very softly.**

affirmative statement A positive sentence that does not have a negative verb.

> Sylvia went to the movies.

agreement The subject and verb of a clause must agree in number. If the subject is singular, the verb form is also singular. If the subject is plural, the verb form is also plural.

Monica **comes** home early.
They **come** home early.

article The words **a, an,** and **the** in English. Articles are used to introduce and identify nouns.

a potato
an onion
the supermarket

auxiliary verb A verb that is used before main verbs (or other auxiliary verbs) in a sentence. Auxiliary verbs are usually used in questions and negative sentences. **Do, have,** and **be** can act as auxiliary verbs. Modals (**may, can, will,** and so on) are also auxiliary verbs.

Do you have any change?
I **have** never been to Istanbul.
The suitcase **was** taken.
Visitors **may** not take photographs.

belief modal *See* **modal of belief.**

clause A group of words that has a subject and a verb. *See also* **dependent clause** and **main clause.**

If I leave,....
...when he speaks.
The rain stopped.

common noun A noun that refers to any of a class of people, animals, places, things, or ideas. Common nouns are not capitalized.

man
cat
city
pencil
grammar

communication verb *See* **reporting verb.**

comparative A form of an adjective, adverb, or noun that is used to express differences between two items or situations.

This book is **heavier than** that one.
He runs **more quickly than** his brother.
A CD costs **more money than** a cassette.

complex sentence A sentence that has a main clause and one or more dependent clauses.

When the bell rang, we were finishing dinner.

conditional sentence *See* ***if*** **sentence.**

contraction The combination of two words into one by omitting certain letters and replacing them with an apostrophe.

> I will = **I'll**
> we are = **we're**
> are not = **aren't**

count noun A common noun that can be counted. It usually has both a singular and a plural form.

> orange — oranges
> woman — women

definite article The word **the** in English. It is used to identify nouns based on assumptions about what information the speaker and listener share about the noun. The definite article is also used for making general statements about a whole class or group of nouns.

> Please give me **the** key.
> **The** boa constrictor is dangerous.

dependent clause A clause that cannot stand alone as a sentence because it depends on the main clause to complete the meaning of the sentence. Also called *subordinate clause*.

> I'm going home **after he calls.**

determiner A word such as **a, an, the, this, that, these, those, my, some, a few, three,** that is used before a noun to limit its meaning in some way.

> **those** videos

direct speech *See* quoted speech.

embedded question *See wh-* clause.

frequency adverb *See* adverb of frequency.

future A time that is to come. The future is expressed in English with **will, be going to,** the simple present, or the present continuous. These different forms of the future often have different meanings and uses.

> **I'll** help you later.
> Brian **is going to** call later.
> The train **leaves** at 6:05 this evening.
> **I'm driving** to Toronto tomorrow.

general quantity expression A quantity expression that indicates whether a quantity or an amount is large or small. It does not give an exact amount.

> **a lot of** cookies
> **a little** flour

general statement A generalization about a whole class or group of nouns.

> Whales are mammals.
> The giant panda is endangered.
> A daffodil is a flower that grows from a bulb.

gerund An –ing form of a verb that is used in place of a noun or a pronoun to name an activity or a situation.

> **Skiing** is fun.
> He doesn't like **being sick.**

if clause A dependent clause that begins with **if** and expresses a real or unreal situation.

> **If I have the time,** I'll paint the kitchen.
> **If I had the time,** I'd paint the kitchen.

if/whether clause A noun clause that begins with either **if** or **whether.**

> I don't know **if they're here.**
> I don't know **whether or not they're here.**

if sentence A sentence that expresses a real or unreal situation in the **if** clause, and the expected result in the main clause. Also called *conditional sentence.*

> If I have time, I will travel to Africa.
> If I had time, I would travel to Africa.

imaginary if sentence An if sentence that expresses an imaginary situation that is not true at the present time, and its imaginary result. It has an **if** clause in the simple past and a main clause with **would** + main verb.

> If I had more time, I would travel to Africa.

imperative A type of sentence, usually without a subject, that tells someone to do something. The verb is in the simple form.

> Please **open** your books to page 36.

impersonal *you* The use of the pronoun **you** to refer to people in general rather than a particular person or group of people.

> Nowadays, **you** can buy anything at the supermarket.

indefinite article The words **a** and **an** in English. Indefinite articles are used to introduce a noun as a member of a class of nouns, or to make generalizations about a whole class or group of nouns.

> Please hand me **a** pencil.
> **An** ocean is a large body of water.

independent clause *See* main clause.

indirect question *See wh-* clause.

indirect speech *See* reported speech.

infinitive A verb form that includes **to** + the simple form of a verb. An infinitive is used in place of a noun or pronoun to name an activity or situation expressed by a verb.

> Do you like **to swim?**

information question A question that begins with a **wh–** word.

> **Where** does your sister live?
> **Who** lives here?

intransitive verb A verb that cannot be followed by an object.

> We finally **arrived.**

irregular verb A verb that forms the simple past in a different way than regular verbs. Some irregular verbs use the simple form as their simple past and past participle form (**put — put — put**); others have one irregular form for both the simple past and the past participle (**buy — bought — bought**); and others have different simple past and past participle forms (**sing — sang — sung**).

main clause A clause that can be used by itself as a sentence. Also called *independent clause.*

> I'm going home.

main verb A verb that can be used as the only verb in a sentence. A main verb often occurs with an auxiliary verb.

> I **ate** lunch at 11:30.
> Sharon can't **eat** lunch today.

mental activity verb A verb such as **decide, know,** and **understand,** that expresses an opinion, thought, or feeling.

> I don't **know** why she left.

modal The auxiliary verbs **can, could, may, might, must, should, will,** and **would.** They modify the meaning of a main verb by expressing ability, authority, formality, politeness, or various degrees of certainty. Also called *modal auxiliary.*

> You **should** take something for your headache.
> Applicants **must** have a high school diploma.

modal of ability **Can** and **could** are called modals of ability when they express knowledge, skill, opportunity, and capability.

> He **can** speak Arabic and English.
> **Can** you play the piano?
> Yesterday we **couldn't** leave during the storm.
> Seatbelts **can** save lives.

modal of belief **Could, might, may, should, must,** and **will** are called modals of belief when they express various degrees of certainty ranging from slight possibility to strong certainty.

> It **could** rain later.
> It **might** rain later.
> It **may** rain later.
> It **will** rain later.

modal auxiliary *See* modal.

modify To add to or change the meaning of a word. For example, in the phrase **expensive cars,** the adjective **expensive** modifies **cars.**

noncount noun A common noun that cannot be counted. A noncount noun has no plural form and cannot occur with **a, an,** or a number.

> information
> mathematics
> weather

nonrestrictive relative clause A relative clause that adds extra information about the noun that it modifies. This information is not necessary to identify the noun, and it can be omitted.

> Ben, **who is seven,** plays hockey.

nonseparable Refers to two- or three-word verbs that allow a noun or pronoun object to separate the two or three words in the verb phrase. Certain two-word verbs and almost all three-word verbs are nonseparable.

> Ella **got off** the bus.
> We **cut down on** fat in our diet.

noun A word that typically refers to a person, animal, place, thing, or idea.

> Joe
> rabbit
> store
> computer
> mathematics

noun clause A dependent clause that can occur in the same place as a noun, pronoun or noun phrase in a sentence. Noun clauses begin with **wh-** words, **if, whether,** or **that.**

> I don't know **where he is.**
> I wonder **if he's coming.**
> I don't know **whether it's true.**
> I think **that it's a lie.**

noun phrase A phrase formed by a noun and its modifiers. A noun phrase can substitute for a noun in a sentence.

object A noun, pronoun, or noun phrase that follows a transitive verb.

> John threw **the ball.**
> She likes **him.**

object relative pronoun A relative pronoun that is the object of a relative clause. It comes before the subject noun or pronoun of the relative clause.

> the letter **that** I wrote

passive voice The passive voice emphasizes the receiver of an action by changing the usual order of the subject and object in a sentence. A sentence is in the passive voice when the subject does not perform the action; it receives the action or is the result of an action. The passive voice is formed with a form of **be** + the past participle of a transitive verb.

The letter **was mailed** yesterday.

past continuous A verb form that expresses an action or situation in progress at a specific time in the past. The past continuous is formed with **was** or **were** + verb + **-ing**. Also called *past progressive*.

A: What **were** you **doing** last night at eight o'clock?
B: I **was studying**.

past imaginary *if* sentence An imaginary **if** sentence that expresses an unreal condition about the past and its imaginary result. It has an **if** clause in the past perfect and a main clause with **would have** + the past participle of the main verb.

If I had been smarter, I would have complained to the manager.

past modal A modal that is used to express past certainty, past obligations, and past abilities and opportunities. It is formed with a modal + **have** + past participle of the main verb. Also called *perfect modal*.

He **must have** arrived late.
I **should have** called, but I forgot.
We **could have** come, but no one told us.

past participle A past verb form that may differ from the simple past form of some irregular verbs. It is used to form the present perfect, present perfect continuous, past perfect, past perfect continuous, and the passive.

I have never **seen** that movie.
He's **been** working too much lately.
By noon, we had already **taken** the exam.
She had **been** working since 8:30.
The letter was **sent** on Monday.

past perfect A past tense that expresses a relationship between two past times. The past perfect indicates the earlier event or situation. It is formed with **had** + the past participle of the main verb.

I **had** already **left** when Barbara called.

past perfect continuous A past form that is like the past perfect, but it emphasizes the duration of the earlier event or situation. It is formed with **had** + **been** + main verb + **–ing**.

When I was offered the position, I **had been looking** for a new job for several months.

past perfect progressive *See* past perfect continuous.

past progressive *See* past continuous.

past *wish* sentence A **wish** sentence that expresses a desire for something that didn't happen in the past. It is formed with a **wish** clause + a past perfect clause.

> I wish I had moved to Colorado.

perfect modal *See* **past modal.**

phrasal verb A two- or three-word verb such as **turn down** or **run out of.** The meaning of a phrasal verb is usually different from the meanings of its individual words.

> She **turned down** the job offer.
> Don't **run out of** gas on the freeway.

phrase A group of words that can form a grammatical unit. A phrase can take the form of a noun phrase, verb phrase, adjective phrase, adverbial phrase, or prepositional phrase. This means it can act as a noun, a verb, an adjective, an adverb, or a preposition.

> **The tall man** left.
> John **hit the ball.**
> The child was **very quiet.**
> She spoke **too quickly.**
> They walked **down the stairs.**

possessive relative pronoun A relative pronoun that expresses possession or a relationship. The possessive relative pronoun is **whose.** It always comes before a noun that belongs to or is related to a noun in the main clause.

> the man **whose** leg was broken
> a man **whose** wife I know

preposition A word such as **at, in, on, to,** that links nouns, pronouns, and gerunds to other words.

prepositional phrase A phrase that consists of a preposition followed by a noun or noun phrase.

> on Sunday
> under the table

present continuous A verb form that indicates that an action is incomplete, in progress, or changing. It is formed with **be** + verb + **-ing.** Also called *present progressive.*

> **I'm watering** the garden.
> Andrea **is sleeping.**
> He's **not working** right now.

present perfect A verb form that expresses a connection between the past and the present. It indicates indefinite past time, recent past time, or continuing past time. The present perfect is formed with **have** + the past participle of the main verb.

> **I've seen** that movie.
> The manager **has** just **resigned.**
> We've **been** here for three hours.

present perfect continuous A verb form that focuses on the duration of actions that began in the past and continue into the present moment or have just ended. It is formed with **have + been + verb + -ing.**

They've **been waiting** for an hour.
I've **been watering** the garden.

present perfect progressive *See* present perfect continuous.

present progressive *See* present continuous.

pronoun A word that can replace a noun or noun phrase. **I, you, he, she, it, mine,** and **yours** are some examples of pronouns.

proper noun A noun that is the name of a particular person, animal, place, thing, or idea. Proper nouns begin with capital letters and are usually not preceded by **the.**

Jonathan
Rover
India
Apollo 13
Buddhism

purpose infinitive An infinitive that expresses the reason or purpose for doing something.

In order to operate this machine, press the green button.

quantity expression A word or words that occur before a noun to express a quantity or amount of that noun.

a lot of rain
few books
four trucks
a pound of broccoli

quoted speech The form of a sentence that uses the exact words of a speaker or writer. Written quoted speech uses quotation marks. Also called *direct speech.*

"Where did you go?" he asked.

real *if* sentence An if sentence that expresses a real or possible situation in the **if** clause and the expected result in the main clause. It has an **if** clause in the simple present, and the **will** future in the main clause.

If I get a raise, I won't look for a new job.

regular verb A verb that forms the simple past by adding **-ed, -d,** or changing **y** to **i** and then adding **-ed** to the simple form.

hunt — hunted
love — loved
cry — cried

rejoinder A short response used in conversation.

A: I like sushi.
B: **Me too.**
C: **So do I.**

relative clause A clause that modifies a noun that it follows. Relative clauses generally begin with **who, whom, that, which,** and **whose.**

The man **who called** is my cousin.
We saw the elephant **that was just born.**

relative pronoun A pronoun that begins a relative clause and refers to a noun in the main clause. The words **who, whom, that, which,** and **whose** are relative pronouns.

reported speech A form of a sentence that expresses the meaning of quoted speech or writing from the point of view of the reporter. **Wh-** clauses, **if/whether** clauses, and **that** clauses are used to express reported speech after a communication verb.

He said that he was tired.
We asked if they could come early.

reporting verb A verb such as **say, tell, ask, explain,** and **complain** that is used to express what has been said or written in both quoted speech and reported speech.

John **complained,** "I'm tired."
John **complained** that he was tired.

restrictive relative clause A relative clause that gives information that helps identify or define the noun that it modifies. Also called *defining* or *identifying relative clause.* In the following sentence, the speaker has more than one aunt. The relative clause **who speaks Russian** identifies which aunt the speaker is talking about.

My aunt **who speaks Russian** is an interpreter.

separable Refers to certain two-word verbs that allow a noun or pronoun object to separate the two words in the verb phrase.

She **gave** her job **up.**

simple form The form of a verb without any verb endings. **Sleep, be,** and **stop** are examples of simple forms. Also called *root, stem,* or *base form* of the verb.

simple past A tense that expresses actions and situations that were completed at a definite time in the past.

Jenna **ate** lunch.
She **was** hungry.

short answer An answer to a *yes/no* question that has *yes* or *no* plus the subject and an auxiliary verb.

A: Do you speak Chinese?
B: **Yes, I do.** OR
   No, I don't.

simple present A verb tense that expresses general statements, especially about habitual or repeated activities and permanent situations.

Sophie **eats** pasta for lunch.
The earth **is** round.

social modals Modal auxiliaries that are used to express politeness, formality, and authority.

Would you please open the window?
May I help you?
Visitors **must** obey the rules.

specific quantity expression A quantity expression that indicates a precise amount of the noun it modifies.

a box of cookies
a pound of rice
seventeen cents

stative verb A type of verb that is not usually used in the continuous form because it expresses a condition or a state that is not changing. **Know, resemble, love, see,** and **smell** are some examples.

subject A noun, pronoun, or noun phrase that precedes the main verb in a sentence. The subject is closely related to the verb as the doer or experiencer of the action or state, or as the noun that is being described.

Sam kicked the ball.
He feels dizzy.
The park is huge.

subject relative pronoun A relative pronoun that is the subject of a relative clause. It comes before the verb in the relative clause.

the man **who** called

subordinate clause *See* dependent clause.

superlative A form of an adjective, adverb, or noun that is used to rank an item or situation first or last in a group of three or more.

This perfume has **the strongest** scent.
He speaks **the fastest** of all.
That machine makes **the most noise** of the three.

***that* clause** A noun clause beginning with **that.**

I think **that the bus is late.**

three-word verb A phrasal verb such as **break up with, cut down on,** and **look out for.** The meaning of a three-word verb is usually different from the individual meanings of the three words.

time clause A dependent clause that begins with a time word such as **while, when, before,** or **after.** It expresses the relationship in time between two different events in the same sentence.

Before Paul left, he fixed the copy machine.

transitive verb A verb that can be followed by an object.

> I **read** the book.

two-word verb A phrasal verb such as **blow up, cross out,** and **hand in.** The meaning of a two-word verb is usually different from the individual meanings of the two words.

verb A word that describes an action or a state.

> Tara **closed** the window.
> He **loves** classical music.

verb phrase A phrase that has a main verb and any objects, adverbs, or dependent clauses that complete the meaning of the verb in the sentence.

> Who **called you?**
> He **walked slowly.**
> I **know what his name is.**

voice Distinction of the form of a verb to show the relation of the subject of the verb to the action which the verb expresses. *See also* **active voice** and **passive voice.**

voiced Refers to speech sounds that are made by vibrating the vocal cords. Examples of voiced sounds are **/b/, /d/,** and **/g/.**

> bat
> dot
> get

voiceless Refers to speech sounds that are made without vibrating the vocal cords. Examples of voiceless sounds are **/p/, /t/,** and **/f/.**

> up
> it
> if

wh- clause A noun clause that begins with a **wh-** word: **who, whom, what, where, when, why, how** and **which.** Also called *indirect question* or *embedded question.*

> I would like to know **where he is.**
> Could you tell me **how long it takes?**

wh- word Who, whom, what, where, when, why, how, and which are wh- words. They are used to ask questions and to connect clauses.

wish sentence A sentence that has a **wish** clause in the simple present and a simple past clause. A **wish** sentence expresses a desire to change a real situation into an unreal or impossible one.

> I wish I had more time.

yes/no question A question that can be answered with the words *yes* or *no.*

> Can you drive a car?
> Does he live here?

Index

A

a/an, 285, 296, 297
  with count nouns, 270
  in general statements, 306
  and noncount nouns, 273
  in reported speech, 466
  in specific quantity expressions, for prices, 294
Ability, *see also* Possibility
  exercises on, 202–208
  and modals of ability, 199, 200–204, 226–227
a bit, 286
able, see *be able to*
Abstract nouns, 275, 294
Accomplishments, 394
Accusing, 54
  exercises on, 59
ache, 16
Actions, *see also* Activities in progress; Receiver of
      action, in passive sentences; Verbs
  activities, 357, 362–363
  definite completed actions, 53–54
  in passive sentences, 415, 417–418, 434
  recent actions, 153–154
  repeated actions, 64, 137, 154
  and simple past, 53–54
  simultaneous events, 112
  and stative verbs, 19
Active sentences, 415
Activities, 357, 362–363, *see also* Actions;
     Activities in progress
Activities in progress
  and past continuous, 69
  and past perfect continuous, 400
  and present continuous, 1, 12–13, 18–19, 212
Adjective clauses, *see* Relative clauses
Adjectives
  in *be* + adjective + preposition + gerund, 367
  in comparisons, 313
    with *as...as*, 323

    comparatives of, 314, 316
    with *so...that* and *such (a)...that*, 332, 333
    superlatives of, 318–319, 320–321
  with *is being, am being,* or *are being*, 18–19
  in *it... + be* + adjective + infinitive, 380
  vs. relative clauses, 239
  with *should be* and *ought to be*, 212
admit, 466, 467
adore, 16
Advantages, 123
Adverbial clauses, *see* Time clauses
Adverbial phrases, with present continuous, 12
Adverbs, *see also* Adverbs of frequency
  in comparisons, 313
    with *as...as*, 323
    comparatives of, 314, 316
    with *so...that*, 332, 333
    superlatives of, 318–319, 320–321
  maybe as, 212
  and past perfect, 394
  position of, with present perfect, 138, 142
  of possibility, with *will*, 222
  with present continuous, 12, 16
  in reported speech, 462, 466
Adverbs of frequency
  meaning of, 26
  position of, 27–28, 138
  and present continuous, 13, 29
  use of, 29
Advice
  exercises on, 38, 39, 126–127, 178–180, 350,
      379–380, 409, 470
  and imaginary *if* sentences, 347
  and imperatives, 37
  and past imaginary *if* sentences, 408
  and real *if* sentences, 123
  in reported speech, 468
  and social modals, 176–177
advise, 468

a few, 138, 270, 286, 288, 290
Affirmatives
  adverbs of frequency, 26
  with *and so...,* 101
  with *and...too,* 99
  in answers to requests for permission, 172
  gerunds as, 356
  with infinitives, 369, 371, 383
Affirmative statements, *see* Statements
afraid not, 459
afraid so, 459
after
  in dependent clauses, 109
  in future time clauses, 118, 119–120
  in past time clauses, 110, 111, 394
after next, 79
Agent of action, in passive sentences, 417–418,
      434
ago, 148
a great deal of, 273, 286, 288, 290
agree, 458
Agreeing, 54
Agreement, see Subject-verb agreement
a little, 273, 286, 288, 290
all, 146
almost always, 26
almost never, 26
a lot of, 273, 286, 288
already, 138, 148, 394
Alternatives, 365, 454, *see also* Choices
always, 13, 25, 26, 29
am, 9–10, 420–421, 431, see *also I'm; "what'm"*
am being, 18–19
an, see *a/an*
and, infinitives shortened after, 371
and...either, 99, 102
and neither..., 101, 102, 103
and so..., 101, 102, 103
and...too, 99, 102
announce, 377, 467
Announcements
  with passive sentences, 418
  in reported speech, 465
  with simple present, to express future, 95–96
  and *there is/there are,* 25, 34
answer, 467
Answers, *see also* Questions; Short answers
  to choice questions with infinitives, 371
  in future, 76–77, 82, 429
  with modals
    with modals of ability, 200, 201
    with modals of belief, 210
    in passive sentences, 438
    with past modals, 224

  with social modals, 165
  with passive sentences, 421, 429, 432, 438
  in past continuous, 67–68, 432
  in past perfect, 390, 432
  in past perfect continuous, 398
  in present continuous, 9–10, 432
  in present perfect, 135, 432
  in present perfect continuous, 151
  in simple past, 45, 50–51, 63, 421
  in simple present, 2–3, 421
  with *so* or *not,* instead of *that* clauses, 459
  with *there is/there are,* 33
any, 32, 286, 290, see also *not any*
a piece of, 294
Apologizing, 153
  exercises on, 156
appear, 416
  in *it appears,* 459
  in *it...* + adjective + infinitive, 380, 381
  as stative verb, 15
appreciate, 16, 360
approve of, 366
are, see also *aren't; they're; we're; "when're";*
      you're
  in passive sentences, 420–421, 431
  in present continuous, 9–10, 431
  in *there is/there are,* 25, 32–33, 34
are being, 18–19
aren't, 9, 32–33, 76, 421, 431
arrive, 94, 416
Articles, 269, 285, see also *a/an;* Definite articles;
      Indefinite articles; *the*
  forms of, 296
  meaning and use of, 270, 297–299, 306–307
as, 323, 324, 326, 328
as...as, 323, 324
ask, 466, 467, 468
assume, 458, 459
Assumptions, exercises on, 214–215, 301–303
assure, 467
at, 60, 321
at this moment, 12
Attitudes, 16, 306, 362–363, 374, *see also*
      Feelings; Opinions
Auxiliary verbs, *see also* Modals
  with adverbs of frequency, 27
  with *and...either,* 99
  with *and neither...,* 101
  with *and so...,* 101
  with *and...too,* 99
  with *as...as,* 323
  with *but,* in affirmative and negative sentences,
      98
  in comparatives, 314, 325, 326

Auxiliary verbs *(continued)*
    do as, in simple present, 2
    in passive sentences, 416
        in continuous and perfect tenses, 431, 432
        in future, 429
        with modals, 438
        in simple present and simple past, 420
avoid, 360

B

Background information, 69
be, see also *am; are; be able to; been; be going to;*
       is; Past continuous; Present continuous;
       was; were
    with adverbs of frequency, 28
    as auxiliary verb, in passive sentences, 416
        in continuous and perfect tenses, 431, 432
        in future, 429
        with modals, 438
        in simple present and simple past, 420
    and *being*, 18–19, 431–432
    in *be* + adjective + preposition + gerund, 367
    contractions with forms of, see also *aren't; he's*
       (he + is); I'm; isn't; it's (is + is); she's (she +
       is); they're; wasn't; we're; weren't;
       "what'm"; what's (what + is); "when're";
       who's (who + is); you're
       with *be going to*, 76
       in passive sentences, 420–421, 431–432
       in past continuous, 67, 431–432
       in present continuous, 9–10, 431–432
       in simple past, 50, 51, 420–421
       with *there is/there are*, 32–33
    in *it...* + adjective + infinitive, 380, 381
    in passive sentences, 416
        in continuous and perfect tenses, 431–432
        in future, 429
        with modals, 438
        in simple present and simple past, 420–421
    in past perfect continuous, 389, 398, 400
    in present perfect continuous, 133, 150–151,
       153–154
    in *should be* and *ought to be*, 212
    simple past of, 50–51
    as stative verb, 15
    in *there is/there are*, 25, 32–33, 34
    with *will*, 86
be able to, 199, 203–204
    in imaginary *if* sentences, 347
    in past *wish* sentences, 403
because, 400
become, 416
been
    in modal passives, 438

in past perfect continuous, 398, 431–432
in present perfect continuous, 150–151,
    431–432
before
    in dependent clauses, 109
    in future time clauses, 118, 119–120
    in past time clauses, 110, 111, 393, 394
begin, 375, 376
be going to, 75–81
    forms of, 76–77
    meaning and use of, 80
       and future time phrases, 78–79
       in passive sentences, 429
       vs. present continuous, with *go* and *come*, 94
       in real *if* sentences, 122, 123–124
       with *that* clauses, 458
       vs. *will*, 85, 86, 124
being, 18–19, 431–432
Belief, *see also* Modals of belief
    exercises on, 219–220
believe, 16, 458, 459
believe in, 367
belong to, 15
bet, 458
better, in *had better*, 163, 176, 177, 178
bit, in *a bit*, 286
bother, 348
busy, 361
but
    in affirmative and negative sentences, 98, 102
    infinitives shortened after, 371
    in *wish* sentences, 340, 403
by
    plus object gerunds, 365
    in passive sentences, 415, 416, 420, 429
by the time, 393

C

can, see also *could*
    as modal of ability, 199, 200–201, 203, 218
    pronunciation of, vs. *can't*, 201
    as social modal, 163, 164, 166, 171–172
cannot, 164, 200, see also *can't*
can't
    with impersonal *you*, 203
    as modal of ability, 200
    in modal passives, 438
    as negative modal of belief, 218
    pronunciation of, vs. *can*, 201
    as social modal, 164
can't help, 361
care for, 16
Categorizing, exercises on, 282–283
Category names, noncount nouns for, 275

Cause and effect, 112, 333, *see also* Results
Certainty
  about future, 221–222
  about past, 226, 229
  about present, 211–212, 218
  exercises on, 213, 217–218, 220–221, 222–223
Changes, and past perfect, 394
Choice questions, with infinitives, 371
Choices, 85, 328, *see also* Alternatives
Clauses, *see* Dependent clauses; Main clauses;
    Result clauses
come, 94, 416
Comma
  with future time clauses, 118
  and *if/whether* clauses, 452
  in imaginary *if* sentences, 346, 406
  and nonrestrictive relative clauses, 261
  with past time clauses, 110
  with purpose infinitives, 383
  in real *if* sentences, 122
  and restrictive relative clauses, 240
  and *that* clauses, 457
  and *wh-* clauses, 448
Commands, with imperatives, 37
comment, 467
Common nouns, 269
Communication, verbs of (reporting verbs), 447,
    461, 465–468
Comparatives, 314, 316, 325, 328
Comparing, 102, 313–338, 323, 324, *see also*
    Comparatives; Differences; Similarities;
    Superlatives
  exercises on, 66, 205, 207–209
complain, 466, 467
Complaining
  and adverbs of frequency, 29
  with *always,* 13, 29
  exercises on, 32, 187, 334, 405–406
  with *must,* 185
  with *so...that* and *such (a)...that,* 333
  in *wish* sentences with *would,* 341
Complex sentences, 69, 109–131
  imaginary *if* sentences, 339, 346–348, 389,
    406–408
  real *if* sentences, 109, 122, 123–124, 339
  wish sentences, 339, 340, 341
    past *wish* sentences, 389, 403, 404
Complimenting, 316
  exercises on, 17, 317–318
Conclusions, 142, 154, 400
  exercises on, 144–145, 157, 216–217, 402
Conditional sentences
  imaginary *if* sentences, 339, 346–348, 389,
    406–408

  real *if* sentences, 109, 122, 123–124, 339
Conditions, 15–16, 18–19, 347, *see also*
    Possibility
confess, 467
Conjunctions, see *and; and...either; and so...;*
    and neither...; and...too; but; or
Consequences, 177, *see also* Results
consider, 360
consist of, 15
constantly, 26, 29
contain, 15
Containers, and specific quantity expressions,
    292
continually, 26
continue, 375, 376
Continuing time up to now, 146, 147,
    153–154
Continuous tenses, 375, *see also* Past continuous;
    Present continuous
  past perfect continuous, 389, 398, 400
  present perfect continuous, 133, 150–151,
    153–154
Contractions, *see also* Negative contractions
  with forms of *be,* see also *aren't; he's (he + is);*
    I'm; isn't; it's (it + is); she's (she + is);
    they're; wasn't; we're; weren't; "what'm";
    what's (what + is); "when're"; who's
    (who + is); you're
  with *be going to,* 76–77
  in past continuous, 67, 431, 432
  in present continuous, 9–10, 431, 432
  in simple past, 50, 51, 420–421
  with *there is/there are,* 32–33
  with forms of *do,* see also *"didja"; didn't;*
    doesn't; don't; "what'd"; "where'd"
  in negative imperatives, 36
  in simple past, 44, 45
  in simple present, 2–3
  with *used to,* 62–63
  with forms of *have,* see also *could've; hadn't;*
    hasn't; haven't; he'd; he's (he + has); I'd;
    it's (it + has); I've; she'd; she's (she + has);
    they'd; they've; we'd (we + had); we've;
    what's (what + has); "what've"; who's
    (who + has); would've; you'd (you + had);
    you've
  in past imaginary *if* sentences, 407
  in past perfect, 390, 391, 431, 432
  in past perfect continuous, 398
  in present perfect, 134–135, 431, 432
  in present perfect continuous, 150–151
  with forms of *will,* see *he'll; I'll; it'll;*
    she'll; they'll; we'll; "what'll";
    won't; you'll

Contractions *(continued)*
  with modals, see also *can't; couldn't; could've;*
      "gotta"; "hafta"; "hasta"; mustn't;
      "oughtta"; shouldn't; we'd (we + would);
      would've
    'd (for *would*), 340
    in passive sentences, 438
  with nouns, 10, 83, 135, 391
  in passive sentences, 420–421, 429, 431–432,
      438
  with pronouns
    in future, 76, 82, 83, 429
    in passive sentences, 420–421, 429, 431–432
    in past perfect, 390, 391, 431–432
    in past perfect continuous, 398
    in present continuous, 9, 10, 431–432
    in present perfect, 134, 135, 431–432
    in present perfect continuous, 150
  with *wh-* words, see *"what'd"; "what'll";*
      "what'm"; what's; "what've"; "when're";
      "where'd"; who's; why's
Contrary-to-fact conditionals (imaginary *if*
      sentences), 339, 346–348, 389, 406–408
Conversation, *see* Speech
convince, 467
Coordinating conjunctions, see *and; and...either;*
      and so...; and neither...; and...too;
      but; or
Correcting, and simple past, 54
  exercises on, 60–61
cost, 16, 380, 381, 416
could
  as modal of ability, 199, 201–202, 204
    and imaginary *if* sentences, 346, 347, 348
    in passive sentences, 440
    as past modal, 226–227
    in *wish* sentences, 340
  as modal of belief, 199, 209–210
    and certainty, 211–212, 221–222
    vs. *couldn't,* 218
    vs. *might,* in questions about possibility, 210
    as past modal, 226–227
  as social modal, 163, 164, 165
    for permission, 171–172
    in requests, 166
    in suggestions, 176
could have, 224–227, 229, 403, 406–408
could not have, 225
couldn't, 202, 210, 218, 224, 225, 227, 438
couldn't have, 227
"couldn't-of," 225
"could-of," 225
could've, 407
Countable nouns, *see* Count nouns

Count nouns, 269
  forms of, 270–272
  meaning and use of, 277–278
    with articles, 296
    in comparisons, 332
    with *fewer,* 325
    with *few* vs. *a few,* 288
    in general statements, 306–307
    with quantity expressions, 286, 292
    with *the fewest* and *the most,* 326
Criticizing, exercises on, 17
cry, 416
Curiosity, and *wh-* clauses, 450
  exercises on, 451

D

-*'d*
  as contraction of *did,* 45
  as contraction of *had,* 178, 390, 391, 398, see
      also *he'd; I'd; she'd; they'd; we'd; you'd*
  as contraction of *would,* 340, 407
deal, in *a great deal of,* 273, 286, 288, 290
decide, 373, 458, 459
Decisions, with *will,* 85–86
Defining
  articles in, 285, 306
  exercises on, 8, 245, 248–249, 308, 425
  with passive sentences, 418, 423
  with relative clauses, 239, 241–242
  with simple present, 5
Defining relative clauses, *see* Restrictive relative
      clauses
Definite articles, 285, 296, 297–299, 306–307, see
      also *the*
Definite completed actions, 53–54
Definite time, 147, 394
Degree expressions, 316, 320, 332, 333
delay, 360
demand, 468
deny, 360
Denying, and simple past, 54
  exercises on, 59
Dependent clauses, *see also* Noun clauses; Relative
      clauses; Time clauses
  imaginary *if* clauses, 346, 347, 406, 407–408
  real *if* clauses, 109, 122
depend on, 15
Describing, 15, 25, 34, 288
  exercises on, 16–17, 35, 69–71, 281–282,
      290–291, 434–435
Determiners, 269, 270, 273, 277, *see also* Articles
did, 44, 45, 62, 63, 102, 103
"didja," 45
didn't, 44, 45, 62, 63

did you, 44, 45
die, 416
Differences, 102, 316, 324, 328
Directions, 37, 239
Directness/indirectness, 347–348, 408, 450, *see also* Politeness
Disadvantages, with real *if* sentences, 123
Disagreeing, and simple past, 54
  exercises on, 59–60
Disapproval, 185, 210
  exercises on, 187
disapprove of, 366
Disbelief, exercises on, 219–220, 229
discover, 458, 459
dislike, 16, 360
Dislikes and likes, 306, 362–363
Dissatisfaction, with past *wish* sentences, 404
do, see also *did*; Simple past; Simple present
  with adverbs of frequency, 28
  contractions with forms of, see also *"didja"*; *didn't*; *doesn't*; *don't*; *"what'd"*; *"where'd"*
    in negative imperatives, 36
    in simple past, 44, 45
    in simple present, 2–3
    with *used to*, 62–63
  in present continuous, to express future, 94
does, 2–3
doesn't, 2–3
do not, 2, 36, 37
don't, 2, 3, 36, 37
don't have to, 191
doubt, 458
dream, 458

E
-ed, 44, 134, 390
Effects, *see* Results
either, 99, 102
Embedded questions (*wh-* clauses), 447, 448, 450, 461
Embedded *yes/no* questions (*if/whether* clauses), 447, 452–453, 454, 461
Emotions, 16, *see also* Feelings
Emphasis, 2, 16
enjoy, 360
equal, 16
Equatives (*as...as*), 323, 324
equipment, 278
-er, in comparatives, 314, 316
-es (for plurals), 271
-es (for simple present), 2
-est, in superlatives, 318–319, 320–321
estimate, 458

Events, *see also* Actions
  order of events, 111–112, 119–120, 377, 393–394
  simultaneous events, 112
ever, 25, 26
  with past perfect, 394
  with present perfect, 137, 138
Excuses, and simple past, 54
  exercises on, 55
expect, 373, 374, 458
Expectations/expected results, 80, 122, 123, *see also* Predicting
explain, 467
Expletive *there (there is/there are)*, 25, 32-33, 34
Expressions of quantity, *see* Quantity expressions
"Extra information" clauses (nonrestrictive relative clauses), 239, 260–261, 262–263

F
Facts, *see also* Information; New information
  background information, 69
  exercises on, 6, 426
  with passive sentences, 423
  and simple present, 1, 5
  and *there is/there are*, 25, 34
Factual conditionals (real *if* sentences), 109, 122, 123–124, 339
fear, 458
feel, 16, 154, 204, 458
Feelings, 362–363, 374, 458, 459, *see also* Attitudes; Emotions; Likes and dislikes; Opinions
  exercises on, 378–379, 460
few, 286, 288, 290, see also *a few*
fewer, 325, 328
fewest, 326, 328
Fields of study, noncount nouns for, 275
figure out, 458, 459
find, 458
find out, 458, 459
finish, 360
fit, 416
fly, 94
Food, and *a piece of*, 294
for, 146, 153–154, 394, 400
forever, 26
forget, 375, 377, 458, 459
Formality/informality, *see also* Politeness; Speech; Writing
  and *and...too, and...either, and so..., and neither..., me too*, and *me neither*, 102–103
  and comparatives, 316

Formality/informality *(continued)*
  and contractions
    with *be going to*, 77
    with forms of *be*, 10, 51
    with forms of *do*, 3, 45
    with forms of *have*, 135
    with social modals, 177–178
    with *will*, 83
  and directness/indirectness, 347–348, 408, 450
  and future, forms of, 75, 95
  and *have to* and *have got to* vs. *must*, 185
  and *if/whether* clauses, 454
  and *lots of* vs. *a lot of* and *a great deal of*, 288
  and *may*, 172
  and nonrestrictive relative clauses, 261, 263
  and passive sentences, 418
  and restrictive relative clauses with
    prepositions, 254
  and social modals, 163, 166, 171–172,
    177–178
  and *was* vs. *were*, 340, 346
  and *whom*, 242, 250
  and *will*, 83, 86
forward, in *look forward to*, 366
Frequency, adverbs of, *see* Adverbs of frequency
frequently, 26, 28
from…to…, 148
Future, 75–98, see also *be going to; will,* for future
  and future time clauses, 118, 119–120
  and future time phrases, 78–79
  with modals of ability, 203
  with modals of belief, 221–222
  passive sentences in, 416, 429, 434
  present continuous as, 94–96
  in reported speech, 465
  in *wish* sentences with *would*, 341
Future time clauses, 118, 119–120
Future time phrases, 78–79

G

Gases, noncount nouns for, 275
Generalizing, *see also* General statements
  and adverbs of frequency, 25, 28
  with *a* or *an*, in definitions, 306
  exercises on, 7, 308–309
  in reported speech, 465
  and simple present, 5
  and *that* clauses, 458
generally, 26, 28
General quantity expressions, 285, 286, 288, 290
General statements, *see also* Generalizing
  and articles, 285, 306–307
  with impersonal *they*, 418
  with impersonal *you*, 203, 418

  and present perfect, followed by simple past,
    148
  and simple present, 5
  and subject gerunds, 357
Generic statements, *see* Generalizing; General
    statements
Gerunds, 355, 356–369, *see also* Object gerunds
  as noncount nouns, 275
  subject gerunds, 356, 357, 381
go, 94, 360, 362, 416
going, see *be going to*
"*gonna*," 77
got, see *have got to*
"*gotta*," 177
Grains, noncount nouns for, 275
great deal, 273, 286, 288, 290
guess, 85, 458, 459
Guessing, 54
  exercises on, 57–58, 219

H

h, words beginning with, 296
Habits, *see also* Repeated actions; Routines
  and adverbs of frequency, 25, 29
  and simple present, 1, 5
  and *used to*, 64
Habitual past *(used to)*, 43, 62–63, 64
had, see *-'d; hadn't; he'd; I'd;* Past perfect; Past
    perfect continuous; *she'd; they'd; we'd;*
    you'd
had been able to, 403
had better, 163, 176, 177, 178
hadn't, 178, 390, 398, 431, 432
had to, 230
"*hafta*," 177
happen, 416
hardly ever, 26
has, see *hasn't;* "*hasta*"; *he's; it's;* Present perfect;
    Present perfect continuous; *she's; what's;*
    who's
hasn't, 134, 151, 431, 432
"*hasta*," 177
has to, 177
hate, 16, 375, 376
have, *see also* Past perfect; Present perfect
  contractions with forms of, see also *could've;*
    hadn't; "*hafta*"; *hasn't;* "*hasta*"; *haven't;*
    he'd; he's (he + has); I'd; it's (it + has); I've;
    she'd; she's (she + has); they'd; they've;
    we've; what's (what + has); "*what've*";
    who's (who + has); would've; you'd
    (you + had); you've
  to "*of*," with past modals, 225
  and passive sentences, 416

have (continued)
    and past modals, 224–227, 229–230, 416, 438
    in past perfect continuous, 389, 398, 400
    in phrases with gerunds, 361
    in present continuous as future, 94
    in present perfect continuous, 133, 150–151, 153–154, 438
    as stative verb, 15, 19, 154
have got to, 163, 199, 222
    in advice, 176, 177
    for certainty about present, 211, 212
    for necessity, requirements, rules, and laws, 184–186
    in speech, 177
haven't, 134, 151, 431
have to, 163, 199, 222
    in advice, 176, 177
    for certainty about present, 211, 212
    for necessity, requirements, rules, and laws, 184–186
    in negative, for lack of necessity, 191
    in speech, 177
Headlines, 5, 417, 434
hear, 16, 204
he'd, 390
he'll, 82, 83, 429
Help, offers of, 85
he's (he + has), 134, 150, 431
he's (he + is), 9, 76, 420, 421, 431
Historical events, simple past for, 147
hope, 458, 459
    in *I hope,* 85
    infinitives with, 373, 374
    vs. *wish,* 341
Hopes, exercises on, 345–346
how, see Information questions
how long, 82
how much, 273
hurt, 16
Hypothetical conditionals (imaginary *if* sentences), 339, 346–348, 389, 406–408
Hypothetical statements, see *wish* sentences

I

I'd, 390, 398, 431
Ideas, 16, *see also* Attitudes; Generalizing; Opinions; Thoughts
Identifying, 241–242
    exercises on, 243–244, 248–249, 259, 300–301
Identifying relative clauses, *see* Restrictive relative clauses
if
    in *if/whether* clauses, 447, 452–453, 454, 461
    in imaginary *if* clauses, 346, 347, 406, 407–408

    in imaginary *if* sentences, 339, 346–348, 389, 406–408
    in real *if* clauses, 109, 122
    in real *if* sentences, 109, 122, 123–124, 339
if/whether clauses, 447, 452–453, 454, 461
I guess, 85
I hope, 85
I'll, 82, 429
I'm, 9, 76, 420, 421, 431
Imaginary *if* clauses, 346, 347, 406, 407–408
Imaginary *if* sentences, 339, 346–348, 389, 406–408
imagine, 360, 458, 459
Imperatives, 36, 37, 461, 468
Impersonal *they,* 418
Impersonal *you,* 203, 418
Impossibility, *see also* Possibility
    exercises on, 229
in, 60, 78, 254, 321
include, 15
Indefinite articles, 285, 296, 297, 306, see also *a/an*
Indefinite time, with present perfect, 137–138, 148
Independent clauses, *see* Main clauses
indicate, 467
Indirectness/directness, 347–348, 408, 450, *see also* Politeness
Indirect questions (*wh-* clauses), 447, 448, 450, 461
Indirect speech (reported speech), 447, 461, 462–463, 465–468
Indirect *yes/no* questions (*if/whether* clauses), 447, 452–453, 454, 461
Inferences, exercises on, 303
Infinitives, 355, 369–386
    with *in order,* 383, 384
    after *it...,* 380, 381
    in reported speech, 461
    in verb + infinitive, 371, 373, 374, 375, 376–377
    verbs not used with, but with object gerunds, 360–361, 366–367
inform, 377, 467
Informality, *see* Formality/informality
Information, *see also* Answers; Facts; Generalizing; Information questions; Information questions (subject); Questions; Short answers; Statements
    background information, 69
    knowledge, 203
    new information, 34, 242, 297
    and nonrestrictive relative clauses, 262–263
    old information, 418, 423
    and restrictive relative clauses, 241–242

Information questions, *see also* Information
    questions (subject)
  adverbs of frequency in, 27
  in future, 77, 82, 429
  with modals
    with modals of ability, 200, 202
    with modals of belief, 210
    in passive sentences, 438
    with past modals, 224
    with social modals, 165
  with passive sentences, 421, 429, 432, 438
  in past continuous, 67, 432
  in past perfect, 390, 432
  in past perfect continuous, 398
  in present continuous, 10, 432
  in present perfect, 135, 432
  in present perfect continuous, 151
  with reported speech, 461
  in simple past, 45, 50, 63, 421
  in simple present, 3, 421
Information questions (subject)
  adverbs of frequency in, 27, 28
  in future, 77, 82, 429
  with modals
    with modals of ability, 200, 202
    with modals of belief, 210
    in passive sentences, 438
    with past modals, 224
    with social modals, 165
  with passive sentences, 421, 429, 432, 438
  in past continuous, 68, 432
  in past perfect, 390, 432
  in past perfect continuous, 398
  in present continuous, 10, 432
  in present perfect, 135, 432
  in present perfect continuous, 151
  in simple past, 45, 51, 63, 421
  in simple present, 3, 421
  with *there is/there are,* 33
-*ing, see* Gerunds; Past continuous; Past perfect
    continuous; Present continuous; Present
    perfect continuous
in order, with infinitives, 370, 383, 384
insist, 468
Instructions, 37, 176, 384
  exercises on, 38, 180–183, 385
Intentions, and *be going to,* 80
  exercises on, 80–81
Intonation, to express intensity or emotion, 16
Intransitive verbs, 416
involve, 15
Irregular plurals of count nouns, 271–272
Irregular verbs, 44, 134, *see also* **specific verbs —**
    e.g., *be, do, have*

is
  contractions with, see *he's; isn't; it's; she's;*
    "there's"; what's; who's
  in passive sentences, 420–421, 431,
    432
  in present continuous, 9–10, 431, 432
  in *there is/there are,* 25, 32–33, 34
is being, 18–19
isn't, 9, 32, 33, 76, 421, 431, 432
it, 356, 370, 380, 381
it appears, 459
itch, 16
it'd, 390
I think, 85
Itineraries, 95–96
it'll, 82, 429
it seems, 459
it's (it + has), 134, 150
it's (it + is), 9, 76, 420
it's (not) worth, 361
it's no use, 361
I've, 134, 150, 186, 431

J
Jokes, 54
just
  with past perfect, 394
  with present perfect, 142, 148
  with present perfect continuous, 153
  with simple past, 148
  with stative verbs, 16

K
keep, 360
know
  in *want to know,* 467
  in present perfect, 154
  as stative verb, 16
  with *that* clauses, 458
  with *wh-* clauses, 450
Knowledge, 203, *see also* Information

L
lack, 15
Lack of necessity, 191
Languages, noncount nouns for, 275
lately, 153
Laws, with social modals, 184, 185, 191
learn, 373, 458, 459
least, 318, 319, 320, 328
leave, 94
less, in comparatives, 314, 316
  with comparative nouns, 325, 328
  vs. negative of *as...as,* 324

like
    as stative verb, 15, 16
    in verb + infinitive or gerund, 375, 376
    in *would like*, 373, 374
Likes and dislikes, 306, 362–363
Liquids, noncount nouns for, 275
Listener, in reported speech, 467
little, 273, 286, 288, 290
live, 154
-*'ll*, 82, 83, 429
look, 15, 381
look forward to, 367
look like, 15
lots of, 286, 288, see also *a lot of*
love, 16, 376

M

Main clauses, 109, *see also* Result clauses
    with future time clauses, 118, 119–120
    with *if/whether* clauses, 452–453
    and past perfect, 393, 394
    with past time clauses, 110, 111–112
    with *that* clauses, 457
    with *wh-* clauses, 448
manage, 373
many, 286, 290
many times, 138
Materials, and *a piece of*, 294
may
    as modal of belief, 199, 209–210
        and certainty about future, 221
        and certainty about present, 211, 212
        in passive sentences, 440
    as social modal, 163, 164, 165
        vs. imaginary *if* sentences, 348
        for permission, 171–172, 230
maybe, 85, 212, 222
may be, 212
may have, 225
may not, 164, 209
may not have, 225
"*may not-of*," 225
"*may-of*," 225
mean, 16
measure, 16
Measure expressions, *see* Specific quantity
        expressions
Measurements, 16, 292
Memories, and *used to*, 64
me neither, 103
Mental activity verbs, 447, 450, 454,
        458–459
mention, 467
me too, 103

might
    as modal of belief, 199, 209–210
        and certainty about future, 221–222
        and certainty about present, 211–212
        in passive sentences, 440
    as social modal, 164, 176
might have, 225
might not, 209
might not have, 225, 227
"*might not-of*," 225
"*might-of*," 225
mind, 16, 348, 360, 363
miss, 361
Modal auxiliaries, *see* Modals
Modals, *see also* Modals of belief; Social modals;
        specific modals — **e.g.,** *can, could, have*
        got to, have to, may, might, must, ought
        to, should, will, would
    with adverbs of frequency, 27
    contractions with, see *can't; couldn't; could've;*
        "*gotta*"; "*hafta*"; "*hasta*"; *mustn't;*
        "*oughtta*"; *shouldn't; we'd* (*we* + *would*);
        would've; you'd (*you* + *would*)
    modals of ability, 199, 200–204, 226–227
    in passive sentences, 416, 438, 440
    past modals, 224–227, 229–230, 416, 438
    in reported speech, 463
Modals of ability, 199, 200–204, 226–227
Modals of belief
    forms of, 209–210
    meaning and use of
        and *be able to*, 203
        for certainty about future, 221–222
        for certainty about present, 211–212
        for certainty about present (negative), 218
        as past modals, 226–227
more, 314, 316, 325, 328
most, 318–321, 326, 328
much, 268, 273, 288, 290
Musical instruments, and *the,* 307
must
    as modal of belief, 199, 209–210, 222
        and certainty about present, 211, 212
        in *yes/no* questions, 210
    as social modal, 163, 164
        in advice, 176, 177
        in instructions, 176
        for necessity, requirements, rules, and laws,
            184–185, 230
        in negative, for prohibition, 191
        in passive sentences, 440
must be, 212
must have, 225, 226
must not, 191, 209

must not have, 225, 227
"must not-of," 225
mustn't, 164
"must-of," 225
my, 269

N

Names (proper nouns), 263, 269
Necessity, 184, 185, 191, 229, 230, *see also*
        Obligations; Requirements; Rules
need, 16, 373
Negative contractions, see also *aren't; can't;*
        couldn't; didn't; doesn't; don't; hadn't;
        hasn't; haven't; isn't; mustn't; shouldn't;
        wasn't; weren't; won't
  in future, 76, 82, 429
  with imperatives, 36
  with modals
    with modals of ability, 200, 202
    with modals of belief, 209–210
    in passive sentences, 438
    with past modals, 224
    with social modals, 164
  in passive sentences, 421, 429, 431–432, 438
  in past continuous, 67, 431, 432
  in past perfect, 390, 431, 432
  in past perfect continuous, 398
  in present continuous, 9, 431, 432
  in present perfect, 134, 431, 432
  in present perfect continuous, 151
  in simple past, 44, 50, 421
  in simple present, 9, 421
  with *there is/there are,* 9
  with *used to,* 62–63
Negative questions, with *had better,* 177, 178
Negatives, *see also* Negative contractions;
        Negative statements; *never; no; not;* **other**
        specific negative words and phrases
  adverbs of frequency as, 26
  as answers, with *so* or *not,* 459
  in answers to requests for permission, 172
  of *as...as,* 324
  gerunds as, 356
  with imperatives, 36, 461
  with infinitives, 369, 383
  modals of belief as, 218, 227
  negative questions, with *had better,* 177, 178
  of verb + infinitive, 371
Negative statements
  adverbs of frequency in, 26, 27, 28
  with *and...either,* 99
  with *and neither...,* 101
  with *but,* 98
  in future, 76, 82, 429

  with *many* and *much,* 286
mind in, plus object gerunds, 363
  with modals
    with modals of ability, 200, 201, 204
    with modals of belief, 209
    in passive sentences, 438
    with past modals, 224, 225
    with social modals, 164, 177, 178, 191
  with passive sentences, 421, 429, 431, 438
  in past continuous, 67, 431
  in past perfect, 390, 431
  in past perfect continuous, 398
  in present continuous, 9, 431
  in present perfect, 134, 431
  in present perfect continuous, 151
  in simple past, 44, 50, 62, 421
  in simple present, 2, 421
  with *there is/there are,* 32
neither, 101, 102, 103
neither did I, 103
never, 26, 138, 394
New information, 34, 242, 297
News reports
  headlines in, 5, 415, 417, 434
  noun clauses in, 447
  passive sentences in, 415, 417
  present perfect in, 142
  reported speech in, 467
  which in, 242
next, 79
no, 32, 286, 290
Nonaction verbs, *see* Stative verbs
Noncount nouns, 269
  forms of, 273
  meaning and use of, 277–278
    with articles, 296
    in comparisons with *such...that,* 332
    in general statements, 306
    gerunds as, 356
    groups of, 275
    with *less,* 325
    with *little* vs. *a little,* 288
    with quantity expressions, 286, 292
    with *the least,* 326
Nonprogressive verbs, *see* Stative verbs
Nonrestrictive relative clauses, 239, 260–261,
        262–263
normally, 26, 28
not, see also Negative contractions; Negative
        statements; Negatives
  with adverbs of frequency, 26
  in answers, with verbs that take *so,* 459
  with gerunds, 356
  with imperatives, in reported speech, 461

not (continued)
    with infinitives, 369
    for refusals, with *will*, 85
not any, 32, 286, 290
not as...as, 324
notice, 458, 459
notify, 467
not many, 286, 290
not much, 286, 288, 290
not...much, 273
not too many, 290
not too much, 290
Noun clauses, 447, 461, see also *that* clauses
    if/whether clauses, 447, 452–453, 454, 461
    wh- clauses, 447, 448, 450, 461
Noun complements, *see* Noun clauses
Nouns, 269–284, *see also* Count nouns; Noncount
        nouns; Noun clauses
    abstract nouns, 275, 294
    articles with, 296, 297–299, 306–307
    common nouns, 269
    in comparisons, 313
        comparatives of, 325, 328
        with *the same...as,* 326, 328
        with *so...that* and *such (a)...that,* 332, 333
        superlatives of, 326, 328
    contractions with, 10, 83, 135, 391
    count nouns vs. noncount nouns, 277–278
    vs. gerunds, 355
    vs. infinitives, 355
    proper nouns, 263, 269
    with quantity expressions, 286, 292, 293
now, with present continuous, 12
-n't, contractions with, see *aren't; can't; couldn't;*
        didn't; doesn't; don't; hadn't; hasn't;
        haven't; isn't; mustn't; shouldn't; wasn't;
        weren't; won't
Numbers, 270, 273

O

Object gerunds, 356, 359–369
    forms of, 359
    meaning and use of, 362–363
        with prepositions, 356, 365–367, 374
        verbs and phrases commonly used with,
            360–361, 375, 376–377
Object pronouns, 314, 323, 325, 326
    object relative pronouns, 250, 254, 260–261
Object relative pronouns, 250, 254, 260–261
Objects (grammatical), 415, *see also* Object
        pronouns
Objects (physical objects), and *a piece of,* 294
Obligations, and social modals, 184, 185, 229
    exercises on, 188, 195

occasionally, 26, 28
occur, 416
of, 292, 321
"*of,*" (as contraction of *have*), with past modals,
    225
offer, 373
Offers, 37, 85–86
often, 25, 26, 29
Old information, in passive sentences, 418, 423
Omitted elements, *see* Optional/omitted elements
on, 60, 321
once, with present perfect, 138
one of, 321
only a few, 290
only a little, 290
Opinions, *see also* Feelings; Thoughts
    attitudes, 16, 306, 362–363, 374
    with comparatives of adjectives and adverbs,
        316
    exercises on, 186, 291–292, 307, 317, 322,
        359, 382–383, 442, 460
    with general quantity expressions, 288
    general statements for, 306
    likes and dislikes, 306, 362–363
    with passive sentences, 417, 440
    with social modals, 184–185, 440
    with superlatives, 320–321
    with *that* clauses, 458
    with verb + infinitive, 374
Opportunity, 203, 226
Optional/omitted elements
    by + noun, in passive sentences, 416, 417, 420,
        429
    h sound in *had,* 391
    in order, with infinitives, 383, 384
    listener, with *answer* and *promise,* 467
    nouns, with *the same...as,* 328
    object relative pronouns, 250, 254
    or not, in *if/whether* clauses, 452, 453
    that
        in *such (a)...that,* 332
        in *that* clauses, 457, 458
        in *wish* sentences, 340, 403
    then, in imaginary *if* sentences, 346, 406
    verbs
        in comparisons, 314, 316, 323, 325, 326
        in infinitives, 371
or, after *had better,* 177
order, in *in order,* 370, 383, 384
Order of events, 111–112, 119–120, 377,
    393–394
ordinarily, 28
or not, in *if/whether* clauses, 452, 453
"*oughtta,*" 177

ought to, 163, 199
   in advice, 176, 177
   and certainty about future, 221, 222
   and certainty about present, 211, 212
   vs. imaginary *if* sentences, 347
   for opinions and obligations, 184–185
   as past modal, 229
   in reported speech, 463
   in speech, 177
ought to be, 212
ought to have, 229
owe, 15
own, 15, 154

P
Participles, *see* Past participles
Passive sentences, 415–445
   forms of, 416
      in continuous and perfect tenses, 431–432
      in future, 429
      with modals, 438
      in simple present and simple past, 420–421
   meaning and use of, 417–418
      in future, continuous, and perfect tenses, 434
      with modals, 440
      in simple present and simple past, 423
Past, 43–73, 389–413, *see also* Past continuous;
        Past participles; Perfect tenses; Simple past
   past ability, with *could*, 201–202, 203–204
   past imaginary *if* sentences, 389, 406–408
   past modals, 224–227, 229–230, 416, 438
   past time clauses, 110, 111–112, 393, 394
   past *wish* sentences, 389, 403, 404
Past continuous, 43
   forms of, 67–68
   meaning and use of, 69
      in complex sentences with past time clauses,
        112
      in imaginary *if* sentences, 346, 347
      in passive sentences, 416, 431–432, 434
Past habitual *(used to)*, 43, 62–63, 64
Past imaginary *if* clauses, 406, 407–408
Past imaginary *if* sentences, 389, 406–408
Past modals, 224–227, 229–230, 416, 438
Past participles, 134, *see also* Past perfect; Present
      perfect
   and adverbs, position of, 138, 142
   in passive sentences, 416
      in continuous and perfect tenses, 431
      in future, 429
      with modals, 438
      in simple present and simple past, 420
   in past imaginary *if* sentences, 406
   with past modals, 224–227, 229–230, 416, 438

Past perfect, 389, 390–397
   forms of, 390–391, 398
   meaning and use of, 393–394
      in passive sentences, 416, 431–432, 434
      in past imaginary *if* sentences, 406,
        407–408
      in past *wish* sentences, 403, 404
      with stative verbs, 400
      with *that* clauses, 458
Past perfect continuous, 389, 398, 400
Past progressive, *see* Past continuous
Past tense, *see* Simple past
Past time clauses, 111–112, 393, 394
Past unreal conditional sentences (past imaginary
      if sentences), 389, 406–408
Past *wish* sentences, 389, 403, 404
people, as subject, 418
Perception, verbs of, 204
Perfect modals (past modals), 224–227, 229–230,
      416, 438
Perfect tenses, *see also* Past perfect; Present perfect
   past perfect continuous, 389, 398, 400
   present perfect continuous, 133, 150–151,
      153–154
perhaps, with *will*, 222
Period (punctuation), 45, 448
Permission, 171–172, 230, 348
   exercises on, 173–174, 180, 351
permitted, 230
persuade, 467
Phrases
   adverbial phrases, 12
   future time phrases, 78–79
   gerunds as, 356
   with object gerunds, 361
   prepositional phrases, 365, 367
   verb phrases, 365–367, 369
Physical sensations, and stative verbs, 16, 18
piece, in *a piece of*, 294
plan, 373
Plans, 80, 94
   exercises on, 81, 94–95
please, 36, 37, 166, 171
plenty of, 286, 290
Plural
   with articles, 296
   of count nouns, 270–273, 277
      with *the*, 307
      for general statements, 306
      with *such...that*, 332
   and noncount nouns, 273, 277
   with *of*, with superlatives, 321
   and "*there's*," 33
point out, 467

Politeness, *see also* Formality/informality
  and directness/indirectness, 347–348, 408, 450
  with *if/whether* clauses, 454
  and imperatives, 37
  and social modals, 163, 166
  and *wh-* clauses, 450
  with *would you mind,* 363
possess, 15
Possession, and stative verbs, 15
Possessive relative pronouns, 258
Possessives, 258, 319
Possibility
  exercises on, 124, 229, 442
  with *maybe,* 212
  and modals
    modals of ability, 203–204
    modals of belief, 210, 221–222, 440
    past modals, 227
  and real *if* sentences, 122, 123
  and *wish* sentences, 341–342
postpone, 361
Powders, noncount nouns for, 275
practice, 361
Precise time, 147, 394
predict, 458
Predicting, 80, *see also* Expectations/expected
    results
  exercises on, 81, 89–90, 223
prefer, 16, 375, 376
Preferences, 316
  exercises on, 317, 378–379
Prepositional phrases, with object gerunds, 365,
    367
Prepositions
  in nonrestrictive relative clauses, 261
  with object gerunds, 356, 365–367, 374
  with object relative pronouns, 254
  in restrictive relative clauses, 254
  with superlatives, 321
  of time, 60
Present, 1–23, *see also* Present continuous; Present
    perfect; Simple present
  with modals of ability, 200–201, 203–204
  with modals of belief, for certainty, 211–212,
    218
  and present perfect continuous, 133, 150–151,
    153–154
Present continuous, 1, 9–15
  forms of, 9
  meaning and use of, 12–13
    with adverbs of frequency, 29
    as future form, 94–95
    with modals of belief, 212
    in passive sentences, 416, 431–432, 434

    vs. simple present, 12–13, 18–19, 29
    with stative verbs, 16, 18–19
Present perfect, 133, 134–150
  forms of, 134–135, 150–151
  meaning and use of, 137–138
    for continuing time up to now, 146
    in passive sentences, 416, 431–432, 434
    vs. past perfect, 394
    vs. present perfect continuous, 154
    for recent time, 142
    vs. simple past, 133, 147–148
    with stative verbs, 154
Present perfect continuous, 133, 150–151,
    153–154
Present progressive, *see* Present continuous
presume, 458
pretend, 458
Prices, 294
probably, 85, 222
Procrastinating, and future time clauses, 120
  exercises on, 121–122
Prohibition, with social modals, 191
promise, 373, 467
Promising, 85–86, 123, 324
  exercises on, 86–87, 127, 324–325
Pronouns, *see also* **specific pronouns**
  after *as...as,* 323
  in comparatives, 314, 316
  contractions with
    in future, 76, 82, 83, 429
    in passive sentences, 420–421, 429, 431–432
    in past perfect, 390, 391, 431–432
    in past perfect continuous, 398
    in present continuous, 9, 10, 431–432
    in present perfect, 134, 135, 431–432
    in present perfect continuous, 150
  and count nouns, 270
  repetition of, vs. nonrestrictive relative clauses,
    263
  in reported speech, 462, 466
Pronunciation, 201, 271, 272, 296, *see also*
    Speech
Proper nouns, 263, 269
propose, 468
prove, 458, 459
Punctuation, *see also* Comma
  period and question mark, 45, 448
Purpose infinitives, 383, 384

Q

Quantifiers, *see* Quantity expressions
Quantity expressions, 273, 285, 321, 328
  general quantity expressions, 285, 286, 288,
    290

Quantity expressions *(continued)*
    specific quantity expressions, 285, 292,
        293–294
Question mark, 45, 448
Questions, *see also* Answers; Information
        questions; Information questions (subject);
        Requesting; *Yes/no* questions
    choice questions, with infinitives, 371
    with *ever*, 26, 137
    with *if/whether* clauses, 454
    with *mind*, plus object gerunds, 363
    with *much*, 286
    negative questions, with *had better*, 177, 178
    in reported speech, 467
    with *shall*, as suggestions, 177
    with *should*, not *ought to*, 177
    and *wh-* clauses, 450
    with *when*, simple past for, 147
Question words, *see* Information questions;
        Information questions (subject); *what;*
        "what'd"; "what'll"; "what'm"; what's;
        "what've"; wh- clauses; *when; "when're";*
        "where'd"; who; who's; wh- words; *why's*
quit, 361
quite a bit of, 286
quite a few, 286, 290
Quotation marks, and reported speech, 462
Quoted speech, vs. reported speech, 462–463

R
rain, 416
Ranking, exercises on, 322
rarely, 26
Real conditional sentences (real *if* sentences), 109,
        122, 123–124, 339
Real *if* clauses, 109, 122
Real *if* sentences, 109, 122, 123–124, 339
realize, 458, 459
really, 16
Reasons, 400
    exercises on, 401–402
    and purpose infinitives, 383, 384
recall, 458, 459
Receiver of action, in passive sentences, 415,
        417–418
    in future, continuous, and perfect tenses, 434
    with modals, 440
    in simple present and simple past, 423
Recent actions, with present perfect continuous,
        153–154
recently, 142, 153
Recent time, 142, 153–154
recognize, 16, 458
recommend, 468

Recommending, 320–321
    exercises on, 189–190, 321
Recreational activities, with *go* plus object
        gerunds, 362
refuse, 373
Refusing, 85–86
    exercises on, 90, 141–142
Regret, 230, 341, 404
    exercises on, 231–232, 342–343, 405–406
regret, 361, 375, 377, 458
Regular verbs, *see* Verbs
Rejoinders, 102–103
Relationships, and stative verbs, 15
Relative clauses, 239–268, *see also* Relative
        pronouns; Restrictive relative clauses
    nonrestrictive, 239, 260–261, 262–263
Relative pronouns, 239
    in nonrestrictive relative clauses, 260–261
    object relative pronouns, 250, 260–261
    possessive relative pronouns, 258
    in restrictive relative clauses, 240
    subject relative pronouns, 246, 250, 260–261
remain, 94
remark, 467
remember
    with *could* or *was able to*, 204
    with infinitives or object gerunds, 375, 377
    as stative verb, 16
    with *that* clauses, 458, 459
    with *wh-* clauses, 450
remind, 467
Reminding, 54
    exercises on, 54–55, 141
Repeated actions, 64, 137, 154, *see also* Habits;
        Routines
reply, 467
report, 467
Reported questions (*wh-* clauses), 447, 448, 450,
        461
Reported speech, 447, 461, 462–463, 465–468
Reporting verbs, 447, 461, 465–468
Requesting, 37, 166, 348, 363
    exercises on, 167–170, 173–174, 364
require, 468
Requirements, 184, 185, 230, 440, *see also* Laws;
        Necessity; Obligations; Rules
    exercises on, 188–191, 193–194
resemble, 15, 416
Restrictive relative clauses, 239
    forms of, 240
    meaning and use of, 241–242
        and names of people and places, 263
        with relative pronouns, 246, 250, 254,
        258

Result clauses
  in imaginary *if* sentences, 346, 347, 406,
    407–408
  in real *if* sentences, 122, 123
Results, *see also* Result clauses
  and cause and effect, 112, 333
  and conclusions, 142, 154
  expectations/expected results, 80, 122, 123
  and passive sentences, 417, 423
  with *so...that* and *such (a)...that,* 333
right now, 12
Routines, *see also* Habits; Repeated actions
  and adverbs of frequency, 25, 29
  and simple present, 1, 5
  and *used to,* 64
Rules, 184, 185, 191
  exercises on, 441

S
-s (for plural), 271, 272
-s (for simple present), 2
-'s, see *he's; it's; she's; "there's"; what's; who's;
    why's*
same, in *the same...as,* 326, 328
say, 377, 466, 467
Schedules, 1, 5, 95–96, *see also* Routines
Scientific writing, passive sentences in, 417
see, 16, 19, 204
seem
  infinitives with, 373, 374
  in *it... + adjective + infinitive,* 381
  in *it seems,* 459
  as stative verb, 15
seldom, 26
Sensations, and stative verbs, 16, 18
Senses, and stative verbs, 16
Sentences, *see also* Complex sentences; Passive
    sentences; Questions; Statements; *wish*
    sentences
  imaginary *if* sentences, 339, 346–348, 389,
    406–408
  real *if* sentences, 109, 122, 123–124, 339
Sequence of events, 111–112, 119–120, 377,
    393–394
several, 269, 270, 286, 290
shall, in suggestions, 177
she'd, 390
she'll, 82, 429
she's (she + has), 134, 150, 186
she's (she + is), 9, 76, 420, 421, 431
shopping, 362
Short answers
  and adverbs of frequency, 28
  in future, 76–77, 82, 429

with modals
  with modals of ability, 200, 202
  with modals of belief, 210
  in passive sentences, 438
  with past modals, 224
  with social modals, 164
with passive sentences, 421, 429, 432, 438
in past continuous, 67, 432
in past perfect, 390, 432
in past perfect continuous, 398
in present continuous, 9, 432
in present perfect, 134, 432
in present perfect continuous, 151
in simple past, 44
  with *be,* 50
  with passive sentences, 421
  with *used to,* 63
in simple present, 2, 421
with *there is/there are,* 33
to *yes/no* questions, with infinitives, 371
should
  as modal of belief, 199, 209–210
    and certainty about future, 221, 222
    and certainty about present, 211, 212
  as social modal, 163, 164, 165
    for advice, 176, 177
    vs. imaginary *if* sentences, 347
    for instructions, 176
    for opinions and obligations, 184–185
    in passive sentences, 440
    as past modal, 229
    in reported speech, 463, 468
    for rules and laws, 185
should be, with adjectives, 212
should have, 224, 225, 229–230, 408
should not have, 224, 225
shouldn't, 164, 209, 224, 225, 438
"shouldn't-of," 225
"should-of," 225
shout, 467
Signs
  definite articles in, 298
  imperatives in, 37
  passive sentences in, 415, 417, 423
  social modals in, 172
  will in, 86
Similarities, 102, 313, 324, 328
Simple future, see *will,* for future
Simple past, 43–66
  forms of, 44–45, 50–51, 420–421
  meaning and use of, 53–54
    with *before* and *after,* 394
    in complex sentences with past time clauses,
      111–112

Simple past *(continued)*
    in imaginary *if* sentences, 346, 347
    in passive sentences, 416, 423
    with past perfect, 389, 393
    with prepositions of time, 60
    vs. present perfect, 133, 147–148
    in reported speech, 463
    with *that* clauses, 458–459
    in *wish* sentences, 340, 341
  with *used to,* 43, 62–63, 64
Simple present, 1–8
  forms of, 2–3, 420–421
  meaning and use of, 5
    with adverbs of frequency, 25, 29
    with *be going to,* 76
    as future, 95–98, 118
    of *have,* in present perfect, 134
    in passive sentences, 416, 423
    for physical sensations, 18
    vs. present continuous, 12–13, 18–19, 29
    in real *if* sentences, 122
    in reported speech, 463, 465, 468
    with stative verbs, 15–16
    with *that* clauses, 458, 459
    vs. *used to,* 64
    in *wish* sentences, 340, 403
Simultaneous events, 112
since, 146, 153–154, 394, 400
Singular, 3, 270–273, 296, 356
Skill, and modals of ability, 203
sleep, 416
smell, 16, 19, 204
so
  in *and so…,* 101, 102, 103
  in *so did I,* 103
  in *so far,* 138
  in *so many* and *so much,* 286
  in *so…that,* 332, 333
  that clauses replaced by, 459
Social modals, 163–198, see also *can; could; may;*
    might; must; should; will; would
  contractions with, 164, 177–178
  meaning and use of
    vs. imaginary *if* sentences, 347, 348
    vs. imperatives, 37
    for lack of necessity and prohibition, 191
    for opinions, obligations, necessity,
      requirements, rules, and laws, 184–186
    as past modals, 226, 229–230
    for permission, 171–172
    for requests, 166
    for suggestions, advice, warnings, and
      instructions, 176–178
so did I, 103

so far, 138
Solids, noncount nouns for, 275
so many, 286
some
  vs. *any,* 32
  with count nouns, 270, 278, 286
  and proper nouns, 269
somebody, 418
someone, 418
sometimes, 26, 28
so much, 286
so…that, 332, 333
sound, 15
sound like, 15
Speaking, *see* Speech
Specific quantity expressions, 285, 292, 293–294
Speech, *see also* Pronunciation
  with *be going to,* 77, 80
  contractions in
    "didja," didn't, "what'd," and "where'd," 45
    doesn't and *don't,* 3, 37
    "gonna," 77
    "gotta," "hafta," "hasta," and "oughtta,"
      177
    of *had,* in past perfect, 391
    with *-'ll,* 83
    with past modals, 225
    "there's," 33
    wasn't and *weren't,* 51
    "what'm" and "when're," 10
    "what've," 135
    who's, 10, 135
  had better in, 178
  imaginary *if* sentences in, with *was,* 347
  imperatives in, 37
  intonation in, to express intensity or emotion,
    16
  lots of in, 288
  must be in, 212
  nonrestrictive relative clauses in, 263
  present continuous in, 10
  present perfect in, 135, 142, 148
  purpose infinitives in, 384
  rejoinders in, 102–103
  simple past in, 45, 51, 148
  simple present in, to express future, 95–96
  social modals in, 177–178
  so in, for *that* clauses, 459
  stative verbs in, 16
  that clauses in, 458, 459
  wish sentences in, with *was,* 340
spend time, 361
Spoken forms, *see* Speech
start, 375, 376

state, 467
Statements, *see also* General statements; Negative
     statements
   adverbs of frequency in, 27, 28
   in future, 76, 82, 429
   with modals
      with modals of ability, 200, 201
      with modals of belief, 209
      in passive sentences, 438
      with past modals, 224
      with social modals, 164
   with passive sentences, 420, 429, 431, 438
   in past continuous, 67, 431
   in past perfect, 390, 431
   in past perfect continuous, 398
   in present continuous, 9, 431
   in present perfect, 134, 431
   with reported speech, 461
   in simple past, 44, 50, 62, 420
   in simple present, 2, 420
   with *there is/there are*, 32
States, 15–16, 18–19
Stative verbs, 1, 15–21
   with *could* or *was able to*, 204
   with *it...* + infinitive, 381
   and passive sentences, 416
   and past perfect continuous, 400
   in present perfect, 154
stay, 94, 154, 416
still, 138, 394
stop, 375, 377
Stories, 64, 69, 400
Stress, 201
study, 154
Subject gerunds, 356, 357, 381
Subject pronouns, 314, 323, 325, 326
   subject relative pronouns, 246, 250, 260–261
Subject relative pronouns, 246, 250, 260–261
Subjects, *see also* Information questions (subject);
        Subject pronouns; Subject-verb agreement
   in *it...* + infinitive, 380, 381
   old information as, 418
   in passive sentences, 415
   subject gerunds, 356, 357, 381
   in *there is/there are*, 34
   with *were*, 340, 346
   in *wh-* clauses, 448
Subject-verb agreement
   and *can*, 200
   and *could*, 201
   and social modals, 164
   and subject relative pronouns, 246
   and *will*, 82
Subordinate clauses, *see* Dependent clauses

such (a)...that, 332, 333
suggest, 361, 468
Suggesting, 176–177, 229
   exercises on, 178–179, 230–231
Summarizing, with relative clauses, 239, 241–242
   exercises on, 246
Superlatives, 313, 318–321, 326, 328
suppose, 458, 459
suspect, 458
swear, 467

T
-'t, contractions with, see *aren't; can't; couldn't;
        didn't; doesn't; don't; hadn't; hasn't;
        haven't; isn't; mustn't; shouldn't; wasn't;
        weren't; won't*
take, 380, 381
Talk, *see* Speech
talk about, 367
taste, 16, 19, 204
teach, 154
Telephone recordings, present perfect in, 142
tell, 377, 466, 467
Tense, *see also* Continuous tenses; Future; Past;
        Perfect tenses; Present
   in reported speech, 465
than, 314, 325
that, 239, see also *that* clauses
   and nonrestrictive relative clauses, 261
   as object relative pronoun, 250, 254
   omission of
      in *such (a)...that*, 332
      in *that* clauses, 457, 458
      in *wish* sentences, 340, 403
   in reported speech, 466
   in restrictive relative clauses, 240, 242, 250
   in *so...that*, 332, 333
   as subject relative pronoun, 246
   in *such (a)...that*, 332, 333
that clauses, 109, 447
   forms of, 457
   meaning and use of, 458–459
      in reported speech, 461, 462–463, 465,
         468
      in *wish* sentences, 340, 403
the, 285, 296, 297–299
   with *after next*, in future time phrases, 79
   with count nouns vs. noncount nouns, 278
   in general statements, 306–307
   with plural nouns, 307
   in reported speech, 466
   in superlatives, 318–319
the fewest, 326, 328
the least, 318, 319, 326, 328

the most, 318–319, 326, 328
then, 122, 346, 406
there aren't, 32, 33
there isn't, 32, 33
there is/there are, 25, 32–33, 34
"there's," 32, 33
there's no, 32
there's not, 32
the same...as, 326, 328
these, in reported speech, 466
they'd, 390
they'll, 82, 83, 429
they're, 9, 76, 420
they've, 134, 150
think, 16, 85, 458, 459
think about, 367
this, 12, 78, 269, 466
those, in reported speech, 466
Thoughts, with *that* clauses, 458, 459
    exercises on, 460
Threats, with real *if* sentences, 123, 124
    exercises on, 126
Time, *see also* Future; Past; Present; Time clauses;
       Time words
    continuing time up to now, 146, 147,
       153–154
    indefinite time, 137–138, 148
    and modals of ability, 203–204
    precise time, 147, 394
    recent time, 142, 153–154
Time adverbials, *see* Time words
Time clauses, 69, 109
    future time clauses, 118, 119–120
    past time clauses, 110, 111–112, 393, 394
time/times, 138, 361, 393
Time words, *see also* Adverbs of frequency; Time
       clauses; **specific time words** — e.g., *after,*
       before, when, while
    ago, with simple past, 148
    for definite time period, 78–79
    for and *since,* with present perfect, 146
    from...to..., with simple past, 148
    future time phrases, 78–79
    of with, with superlatives, 321
    prepositions of time, 60
    for quantity of time, 78
    the + after next, 79
tingle, 16
to, 254, 467, *see also* Infinitives
too, 99, 102, 103, 290
too many, 286
too much, 286
Transitive verbs, 416
Travel verbs, 94

try, 375, 377
typically, 26

U
Uncertainty, 450, 454
    exercises on, 450–451, 454–455
Uncountable nouns, *see* Noncount nouns
understand, 16, 204, 450, 458
Unreal conditionals (imaginary *if* sentences), 339,
       346–348, 389, 406–408
Unreal situations, expression of, see also *wish*
       sentences
    with imaginary *if* sentences, 339, 346–348, 389,
       406–408
until, 393
use, in *it's no use*, 361
used to, 43, 62–63, 64
use to, 62–63
usually, 25, 26, 28, 29

V
value, 16
-'ve, see *I've; they've; we've; you've*
Verb phrases, 365–367, 369
Verbs, *see also* Auxiliary verbs; *be; do;* Gerunds;
       have; Infinitives; Modals; Past participles;
       Stative verbs; Subject-verb agreement;
       Tense; **other specific verbs**
    and adverbs of frequency, 27
    with *for* and *since*, 154
    in imperatives, 36, 37, 461, 468
    infinitives with, 373
        forms of, 371, 375
        meaning and use of, 374, 376, 380, 381
    intransitive verbs, 416
    mental activity verbs, 447, 450, 454, 458–459
    in nonrestrictive relative clauses, 260–261
    object gerunds with, 359–367, 374–377
    perception, verbs of, 204
    regular vs. irregular, 44
    reporting verbs, 447, 461, 465–468
    in restrictive relative clauses, 246, 250, 254, 258
    with *than*, in comparatives, 314, 325
    transitive verbs, 416
    travel verbs, 94
    verb phrases, 365–367, 369
very few, 286, 288, 290
very little, 286, 288, 290
Volunteering, exercises on, 88

W
wait, 373
walk, 416
want, 16, 373, 374

want to know, 467
Warning, 37, 123, 176–178
  exercises on, 124–125, 183–184
was, 50–51
  in imaginary *if* sentences, 346
  in passive sentences, 420–421, 431, 432
  and past continuous, 67–68, 431, 432
  in *wish* sentences, 340
was able to, 204
was going to, 458
wasn't, 50, 51, 67, 421, 431, 432
waste time, 361
wear, 154
Weather, noncount nouns for, 275
we'd (we + had), 390, 398
we'd (we + would), 407
weigh, 16, 19, 416
we'll, 82, 429
were, 50–51
  in imaginary *if* sentences, 346
  in passive sentences, 420–421, 431, 432
  and past continuous, 67–68, 431, 432
  in *wish* sentences, 340
we're, 9, 76, 420, 431
were able to, 204
were going to, 458
weren't, 50, 51, 67, 421, 431
we've, 134, 150
what, 448, *see also* Information questions;
    Information questions (subject)
"what'd," 45
"what'll," 83
"what'm," 10
what's (what + has), 135, 151
what's (what + is), 10, 33, 77, 432
"what've," 135
wh- clauses, 447, 448, 450, 461
when, see also Information questions
  in dependent clauses, 109
  in future time clauses, 118, 119–120
  in past time clauses, 69, 110, 111–112, 393
"when're," 10
where, see Information questions
"where'd," 45
whether, in *if/whether* clauses, 447, 452–453,
    454, 461
which, 239
  in nonrestrictive relative clauses,
    260–261
  as object relative pronoun, 250, 254
  in restrictive relative clauses, 240, 242
  as subject relative pronoun, 246
while, 69, 109, 110, 111–112
whisper, 467

who, 239, *see also* Information questions;
    Information questions (subject)
  in dependent clauses, 109
  in nonrestrictive relative clauses, 260, 261
  as object relative pronoun, 250, 254
  in restrictive relative clauses, 240, 242
  as subject relative pronoun, 246
  in *wh-* clauses, 448
whom, 239
  in nonrestrictive relative clauses, 260, 261
  as object relative pronoun, 250, 254
  in restrictive relative clauses, 240, 242, 250
who's (who + has), 135, 151, 432
who's (who + is), 10, 77, 421
whose, 239, 240, 258, 261
wh- words, *see also* Information questions;
    Information questions (subject); *what*;
    "what'd"; *"what'll"*; *"what'm"*; *what's*;
    "what've"; *when*; *"when're"*; *"where'd"*;
    who; *who's*; *why's*
  in *wh-* clauses, 447, 448, 450, 461
why, see Information questions
why's, 432
will, see also would
  contractions with forms of, *see he'll; I'll; it'll;
    she'll; they'll; "what'll"; won't; would've*
  for future, 75, 82–93
    with *be able to*, 203
    vs. *be going to*, 85, 86, 124
    in passive sentences, 429
    in real *if* sentences, 122, 123–124
  as modal of belief, 199, 209–210, 221, 222
  as social modal, 164, 166
wish, 16, *see also* Past *wish* sentences; *wish*
    sentences
Wishes, 408, *see also* Past *wish* sentences; *wish*
    sentences
  exercises on, 342, 343–344, 345–346, 410
wish sentences, 339, 340, 341
  past *wish* sentences, 389, 403, 404
women, pronunciation of, 272
wonder, with *wh-* clauses, 450
won't, 82, 85, 90, 429
work, 154
worry about, 367
worth, in *it's (not) worth*, 361
would, 163, 164
  -*'d* as contraction of, 340, 407
  in imaginary *if* sentences, 346, 347
  for repeated actions, 43, 64
  in requests, 166
  with *that* clauses, 458
  vs. *used to*, 64
  in *wish* sentences, 340, 341–342

would have, 406–407, 407–408
would like, 373, 374
would've, 407
would you mind, 348, 363
Writing
  with *be going to,* 77
  contractions in
    didn't, 45
    doesn't, 3
    don't, 3
    of *had,* in past perfect, 391
    he's, 10
    who's, 10, 135
    with *wh-* words, 10
    with *will,* 83
  nonrestrictive relative clauses in, 263
  passive sentences in, 415, 417–418
  past modals in, 225
  present continuous in, 10
  present perfect in, 135, 148
  simple past in, 45, 148
  social modals in, 172, 177–178

Y

Yes/no questions
  adverbs of frequency in, 27, 28
  and answers with infinitives, 371

in future, 76–77, 82, 429
with modals
  with modals of ability, 200, 202
  with modals of belief, 210
  in passive sentences, 438
  with past modals, 224
  with social modals, 164
with passive sentences, 421, 429, 432, 438
in past continuous, 67, 432
in past perfect, 390, 432
in past perfect continuous, 398
permission requests as, 172
in present continuous, 9, 432
in present perfect, 134, 432
in present perfect continuous, 151
with reported speech, 461
in simple past, 44, 50, 63, 421
in simple present, 2, 421
so in responses to, 459
with *there is/there are,* 33
yet, 138, 148, 394
you, 36, 37, 203, 418
you'd (you + had), 390
you'd (you + would), 340
you'll, 82, 429
you're, 9, 76, 420, 421
you've, 134, 150